Rob J Hyndman and George Athanasopoulos

Forecasting

Principles and Practice

Forecasting: Principles and Practice

ISBN 978-0-9875071-1-2

Available online at *http://OTexts.com/fpp2/*

Second print edition, May 2018

PUBLISHED BY OTEXTS

Contents

Preface

This textbook is intended to provide a comprehensive introduction to forecasting methods and to present enough information about each method for readers to be able to use them sensibly. We don't attempt to give a thorough discussion of the theoretical details behind each method, although the references at the end of each chapter will fill in many of those details.

The book is written for three audiences: (1) people finding themselves doing forecasting in business when they may not have had any formal training in the area; (2) undergraduate students studying business; (3) MBA students doing a forecasting elective. We use it ourselves for a third-year subject for students undertaking a Bachelor of Commerce or a Bachelor of Business degree at Monash University, Australia.

For most sections, we only assume that readers are familiar with introductory statistics, and with high-school algebra. There are a couple of sections that also require knowledge of matrices, but these are flagged.

At the end of each chapter we provide a list of "further reading". In general, these lists comprise suggested textbooks that provide a more advanced or detailed treatment of the subject. Where there is no suitable textbook, we suggest journal articles that provide more information.

We use R throughout the book and we intend students to learn how to forecast with R. R is free and available on almost every operating system. It is a wonderful tool for all statistical analysis, not just for forecasting. See the Using R appendix for instructions on installing and using R.

All R examples in the book assume you have loaded the **fpp2** package, available on CRAN, using `library(fpp2)`. This will automatically load several other packages including **forecast** and **ggplot2**, as well as all the data used in the book. We have used v2.3 of the **fpp2** package and v8.3 of the **forecast** package in preparing this book. These can be installed from CRAN in the usual way. Earlier versions of the packages will not necessarily give the same results as those shown in this book.

We will use the **ggplot2** package for all graphics. If you want to learn how to modify the graphs, or create your own ggplot2 graphics that are different from the examples shown in this book, please either read the ggplot2 book (Wickham 2016), or do the ggplot2 course[1] on the DataCamp online learning platform.

[1] `http://bit.ly/dcggplot2`

There is also a DataCamp course based on this book[2] which provides an introduction to some of the ideas in Chapters 2, 3, 7 and 8, plus a brief glimpse at a few of the topics in Chapters 9 and 11.

[2] `http://bit.ly/dcforecasting`

The book is different from other forecasting textbooks in several ways.

- It is free and online, making it accessible to a wide audience.
- It uses R, which is free, open-source, and extremely powerful software.
- The online version is continuously updated. You don't have to wait until the next edition for errors to be removed or new methods to be discussed. We will update the book frequently.
- There are dozens of real data examples taken from our own consulting practice. We have worked with hundreds of businesses and organizations helping them with forecasting issues, and this experience has contributed directly to many of the examples given here, as well as guiding our general philosophy of forecasting.
- We emphasise graphical methods more than most forecasters. We use graphs to explore the data, analyse the validity of the models fitted and present the forecasting results.

Changes in the second edition

The most important change in edition 2 of the book is that we have restricted our focus to *time series forecasting*. That is, we no longer consider the problem of cross-sectional prediction. Instead, all forecasting in this book concerns prediction of data at future times using observations collected in the past.

We have also simplified the chapter on exponential smoothing, and added new chapters on dynamic regression forecasting, hierarchical forecasting and practical forecasting issues. We have added new material on combining forecasts, handling complicated seasonality patterns, dealing with hourly, daily and weekly data, forecasting count time series, and we have many new examples. We have also revised all existing chapters to bring them up-to-date with the latest research, and we have carefully gone through every chapter to improve the explanations where possible, to add newer references, to add more exercises, and to make the R code simpler.

Helpful readers of the earlier versions of the book let us know of any typos or errors they had found. These were updated immediately online. No doubt we have introduced some new mistakes, and we will correct them online as soon as they are spotted. Please continue to let us know[3] about such things.

[3] `http://bit.ly/fpptypo`

Happy forecasting!

Rob J Hyndman and George Athanasopoulos

April 2018

Chapter 1
Getting started

Forecasting has fascinated people for thousands of years, sometimes being considered a sign of divine inspiration, and sometimes being seen as a criminal activity. The Jewish prophet Isaiah wrote in about 700 BC

> *Tell us what the future holds, so we may know that you are gods.* (Isaiah 41:23)

One hundred years later, in ancient Babylon, forecasters would foretell the future based on the distribution of maggots in a rotten sheep's liver. By 300 BC, people wanting forecasts would journey to Delphi in Greece to consult the Oracle, who would provide her predictions while intoxicated by ethylene vapours. Forecasters had a tougher time under the emperor Constantine, who issued a decree in AD357 forbidding anyone "to consult a soothsayer, a mathematician, or a forecaster ... May curiosity to foretell the future be silenced forever." A similar ban on forecasting occurred in England in 1736 when it became an offence to defraud by charging money for predictions. The punishment was three months' imprisonment with hard labour!

The varying fortunes of forecasters arise because good forecasts can seem almost magical, while bad forecasts may be dangerous. Consider the following famous predictions about computing.

- *I think there is a world market for maybe five computers.* (Chairman of IBM, 1943)
- *Computers in the future may weigh no more than 1.5 tons.* (Popular Mechanics, 1949)

- *There is no reason anyone would want a computer in their home.* (President, DEC, 1977)

The last of these was made only three years before IBM produced the first personal computer. Not surprisingly, you can no longer buy a DEC computer. Forecasting is obviously a difficult activity, and businesses that do it well have a big advantage over those whose forecasts fail.

In this book, we will explore the most reliable methods for producing forecasts. The emphasis will be on methods that are replicable and testable, and have been shown to work.

1.1 What can be forecast?

Forecasting is required in many situations: deciding whether to build another power generation plant in the next five years requires forecasts of future demand; scheduling staff in a call centre next week requires forecasts of call volumes; stocking an inventory requires forecasts of stock requirements. Forecasts can be required several years in advance (for the case of capital investments), or only a few minutes beforehand (for telecommunication routing). Whatever the circumstances or time horizons involved, forecasting is an important aid to effective and efficient planning.

Some things are easier to forecast than others. The time of the sunrise tomorrow morning can be forecast very precisely. On the other hand, tomorrow's lotto numbers cannot be forecast with any accuracy. The predictability of an event or a quantity depends on several factors including:

1. how well we understand the factors that contribute to it;
2. how much data are available;
3. whether the forecasts can affect the thing we are trying to forecast.

For example, forecasts of electricity demand can be highly accurate because all three conditions are usually satisfied. We have a good idea of the contributing factors: electricity demand is driven largely by temperatures, with smaller effects for calendar variation such as holidays, and economic conditions. Provided there is a sufficient history of data on electricity demand and weather conditions, and we have the skills to develop a good model linking electricity demand and the key driver variables, the forecasts can be remarkably accurate.

On the other hand, when forecasting currency exchange rates, only one of the conditions is satisfied: there is plenty of available data. However, we have a very limited understanding of the factors that affect exchange rates, and forecasts of the exchange rate have a direct effect on the rates themselves. If there are well-publicized forecasts that the exchange rate will increase, then people will immediately adjust the price they are willing to pay and so the forecasts are self-fulfilling. In a sense, the exchange rates become their own forecasts. This is an example of the "efficient market hypothesis". Consequently, forecasting whether the exchange rate will rise or fall tomorrow is about as predictable as forecasting whether a tossed coin will come down as a head or a tail. In both situations, you will be correct about 50% of the time, whatever you forecast. In situations like this, forecasters need to be aware of their own limitations, and not claim more than is possible.

Often in forecasting, a key step is knowing when something can be forecast accurately, and when forecasts will be no better than tossing a coin. Good forecasts capture the genuine patterns and relationships which exist in the historical data, but do not replicate past events that will not occur again. In this book, we will learn how to tell the difference between a random fluctuation in the past data that should be ignored, and a genuine pattern that should be modelled and extrapolated.

Many people wrongly assume that forecasts are not possible in a changing environment. Every environment is changing, and a good forecasting model captures the way in which things are changing. Forecasts rarely assume that the environment is unchanging. What is normally assumed is that *the way in which the environment is changing* will continue into the future. That is, a highly volatile environment will continue to be highly volatile; a business with fluctuating sales will continue to have fluctuating sales; and an economy that has gone through booms and busts will continue to go through booms and busts. A forecasting model is intended to capture the way things move, not just where things are. As Abraham Lincoln said, "If we could first know where we are and whither we are tending, we could better judge what to do and how to do it".

Forecasting situations vary widely in their time horizons, factors determining actual outcomes, types of data patterns, and many other aspects. Forecasting methods can be very simple, such as using the most recent observation as a forecast (which is called the **naïve method**), or highly complex, such as neural nets and econometric systems of simultaneous equations. Sometimes, there will be no data available at all. For example, we may wish to forecast the sales of a new product in its first year, but there are obviously no data to work with. In situations like this, we use judgmental forecasting, discussed in Chapter 4. The choice of method depends on what data are available and the predictability of the quantity to be forecast.

1.2 Forecasting, planning and goals

Forecasting is a common statistical task in business, where it helps to inform decisions about the scheduling of production, transportation and personnel, and provides a guide to long-term strategic planning. However, business forecasting is often done poorly, and is frequently confused with planning and goals. They are three different things.

Forecasting is about predicting the future as accurately as possible, given all of the information available, including historical data and knowledge of any future events that might impact the forecasts.

Goals are what you would like to have happen. Goals should be linked to forecasts and plans, but this does not always occur. Too often, goals are set without any plan for how to achieve them, and no forecasts for whether they are realistic.

Planning is a response to forecasts and goals. Planning involves determining the appropriate actions that are required to make your forecasts match your goals.

Forecasting should be an integral part of the decision-making activities of management, as it can play an important role in many areas of a company. Modern organizations require short-term, medium-term and long-term forecasts, depending on the specific application.

Short-term forecasts are needed for the scheduling of personnel, production and transportation. As part of the scheduling process, forecasts of demand are often also required.

Medium-term forecasts are needed to determine future resource requirements, in order to purchase raw materials, hire personnel, or buy machinery and equipment.

Long-term forecasts are used in strategic planning. Such decisions must take account of market opportunities, environmental factors and internal resources.

An organization needs to develop a forecasting system that involves several approaches to predicting uncertain events. Such forecasting systems require the development of expertise in identifying forecasting problems, applying a range of forecasting methods, selecting appropriate methods for each problem, and evaluating and refining forecasting methods over time. It is also important to have strong organizational support for the use of formal forecasting methods if they are to be used successfully.

1.3 Determining what to forecast

In the early stages of a forecasting project, decisions need to be made about what should be forecast. For example, if forecasts are required for items in a manufacturing environment, it is necessary to ask whether forecasts are needed for:

1. every product line, or for groups of products?
2. every sales outlet, or for outlets grouped by region, or only for total sales?
3. weekly data, monthly data or annual data?

It is also necessary to consider the forecasting horizon. Will forecasts be required for one month in advance, for 6 months, or for ten years? Different types of models will be necessary, depending on what forecast horizon is most important.

How frequently are forecasts required? Forecasts that need to be produced frequently are better done using an automated system than with methods that require careful manual work.

It is worth spending time talking to the people who will use the forecasts to ensure that you understand their needs, and how the forecasts are to be used, before embarking on extensive work in producing the forecasts.

Once it has been determined what forecasts are required, it is then necessary to find or collect the data on which the forecasts will be based. The data required for forecasting may already exist. These days, a lot of data are recorded, and the forecaster's task is often to identify where and how the required data are stored. The data may include sales records of a company, the historical demand for a product, or the unemployment rate for a geographical region. A large part of a forecaster's time can be spent in locating and collating the available data prior to developing suitable forecasting methods.

1.4 Forecasting data and methods

The appropriate forecasting methods depend largely on what data are available.

If there are no data available, or if the data available are not relevant to the forecasts, then **qualitative forecasting** methods must be used. These methods are not purely guesswork—there are well-developed structured approaches to obtaining good forecasts without using historical data. These methods are discussed in Chapter 4.

Quantitative forecasting can be applied when two conditions are satisfied:

1. numerical information about the past is available;
2. it is reasonable to assume that some aspects of the past patterns will continue into the future.

There is a wide range of quantitative forecasting methods, often developed within specific disciplines for specific purposes. Each method has its own properties, accuracies, and costs that must be considered when choosing a specific method.

Most quantitative prediction problems use either time series data (collected at regular intervals over time) or cross-sectional data (collected at a single point in time). In this book we are concerned with forecasting future data, and we concentrate on the time series domain.

Time series forecasting

Examples of time series data include:

- Daily IBM stock prices
- Monthly rainfall
- Quarterly sales results for Amazon
- Annual Google profits

Anything that is observed sequentially over time is a time series. In this book, we will only consider time series that are observed at regular intervals of time (e.g., hourly, daily, weekly, monthly, quarterly, annually). Irregularly spaced time series can also occur, but are beyond the scope of this book.

When forecasting time series data, the aim is to estimate how the sequence of observations will continue into the future. Figure 1.1 shows the quarterly Australian beer production from 1992 to the second quarter of 2010.

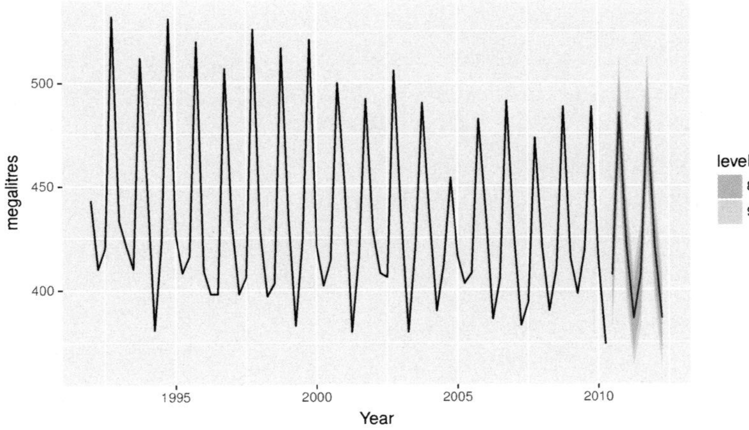

Figure 1.1: Australian quarterly beer production: 1992Q1–2010Q2, with two years of forecasts.

The blue lines show forecasts for the next two years. Notice how the forecasts have captured the seasonal pattern seen in the historical data and replicated it for the next two years. The dark shaded region shows 80% prediction intervals. That is, each future value is expected to lie in the dark shaded region with a probability of 80%. The light shaded region shows 95% prediction intervals. These prediction intervals are a very useful way of displaying the uncertainty in forecasts. In this case the forecasts are expected to be very accurate, and hence the prediction intervals are quite narrow.

The simplest time series forecasting methods use only information on the variable to be forecast, and make no attempt to discover the factors that affect its behaviour. Therefore they will extrapolate trend and seasonal patterns, but they ignore all other information such as marketing initiatives, competitor activity, changes in economic conditions, and so on.

Time series models used for forecasting include decomposition models, exponential smoothing models and ARIMA models. These models are discussed in Chapters 6, 7 and 8, respectively.

Predictor variables and time series forecasting

Predictor variables are often useful in time series forecasting. For example, suppose we wish to forecast the hourly electricity demand (ED) of a hot region during the summer period. A model with predictor variables might be of the form

$$\begin{aligned}\text{ED} = & f(\text{current temperature, strength of economy, population,} \\ & \text{time of day, day of week, error}).\end{aligned}$$

The relationship is not exact — there will always be changes in electricity demand that cannot be accounted for by the predictor variables. The "error" term on the right allows for random variation and the effects of relevant variables that are not included in the model. We call this an **explanatory model** because it helps explain what causes the variation in electricity demand.

Because the electricity demand data form a time series, we could also use a time series model for forecasting. In this case, a suitable time series forecasting equation is of the form

$$\text{ED}_{t+1} = f(\text{ED}_t, \text{ED}_{t-1}, \text{ED}_{t-2}, \text{ED}_{t-3}, \ldots, \text{error}),$$

where t is the present hour, $t+1$ is the next hour, $t-1$ is the previous hour, $t-2$ is two hours ago, and so on. Here, prediction of the future is based on past values of a variable, but not on external variables which may affect the system. Again, the "error" term on the right allows for random variation and the effects of relevant variables that are not included in the model.

There is also a third type of model which combines the features of the above two models. For example, it might be given by

$$\text{ED}_{t+1} = f(\text{ED}_t, \text{current temperature, time of day, day of week, error}).$$

These types of "mixed models" have been given various names in different disciplines. They are known as dynamic regression models, panel data models, longitudinal models, transfer function models, and linear system models (assuming that f is linear). These models are discussed in Chapter 9.

An explanatory model is very useful because it incorporates information about other variables, rather than only historical values of the variable to be forecast. However, there are several reasons a forecaster might select a time series model rather than an explanatory or mixed model. First, the system may not be understood, and even if it was understood it may be extremely difficult to measure the relationships that are assumed to govern its behaviour. Second, it is necessary to know or forecast the future values of the various predictors in order to be able to forecast the variable of interest, and this may be too difficult. Third, the main concern may be only to predict what will happen, not to know why it happens. Finally, the time series model may give more accurate forecasts than an explanatory or mixed model.

The model to be used in forecasting depends on the resources and data available, the accuracy of the competing models, and the way in which the forecasting model is to be used.

1.5 Some case studies

The following four cases are from our consulting practice and demonstrate different types of forecasting situations and the associated problems that often arise.

Case 1 The client was a large company manufacturing disposable tableware such as napkins and paper plates. They needed forecasts of each of hundreds of items every month. The time series data showed a range of patterns, some with trends, some seasonal, and some with neither. At the time, they were using their own software, written in-house, but it often produced forecasts that did not seem sensible. The methods that were being used were the following:

1. average of the last 12 months data;
2. average of the last 6 months data;

3. prediction from a straight line regression over the last 12 months;
4. prediction from a straight line regression over the last 6 months;
5. prediction obtained by a straight line through the last observation with slope equal to the average slope of the lines connecting last year's and this year's values;
6. prediction obtained by a straight line through the last observation with slope equal to the average slope of the lines connecting last year's and this year's values, where the average is taken only over the last 6 months.

They required us to tell them what was going wrong and to modify the software to provide more accurate forecasts. The software was written in COBOL, making it difficult to do any sophisticated numerical computation.

Case 2 In this case, the client was the Australian federal government, who needed to forecast the annual budget for the Pharmaceutical Benefit Scheme (PBS). The PBS provides a subsidy for many pharmaceutical products sold in Australia, and the expenditure depends on what people purchase during the year. The total expenditure was around A$7 billion in 2009, and had been underestimated by nearly $1 billion in each of the two years before we were asked to assist in developing a more accurate forecasting approach.

In order to forecast the total expenditure, it is necessary to forecast the sales volumes of hundreds of groups of pharmaceutical products using monthly data. Almost all of the groups have trends and seasonal patterns. The sales volumes for many groups have sudden jumps up or down due to changes in what drugs are subsidised. The expenditures for many groups also have sudden changes due to cheaper competitor drugs becoming available.

Thus we needed to find a forecasting method that allowed for trend and seasonality if they were present, and at the same time was robust to sudden changes in the underlying patterns. It also needed to be able to be applied automatically to a large number of time series.

Case 3 A large car fleet company asked us to help them forecast vehicle re-sale values. They purchase new vehicles, lease them out for three years, and then sell them. Better forecasts of vehicle sales values would mean better control of profits; understanding what affects resale values may allow leasing and sales policies to be developed in order to maximize profits.

At the time, the resale values were being forecast by a group of specialists. Unfortunately, they saw any statistical model as a threat to their jobs, and were uncooperative in providing information. Nevertheless, the company provided a large amount of data on previous vehicles and their eventual resale values.

Case 4 In this project, we needed to develop a model for forecasting weekly air passenger traffic on major domestic routes for one of Australia's leading airlines. The company required forecasts of passenger numbers for each major domestic route and for each class of passenger (economy class, business class and first class). The company provided weekly traffic data from the previous six years.

Air passenger numbers are affected by school holidays, major sporting events, advertising campaigns, competition behaviour, etc. School holidays often do not coincide in different Australian cities, and sporting events sometimes move from one city to another. During the period of the historical data, there was a major pilots' strike during which there was no traffic for several months. A new cut-price airline also launched and folded. Towards the end of the historical data, the airline had trialled a redistribution of some economy class seats to business class, and some business class seats to first class. After several months, however, the seat classifications reverted to the original distribution.

1.6 The basic steps in a forecasting task

A forecasting task usually involves five basic steps.

Step 1: Problem definition. Often this is the most difficult part of forecasting. Defining the problem carefully requires an understanding of the way the forecasts will be used, who requires the forecasts, and how the forecasting function fits within the organization requiring the forecasts. A forecaster needs to spend time talking to everyone who will be involved in collecting data, maintaining databases, and using the forecasts for future planning.

Step 2: Gathering information. There are always at least two kinds of information required: (a) statistical data, and (b) the accumulated expertise of the people who collect the data and use the forecasts. Often, it will be difficult to obtain enough historical data to be able to fit a good statistical model. In that case, the judgmental forecasting methods of Chapter 4 can be used. Occasionally, very old data will be less useful due to structural changes in the system being forecast; then we may choose to use only the most recent data. However, remember that good statistical models will handle evolutionary changes in the system; don't throw away good data unnecessarily.

Step 3: Preliminary (exploratory) analysis. Always start by graphing the data. Are there consistent patterns? Is there a significant trend? Is seasonality important? Is there evidence of the presence of business cycles? Are there any outliers in the data that need to be explained by those with expert knowledge? How strong are the relationships among the variables available for analysis? Various tools have been developed to help with this analysis. These are discussed in Chapters 2 and 6.

Step 4: Choosing and fitting models. The best model to use depends on the availability of historical data, the strength of relationships between the forecast variable and any explanatory variables, and the way in which the forecasts are to be used. It is common to compare two or three potential models. Each model is itself an artificial construct that is based on a set of assumptions (explicit and implicit) and usually involves one or more parameters which must be estimated using the known historical data. We will discuss regression models (Chapter 5), exponential smoothing methods (Chapter 7), Box-Jenkins ARIMA models (Chapter 8), Dynamic regression models (Chapter 9), Hierarchical forecasting (Chapter 10), and several advanced methods including neural networks and vector autoregression in Chapter 11.

Step 5: Using and evaluating a forecasting model. Once a model has been selected and its parameters estimated, the model is used to make forecasts. The performance of the model can only be properly evaluated after the data for the forecast period have become available. A number of methods have been developed to help in assessing the accuracy of forecasts. There are also organizational issues in using and acting on the forecasts. A brief discussion of some of these issues is given in Chapter 3. When using a forecasting model in practice, numerous practical issues arise such as how to handle missing values and outliers, or how to deal with very short time series. These are discussed in Chapter 12.

1.7 The statistical forecasting perspective

The thing we are trying to forecast is unknown (or we wouldn't be forecasting it), and so we can think of it as a *random variable*. For example, the total sales for next month could take a range of possible values, and until we add up the actual sales at the end of the month, we don't know what the value will be. So until we know the sales for next month, it is a random quantity.

Because next month is relatively close, we usually have a good idea what the likely sales values could be. On the other hand, if we are forecasting the sales for the same month next year, the possible values it could take are much more variable. In most forecasting situations, the variation associated with the thing we are forecasting will shrink as the event approaches. In other words, the further ahead we forecast, the more uncertain we are.

We can imagine many possible futures, each yielding a different value for the thing we wish to forecast. Plotted in black in Figure 1.2 are the total international visitors to Australia from 1980 to 2015. Also shown are ten possible futures from 2016–2025.

When we obtain a forecast, we are estimating the *middle* of the range of possible values the random variable could take. Very often, a forecast is accompanied by a **prediction interval** giving a *range* of values the random variable could take with relatively high probability. For example, a 95% prediction

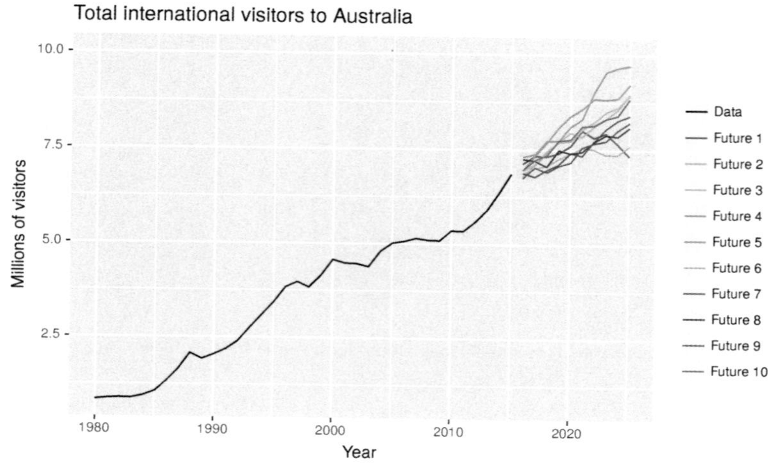

Figure 1.2: Total international visitors to Australia (1980-2015) along with ten possible futures.

interval contains a range of values which should include the actual future value with probability 95%.

Instead of plotting individual possible futures as shown in Figure 1.2, we usually show these prediction intervals instead. The plot below shows 80% and 95% intervals for the future Australian international visitors. The blue line is the average of the possible future values, which we call the **point forecasts**.

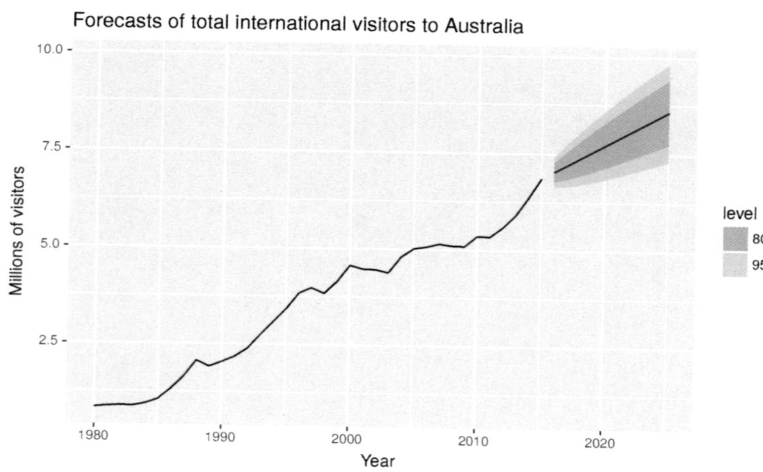

Figure 1.3: Total international visitors to Australia (1980–2015) along with 10-year forecasts and 80% and 95% prediction intervals.

We will use the subscript t for time. For example, y_t will denote the observation at time t. Suppose we denote all the information we have observed as $\mathcal{I}$ and we want to forecast y_t. We then write $y_t|\mathcal{I}$ meaning "the random variable y_t given what we know in $\mathcal{I}$". The set of values that this random variable could take, along with their relative probabilities, is known as the "probability distribution" of $y_t|\mathcal{I}$. In forecasting, we call this the **forecast distribution**.

When we talk about the "forecast", we usually mean the average value of the forecast distribution, and we put a "hat" over y to show this. Thus, we write the forecast of y_t as $\hat{y}_t$, meaning the average of the possible values that y_t could take given everything we know. Occasionally, we will use $\hat{y}_t$ to refer to the *median* (or middle value) of the forecast distribution instead.

It is often useful to specify exactly what information we have used in calculating the forecast. Then we will write, for example, $\hat{y}_{t|t-1}$ to mean the forecast of y_t taking account of all previous observations $(y_1,\dots,y_{t-1})$. Similarly, $\hat{y}_{T+h|T}$ means the forecast of y_{T+h} taking account of $y_1,\dots,y_T$ (i.e., an h-step forecast taking account of all observations up to time T).

1.8 Exercises

1. For cases 3 and 4 in Section 1.5, list the possible predictor variables that might be useful, assuming that the relevant data are available.
2. For case 3 in Section 1.5, describe the five steps of forecasting in the context of this project.

1.9 Further reading

- Armstrong (2001) covers the whole field of forecasting, with each chapter written by different experts. It is highly opinionated at times (and we don't agree with everything in it), but it is full of excellent general advice on tackling forecasting problems.
- Ord, Fildes, and Kourentzes (2017) is a forecasting textbook covering some of the same areas as this book, but with a different emphasis and not focussed around any particular software environment. It is written by three highly respected forecasters, with many decades of experience between them.

Chapter 2

Time series graphics

The first thing to do in any data analysis task is to plot the data. Graphs enable many features of the data to be visualized, including patterns, unusual observations, changes over time, and relationships between variables. The features that are seen in plots of the data must then be incorporated, as much as possible, into the forecasting methods to be used. Just as the type of data determines what forecasting method to use, it also determines what graphs are appropriate.

But before we produce graphs, we need to set up our time series in R.

2.1 `ts` objects

A time series can be thought of as a list of numbers, along with some information about what times those numbers were recorded. This information can be stored as a `ts` object in R.

Suppose you have annual observations for the last few years:

Year	Observation
2012	123
2013	39
2014	78
2015	52
2016	110

We turn this into a `ts` object using the `ts()` function:

```
y <- ts(c(123,39,78,52,110), start=2012)
```

If you have annual data, with one observation per year, you only need to provide the starting year (or the ending year).

For observations that are more frequent than once per year, you simply add a `frequency` argument. For example, if your monthly data is already stored as a numerical vector `z`, then it can be converted to a `ts` object like this:

```
y <- ts(z, start=2003, frequency=12)
```

Almost all of the data used in this book is already stored as `ts` objects. But if you want to work with your own data, you will need to use the `ts()` function before proceeding with the analysis.

Frequency of a time series

The "frequency" is the number of observations before the seasonal pattern repeats.[1] When using the `ts()` function in R, the following choices should be used.

[1] This is the opposite of the definition of frequency in physics, or in Fourier analysis, where this would be called the "period".

Data	frequency
Annual	1
Quarterly	4
Monthly	12
Weekly	52

Actually, there are not 52 weeks in a year, but $365.25/7 = 52.18$ on average, allowing for a leap year every fourth year. But most functions which use `ts` objects require integer frequency.

If the frequency of observations is greater than once per week, then there is usually more than one way of handling the frequency. For example, data with daily observations might have a weekly seasonality (frequency$=7$) or an annual seasonality (frequency$=365.25$). Similarly, data that are observed every minute might have an hourly seasonality (frequency$=60$), a daily seasonality (frequency$=24\times60=1440$), a weekly seasonality (frequency$=24\times60\times7=10080$) and an annual seasonality (frequency$=24\times60\times365.25=525960$). If you want to use a `ts` object, then you need to decide which of these is the most important.

In chapter 11 we will look at handling these types of multiple seasonality, without having to choose just one of the frequencies.

2.2 Time plots

For time series data, the obvious graph to start with is a time plot. That is, the observations are plotted against the time of observation, with consecutive observations joined by straight lines. Figure 2.1 below shows the weekly economy passenger load on Ansett Airlines between Australia's two largest cities.

```
autoplot(melsyd[,"Economy.Class"]) +
  ggtitle("Economy class passengers: Melbourne-Sydney") +
  xlab("Year") +
  ylab("Thousands")
```

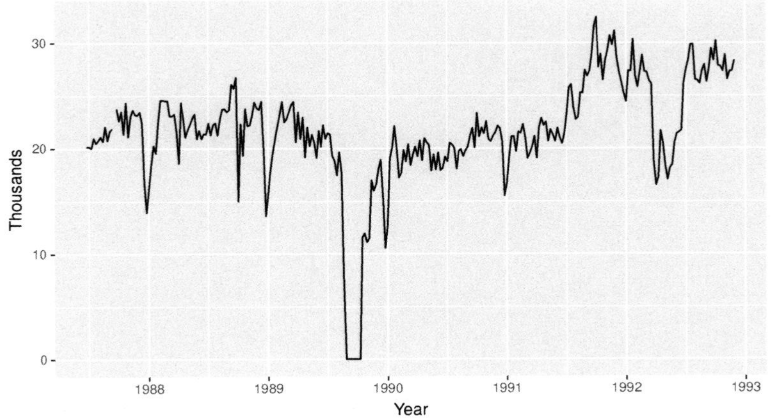

Figure 2.1: Weekly economy passenger load on Ansett Airlines.

We will use the `autoplot()` command frequently. It automatically produces an appropriate plot of whatever you pass to it in the first argument. In this case, it recognizes `melsyd[,"Economy.Class"]` as a time series and produces a time plot.

The time plot immediately reveals some interesting features.

- There was a period in 1989 when no passengers were carried — this was due to an industrial dispute.

- There was a period of reduced load in 1992. This was due to a trial in which some economy class seats were replaced by business class seats.
- A large increase in passenger load occurred in the second half of 1991.
- There are some large dips in load around the start of each year. These are due to holiday effects.
- There is a long-term fluctuation in the level of the series which increases during 1987, decreases in 1989, and increases again through 1990 and 1991.
- There are some periods of missing observations.

Any model will need to take all these features into account in order to effectively forecast the passenger load into the future.

A simpler time series is shown in Figure 2.2.

```
autoplot(a10) +
  ggtitle("Antidiabetic drug sales") +
  ylab("$ million") +
  xlab("Year")
```

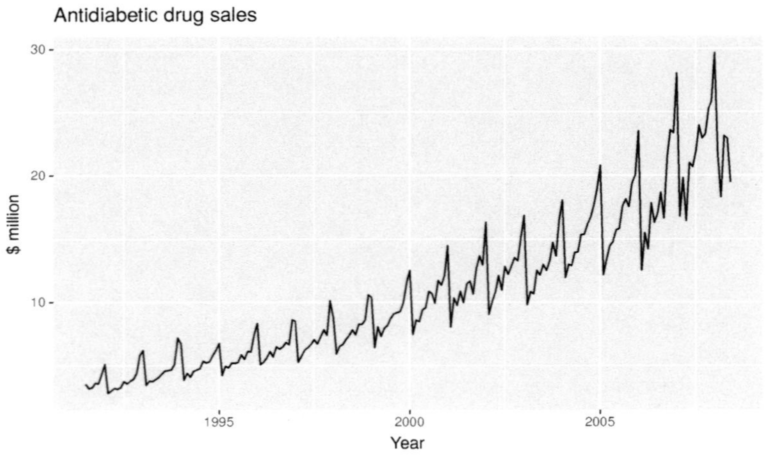

Figure 2.2: Monthly sales of antidiabetic drugs in Australia.

Here, there is a clear and increasing trend. There is also a strong seasonal pattern that increases in size as the level of the series increases. The sudden drop at the start of each year is caused by a government subsidisation scheme that makes it cost-effective for patients to stockpile drugs at the end of the calendar year. Any forecasts of this series would need to capture the seasonal pattern, and the fact that the trend is changing slowly.

2.3 Time series patterns

In describing these time series, we have used words such as "trend" and "seasonal" which need to be defined more carefully.

Trend A *trend* exists when there is a long-term increase or decrease in the data. It does not have to be linear. Sometimes we will refer to a trend as "changing direction", when it might go from an increasing trend to a decreasing trend. There is a trend in the antidiabetic drug sales data shown in Figure 2.2.

Seasonal A *seasonal* pattern occurs when a time series is affected by seasonal factors such as the time of the year or the day of the week. Seasonality is always of a fixed and known frequency. The monthly sales of antidiabetic drugs above shows seasonality which is induced partly by the change in the cost of the drugs at the end of the calendar year.

Cyclic A *cycle* occurs when the data exhibit rises and falls that are not of a fixed frequency. These fluctuations are usually due to economic conditions, and are often related to the "business cycle". The duration of these fluctuations is usually at least 2 years.

Many people confuse cyclic behaviour with seasonal behaviour, but they are really quite different. If the fluctuations are not of a fixed frequency then they are cyclic; if the frequency is unchanging and associated with some aspect of the calendar, then the pattern is seasonal. In general, the average length of cycles is longer than the length of a seasonal pattern, and the magnitudes of cycles tend to be more variable than the magnitudes of seasonal patterns.

Many time series include trend, cycles and seasonality. When choosing a forecasting method, we will first need to identify the time series patterns in the data, and then choose a method that is able to capture the patterns properly.

The examples in Figure 2.3 show different combinations of the above components.

1. The monthly housing sales (top left) show strong seasonality within each year, as well as some strong cyclic behaviour

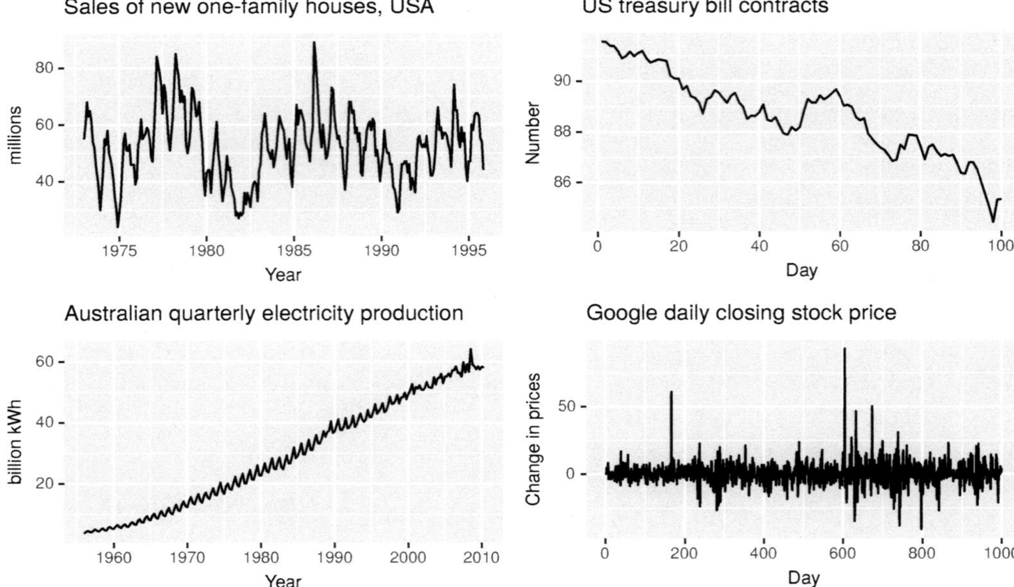

Figure 2.3: Four examples of time series showing different patterns.

with a period of about 6–10 years. There is no apparent trend in the data over this period.

2. The US treasury bill contracts (top right) show results from the Chicago market for 100 consecutive trading days in 1981. Here there is no seasonality, but an obvious downward trend. Possibly, if we had a much longer series, we would see that this downward trend is actually part of a long cycle, but when viewed over only 100 days it appears to be a trend.
3. The Australian monthly electricity production (bottom left) shows a strong increasing trend, with strong seasonality. There is no evidence of any cyclic behaviour here.
4. The daily change in the Google closing stock price (bottom right) has no trend, seasonality or cyclic behaviour. There are random fluctuations which do not appear to be very predictable, and no strong patterns that would help with developing a forecasting model.

2.4 Seasonal plots

A seasonal plot is similar to a time plot except that the data are plotted against the individual "seasons" in which the data were observed. An example is given below showing the antidiabetic drug sales.

```
ggseasonplot(a10, year.labels=TRUE, year.labels.left=TRUE) +
  ylab("$ million") +
  ggtitle("Seasonal plot: antidiabetic drug sales")
```

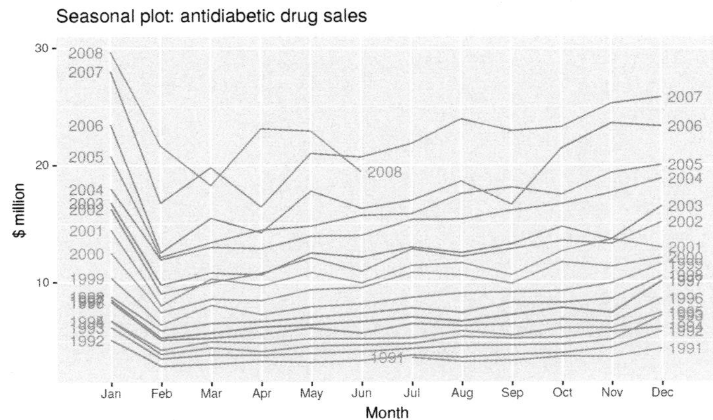

Figure 2.4: Seasonal plot of monthly antidiabetic drug sales in Australia.

These are exactly the same data as were shown earlier, but now the data from each season are overlapped. A seasonal plot allows the underlying seasonal pattern to be seen more clearly, and is especially useful in identifying years in which the pattern changes.

In this case, it is clear that there is a large jump in sales in January each year. Actually, these are probably sales in late December as customers stockpile before the end of the calendar year, but the sales are not registered with the government until a week or two later. The graph also shows that there was an unusually small number of sales in March 2008 (most other years show an increase between February and March). The small number of sales in June 2008 is probably due to incomplete counting of sales at the time the data were collected.

A useful variation on the seasonal plot uses polar coordinates. Setting `polar=TRUE` makes the time series axis circular rather than horizontal, as shown below.

```
ggseasonplot(a10, polar=TRUE) +
  ylab("$ million") +
  ggtitle("Polar seasonal plot: antidiabetic drug sales")
```

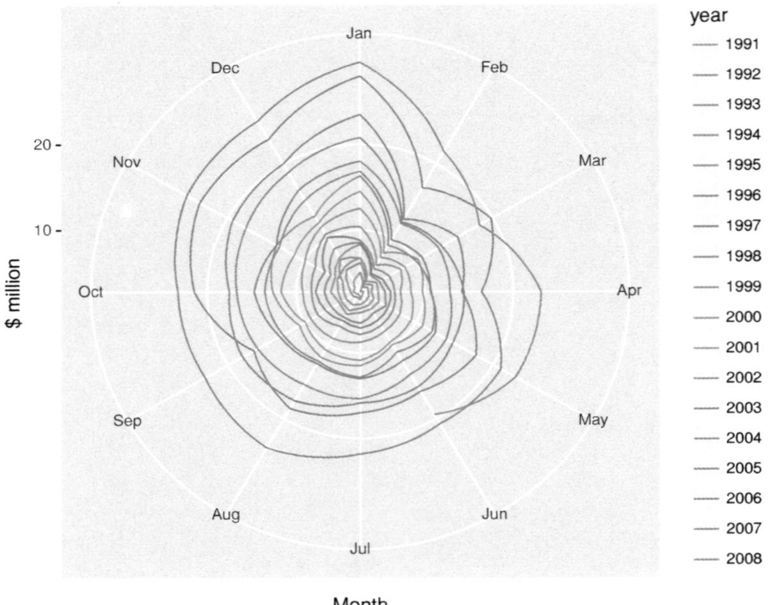

Figure 2.5: Polar seasonal plot of monthly antidiabetic drug sales in Australia.

2.5 Seasonal subseries plots

An alternative plot that emphasises the seasonal patterns is where the data for each season are collected together in separate mini time plots.

```
ggsubseriesplot(a10) +
  ylab("$ million") +
  ggtitle("Seasonal subseries plot: antidiabetic drug sales")
```

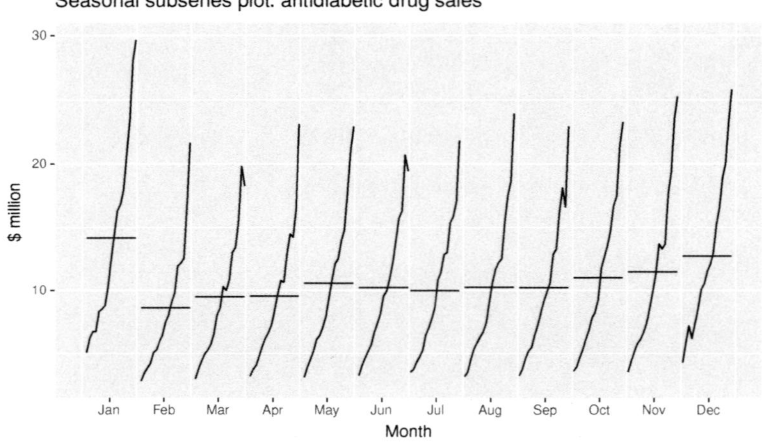

Figure 2.6: Seasonal subseries plot of monthly antidiabetic drug sales in Australia.

The horizontal lines indicate the means for each month. This form of plot enables the underlying seasonal pattern to be seen clearly, and also shows the changes in seasonality over time. It is especially useful in identifying changes within particular seasons. In this example, the plot is not particularly revealing; but in some cases, this is the most useful way of viewing seasonal changes over time.

2.6 Scatterplots

The graphs discussed so far are useful for visualizing individual time series. It is also useful to explore relationships *between* time series.

Figure 2.7 shows two time series: half-hourly electricity demand (in GigaWatts) and temperature (in degrees Celsius), for 2014 in Victoria, Australia. The temperatures are for Melbourne, the largest city in Victoria, while the demand values are for the entire state.

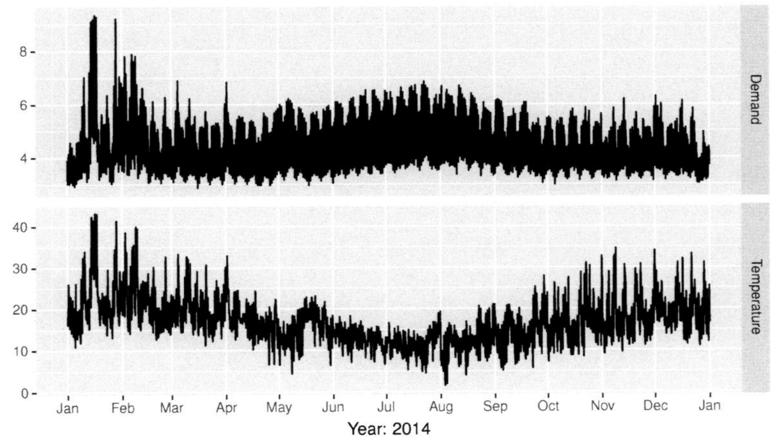

Figure 2.7: Half hourly electricity demand and temperatures in Victoria, Australia, for 2014.

We can study the relationship between demand and temperature by plotting one series against the other.

```
qplot(Temperature, Demand, data=as.data.frame(elecdemand)) +
  ylab("Demand (GW)") + xlab("Temperature (Celsius)")
```

This scatterplot helps us to visualize the relationship between the variables. It is clear that high demand occurs when temperatures are high due to the effect of air-conditioning. But there

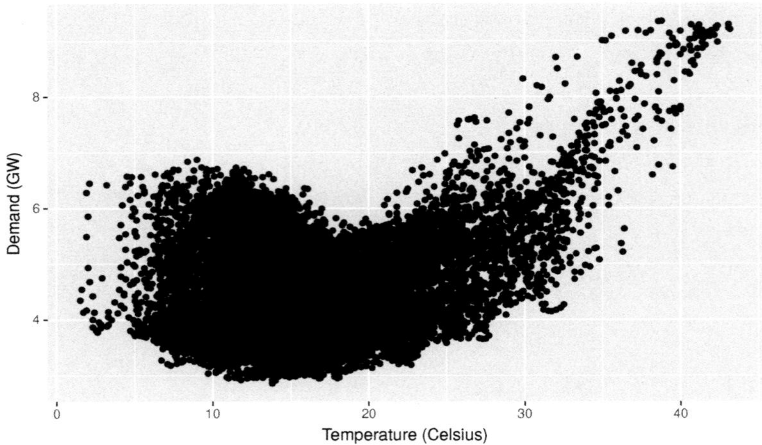

Figure 2.8: Half-hourly electricity demand plotted against temperature for 2014 in Victoria, Australia.

is also a heating effect, where demand increases for very low temperatures.

Correlation

It is common to compute *correlation coefficients* to measure the strength of the relationship between two variables. The correlation between variables x and y is given by

$$r = \frac{\sum(x_t - \bar{x})(y_t - \bar{y})}{\sqrt{\sum(x_t - \bar{x})^2}\sqrt{\sum(y_t - \bar{y})^2}}.$$

The value of r always lies between -1 and 1 with negative values indicating a negative relationship and positive values indicating a postive relationship. The graphs in Figure 2.9 show examples of data sets with varying levels of correlation.

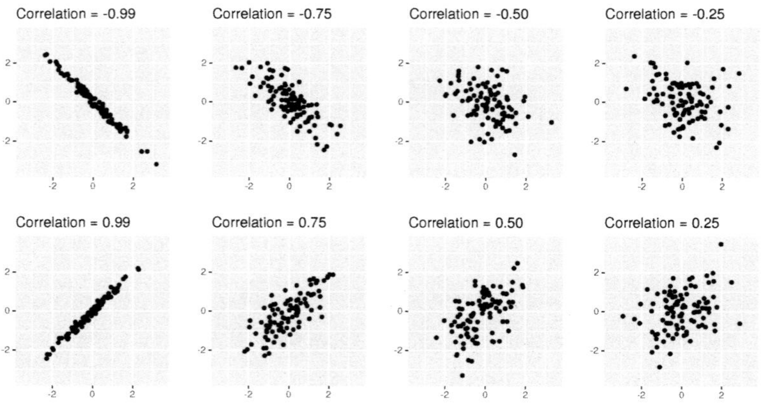

Figure 2.9: Examples of data sets with different levels of correlation.

The correlation coefficient only measures the strength of the *linear* relationship, and can sometimes be misleading. For example, the correlation for the electricity demand and temperature data shown in Figure 2.8 is 0.28, but the *non-linear* relationship is stronger than that.

The plots in Figure 2.10 all have correlation coefficients of 0.82, but they have very different relationships. This shows how important it is look at the plots of the data and not simply rely on correlation values.

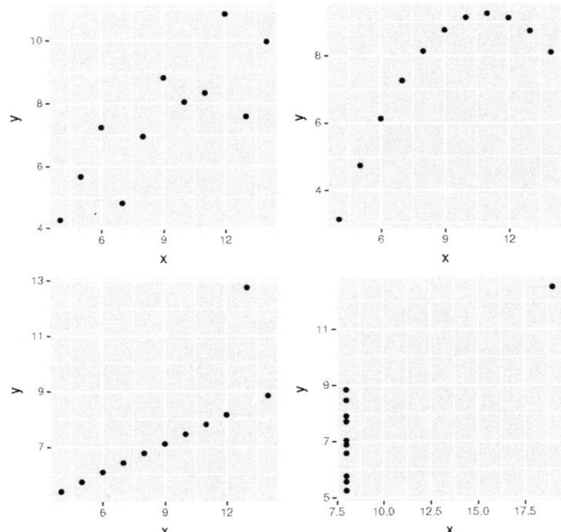

Figure 2.10: Each of these plots has a correlation coefficient of 0.82. Data from FJ Anscombe (1973) Graphs in statistical analysis. *American Statistician*, **27**, 17–21.

Scatterplot matrices

When there are several potential predictor variables, it is useful to plot each variable against each other variable. Consider the five time series shown in Figure 2.11, showing quarterly visitor numbers for five regions of New South Wales, Australia.

```
autoplot(visnights[,1:5], facets=TRUE) +
  ylab("Number of visitor nights each quarter (millions)")
```

To see the relationships between these five time series, we can plot each time series against the others. These plots can be arranged in a scatterplot matrix, as shown in Figure 2.12.

```
visnights[,1:5] %>% as.data.frame() %>% GGally::ggpairs()
```

For each panel, the variable on the vertical axis is given by the variable name in that row, and the variable on the horizontal axis is given by the variable name in that column. There are many options available to produce different plots within each

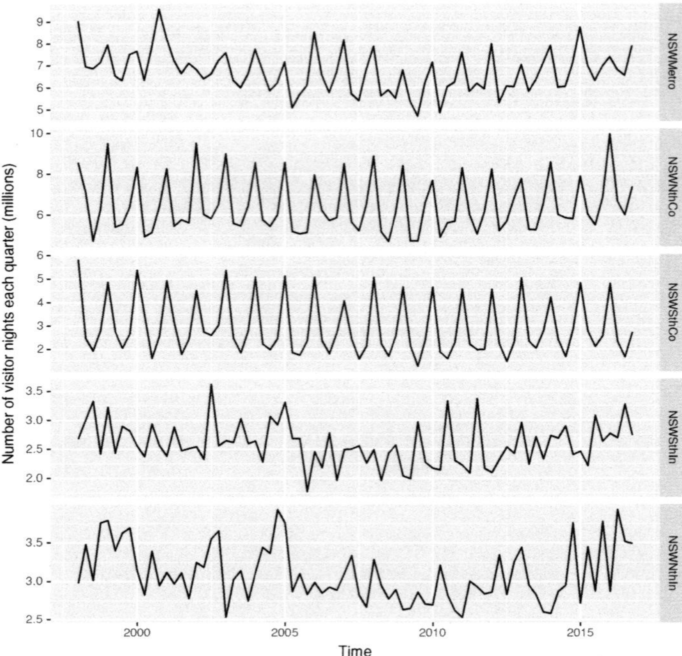

Figure 2.11: Quarterly visitor nights for various regions of NSW, Australia.

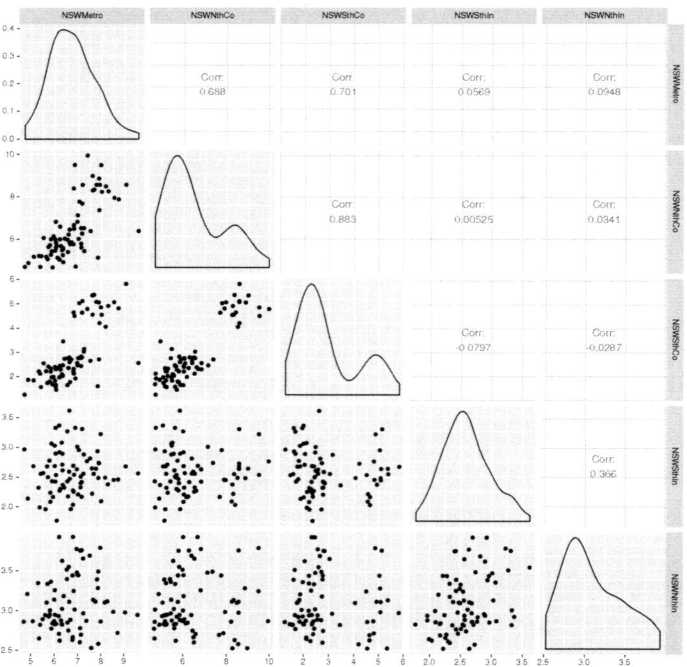

Figure 2.12: A scatterplot matrix of the quarterly visitor nights in five regions of NSW, Australia.

panel. In the default version, the correlations are shown in the upper right half of the plot, while the scatterplots are shown in the lower half. On the diagonal are shown density plots.

The value of the scatterplot matrix is that it enables a quick view of the relationships between all pairs of variables. In this example, the second column of plots shows there is a strong positive relationship between visitors to the NSW north coast and visitors to the NSW south coast, but no detectable relationship between visitors to the NSW north coast and visitors to the NSW south inland. Outliers can also be seen. There is one unusually high quarter for the NSW Metropolitan region, corresponding to the 2000 Sydney Olympics. This is most easily seen in the first two plots in the left column of Figure 2.12, where the largest value for NSW Metro is separate from the main cloud of observations.

2.7 Lag plots

Figure 2.13 displays scatterplots of quarterly Australian beer production, where the horizontal axis shows lagged values of the time series. Each graph shows y_t plotted against y_{t-k} for different values of k.

```
beer2 <- window(ausbeer, start=1992)
gglagplot(beer2)
```

Here the colours indicate the quarter of the variable on the vertical axis. The lines connect points in chronological order. The relationship is strongly positive at lags 4 and 8, reflecting the strong quarterly seasonality in the data. The negative relationship seen for lags 2 and 6 occurs because peaks (in Q4) are plotted against troughs (in Q2)

The `window()` function used here is very useful when extracting a portion of a time series. In this case, we have extracted the data from `ausbeer`, beginning in 1992.

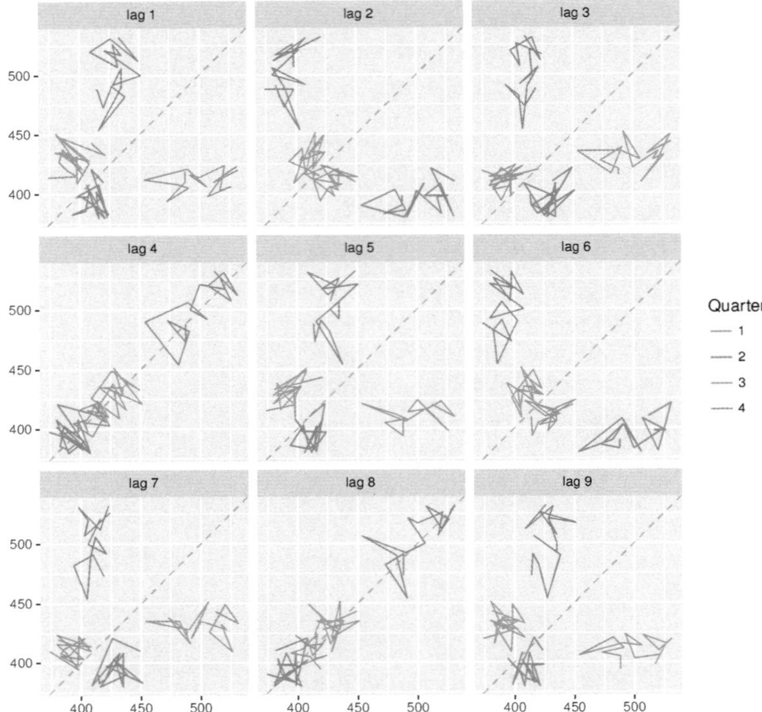

Figure 2.13: Lagged scatterplots for quarterly beer production.

2.8 Autocorrelation

Just as correlation measures the extent of a linear relationship between two variables, autocorrelation measures the linear relationship between *lagged values* of a time series.

There are several autocorrelation coefficients, corresponding to each panel in the lag plot. For example, r_1 measures the relationship between y_t and y_{t-1}, r_2 measures the relationship between y_t and y_{t-2}, and so on.

The value of r_k can be written as

$$r_k = \frac{\sum\limits_{t=k+1}^{T} (y_t - \bar{y})(y_{t-k} - \bar{y})}{\sum\limits_{t=1}^{T} (y_t - \bar{y})^2},$$

where T is the length of the time series.

The first nine autocorrelation coefficients for the beer production data are given in the following table.

r_1	r_2	r_3	r_4	r_5	r_6	r_7	r_8	r_9
-0.102	-0.657	-0.060	0.869	-0.089	-0.635	-0.054	0.832	-0.108

These correspond to the nine scatterplots in Figure 2.13. The autocorrelation coefficients are plotted to show the *autocorrelation function* or ACF. The plot is also known as a *correlogram*.

```
ggAcf(beer2)
```

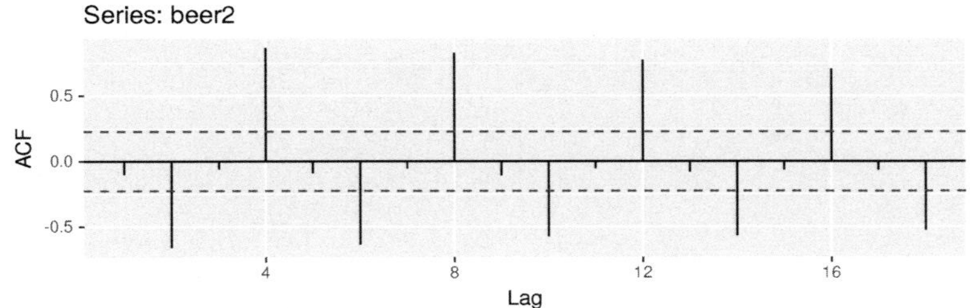

Figure 2.14: Autocorrelation function of quarterly beer production.

In this graph:

- r_4 is higher than for the other lags. This is due to the seasonal pattern in the data: the peaks tend to be four quarters apart and the troughs tend to be two quarters apart.
- r_2 is more negative than for the other lags because troughs tend to be two quarters behind peaks.
- The dashed blue lines indicate whether the correlations are significantly different from zero. These are explained in Section 2.9.

Trend and seasonality in ACF plots

When data have a trend, the autocorrelations for small lags tend to be large and positive because observations nearby in time are also nearby in size. So the ACF of trended time series tend to have positive values that slowly decrease as the lags increase.

When data are seasonal, the autocorrelations will be larger for the seasonal lags (at multiples of the seasonal frequency) than for other lags.

When data are both trended and seasonal, you see a combination of these effects. The monthly Australian electricity demand series plotted in Figure 2.15 shows both trend and seasonality. Its ACF is shown in Figure 2.16.

```
aelec <- window(elec, start=1980)
autoplot(aelec) + xlab("Year") + ylab("GWh")
```

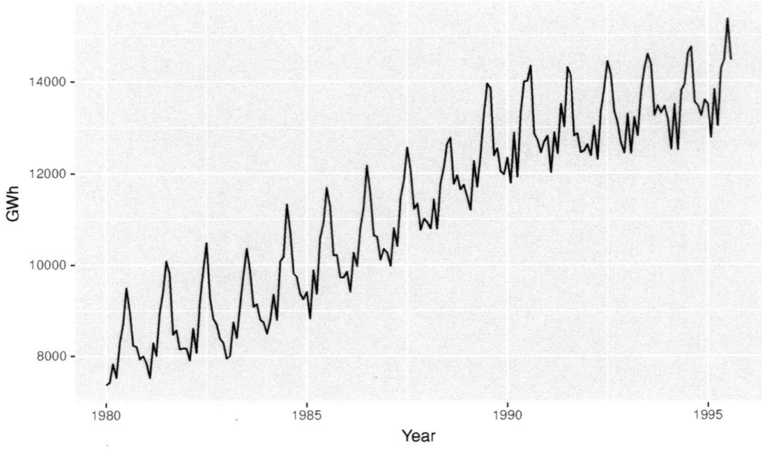

Figure 2.15: Monthly Australian electricity demand from 1980–1995.

```
ggAcf(aelec, lag=48)
```

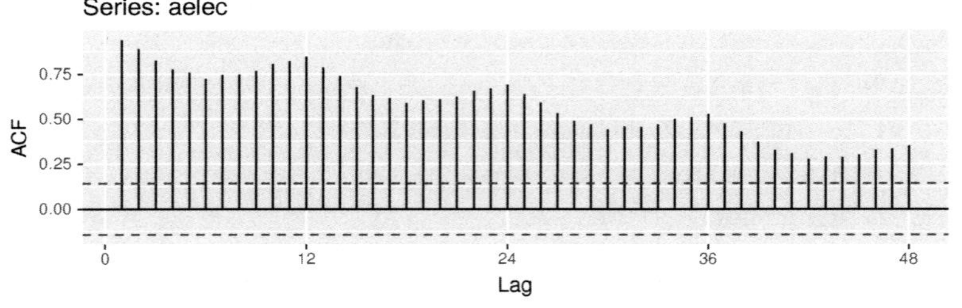

Figure 2.16: ACF of monthly Australian electricity demand.

The slow decrease in the ACF as the lags increase is due to the trend, while the "scalloped" shape is due the seasonality.

2.9 White noise

Time series that show no autocorrelation are called **white noise**. Figure 2.17 gives an example of a white noise series.

```
set.seed(30)
y <- ts(rnorm(50))
autoplot(y) + ggtitle("White noise")
```

```
ggAcf(y)
```

For white noise series, we expect each autocorrelation to be close to zero. Of course, they will not be exactly equal to zero

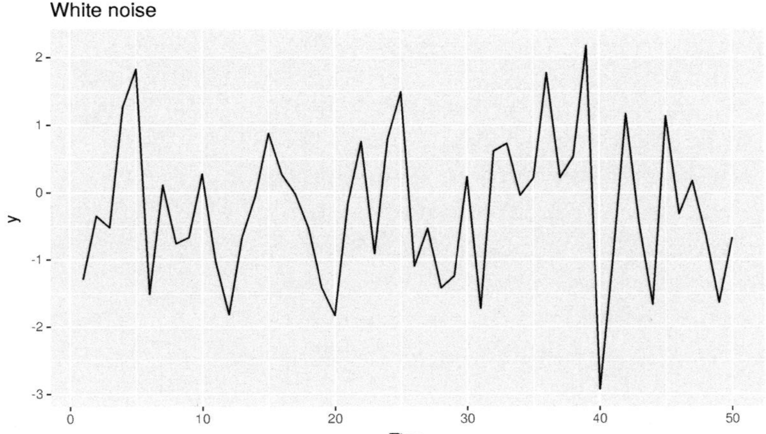

Figure 2.17: A white noise time series.

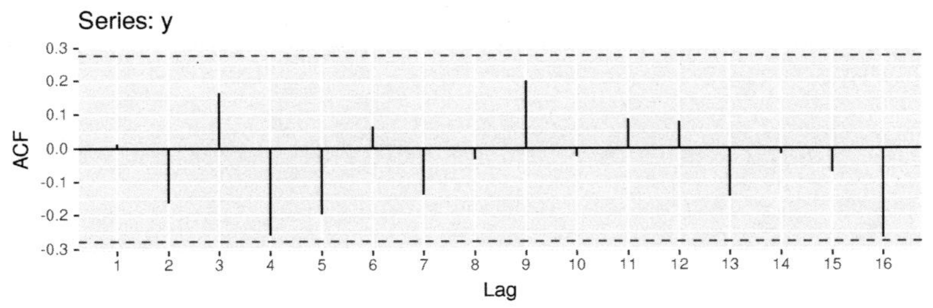

Figure 2.18: Autocorrelation function for the white noise series.

as there is some random variation. For a white noise series, we expect 95% of the spikes in the ACF to lie within $\pm 2/\sqrt{T}$ where T is the length of the time series. It is common to plot these bounds on a graph of the ACF (the blue dashed lines above). If one or more large spikes are outside these bounds, or if substantially more than 5% of spikes are outside these bounds, then the series is probably not white noise.

In this example, $T = 50$ and so the bounds are at $\pm 2/\sqrt{50} = \pm 0.28$. All of the autocorrelation coefficients lie within these limits, confirming that the data are white noise.

2.10 Exercises

1. Use the help function to explore what the series `gold`, `woolyrnq` and `gas` represent.

   a. Use `autoplot()` to plot each of these in separate plots.
   b. What is the frequency of each series? Hint: apply the `frequency()` function.

c. Use `which.max()` to spot the outlier in the `gold` series. Which observation was it?

2. Download the file `tute1.csv` from the book website[2], open it in Excel (or some other spreadsheet application), and review its contents. You should find four columns of information. Columns B through D each contain a quarterly series, labelled Sales, AdBudget and GDP. Sales contains the quarterly sales for a small company over the period 1981-2005. AdBudget is the advertising budget and GDP is the gross domestic product. All series have been adjusted for inflation.

[2] http://OTexts.org/fpp2/extrafiles/tute1.csv

a. You can read the data into R with the following script:

```
tute1 <- read.csv("tute1.csv", header=TRUE)
View(tute1)
```

b. Convert the data to time series

```
mytimeseries <- ts(tute1[,-1], start=1981, frequency=4)
```

(The `[,-1]` removes the first column which contains the quarters as we don't need them now.)

c. Construct time series plots of each of the three series

```
autoplot(mytimeseries, facets=TRUE)
```

Check what happens when you don't include `facets=TRUE`.

3. Download some monthly Australian retail data from the book website[3]. These represent retail sales in various categories for different Australian states, and are stored in a MS-Excel file.

[3] https://OTexts.org/fpp2/extrafiles/retail.xlsx

a. You can read the data into R with the following script:

```
retaildata <- readxl::read_excel("retail.xlsx", skip=1)
```

The second argument (`skip=1`) is required because the Excel sheet has two header rows.

b. Select one of the time series as follows (but replace the column name with your own chosen column):

```
myts <- ts(retaildata[,"A3349873A"],
  frequency=12, start=c(1982,4))
```

c. Explore your chosen retail time series using the following functions:

   `autoplot()`, `ggseasonplot()`, `ggsubseriesplot()`, `gglagplot()`, `ggAcf()`

   Can you spot any seasonality, cyclicity and trend? What do you learn about the series?

4. Create time plots of the following time series: `bicoal`, `chicken`, `dole`, `usdeaths`, `lynx`, `goog`, `writing`, `fancy`, `a10`, `h02`.

   - Use `help()` to find out about the data in each series.
   - For the `goog` plot, modify the axis labels and title.

5. Use the `ggseasonplot()` and `ggsubseriesplot()` functions to explore the seasonal patterns in the following time series: `writing`, `fancy`, `a10`, `h02`.

   - What can you say about the seasonal patterns?
   - Can you identify any unusual years?

6. Use the following graphics functions: `autoplot()`, `ggseasonplot()`, `ggsubseriesplot()`, `gglagplot()`, `ggAcf()` and explore features from the following time series: `hsales`, `usdeaths`, `bricksq`, `sunspotarea`, `gasoline`.

   - Can you spot any seasonality, cyclicity and trend?
   - What do you learn about the series?

7. The `arrivals` data set comprises quarterly international arrivals (in thousands) to Australia from Japan, New Zealand, UK and the US.

   - Use `autoplot()`, `ggseasonplot()` and `ggsubseriesplot()` to compare the differences between the arrivals from these four countries.
   - Can you identify any unusual observations?

8. The following time plots and ACF plots correspond to four different time series. Your task is to match each time plot in the first row with one of the ACF plots in the second row.

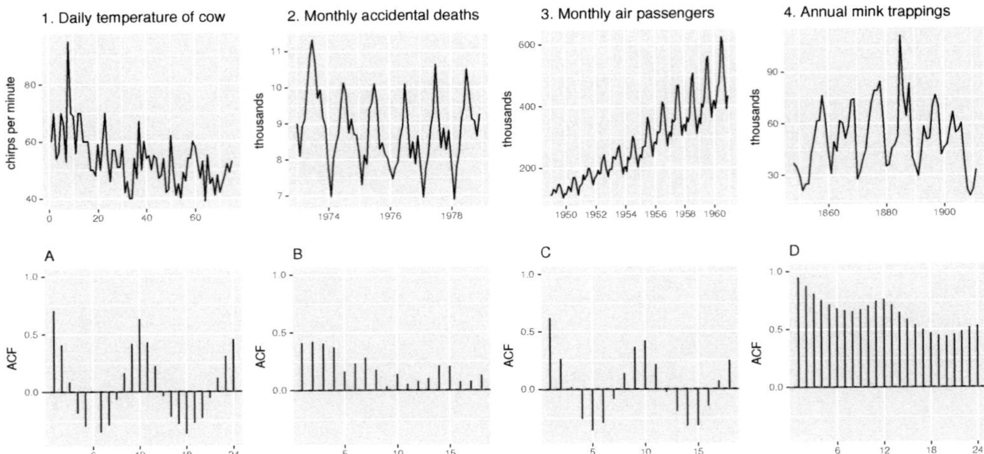

9. The `pigs` data shows the monthly total number of pigs slaughtered in Victoria, Australia, from Jan 1980 to Aug 1995. Use `mypigs <- window(pigs, start=1990)` to select the data starting from 1990. Use `autoplot` and `ggAcf` for `mypigs` series and compare these to white noise plots from Figures 2.17 and 2.18.

10. `dj` contains 292 consecutive trading days of the Dow Jones Index. Use `ddj <- diff(dj)` to compute the daily changes in the index. Plot `ddj` and its ACF. Do the changes in the Dow Jones Index look like white noise?

2.11 Further reading

- Cleveland (1993) is a classic book on the principles of visualization for data analysis. While it is more than 20 years old, the ideas are timeless.
- Unwin (2015) is a modern introduction to graphical data analysis using R. It does not have much information on time series graphics, but plenty of excellent general advice on using graphics for data analysis.

Chapter 3

The forecaster's toolbox

In this chapter, we discuss some general tools that are useful for many different forecasting situations. We will describe some benchmark forecasting methods, ways of making the forecasting task simpler using transformations and adjustments, methods for checking whether a forecasting method has adequately utilized the available information, and techniques for computing prediction intervals.

Each of the tools discussed in this chapter will be used repeatedly in subsequent chapters as we develop and explore a range of forecasting methods.

3.1 Some simple forecasting methods

Some forecasting methods are very simple and surprisingly effective. We will use the following four forecasting methods as benchmarks throughout this book.

Average method

Here, the forecasts of all future values are equal to the average (or "mean") of the historical data. If we let the historical data be denoted by $y_1,\dots,y_T$, then we can write the forecasts as

$$\hat{y}_{T+h|T} = \bar{y} = (y_1 + \cdots + y_T)/T.$$

The notation $\hat{y}_{T+h|T}$ is a short-hand for the estimate of y_{T+h} based on the data $y_1,\dots,y_T$.

```
meanf(y, h)
# y contains the time series
# h is the forecast horizon
```

Naïve method

For naïve forecasts, we simply set all forecasts to be the value of the last observation. That is,

$$\hat{y}_{T+h|T} = y_T.$$

This method works remarkably well for many economic and financial time series.

```
naive(y, h)
rwf(y, h) # Equivalent alternative
```

Because a naïve forecast is optimal when data follow a random walk (see Section 8.1), these are also called **random walk forecasts**.

Seasonal naïve method

A similar method is useful for highly seasonal data. In this case, we set each forecast to be equal to the last observed value from the same season of the year (e.g., the same month of the previous year). Formally, the forecast for time $T + h$ is written as

$$\hat{y}_{T+h|T} = y_{T+h-m(k+1)},$$

where m = the seasonal period, and k is the integer part of $(h-1)/m$ (i.e., the number of complete years in the forecast period prior to time $T+h$). This looks more complicated than it really is. For example, with monthly data, the forecast for all future February values is equal to the last observed February value. With quarterly data, the forecast of all future Q2 values is equal to the last observed Q2 value (where Q2 means the second quarter). Similar rules apply for other months and quarters, and for other seasonal periods.

```
snaive(y, h)
```

Drift method

A variation on the naïve method is to allow the forecasts to increase or decrease over time, where the amount of change over time (called the **drift**) is set to be the average change seen in the historical data. Thus the forecast for time $T+h$ is given by

$$\hat{y}_{T+h|T} = y_T + \frac{h}{T-1}\sum_{t=2}^{T}(y_t - y_{t-1}) = y_T + h\left(\frac{y_T - y_1}{T-1}\right).$$

This is equivalent to drawing a line between the first and last observations, and extrapolating it into the future.

```
rwf(y, h, drift=TRUE)
```

Examples

Figure 3.1 shows the first three methods applied to the quarterly beer production data.

```
# Set training data from 1992-2007
beer2 <- window(ausbeer,start=1992,end=c(2007,4))
# Plot some forecasts
autoplot(beer2) +
  autolayer(meanf(beer2, h=11),
    series="Mean", PI=FALSE) +
  autolayer(naive(beer2, h=11),
    series="Naïve", PI=FALSE) +
  autolayer(snaive(beer2, h=11),
    series="Seasonal naïve", PI=FALSE) +
  ggtitle("Forecasts for quarterly beer production") +
  xlab("Year") + ylab("Megalitres") +
  guides(colour=guide_legend(title="Forecast"))
```

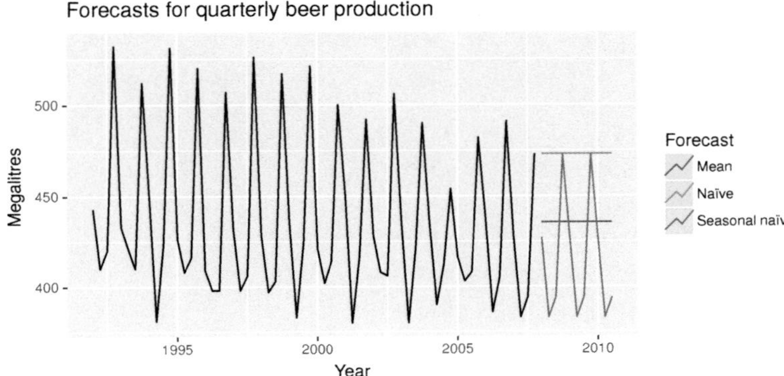

Figure 3.1: Forecasts of Australian quarterly beer production.

In Figure 3.2, the non-seasonal methods are applied to a series of 200 days of the Google daily closing stock price.

```
autoplot(goog200) +
  autolayer(meanf(goog200, h=40),
    series="Mean", PI=FALSE) +
  autolayer(rwf(goog200, h=40),
    series="Naïve", PI=FALSE) +
  autolayer(rwf(goog200, drift=TRUE, h=40),
    series="Drift", PI=FALSE) +
  ggtitle("Google stock (daily ending 6 Dec 2013)") +
  xlab("Day") + ylab("Closing Price (US$)") +
  guides(colour=guide_legend(title="Forecast"))
```

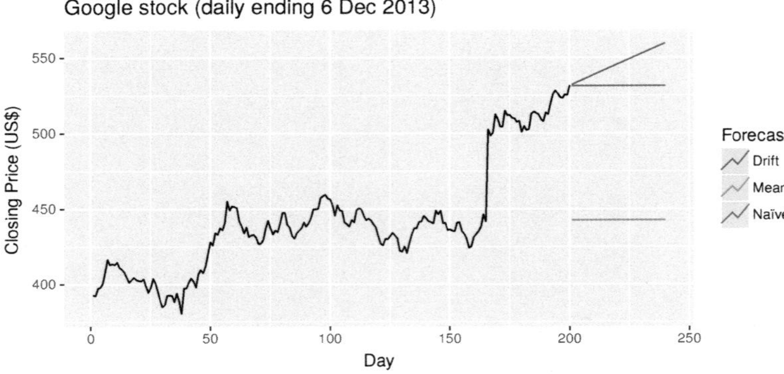

Figure 3.2: Forecasts based on 200 days of the Google daily closing stock price.

Sometimes one of these simple methods will be the best forecasting method available; but in many cases, these methods will serve as benchmarks rather than the method of choice. That is, any forecasting methods we develop will be compared to these simple methods to ensure that the new method is better than these simple alternatives. If not, the new method is not worth considering.

3.2 Transformations and adjustments

Adjusting the historical data can often lead to a simpler forecasting task. Here, we deal with four kinds of adjustments: calendar adjustments, population adjustments, inflation adjustments and mathematical transformations. The purpose of these adjustments and transformations is to simplify the patterns in the historical data by removing known sources of variation or by making the pattern more consistent across the whole data set. Simpler patterns usually lead to more accurate forecasts.

Calendar adjustments

Some of the variation seen in seasonal data may be due to simple calendar effects. In such cases, it is usually much easier to remove the variation before fitting a forecasting model. The `monthdays()` function will compute the number of days in each month or quarter.

For example, if you are studying the monthly milk production on a farm, there will be variation between the months simply because of the different numbers of days in each month, in addition to the seasonal variation across the year.

```
dframe <- cbind(Monthly = milk,
                DailyAverage = milk/monthdays(milk))
  autoplot(dframe, facet=TRUE) +
    xlab("Years") + ylab("Pounds") +
    ggtitle("Milk production per cow")
```

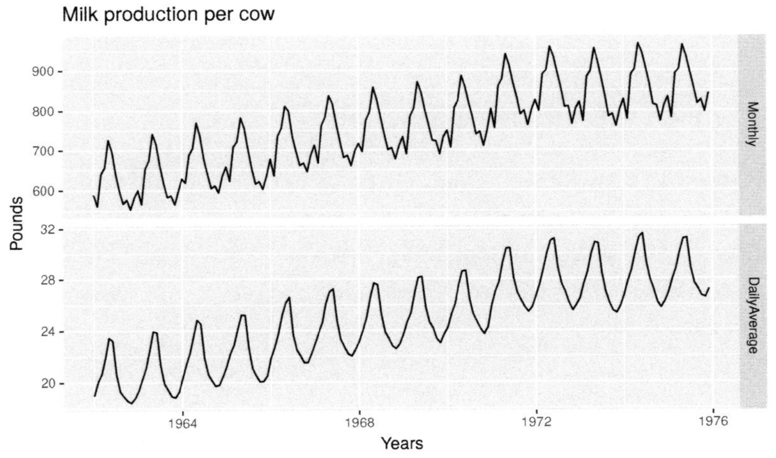

Figure 3.3: Monthly milk production per cow.

Notice how much simpler the seasonal pattern is in the average daily production plot compared to the average monthly production plot. By looking at the average daily production instead of the average monthly production, we effectively remove the variation due to the different month lengths. Simpler patterns are usually easier to model and lead to more accurate forecasts.

A similar adjustment can be done for sales data when the number of trading days in each month varies. In this case, the sales per trading day can be modelled instead of the total sales for each month.

Population adjustments

Any data that are affected by population changes can be adjusted to give per-capita data. That is, consider the data per person (or per thousand people, or per million people) rather than the total. For example, if you are studying the number of hospital beds in a particular region over time, the results are much easier to interpret if you remove the effects of population changes by considering the number of beds per thousand people. Then you can see whether there have been real increases in the number of beds, or whether the increases are due entirely to population increases. It is possible for the total number of beds to increase, but the number of beds per thousand people to decrease. This occurs when the population is increasing faster than the number of hospital beds. For most data that are affected by population changes, it is best to use per-capita data rather than the totals.

Inflation adjustments

Data which are affected by the value of money are best adjusted before modelling. For example, the average cost of a new house will have increased over the last few decades due to inflation. A $200,000 house this year is not the same as a $200,000 house twenty years ago. For this reason, financial time series are usually adjusted so that all values are stated in dollar values from a particular year. For example, the house price data may be stated in year 2000 dollars.

To make these adjustments, a price index is used. If z_t denotes the price index and y_t denotes the original house price in year t, then $x_t = y_t/z_t * z_{2000}$ gives the adjusted house price at year 2000 dollar values. Price indexes are often constructed by government agencies. For consumer goods, a common price index is the Consumer Price Index (or CPI).

Mathematical transformations

If the data show variation that increases or decreases with the level of the series, then a transformation can be useful. For example, a logarithmic transformation is often useful. If we denote the original observations as $y_1, \dots, y_T$ and the transformed observations as $w_1, \dots, w_T$, then $w_t = \log(y_t)$. Logarithms are useful because they are interpretable: changes in a log value are relative (or percentage) changes on the original scale. So if log base 10 is used, then an increase of 1 on the log scale corresponds to a multiplication of 10 on the original scale. Another useful feature of log transformations is that they constrain the forecasts to stay positive on the original scale.

Sometimes other transformations are also used (although they are not so interpretable). For example, square roots and cube roots can be used. These are called **power transformations** because they can be written in the form $w_t = y_t^p$.

A useful family of transformations, that includes both logarithms and power transformations, is the family of **Box-Cox transformations**, which depend on the parameter λ and are defined as follows:

$$w_t = \begin{cases} \log(y_t) & \text{if } \lambda = 0; \\ (y_t^\lambda - 1)/\lambda & \text{otherwise.} \end{cases}$$

The logarithm in a Box-Cox transformation is always a natural logarithm (i.e., to base e). So if $\lambda = 0$, natural logarithms are used, but if $\lambda \neq 0$, a power transformation is used, followed by some simple scaling.

If $\lambda = 1$, then $w_t = y_t - 1$, so the transformed data is shifted downwards but there is no change in the shape of the time series. But for all other values of λ, the time series will change shape.

A good value of λ is one which makes the size of the seasonal variation about the same across the whole series, as that makes the forecasting model simpler. In this case, $\lambda = 0.30$ works quite well, although any value of λ between 0 and 0.5 would give similar results.

The `BoxCox.lambda()` function will choose a value of lambda for you.

```
(lambda <- BoxCox.lambda(elec))
#> [1] 0.2654
autoplot(BoxCox(elec,lambda))
```

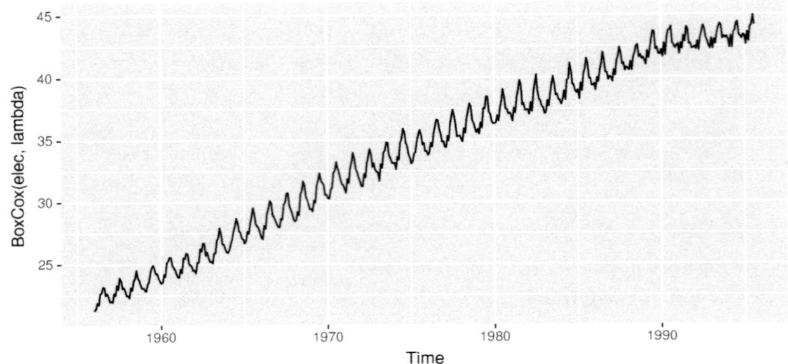

Having chosen a transformation, we need to forecast the transformed data. Then, we need to reverse the transformation (or *back-transform*) to obtain forecasts on the original scale. The reverse Box-Cox transformation is given by

$$y_t = \begin{cases} \exp(w_t) & \text{if } \lambda = 0; \\ (\lambda w_t + 1)^{1/\lambda} & \text{otherwise.} \end{cases} \tag{3.1}$$

Features of power transformations

- If some $y_t \leq 0$, no power transformation is possible unless all observations are adjusted by adding a constant to all values.
- Choose a simple value of λ. It makes explanations easier.
- The forecasting results are relatively insensitive to the value of λ.
- Often no transformation is needed.
- Transformations sometimes make little difference to the forecasts but have a large effect on prediction intervals.

Bias adjustments

One issue with using mathematical transformations such as Box-Cox transformations is that the back-transformed forecast will not be the mean of the forecast distribution. In fact, it will usually be the median of the forecast distribution (assuming that the distribution on the transformed space is symmetric). For many purposes, this is acceptable, but occasionally the mean forecast is required. For example, you may wish to add up sales forecasts from various regions to form a forecast for the whole country. But medians do not add up, whereas means do.

For a Box-Cox transformation, the back-transformed mean is given by

$$y_t = \begin{cases} \exp(w_t)\left[1 + \frac{\sigma_h^2}{2}\right] & \text{if } \lambda = 0; \\ (\lambda w_t + 1)^{1/\lambda}\left[1 + \frac{\sigma_h^2(1-\lambda)}{2(\lambda w_t+1)^2}\right] & \text{otherwise;} \end{cases} \tag{3.2}$$

where σ_h^2 is the h-step forecast variance. The larger the forecast variance, the bigger the difference between the mean and the median.

The difference between the simple back-transformed forecast given by (3.1) and the mean given by (3.2) is called the **bias**. When we use the mean, rather than the median, we say the point forecasts have been **bias-adjusted**.

To see how much difference this bias-adjustment makes, consider the following example, where we forecast average annual price of eggs using the drift method with a log transformation ($\lambda = 0$). The log transformation is useful in this case to ensure the forecasts and the prediction intervals stay positive.

```
fc <- rwf(eggs, drift=TRUE, lambda=0, h=50, level=80)
fc2 <- rwf(eggs, drift=TRUE, lambda=0, h=50, level=80,
  biasadj=TRUE)
autoplot(eggs) +
  autolayer(fc, series="Simple back transformation") +
  autolayer(fc2, series="Bias adjusted", PI=FALSE) +
  guides(colour=guide_legend(title="Forecast"))
```

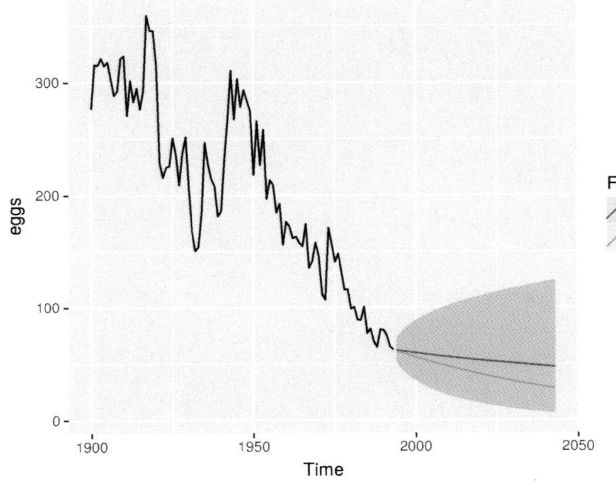

Figure 3.4: Forecasts of egg prices using a random walk with drift applied to the logged data.

The blue line in Figure 3.4 shows the forecast medians while the red line shows the forecast means. Notice how the skewed forecast distribution pulls up the point forecast when we use the bias adjustment.

Bias adjustment is not done by default in the **forecast** package. If you want your forecasts to be means rather than medians, use the argument `biasadj=TRUE` when you select your Box-Cox transformation parameter.

3.3 Residual diagnostics

Fitted values

Each observation in a time series can be forecast using all previous observations. We call these **fitted values** and they are denoted by $\hat{y}_{t|t-1}$, meaning the forecast of y_t based on observations $y_1, \dots, y_{t-1}$. We use these so often, we sometimes drop part of the subscript and just write $\hat{y}_t$ instead of $\hat{y}_{t|t-1}$. Fitted values always involve one-step forecasts.

Actually, fitted values are often not true forecasts because any parameters involved in the forecasting method are estimated using all available observations in the time series, including future observations. For example, if we use the average method, the fitted values are given by

$$\hat{y}_t = \hat{c}$$

where $\hat{c}$ is the average computed over all available observations, including those at times *after* t. Similarly, for the drift method, the drift parameter is estimated using all available observations. In this case, the fitted values are given by

$$\hat{y}_t = y_{t-1} + \hat{c}$$

where $\hat{c} = (y_T - y_1)/(T-1)$. In both cases, there is a parameter to be estimated from the data. The "hat" above the c reminds us that this is an estimate. When the estimate of c involves observations after time t, the fitted values are not true forecasts. On the other hand, naïve or seasonal naïve forecasts do not involve any parameters, and so fitted values are true forecasts in such cases.

Residuals

The "residuals" in a time series model are what is left over after fitting a model. For many (but not all) time series models, the residuals are equal to the difference between the observations and the corresponding fitted values:

$$e_t = y_t - \hat{y}_t.$$

Residuals are useful in checking whether a model has adequately captured the information in the data. A good forecasting method will yield residuals with the following properties:

1. The residuals are uncorrelated. If there are correlations between residuals, then there is information left in the residuals which should be used in computing forecasts.
2. The residuals have zero mean. If the residuals have a mean other than zero, then the forecasts are biased.

Any forecasting method that does not satisfy these properties can be improved. However, that does not mean that forecasting methods that satisfy these properties cannot be improved. It is possible to have several different forecasting methods for the same data set, all of which satisfy these properties. Checking these properties is important in order to see whether a method is using all of the available information, but it is not a good way to select a forecasting method.

If either of these properties is not satisfied, then the forecasting method can be modified to give better forecasts. Adjusting for bias is easy: if the residuals have mean m, then simply add m to all forecasts and the bias problem is solved. Fixing the correlation problem is harder, and we will not address it until Chapter 9.

In addition to these essential properties, it is useful (but not necessary) for the residuals to also have the following two properties.

3. The residuals have constant variance.
4. The residuals are normally distributed.

These two properties make the calculation of prediction intervals easier (see Section 3.5 for an example). However, a forecasting method that does not satisfy these properties cannot necessarily be improved. Sometimes applying a Box-Cox transformation may assist with these properties, but otherwise there is usually little that you can do to ensure that your residuals have constant variance and a normal distribution. Instead, an alternative approach to obtaining prediction intervals is necessary. Again, we will not address how to do this until later in the book.

Example: Forecasting the Google daily closing stock price

For stock market prices and indexes, the best forecasting method is often the naïve method. That is, each forecast is simply equal to the last observed value, or $\hat{y}_t = y_{t-1}$. Hence, the residuals are simply equal to the difference between consecutive observations:

$$e_t = y_t - \hat{y}_t = y_t - y_{t-1}.$$

The following graph shows the Google daily closing stock price (GOOG). The large jump at day 166 corresponds to 18 October 2013 when the price jumped 12% due to unexpectedly strong third quarter results.

```
autoplot(goog200) +
  xlab("Day") + ylab("Closing Price (US$)") +
  ggtitle("Google Stock (daily ending 6 December 2013)")
```

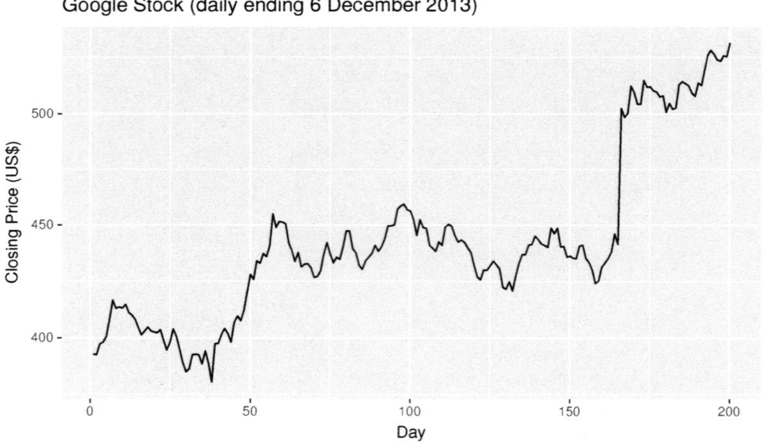

Figure 3.5: The daily Google stock price to 6 Dec 2013.

The residuals obtained from forecasting this series using the naïve method are shown in Figure 3.6. The large positive residual is a result of the unexpected price jump at day 166.

```r
res <- residuals(naive(goog200))
autoplot(res) + xlab("Day") + ylab("") +
  ggtitle("Residuals from naïve method")
```

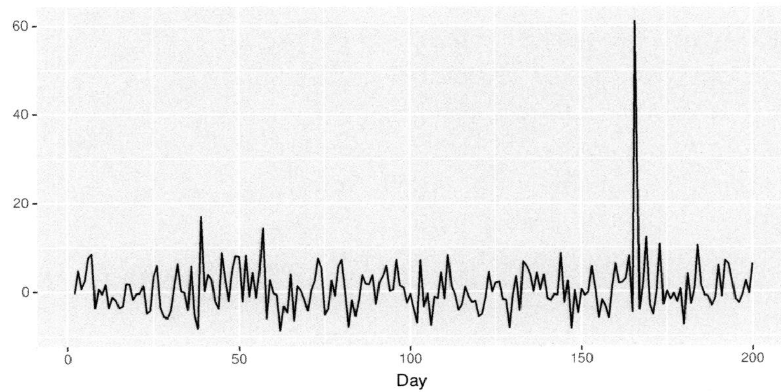

Figure 3.6: Residuals from forecasting the Google stock price using the naïve method.

```r
gghistogram(res) + ggtitle("Histogram of residuals")
```

Figure 3.7: Histogram of the residuals from the naïve method applied to the Google stock price. The right tail seems a little too long for a normal distribution.

```r
ggAcf(res) + ggtitle("ACF of residuals")
```

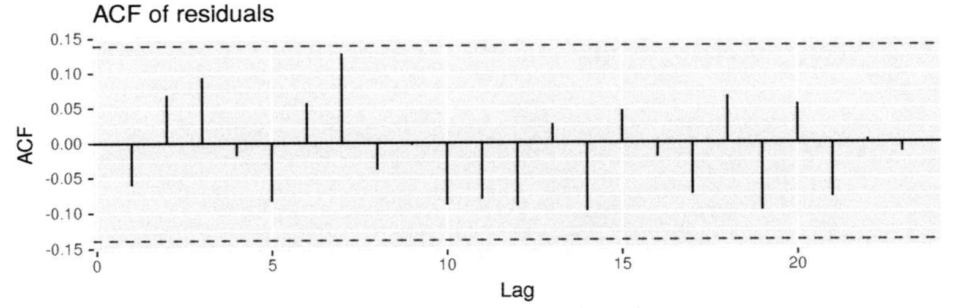

Figure 3.8: ACF of the residuals from the naïve method applied to the Google stock price. The lack of correlation suggesting the forecasts are good.

These graphs show that the naïve method produces forecasts that appear to account for all available information. The mean of the residuals is very close to zero and there is no significant correlation in the residuals series. The time plot of the residuals shows that the variation of the residuals stays much the same across the historical data, apart from the one outlier, and therefore the residual variance can be treated as constant. This can also be seen on the histogram of the residuals. The histogram suggests that the residuals may not be normal — the right tail seems a little too long, even when we ignore the outlier. Consequently, forecasts from this method will probably be quite good, but prediction intervals that are computed assuming a normal distribution may be inaccurate.

Portmanteau tests for autocorrelation

In addition to looking at the ACF plot, we can also do a more formal test for autocorrelation by considering a whole set of r_k values as a group, rather than treating each one separately.

Recall that r_k is the autocorrelation for lag k. When we look at the ACF plot to see whether each spike is within the required limits, we are implicitly carrying out multiple hypothesis tests, each one with a small probability of giving a false positive. When enough of these tests are done, it is likely that at least one will give a false positive, and so we may conclude that the residuals have some remaining autocorrelation, when in fact they do not.

In order to overcome this problem, we test whether the first h autocorrelations are significantly different from what would be expected from a white noise process. A test for a group of autocorrelations is called a **portmanteau test**, from a French word describing a suitcase containing a number of items.

One such test is the **Box-Pierce test**, based on the following statistic

$$Q = T\sum_{k=1}^{h} r_k^2,$$

where h is the maximum lag being considered and T is the number of observations. If each r_k is close to zero, then Q will be small. If some r_k values are large (positive or negative), then Q will be large. We suggest using $h = 10$ for non-seasonal data and $h = 2m$ for seasonal data, where m is the period of seasonality. However, the test is not good when h is large, so if these values are larger than $T/5$, then use $h = T/5$

A related (and more accurate) test is the **Ljung-Box test**, based on

$$Q^* = T(T+2)\sum_{k=1}^{h}(T-k)^{-1}r_k^2.$$

Again, large values of Q^* suggest that the autocorrelations do not come from a white noise series.

How large is too large? If the autocorrelations did come from a white noise series, then both Q and Q^* would have a χ^2 distribution with $(h - K)$ degrees of freedom, where K is the number of parameters in the model. If they are calculated from raw data (rather than the residuals from a model), then set $K = 0$.

For the Google stock price example, the naïve model has no parameters, so $K = 0$ in that case also.

```
# lag=h and fitdf=K
Box.test(res, lag=10, fitdf=0)
#>
#>  Box-Pierce test
#>
#> data:  res
#> X-squared = 11, df = 10, p-value = 0.4

Box.test(res,lag=10, fitdf=0, type="Lj")
#>
#>  Box-Ljung test
#>
#> data:  res
#> X-squared = 11, df = 10, p-value = 0.4
```

For both Q and Q^*, the results are not significant (i.e., the p-values are relatively large). Thus, we can conclude that the residuals are not distinguishable from a white noise series.

All of these methods for checking residuals are conveniently packaged into one R function `checkresiduals()`, which will produce a time plot, ACF plot and histogram of the residuals (with an overlayed normal distribution for comparison), and do a Ljung-Box test with the correct degrees of freedom.

```r
checkresiduals(naive(goog200))
```

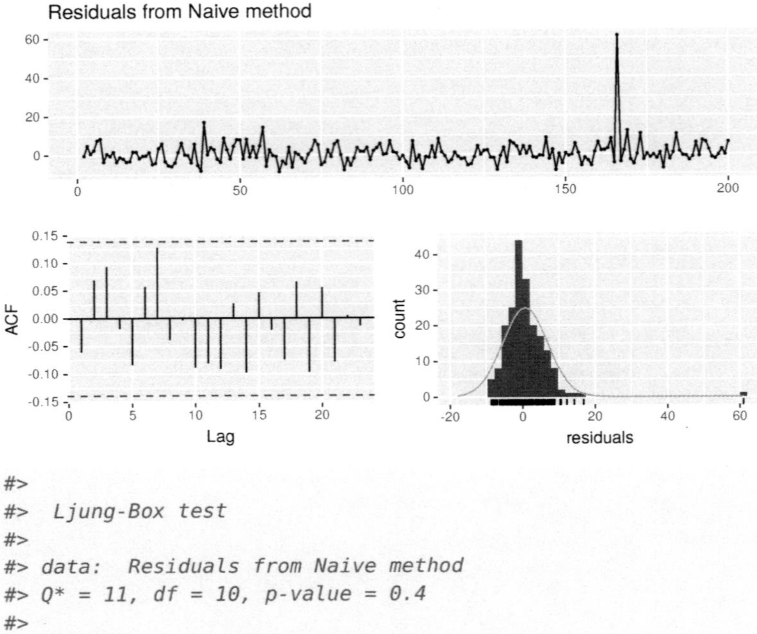


```
#>
#>  Ljung-Box test
#>
#> data:  Residuals from Naive method
#> Q* = 11, df = 10, p-value = 0.4
#>
#> Model df: 0.   Total lags used: 10
```

3.4 Evaluating forecast accuracy

Training and test sets

It is important to evaluate forecast accuracy using genuine forecasts. Consequently, the size of the residuals is not a reliable indication of how large true forecast errors are likely to be. The accuracy of forecasts can only be determined by considering how well a model performs on new data that were not used when fitting the model.

When choosing models, it is common practice to separate the available data into two portions, **training** and **test** data, where the training data is used to estimate any parameters of a forecasting method and the test data is used to evaluate its accuracy. Because the test data is not used in determining the forecasts, it should provide a reliable indication of how well the model is likely to forecast on new data.

The size of the test set is typically about 20% of the total sample, although this value depends on how long the sample is and how far ahead you want to forecast. The test set should ideally be at least as large as the maximum forecast horizon required. The following points should be noted.

- A model which fits the training data well will not necessarily forecast well.
- A perfect fit can always be obtained by using a model with enough parameters.
- Over-fitting a model to data is just as bad as failing to identify a systematic pattern in the data.

Some references describe the test set as the "hold-out set" because these data are "held out" of the data used for fitting. Other references call the training set the "in-sample data" and the test set the "out-of-sample data". We prefer to use "training data" and "test data" in this book.

Functions to subset a time series

The `window()` function introduced in Chapter 2 is very useful when extracting a portion of a time series, such as we need when creating training and test sets. In the `window()` function, we specify the start and/or end of the portion of time series required using time values. For example,

```
window(ausbeer, start=1995)
```

extracts all data from 1995 onwards.

Another useful function is `subset()` which allows for more types of subsetting. A great advantage of this function is that it allows the use of indices to choose a subset. For example,

```
subset(ausbeer, start=length(ausbeer)-4*5)
```

extracts the last 5 years of observations from `ausbeer`. It also allows extracting all values for a specific season. For example,

```
subset(ausbeer, quarter = 1)
```

extracts the first quarters for all years.

Finally, `head` and `tail` are useful for extracting the first few or last few observations. For example, the last 5 years of `ausbeer` can also be obtained using

```
tail(ausbeer, 4*5)
```

Forecast errors

A forecast "error" is the difference between an observed value and its forecast. Here "error" does not mean a mistake, it means the unpredictable part of an observation. It can be written as

$$e_{T+h} = y_{T+h} - \hat{y}_{T+h|T},$$

where the training data is given by $\{y_1, \dots, y_T\}$ and the test data is given by $\{y_{T+1}, y_{T+2}, \dots\}$.

Note that forecast errors are different from residuals in two ways. First, residuals are calculated on the *training* set while forecast errors are calculated on the *test* set. Second, residuals are based on *one-step* forecasts while forecast errors can involve *multi-step* forecasts.

We can measure forecast accuracy by summarising the forecast errors in different ways.

Scale-dependent errors

The forecast errors are on the same scale as the data. Accuracy measures that are based only on e_t are therefore scale-dependent and cannot be used to make comparisons between series that involve different units.

The two most commonly used scale-dependent measures are based on the absolute errors or squared errors:

$$\text{Mean absolute error: MAE} = \text{mean}(|e_t|),$$

$$\text{Root mean squared error: RMSE} = \sqrt{\text{mean}(e_t^2)}.$$

When comparing forecast methods applied to a single time series, or to several time series with the same units, the MAE is popular as it is easy to both understand and compute. A forecast method that minimizes the MAE will lead to forecasts of the median, while minimizing the RMSE will lead to forecasts of the mean. Consequently, the RMSE is also widely used, despite being more difficult to interpret.

Percentage errors

The percentage error is given by $p_t = 100e_t/y_t$. Percentage errors have the advantage of being unit-free, and so are frequently used to compare forecast performances between data sets. The most commonly used measure is:

$$\text{Mean absolute percentage error: MAPE} = \text{mean}(|p_t|).$$

Measures based on percentage errors have the disadvantage of being infinite or undefined if $y_t = 0$ for any t in the period of interest, and having extreme values if any y_t is close to zero. Another problem with percentage errors that is often overlooked is that they assume the unit of measurement has a meaningful zero.[1] For example, a percentage error makes no sense when measuring the accuracy of temperature forecasts on either the Fahrenheit or Celsius scales, because temperature has an arbitrary zero point.

[1] That is, a percentage is valid on a ratio scale, but not on an interval scale. Only ratio scale variables have meaningful zeros.

They also have the disadvantage that they put a heavier penalty on negative errors than on positive errors. This observation led to the use of the so-called "symmetric" MAPE (sMAPE) proposed by Armstrong (1985, p.348), which was used in the M3 forecasting competition. It is defined by

$$\text{sMAPE} = \text{mean}\left(200|y_t - \hat{y}_t|/(y_t + \hat{y}_t)\right).$$

However, if y_t is close to zero, $\hat{y}_t$ is also likely to be close to zero. Thus, the measure still involves division by a number close to zero, making the calculation unstable. Also, the value of sMAPE can be negative, so it is not really a measure of "absolute percentage errors" at all.

Hyndman and Koehler (2006) recommend that the sMAPE not be used. It is included here only because it is widely used, although we will not use it in this book.

Scaled errors

Scaled errors were proposed by Hyndman and Koehler (2006) as an alternative to using percentage errors when comparing forecast accuracy across series with different units. They proposed scaling the errors based on the *training* MAE from a simple forecast method.

For a non-seasonal time series, a useful way to define a scaled error uses naïve forecasts:

$$q_j = \frac{e_j}{\displaystyle\frac{1}{T-1}\sum_{t=2}^{T}|y_t - y_{t-1}|}.$$

Because the numerator and denominator both involve values on the scale of the original data, q_j is independent of the scale of the data. A scaled error is less than one if it arises from a better forecast than the average naïve forecast computed on the training data. Conversely, it is greater than one if the forecast is worse than the average naïve forecast computed on the training data.

For seasonal time series, a scaled error can be defined using seasonal naïve forecasts:

$$q_j = \frac{e_j}{\displaystyle\frac{1}{T-m}\sum_{t=m+1}^{T}|y_t - y_{t-m}|}.$$

The *mean absolute scaled error* is simply

$$\text{MASE} = \text{mean}(|q_j|).$$

Examples

```
beer2 <- window(ausbeer,start=1992,end=c(2007,4))
beerfit1 <- meanf(beer2,h=10)
beerfit2 <- rwf(beer2,h=10)
beerfit3 <- snaive(beer2,h=10)
autoplot(window(ausbeer, start=1992)) +
  autolayer(beerfit1, series="Mean", PI=FALSE) +
  autolayer(beerfit2, series="Naïve", PI=FALSE) +
  autolayer(beerfit3, series="Seasonal naïve", PI=FALSE) +
  xlab("Year") + ylab("Megalitres") +
  ggtitle("Forecasts for quarterly beer production") +
  guides(colour=guide_legend(title="Forecast"))
```

Figure 3.9 shows three forecast methods applied to the quarterly Australian beer production using data only to the end of 2007. The actual values for the period 2008–2010 are also shown. We compute the forecast accuracy measures for this period.

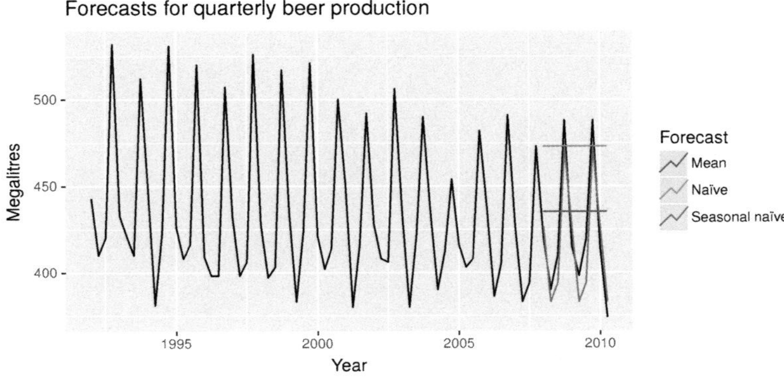

Figure 3.9: Forecasts of Australian quarterly beer production using data up to the end of 2007.

```
beer3 <- window(ausbeer, start=2008)
accuracy(beerfit1, beer3)
accuracy(beerfit2, beer3)
accuracy(beerfit3, beer3)
```

	RMSE	MAE	MAPE	MASE
Mean method	38.45	34.83	8.28	2.44
Naïve method	62.69	57.40	14.18	4.01
Seasonal naïve method	14.31	13.40	3.17	0.94

It is obvious from the graph that the seasonal naïve method is best for these data, although it can still be improved, as we will discover later. Sometimes, different accuracy measures will lead to different results as to which forecast method is best. However, in this case, all of the results point to the seasonal naïve method as the best of these three methods for this data set.

To take a non-seasonal example, consider the Google stock price. The following graph shows the 200 observations ending on 6 Dec 2013, along with forecasts of the next 40 days obtained from three different methods.

```
googfc1 <- meanf(goog200, h=40)
googfc2 <- rwf(goog200, h=40)
googfc3 <- rwf(goog200, drift=TRUE, h=40)
autoplot(subset(goog, end = 240)) +
  autolayer(googfc1, PI=FALSE, series="Mean") +
  autolayer(googfc2, PI=FALSE, series="Naïve") +
  autolayer(googfc3, PI=FALSE, series="Drift") +
  xlab("Day") + ylab("Closing Price (US$)") +
  ggtitle("Google stock price (daily ending 6 Dec 13)") +
  guides(colour=guide_legend(title="Forecast"))
```

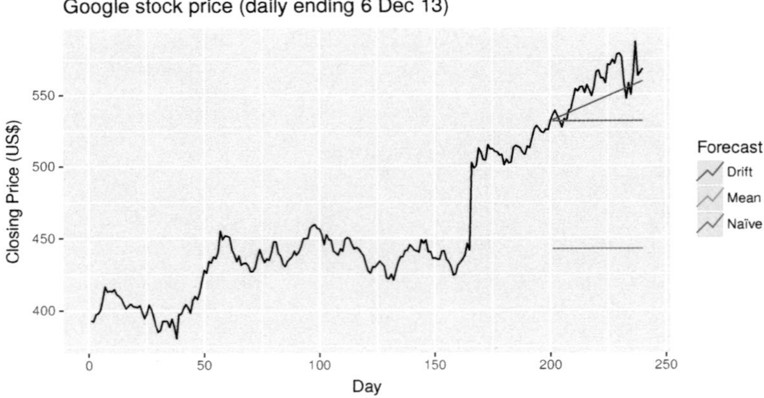

Figure 3.10: Forecasts of the Google stock price from 7 Dec 2013.

```
googtest <- window(goog, start=201, end=240)
accuracy(googfc1, googtest)
accuracy(googfc2, googtest)
accuracy(googfc3, googtest)
```

	RMSE	MAE	MAPE	MASE
Mean method	114.21	113.27	20.32	30.28
Naïve method	28.43	24.59	4.36	6.57
Drift method	14.08	11.67	2.07	3.12

Here, the best method is the drift method (regardless of which accuracy measure is used).

Time series cross-validation

A more sophisticated version of training/test sets is time series cross-validation. In this procedure, there are a series of test sets, each consisting of a single observation. The corresponding training set consists only of observations that occurred *prior* to the observation that forms the test set. Thus, no future observations can be used in constructing the forecast. Since it is not possible to obtain a reliable forecast based on a very small training set, the earliest observations are not considered as test sets.

The following diagram illustrates the series of training and test sets, where the blue observations form the training sets, and the red observations form the test sets.

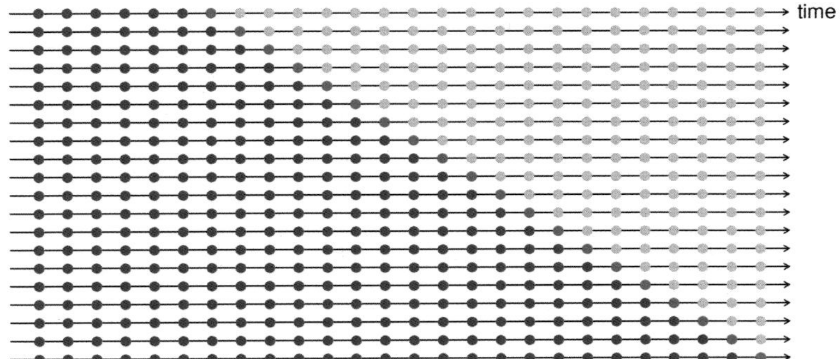

The forecast accuracy is computed by averaging over the test sets. This procedure is sometimes known as "evaluation on a rolling forecasting origin" because the "origin" at which the forecast is based rolls forward in time.

With time series forecasting, one-step forecasts may not be as relevant as multi-step forecasts. In this case, the cross-validation procedure based on a rolling forecasting origin can be modified to allow multi-step errors to be used. Suppose that we are interested in models that produce good 4-step-ahead forecasts. Then the corresponding diagram is shown below.

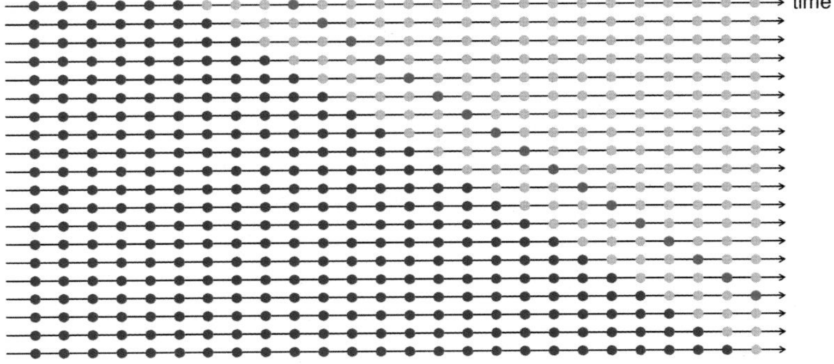

Time series cross-validation is implemented with the `tsCV()` function. In the following example, we compare the RMSE obtained via time series cross-validation with the residual RMSE.

```
e <- tsCV(goog200, rwf, drift=TRUE, h=1)
sqrt(mean(e^2, na.rm=TRUE))
#> [1] 6.233
sqrt(mean(residuals(rwf(goog200, drift=TRUE))^2, na.rm=TRUE))
#> [1] 6.169
```

As expected, the RMSE from the residuals is smaller, as the corresponding "forecasts" are based on a model fitted to the entire data set, rather than being true forecasts.

A good way to choose the best forecasting model is to find the model with the smallest RMSE computed using time series cross-validation.

Pipe operator

The ugliness of the above R code makes this a good opportunity to introduce some alternative ways of stringing R functions together. In the above code, we are nesting functions within functions within functions, so you have to read the code from the inside out, making it difficult to understand what is being computed. Instead, we can use the pipe operator `%>%` as follows.

```
goog200 %>% tsCV(forecastfunction=rwf, drift=TRUE, h=1) -> e
e^2 %>% mean(na.rm=TRUE) %>% sqrt()
#> [1] 6.233
goog200 %>% rwf(drift=TRUE) %>% residuals() -> res
res^2 %>% mean(na.rm=TRUE) %>% sqrt()
#> [1] 6.169
```

The left hand side of each pipe is passed as the first argument to the function on the right hand side. This is consistent with the way we read from left to right in English. When using pipes, all other arguments must be named, which also helps readability. When using pipes, it is natural to use the right arrow assignment `->` rather than the left arrow. For example, the third line above can be read as "Take the `goog200` series, pass it to `rwf()` with `drift=TRUE`, compute the resulting residuals, and store them as `res`".

We will use the pipe operator whenever it makes the code easier to read. In order to be consistent, we will always follow a function with parentheses to differentiate it from other objects, even if it has no arguments. See, for example, the use of `sqrt()` and `residuals()` in the code above.

Example: using tsCV()

The goog200 data, plotted in Figure 3.5, includes daily closing stock price of Google Inc from the NASDAQ exchange for 200 consecutive trading days starting on 25 February 2013.

The code below evaluates the forecasting performance of 1- to 8-step-ahead naïve forecasts with tsCV(), using MSE as the forecast error measure. The plot shows that the forecast error increases as the forecast horizon increases, as we would expect.

```
e <- tsCV(goog200, forecastfunction=naive, h=8)
# Compute the MSE values and remove missing values
mse <- colMeans(e^2, na.rm = T)
# Plot the MSE values against the forecast horizon
data.frame(h = 1:8, MSE = mse) %>%
  ggplot(aes(x = h, y = MSE)) + geom_point()
```

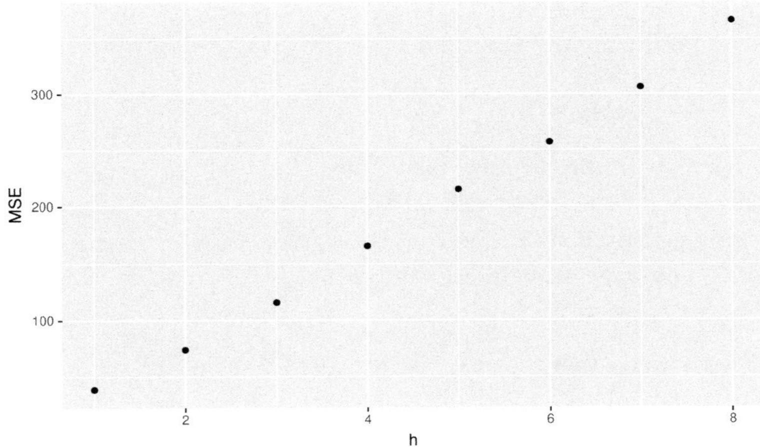

3.5 Prediction intervals

As discussed in Section 1.7, a prediction interval gives an interval within which we expect y_t to lie with a specified probability. For example, assuming that the forecast errors are normally distributed, a 95% prediction interval for the h-step forecast is

$$\hat{y}_{T+h|T} \pm 1.96\hat{\sigma}_h,$$

where $\hat{\sigma}_h$ is an estimate of the standard deviation of the h-step forecast distribution.

Percentage	Multiplier
50	0.67
55	0.76
60	0.84
65	0.93
70	1.04
75	1.15
80	1.28
85	1.44
90	1.64
95	1.96
96	2.05
97	2.17
98	2.33
99	2.58

Table 3.1: Multipliers to be used for prediction intervals.

More generally, a prediction interval can be written as

$$\hat{y}_{T+h|T} \pm c\hat{\sigma}_h$$

where the multiplier c depends on the coverage probability. In this book we usually calculate 80% intervals and 95% intervals, although any percentage may be used. The following table gives the value of c for a range of coverage probabilities assuming normally distributed forecast errors.

The value of prediction intervals is that they express the uncertainty in the forecasts. If we only produce point forecasts, there is no way of telling how accurate the forecasts are. However, if we also produce prediction intervals, then it is clear how much uncertainty is associated with each forecast. For this reason, point forecasts can be of almost no value without the accompanying prediction intervals.

One-step prediction intervals

When forecasting one step ahead, the standard deviation of the forecast distribution is almost the same as the standard deviation of the residuals. (In fact, the two standard deviations are identical if there are no parameters to be estimated, as is the case with the naïve method. For forecasting methods involving parameters to be estimated, the standard deviation of the forecast distribution is slightly larger than the residual standard deviation, although this difference is often ignored.)

For example, consider a naïve forecast for the Google stock price data `goog200` (shown in Figure 3.5). The last value of the observed series is 531.48, so the forecast of the next value of the GSP is 531.48. The standard deviation of the residuals from the naïve method is 6.21. Hence, a 95% prediction interval for the next value of the GSP is

$$531.48 \pm 1.96(6.21) = [519.3, 543.6].$$

Similarly, an 80% prediction interval is given by

$$531.48 \pm 1.28(6.21) = [523.5, 539.4].$$

The value of the multiplier (1.96 or 1.28) is taken from Table 3.1.

Multi-step prediction intervals

A common feature of prediction intervals is that they increase in length as the forecast horizon increases. The further ahead we forecast, the more uncertainty is associated with the forecast, and thus the wider the prediction intervals. That is, σ_h usually increases with h (although there are some non-linear forecasting methods that do not have this property).

To produce a prediction interval, it is necessary to have an estimate of σ_h. As already noted, for one-step forecasts ($h = 1$), the residual standard deviation provides a good estimate of the forecast standard deviation σ_1. For multi-step forecasts, a more complicated method of calculation is required. These calculations assume that the residuals are uncorrelated.

Benchmark methods

For the four benchmark methods, it is possible to mathematically derive the forecast standard deviation under the assumption of uncorrelated residuals. If $\hat{\sigma}_h$ denotes the standard deviation of the h-step forecast distribution, and $\hat{\sigma}$ is the residual standard deviation, then we can use the following expressions.

Mean forecasts: $\hat{\sigma}_h = \hat{\sigma}\sqrt{1 + 1/T}$

Naïve forecasts: $\hat{\sigma}_h = \hat{\sigma}\sqrt{h}$

Seasonal naïve forecasts $\hat{\sigma}_h = \hat{\sigma}\sqrt{k + 1}$, where k is the integer part of $(h - 1)/m$.

Drift forecasts: $\hat{\sigma}_h = \hat{\sigma}\sqrt{h(1 + h/T)}$.

Note that when $h = 1$ and T is large, these all give the same approximate value $\hat{\sigma}$.

Prediction intervals will be computed for you when using any of the benchmark forecasting methods. For example, here is the output when using the naïve method for the Google stock price.

```
naive(goog200)
#>     Point Forecast Lo 80 Hi 80 Lo 95 Hi 95
#> 201          531.5 523.5 539.4 519.3 543.6
#> 202          531.5 520.2 542.7 514.3 548.7
#> 203          531.5 517.7 545.3 510.4 552.6
#> 204          531.5 515.6 547.4 507.1 555.8
#> 205          531.5 513.7 549.3 504.3 558.7
#> 206          531.5 512.0 551.0 501.7 561.3
#> 207          531.5 510.4 552.5 499.3 563.7
#> 208          531.5 509.0 554.0 497.1 565.9
#> 209          531.5 507.6 555.3 495.0 568.0
#> 210          531.5 506.3 556.6 493.0 570.0
```

When plotted, the prediction intervals are shown as shaded region, with the strength of colour indicating the probability associated with the interval.

```
autoplot(naive(goog200))
```

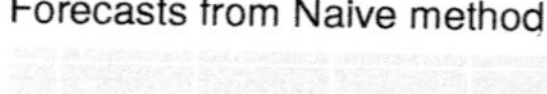

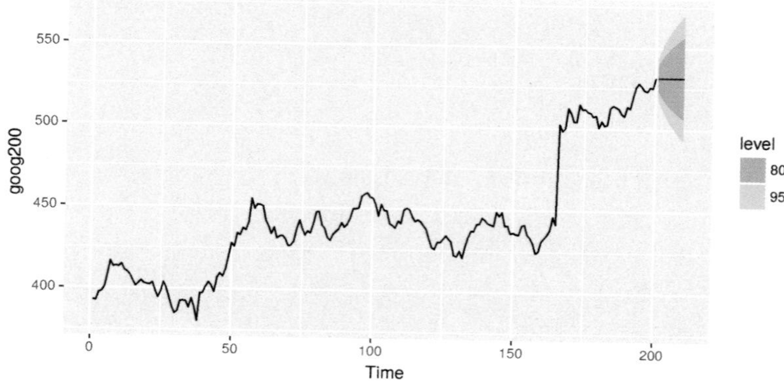

Prediction intervals from bootstrapped residuals

When a normal distribution for the forecast errors is an unreasonable assumption, one alternative is to use bootstrapping, which only assumes that the forecast errors are uncorrelated.

A forecast error is defined as $e_t = y_t - \hat{y}_{t|t-1}$. We can re-write this as

$$y_t = \hat{y}_{t|t-1} + e_t.$$

So we can simulate the next observation of a time series using

$$y_{T+1} = \hat{y}_{T+1|T} + e_{T+1}$$

where $\hat{y}_{T+1|T}$ is the one-step forecast and e_{T+1} is the unknown future error. Assuming future errors will be similar to past errors, we can replace e_{T+1} by sampling from the collection of errors we have seen in the past (i.e., the residuals). Adding the new simulated observation to our data set, we can repeat the process to obtain

$$y_{T+2} = \hat{y}_{T+2|T+1} + e_{T+2}$$

where e_{T+2} is another draw from the collection of residuals. Continuing in this way, we can simulate an entire set of future values for our time series.

Doing this repeatedly, we obtain many possible futures. Then we can compute prediction intervals by calculating percentiles for each forecast horizon. The result is called a **bootstrapped** prediction interval. The name "bootstrap" is a reference to pulling ourselves up by our bootstraps, because the process allows us to measure future uncertainty by only using the historical data.

To generate such intervals, we can simply add the `bootstrap` argument to our forecasting functions. For example:

```
naive(goog200, bootstrap=TRUE)
#>     Point Forecast Lo 80 Hi 80 Lo 95 Hi 95
#> 201          531.5 525.6 537.8 522.9 541.1
#> 202          531.5 523.0 539.4 519.5 546.2
#> 203          531.5 521.0 541.6 516.6 552.1
#> 204          531.5 519.4 543.4 514.1 566.7
#> 205          531.5 517.6 544.8 511.8 581.7
#> 206          531.5 516.2 546.8 509.8 583.4
#> 207          531.5 514.8 547.6 507.3 584.5
```

```
#> 208             531.5 513.2 549.5 505.8 587.7
#> 209             531.5 512.2 550.4 503.7 589.2
#> 210             531.5 510.7 551.7 502.1 591.3
```

In this case, they are very similar (but not identical) to the prediction intervals based on the normal distribution.

Prediction intervals with transformations

If a transformation has been used, then the prediction interval should be computed on the transformed scale, and the end points back-transformed to give a prediction interval on the original scale. This approach preserves the probability coverage of the prediction interval, although it will no longer be symmetric around the point forecast.

The back-transformation of prediction intervals is done automatically using the functions in the **forecast** package in R, provided you have used the `lambda` argument when computing the forecasts.

3.6 The forecast package in R

This book uses the facilities in the **forecast** package in R (which is loaded automatically whenever you load the **fpp2** package). This appendix briefly summarises some of the features of the package. Please refer to the help files for individual functions to learn more, and to see some examples of their use.

Functions that output a forecast object:

Many functions, including `meanf()`, `naive()`, `snaive()` and `rwf()`, produce output in the form of a `forecast` object (i.e., an object of class `forecast`). This allows other functions (such as `autoplot()`) to work consistently across a range of forecasting models.

Objects of class `forecast` contain information about the forecasting method, the data used, the point forecasts obtained, prediction intervals, residuals and fitted values. There are several functions designed to work with these objects including `autoplot()`, `summary()` and `print()`.

The following list shows all the functions that produce `forecast` objects.

- `meanf()`
- `naive()`, `snaive()`
- `rwf()`
- `croston()`
- `stlf()`
- `ses()`
- `holt()`, `hw()`
- `splinef()`
- `thetaf()`
- `forecast()`

`forecast()` function

So far we have used functions which produce a `forecast` object directly. But a more common approach, which we will focus on in the rest of the book, will be to fit a model to the data, and then use the `forecast()` function to produce forecasts from that model.

The `forecast()` function works with many different types of inputs. It generally takes a time series or time series model as its main argument, and produces forecasts appropriately. It always returns objects of class `forecast`.

If the first argument is of class `ts`, it returns forecasts from the automatic ETS algorithm discussed in Chapter 7.

Here is a simple example, applying `forecast()` to the `ausbeer` data:

```
forecast(ausbeer, h=4)
#>         Point Forecast Lo 80 Hi 80 Lo 95 Hi 95
#> 2010 Q3          404.6 385.9 423.3 376.0 433.3
#> 2010 Q4          480.4 457.5 503.3 445.4 515.4
#> 2011 Q1          417.0 396.5 437.6 385.6 448.4
#> 2011 Q2          383.1 363.5 402.7 353.1 413.1
```

That works quite well if you have no idea what sort of model to use. But by the end of this book, you should not need to use `forecast()` in this "blind" fashion. Instead, you will fit a model appropriate to the data, and then use `forecast()` to produce forecasts from that model.

3.7 Exercises

1. For the following series, find an appropriate Box-Cox transformation in order to stabilize the variance.

   - `usnetelec`
   - `usgdp`
   - `mcopper`
   - `enplanements`

2. Why is a Box-Cox transformation unhelpful for the `cangas` data?

3. What Box-Cox transformation would you select for your retail data (from Exercise 3 in Section 2.10)?

4. For each of the following series, make a graph of the data. If transforming seems appropriate, do so and describe the effect. `dole`, `usdeaths`, `bricksq`.

5. Calculate the residuals from a seasonal naïve forecast applied to the quarterly Australian beer production data from 1992. The following code will help.

   ```
   beer <- window(ausbeer, start=1992)
   fc <- snaive(beer)
   autoplot(fc)
   res <- residuals(fc)
   autoplot(res)
   ```

   Test if the residuals are white noise and normally distributed.

   ```
   checkresiduals(fc)
   ```

   What do you conclude?

6. Repeat the exercise for the `WWWusage` and `bricksq` data. Use whichever of `naive()` or `snaive()` is more appropriate in each case.

7. Are the following statements true or false? Explain your answer.

   a. Good forecast methods should have normally distributed residuals.
   b. A model with small residuals will give good forecasts.
   c. The best measure of forecast accuracy is MAPE.

d. If your model doesn't forecast well, you should make it more complicated.
e. Always choose the model with the best forecast accuracy as measured on the test set.

8. For your retail time series (from Exercise 3 in Section 2.10):

a. Split the data into two parts using

```
myts.train <- window(myts, end=c(2010,12))
myts.test <- window(myts, start=2011)
```

b. Check that your data have been split appropriately by producing the following plot.

```
autoplot(myts) +
  autolayer(myts.train, series="Training") +
  autolayer(myts.test, series="Test")
```

c. Calculate forecasts using `snaive` applied to `myts.train`.

```
fc <- snaive(myts.train)
```

d. Compare the accuracy of your forecasts against the actual values stored in `myts.test`.

```
accuracy(fc,myts.test)
```

e. Check the residuals.

```
checkresiduals(fc)
```

Do the residuals appear to be uncorrelated and normally distributed?

f. How sensitive are the accuracy measures to the training/test split?

9. `visnights` contains quarterly visitor nights (in millions) from 1998-2016 for twenty regions of Australia.

a. Use `window()` to create three training sets for `visnights[,"QLDMetro"],` omitting the last 1, 2 and 3 years; call these train1, train2, and train3, respectively. For example `train1 <- window(visnights[, "QLDMetro"], end = c(2015, 4))`.

b. Compute one year of forecasts for each training set using the `snaive()` method. Call these `fc1`, `fc2` and `fc3`, respectively.

c. Use `accuracy()` to compare the MAPE over the three test sets. Comment on these.

10. Use the Dow Jones index (data set `dowjones`) to do the following:

    a. Produce a time plot of the series.
    b. Produce forecasts using the drift method and plot them.
    c. Show that the forecasts are identical to extending the line drawn between the first and last observations.
    d. Try using some of the other benchmark functions to forecast the same data set. Which do you think is best? Why?

11. Consider the daily closing IBM stock prices (data set `ibmclose`).

    a. Produce some plots of the data in order to become familiar with it.
    b. Split the data into a training set of 300 observations and a test set of 69 observations.
    c. Try using various benchmark methods to forecast the training set and compare the results on the test set. Which method did best?
    d. Check the residuals of your preferred method. Do they resemble white noise?

12. Consider the sales of new one-family houses in the USA, Jan 1973 – Nov 1995 (data set `hsales`).

    a. Produce some plots of the data in order to become familiar with it.
    b. Split the `hsales` data set into a training set and a test set, where the test set is the last two years of data.
    c. Try using various benchmark methods to forecast the training set and compare the results on the test set. Which method did best?
    d. Check the residuals of your preferred method. Do they resemble white noise?

3.8 Further reading

- Ord, Fildes, and Kourentzes (2017) provides further discussion of simple benchmark forecasting methods.
- A review of forecast evaluation methods is given in Hyndman and Koehler (2006), looking at the strengths and weaknesses of different approaches. This is the paper that introduced the MASE as a general-purpose forecast accuracy measure.

Chapter 4

Judgmental forecasts

Forecasting using judgement is very common in practice. In many cases, judgmental forecasting is the only option, such as when there is a complete lack of historical data, or when a new product is being launched, or when a new competitor enters the market, or during completely new and unique market conditions. For example, in December 2012, the Australian government was the first in the world to pass legislation that banned the use of company logos on cigarette packets, and required all cigarette packets to be a dark green colour. Judgement must be applied in order to forecast the effect of such a policy, as there are no historical precedents.

There are also situations where the data are incomplete, or only become available after some delay. For example, central banks include judgement when forecasting the current level of economic activity, a procedure known as nowcasting, as GDP is only available on a quarterly basis.

Research in this area[1] has shown that the accuracy of judgmental forecasting improves when the forecaster has (i) important domain knowledge, and (ii) more timely, up-to-date information. A judgmental approach can be quick to adjust to such changes, information or events.

[1] Lawrence et al. (2006)

Over the years, the acceptance of judgmental forecasting as a science has increased, as has the recognition of its need. More importantly, the quality of judgmental forecasts has also improved, as a direct result of recognising that improvements in judgmental forecasting can be achieved by implementing well-structured and systematic approaches. It is important to recognise that judgmental forecasting is subjective and comes with limitations. However, implementing systematic and well-structured approaches can confine these limitations and markedly improve forecast accuracy.

There are three general settings in which judgmental forecasting is used: (i) there are no available data, so that statistical methods are not applicable and judgmental forecasting is the only feasible approach; (ii) data are available, statistical forecasts are generated, and these are then adjusted using judgement; and (iii) data are available and statistical and judgmental forecasts are generated independently and then combined. We should clarify that when data are available, applying statistical methods (such as those discussed in other chapters of this book), is preferable and should, at the very least, be used as a starting point. Statistical forecasts are generally superior to generating forecasts using only judgement. For the majority of the chapter, we focus on the first setting where no data are available, and in the very last section we discuss judgmentally adjusting statistical forecasts. We discuss combining forecasts in Section 12.4.

4.1 Beware of limitations

Judgmental forecasts are subjective, and therefore do not come free of bias or limitations.

Judgmental forecasts can be inconsistent. Unlike statistical forecasts, which can be generated by the same mathematical formulas every time, judgmental forecasts depend heavily on human cognition, and are vulnerable to its limitations. For example, a limited memory may render recent events more important than they actually are and may ignore momentous events from the more distant past; or a limited attention span may result in important information being missed; or a misunderstanding of causal relationships may lead to erroneous inferences. Furthermore, human judgement can vary due to the effect of psychological factors. One can imagine a manager who is in a positive frame of mind one day, generating forecasts that may tend to be somewhat optimistic, and in a negative frame of mind another day, generating somewhat less optimistic forecasts.

Judgement can be clouded by personal or political agendas, where targets and forecasts (as defined in Chapter 1) are not segregated. For example, if a sales manager knows that the forecasts she generates will be used to set sales expectations (targets), she may tend to set these low in order to show a good performance (i.e., exceed the expected targets). Even in cases where targets and forecasts are well segregated, judgement may be plagued by optimism or wishful thinking. For example, it would be highly unlikely that a team working towards launching a new product would forecast its failure. As we will discuss later, this optimism can be accentuated in a group meeting setting. "Beware of the enthusiasm of your marketing and sales colleagues"[2].

[2] Fildes and Goodwin (2007b)

Another undesirable property which is commonly seen in judgmental forecasting is the effect of anchoring. In this case, the subsequent forecasts tend to converge or be very close to an initial familiar reference point. For example, it is common to take the last observed value as a reference point. The forecaster is influenced unduly by prior information, and therefore gives this more weight in the forecasting process. Anchoring may lead to conservatism and undervaluing new and more current information, and thereby create a systematic bias.

4.2 Key principles

Using a systematic and well structured approach in judgmental forecasting helps to reduce the adverse effects of the limitations of judgmental forecasting, some of which we listed in the previous section. Whether this approach involves one individual or many, the following principles should be followed.

Set the forecasting task clearly and concisely

Care is needed when setting the forecasting challenges and expressing the forecasting tasks. It is important that everyone be clear about what the task is. All definitions should be clear and comprehensive, avoiding ambiguous and vague expressions. Also, it is important to avoid incorporating emotive terms and irrelevant information that may distract the forecaster. In the Delphi method that follows (see Section 4.3), it may sometimes be useful to conduct a preliminary round of information gathering before setting the forecasting task.

Implement a systematic approach

Forecast accuracy and consistency can be improved by using a systematic approach to judgmental forecasting involving checklists of categories of information which are relevant to the forecasting task. For example, it is helpful to identify what information is important and how this information is to be weighted. When forecasting the demand for a new product, what factors should we account for and how should we account for them? Should it be the price, the quality and/or quantity of the competition, the economic environment at the time, the target population of the product? It is worthwhile to devote significant effort and resources to put together decision rules that will lead to the best possible systematic approach.

Document and justify

Formalising and documenting the decision rules and assumptions implemented in the systematic approach can promote consistency, as the same rules can be implemented repeatedly. Also, requesting a forecaster to document and justify their forecasts leads to accountability, which can lead to reduced bias. Furthermore, formal documentation aids significantly in the systematic evaluation process that is suggested next.

Systematically evaluate forecasts

Systematically monitoring the forecasting process can identify unforeseen irregularities. In particular, keep records of forecasts and use them to obtain feedback when the corresponding observations become available. Although you may do your best as a forecaster, the environment you operate in is dynamic. Changes occur, and you need to monitor these in order to evaluate the decision rules and assumptions. Feedback and evaluation help forecasters learn and improve their forecast accuracy.

Segregate forecasters and users

Forecast accuracy may be impeded if the forecasting task is carried out by users of the forecasts, such as those responsible for implementing plans of action about which the forecast is concerned. We should clarify again here (as in Section 1.2), that forecasting is about predicting the future as accurately as possible, given all of the information available, including historical data and knowledge of any future events that may impact the forecasts. Forecasters and users should be clearly segregated. A classic case is that of a new product being launched. The forecast should be a reasonable estimate of the sales volume of a new product, which may differ considerably from what management expects or hopes the sales will be in order to meet company financial objectives. In this case, a forecaster may be delivering a reality check to the user.

It is important that forecasters communicate forecasts to potential users thoroughly. As we will see in Section 4.7, users may feel distant and disconnected from forecasts, and may not have full confidence in them. Explaining and clarifying the process and justifying the basic assumptions that led to the forecasts will provide some assurance to users.

The way in which forecasts may then be used and implemented will clearly depend on managerial decision making. For example, management may decide to adjust a forecast upwards (be over-optimistic), as the forecast may be used to guide purchasing and stock keeping levels. Such a decision may be taken after a cost-benefit analysis reveals that the cost of holding excess stock is much lower than that of lost sales. This type of adjustment should be part of setting goals or planning supply, rather than part of the forecasting process. In contrast, if forecasts are used as targets, they may be set low so that they can be exceeded more easily. Again, setting targets is different from producing forecasts, and the two should not be confused.

The example that follows comes from our experience in industry. It exemplifies two contrasting styles of judgmental forecasting — one that adheres to the principles we have just presented and one that does not.

Example: Pharmaceutical Benefits Scheme (PBS)

The Australian government subsidises the cost of a wide range of prescription medicines as part of the PBS. Each subsidised medicine falls into one of four categories: concession copayments, concession safety net, general copayments, and general safety net. Each person with a concession card makes a concession copayment per PBS medicine ($5.80)[3], until they reach a set threshold amount labelled the concession safety net ($348). For the rest of the financial year, all PBS-listed medicines are free. Each general patient makes a general copayment per PBS medicine ($35.40) until the general safety net amount is reached ($1,363.30). For the rest of the financial year, they contribute a small amount per PBS-listed medicine ($5.80). The PBS forecasting process uses 84 groups of PBS-listed medicines, and produces forecasts of the medicine volume and the total expenditure for each group and for each of the four PBS categories, a total of 672 series. This forecasting process aids in setting the government budget allocated to the PBS, which is over $7 billion per year, or approximately 1% of GDP.

[3] These are Australian dollar amounts published by the Australian government for 2012.

Figure 4.1 summarises the forecasting process. Judgmental forecasts are generated for new listings of medicines and for estimating the impact of new policies. These are shown by the green items. The pink items indicate the data used which were obtained from various government departments and associated authorities. The blue items show things that are calculated from the data provided. There were judgmental adjustments to the data to take account of new listings and new policies, and there were also judgmental adjustments to the forecasts. Because of the changing size of both the concession population and the total population, forecasts are produced on a per-capita basis, and then multiplied by the forecast population to obtain forecasts of total volume and expenditure per month.

One of us (Hyndman) was asked to evaluate the forecasting process a few years ago. We found that using judgement for new listings and new policy impacts gave better forecasts than using a statistical model alone. However, we also found that the forecasting accuracy and consistency could be improved through a more structured and systematic process, especially for policy impacts.

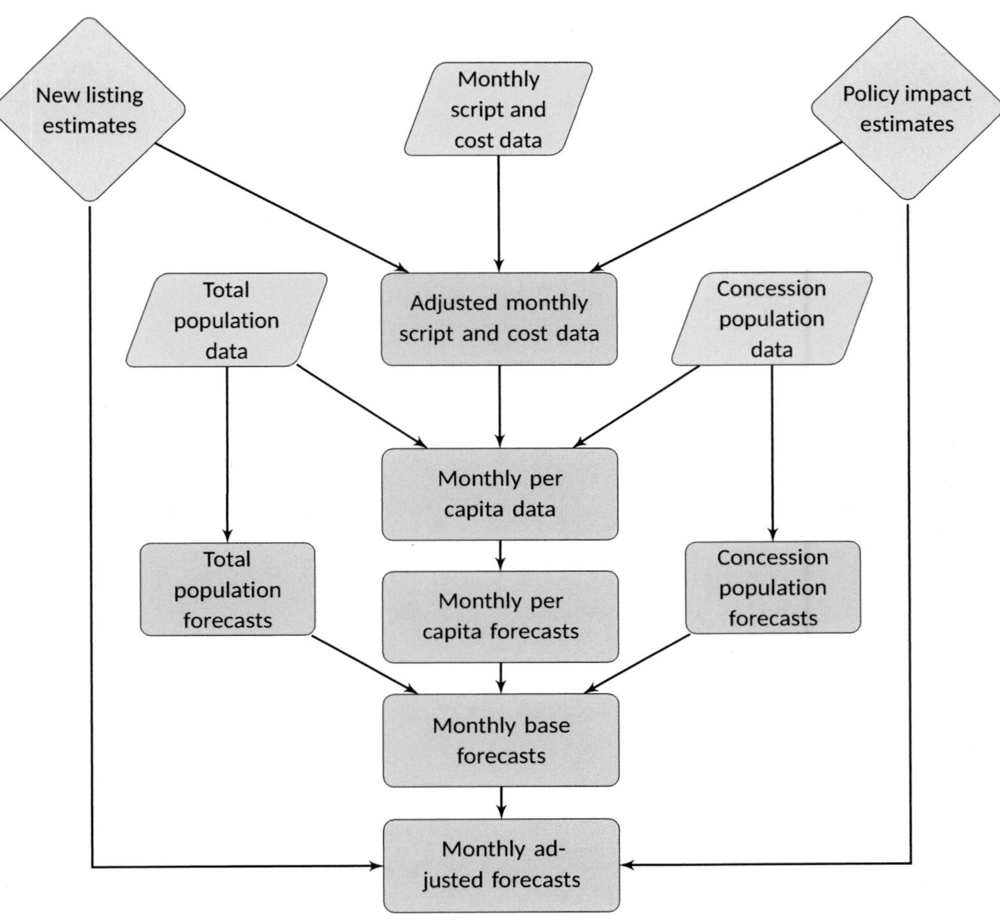

Figure 4.1: Process for producing PBS forecasts.

Forecasting new listings: Companies who apply for their medicine to be added to the PBS are asked to submit detailed forecasts for various aspects of the medicine, such as projected patient numbers, market share of the new medicine, substitution effects, etc. The Pharmaceutical Benefits Advisory Committee provides guidelines describing a highly structured and systematic approach for generating these forecasts, and requires careful documentation for each step of the process. This structured process helps to reduce the likelihood and effects of deliberate self-serving biases. Two detailed evaluation rounds of the company forecasts are implemented by a sub-committee, one before the medicine is added to the PBS and one after it is added. Finally, comparisons of observations versus forecasts for some selected new listings are performed, 12 months and 24 months after the listings, and the results are sent back to the companies for comment.

Policy impact forecasts: In contrast to the highly structured process used for new listings, there were no systematic procedures for policy impact forecasts. On many occasions, forecasts of policy impacts were calculated by a small team, and were often heavily reliant on the work of one person. The forecasts were not usually subject to a formal review process. There were no guidelines for how to construct judgmental forecasts for policy impacts, and there was often a lack of adequate documentation about how these forecasts were obtained, the assumptions underlying them, etc.

Consequently, we recommended several changes:

- that guidelines for forecasting new policy impacts be developed, to encourage a more systematic and structured forecasting approach;
- that the forecast methodology be documented in each case, including all assumptions made in forming the forecasts;
- that new policy forecasts be made by at least two people from different areas of the organisation;
- that a review of forecasts be conducted one year after the implementation of each new policy by a review committee, especially for new policies that have a significant annual projected cost or saving. The review committee should include those involved in generating the forecasts, but also others.

These recommendations reflect the principles outlined in this section.

4.3 The Delphi method

The Delphi method was invented by Olaf Helmer and Norman Dalkey of the Rand Corporation in the 1950s for the purpose of addressing a specific military problem. The method relies on the key assumption that forecasts from a group are generally more accurate than those from individuals. The aim of the Delphi method is to construct consensus forecasts from a group of experts in a structured iterative manner. A facilitator is appointed in order to implement and manage the process. The Delphi method generally involves the following stages:

1. A panel of experts is assembled.
2. Forecasting tasks/challenges are set and distributed to the experts.
3. Experts return initial forecasts and justifications. These are compiled and summarised in order to provide feedback.
4. Feedback is provided to the experts, who now review their forecasts in light of the feedback. This step may be iterated until a satisfactory level of consensus is reached.
5. Final forecasts are constructed by aggregating the experts' forecasts.

Each stage of the Delphi method comes with its own challenges. In what follows, we provide some suggestions and discussions about each one of these.[4]

[4] For further reading, refer to: Rowe (2007); Rowe and Wright (1999)

Experts and anonymity

The first challenge of the facilitator is to identify a group of experts who can contribute to the forecasting task. The usual suggestion is somewhere between 5 and 20 experts with diverse expertise. Experts submit forecasts and also provide detailed qualitative justifications for these.

A key feature of the Delphi method is that the participating experts remain anonymous at all times. This means that the experts cannot be influenced by political and social pressures in their forecasts. Furthermore, all experts are given an equal say and all are held accountable for their forecasts. This avoids the situation where a group meeting is held and some members do not contribute, while others dominate. It also prevents members exerting undue influence based on seniority or personality. There have been suggestions that even something as simple as the seating arrangements in a group setting can influence the group dynamics. Furthermore, there is ample evidence that a group meeting setting promotes enthusiasm and influences individual judgement, leading to optimism and overconfidence.[5]

[5] Buehler, Messervey, and Griffin (2005)

A by-product of anonymity is that the experts do not need to meet as a group in a physical location. An important advantage of this is that it increases the likelihood of gathering experts with diverse skills and expertise from varying locations. Furthermore, it makes the process cost-effective by eliminating the expense and inconvenience of travel, and it makes it flexible, as the experts only have to meet a common deadline for submitting forecasts, rather than having to set a common meeting time.

Setting the forecasting task in a Delphi

In a Delphi setting, it may be useful to conduct a preliminary round of information gathering from the experts before setting the forecasting tasks. Alternatively, as experts submit their initial forecasts and justifications, valuable information which is not shared between all experts can be identified by the facilitator when compiling the feedback.

Feedback

Feedback to the experts should include summary statistics of the forecasts and outlines of qualitative justifications. Numerical data summaries and graphical representations can be used to summarise the experts' forecasts.

As the feedback is controlled by the facilitator, there may be scope to direct attention and information from the experts to areas where it is most required. For example, the facilitator may direct the experts' attention to responses that fall outside the interquartile range, and the qualitative justification for such forecasts.

Iteration

The process of the experts submitting forecasts, receiving feedback, and reviewing their forecasts in light of the feedback, is repeated until a satisfactory level of consensus between the experts is reached. Satisfactory consensus does not mean complete convergence in the forecast value; it simply means that the variability of the responses has decreased to a satisfactory level. Usually two or three rounds are sufficient. Experts are more likely to drop out as the number of iterations increases, so too many rounds should be avoided.

Final forecasts

The final forecasts are usually constructed by giving equal weight to all of the experts' forecasts. However, the facilitator should keep in mind the possibility of extreme values which can distort the final forecast.

Limitations and variations

Applying the Delphi method can be time consuming. In a group meeting, final forecasts can possibly be reached in hours or even minutes — something which is almost impossible to do in a Delphi setting. If it is taking a long time to reach a consensus in a Delphi setting, the panel may lose interest and cohesiveness.

In a group setting, personal interactions can lead to quicker and better clarifications of qualitative justifications. A variation of the Delphi method which is often applied is the "estimate-talk-estimate" method, where the experts can interact between iterations, although the forecast submissions can still remain anonymous. A disadvantage of this variation is the possibility of the loudest person exerting undue influence.

The facilitator

The role of the facilitator is of the utmost importance. The facilitator is largely responsible for the design and administration of the Delphi process. The facilitator is also responsible for providing feedback to the experts and generating the final forecasts. In this role, the facilitator needs to be experienced enough to recognise areas that may need more attention, and to direct the experts' attention to these. Also, as there is no face-to-face interaction between the experts, the facilitator is responsible for disseminating important information. The efficiency and effectiveness of the facilitator can dramatically increase the probability of a successful Delphi method in a judgmental forecasting setting.

4.4 Forecasting by analogy

A useful judgmental approach which is often implemented in practice is forecasting by analogy. A common example is the pricing of a house through an appraisal process. An appraiser estimates the market value of a house by comparing it to similar properties that have sold in the area. The degree of similarity depends on the attributes considered. With house appraisals, attributes such as land size, dwelling size, numbers of bedrooms and bathrooms, and garage space are usually considered.

Even thinking and discussing analogous products or situations can generate useful (and sometimes crucial) information. We illustrate this point with the following example.[6]

[6] This example is extracted from Kahneman and Lovallo (1993)

Example: Designing a high school curriculum

A small group of academics and teachers were assigned the task of developing a curriculum for teaching judgement and decision making under uncertainty for high schools in Israel. Each group member was asked to forecast how long it would take for the curriculum to be completed. Responses ranged between 18 and 30 months. One of the group members who was an expert in curriculum design was asked to consider analogous curricula developments around the world. He concluded that 40% of analogous groups he considered never completed the task. The rest took between 7 to 10 years. The Israel project was completed in 8 years.

Obviously, forecasting by analogy comes with challenges. We should aspire to base forecasts on multiple analogies rather than a single analogy, which may create biases. However, these may be challenging to identify. Similarly, we should aspire to consider multiple attributes. Identifying or even comparing these may not always be straightforward. As always, we suggest performing these comparisons and the forecasting process using a systematic approach. Developing a detailed scoring mechanism to rank attributes and record the process of ranking will always be useful.

A structured analogy

Alternatively, a structured approach comprising a panel of experts can be implemented, as was proposed by Green and Armstrong (2007). The concept is similar to that of a Delphi; however, the forecasting task is completed by considering analogies. First, a facilitator is appointed. Then the structured approach involves the following steps.

1. A panel of experts who are likely to have experience with analogous situations is assembled.
2. Tasks/challenges are set and distributed to the experts.
3. Experts identify and describe as many analogies as they can, and generate forecasts based on each analogy.
4. Experts list similarities and differences of each analogy to the target situation, then rate the similarity of each analogy to the target situation on a scale.
5. Forecasts are derived by the facilitator using a set rule. This can be a weighted average, where the weights can be guided by the ranking scores of each analogy by the experts.

As with the Delphi approach, anonymity of the experts may be an advantage in not suppressing creativity, but could hinder collaboration. Green and Armstrong found no gain in collaboration between the experts in their results. A key finding was that experts with multiple analogies (more than two), and who had direct experience with the analogies, generated the most accurate forecasts.

4.5 Scenario forecasting

A fundamentally different approach to judgmental forecasting is scenario-based forecasting. The aim of this approach is to generate forecasts based on plausible scenarios. In contrast to the two previous approaches (Delphi and forecasting by analogy) where the resulting forecast is intended to be a likely outcome, each scenario-based forecast may have a low probability of occurrence. The scenarios are generated by considering all possible factors or drivers, their relative impacts, the interactions between them, and the targets to be forecasted.

Building forecasts based on scenarios allows a wide range of possible forecasts to be generated and some extremes to be identified. For example it is usual for "best", "middle" and "worst" case scenarios to be presented, although many other scenarios will be generated. Thinking about and documenting these contrasting extremes can lead to early contingency planning.

With scenario forecasting, decision makers often participate in the generation of scenarios. While this may lead to some biases, it can ease the communication of the scenario-based forecasts, and lead to a better understanding of the results.

4.6 New product forecasting

The definition of a new product can vary. It may be an entirely new product which has been launched, a variation of an existing product ("new and improved"), a change in the pricing scheme of an existing product, or even an existing product entering a new market.

Judgmental forecasting is usually the only available method for new product forecasting, as historical data are unavailable. The approaches we have already outlined (Delphi, forecasting by analogy and scenario forecasting) are all applicable when forecasting the demand for a new product.

Other methods which are more specific to the situation are also available. We briefly describe three such methods which are commonly applied in practice. These methods are less structured than those already discussed, and are likely to lead to more biased forecasts as a result.

Sales force composite

In this approach, forecasts for each outlet/branch/store of a company are generated by salespeople, and are then aggregated. This usually involves sales managers forecasting the demand for the outlet they manage. Salespeople are usually closest to the interaction between customers and products, and often develop an intuition about customer purchasing intentions. They bring this valuable experience and expertise to the forecast.

However, having salespeople generate forecasts violates the key principle of segregating forecasters and users, which can create biases in many directions. It is very common for the performance of a salesperson to be evaluated against the sales forecasts or expectations set beforehand. In this case, the salesperson acting as a forecaster may introduce some self-serving bias by generating low forecasts. On the other hand, one can imagine a very enthusiastic salesperson, full of optimism, generating high forecasts.

Moreover a successful salesperson is not necessarily a successful nor well-informed forecaster. A large proportion of salespeople will have no or very limited formal training in forecasting. Finally, salespeople will feel customer displeasure at first hand if, for example, the product runs out or is not introduced in their store. Such interactions will cloud their judgement.

Executive opinion

In contrast to the sales force composite, this approach involves staff at the top of the managerial structure generating aggregate forecasts. Such forecasts are usually generated in a group meeting, where executives contribute information from their own area of the company. Having executives from different functional areas of the company promotes great skill and knowledge diversity in the group.

This process carries all of the advantages and disadvantages of a group meeting setting which we discussed earlier. In this setting, it is important to justify and document the forecasting process. That is, executives need to be held accountable in order to reduce the biases generated by the group meeting setting. There may also be scope to apply variations to a Delphi approach in this setting; for example, the estimate-talk-estimate process described earlier.

Customer intentions

Customer intentions can be used to forecast the demand for a new product or for a variation on an existing product. Questionnaires are filled in by customers on their intentions to buy the product. A structured questionnaire is used, asking customers to rate the likelihood of them purchasing the product on a scale; for example, highly likely, likely, possible, unlikely, highly unlikely.

Survey design challenges, such as collecting a representative sample, applying a time- and cost-effective method, and dealing with non-responses, need to be addressed.[7]

[7] Groves et al. (2009)

Furthermore, in this survey setting we must keep in mind the relationship between purchase intention and purchase behaviour. Customers do not always do what they say they will. Many studies have found a positive correlation between purchase intentions and purchase behaviour; however, the strength of these correlations varies substantially. The factors driving this variation include the timings of data collection and product launch, the definition of "new" for the product, and the type of industry. Behavioural theory tells us that intentions predict behaviour if the intentions are measured just before the behaviour.[8] The time between intention and behaviour will vary depending on whether it is a completely new product or a variation on an existing product. Also, the correlation between intention and behaviour is found to be stronger for variations on existing and familiar products than for completely new products.

[8] Randall and Wolff (1994)

Whichever method of new product forecasting is used, it is important to thoroughly document the forecasts made, and the reasoning behind them, in order to be able to evaluate them when data become available.

4.7 Judgmental adjustments

In this final section, we consider the situation where historical data are available and are used to generate statistical forecasts. It is common for practitioners to then apply judgmental adjustments to these forecasts. These adjustments can potentially provide all of the advantages of judgmental forecasting which have been discussed earlier in this chapter. For example, they provide an avenue for incorporating factors that may not be accounted for in the statistical model, such as promotions, large sporting events, holidays, or recent events that are not yet reflected in the data. However, these advantages come to fruition only when the right conditions are present. Judgmental adjustments, like judgmental forecasts, come with biases and limitations, and we must implement methodical strategies in order to minimise them.

Use adjustments sparingly

Practitioners adjust much more often than they should, and many times for the wrong reasons. By adjusting statistical forecasts, users of forecasts create a feeling of ownership and credibility. Users often do not understand or appreciate the mechanisms that generate the statistical forecasts (as they will usually have no training in this area). By implementing judgmental adjustments, users feel that they have contributed to and completed the forecasts, and they can now relate their own intuition and interpretations to these. The forecasts have become their own.

Judgmental adjustments should not aim to correct for a systematic pattern in the data that is thought to have been missed by the statistical model. This has been proven to be ineffective, as forecasters tend to read non-existent patterns in noisy series. Statistical models are much better at taking account of data patterns, and judgmental adjustments only hinder accuracy.

Judgmental adjustments are most effective when there is significant additional information at hand or strong evidence of the need for an adjustment. We should only adjust when we have important extra information which is not incorporated in the statistical model. Hence, adjustments seem to be most accurate when they are large in size. Small adjustments (especially in the positive direction promoting the illusion of optimism) have been found to hinder accuracy, and should be avoided.

Apply a structured approach

Using a structured and systematic approach will improve the accuracy of judgmental adjustments. Following the key principles outlined in Section 4.2 is vital. In particular, having to document and justify adjustments will make it more challenging to override the statistical forecasts, and will guard against unnecessary adjustments.

It is common for adjustments to be implemented by a panel (see the example that follows). Using a Delphi setting carries great advantages. However, if adjustments are implemented in a group meeting, it is wise to consider the forecasts of key markets or products first, as panel members will get tired during this process. Fewer adjustments tend to be made as the meeting goes on through the day.

Example: Tourism Forecasting Committee (TFC)

Tourism Australia publishes forecasts for all aspects of Australian tourism twice a year. The published forecasts are generated by the TFC, an independent body which comprises experts from various government and private industry sectors; for example, the Australian Commonwealth Treasury, airline companies, consulting firms, banking sector companies, and tourism bodies.

The forecasting methodology applied is an iterative process. First, model-based statistical forecasts are generated by the forecasting unit within Tourism Australia, then judgmental adjustments are made to these in two rounds. In the first round, the TFC Technical Committee[9] (comprising senior researchers, economists and independent advisers) adjusts the model-based forecasts. In the second and final round, the TFC (comprising industry and government experts) makes final adjustments. In both rounds, adjustments are made by consensus.

[9] GA was an observer on this technical committee for a few years.

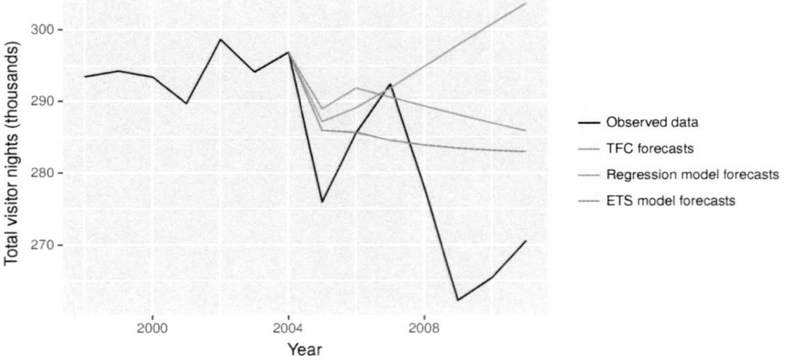

Figure 4.2: Long run annual forecasts for domestic visitor nights for Australia. We study regression models in Chapter 5, and ETS (ExponenTial Smoothing) models in Chapter 7.

In 2008, we[10] analysed forecasts for Australian domestic tourism. We concluded that the published TFC forecasts were optimistic, especially for the long-run, and we proposed alternative model-based forecasts. We now have access to observed data up to and including 2011. In Figure 4.2, we plot the published forecasts against the actual data. We can see that the published TFC forecasts have continued to be optimistic.

[10] Athanasopoulos and Hyndman (2008)

What can we learn from this example? Although the TFC clearly states in its methodology that it produces 'forecasts' rather than 'targets', could this be a case where these have been confused? Are the forecasters and users sufficiently well-segregated in this process? Could the iterative process itself be improved? Could the adjustment process in the meetings be improved? Could it be that the group meetings have promoted optimism? Could it be that domestic tourism should have been considered earlier in the day?

4.8 Further reading

Many forecasting textbooks ignore judgmental forecasting altogether. Here are three which do cover it in some detail.

- Chapter 11 of Ord, Fildes, and Kourentzes (2017) provides an excellent review of some of the same topics as this chapter, but also includes assessing forecast uncertainty judgmentally, and forecasting using prediction markets.
- Goodwin and Wright (2009) is a book-length treatment of the use of judgement in decision marking by two of the leading researchers in the field.
- Kahn (2006) covers techniques for new product forecasting, where judgmental methods play an important role.

There have been some very helpful survey papers on judgemental forecasting published in the last 20 years. We have found these three particularly helpful.

- Fildes and Goodwin (2007b)
- Fildes and Goodwin (2007a)
- Harvey (2001)

Some helpful papers on individual judgmental forecasting methods are listed in the table below.

Forecasting Method	Recommended papers
Delphi	Rowe and Wright (1999)
	Rowe (2007)
Adjustments	Sanders et al. (2005)
	Eroglu and Croxton (2010)
	Franses and Legerstee (2013)
Analogy	Green and Armstrong (2007)
Scenarios	Önkal, Sayım, and Gönül (2012)
Customer intentions	Morwitz, Steckel, and Gupta (2007)

Chapter 5

Time series regression models

In this chapter we discuss regression models. The basic concept is that we forecast the time series of interest y assuming that it has a linear relationship with other time series x.

For example, we might wish to forecast monthly sales y using total advertising spend x as a predictor. Or we might forecast daily electricity demand y using temperature x_1 and the day of week x_2 as predictors.

The **forecast variable** y is sometimes also called the regressand, dependent or explained variable. The **predictor variables** x are sometimes also called the regressors, independent or explanatory variables. In this book we will always refer to them as the "forecast" variable and "predictor" variables.

5.1 The linear model

Simple linear regression

In the simplest case, the regression model allows for a linear relationship between the forecast variable y and a single predictor variable x:

$$y_t = \beta_0 + \beta_1 x_t + \varepsilon_t.$$

An artificial example of data from such a model is shown in Figure 5.1. The coefficients β_0 and β_1 denote the intercept and the slope of the line respectively. The intercept β_0 represents the predicted value of y when $x = 0$. The slope β_1 represents the

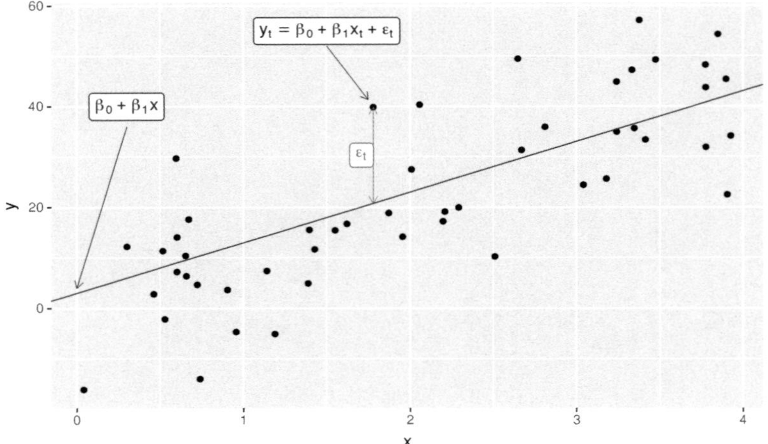

Figure 5.1: An example of data from a simple linear regression model.

average predicted change in y resulting from a one unit increase in x.

Notice that the observations do not lie on the straight line but are scattered around it. We can think of each observation y_t as consisting of the systematic or explained part of the model, $\beta_0 + \beta_1 x_t$, and the random "error", ε_t. The "error" term does not imply a mistake, but a deviation from the underlying straight line model. It captures anything that may affect y_t other than x_t.

Example: US consumption expenditure Figure 5.2 shows time series of quarterly percentage changes (growth rates) of real personal consumption expenditure, y, and real personal disposable income, x, for the US from 1970 Q1 to 2016 Q3.

```
autoplot(uschange[,c("Consumption","Income")]) +
  ylab("% change") + xlab("Year")
```

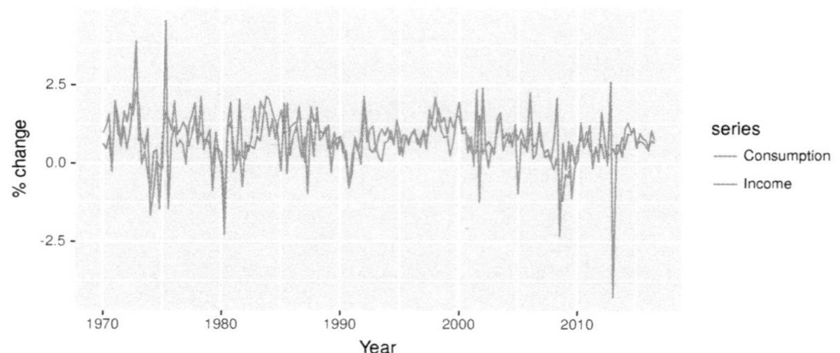

Figure 5.2: Percentage changes in personal consumption expenditure and personal income for the US.

A scatter plot of consumption changes against income changes is shown in Figure 5.3 along with the estimated regression line

$$\hat{y}_t = 0.55 + 0.28x_t.$$

(We put a "hat" above y to indicate that this is the value of y predicted by the model.)

```
uschange %>%
  as.data.frame() %>%
  ggplot(aes(x=Income, y=Consumption)) +
    ylab("Consumption (quarterly % change)") +
    xlab("Income (quarterly % change)") +
    geom_point() +
    geom_smooth(method="lm", se=FALSE)
```

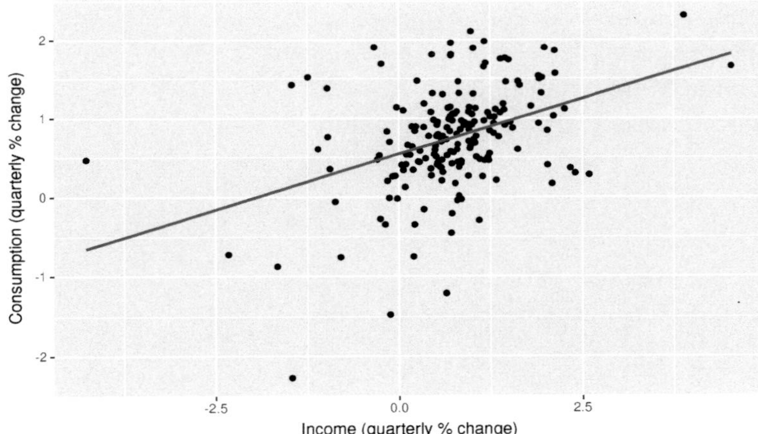

Figure 5.3: Scatterplot of quarterly changes in consumption expenditure versus quarterly changes in personal income and the fitted regression line.

The equation is estimated in R using the `tslm()` function:

```
tslm(Consumption ~ Income, data=uschange)
#>
#> Call:
#> tslm(formula = Consumption ~ Income, data = uschange)
#>
#> Coefficients:
#> (Intercept)       Income
#>       0.545        0.281
```

We will discuss how `tslm()` computes the coefficients in Section 5.2.

The fitted line has a positive slope, reflecting the positive relationship between income and consumption. The slope coefficient shows that a one unit increase in x (a 1% increase in personal disposable income) results on average in 0.28 units increase in y (an average increase of 0.28% in personal consumption expenditure). Alternatively the estimated equation shows that a value of 1 for x (the percentage increase in personal disposable income) will result in a forecast value of $0.55 + 0.28 \times 1 = 0.83$ for y (the percentage increase in personal consumption expenditure).

The interpretation of the intercept requires that a value of $x = 0$ makes sense. In this case when $x = 0$ (i.e., when there is no change in personal disposable income since the last quarter) the predicted value of y is 0.55 (i.e., an average increase in personal consumption expenditure of 0.55%). Even when $x = 0$ does not make sense, the intercept is an important part of the model. Without it, the slope coefficient can be distorted unnecessarily. The intercept should always be included unless the requirement is to force the regression line "through the origin". In what follows we assume that an intercept is always included in the model.

Multiple linear regression

When there are two or more predictor variables, the model is called a **multiple regression model**. The general form of a multiple regression model is

$$y_t = \beta_0 + \beta_1 x_{1,t} + \beta_2 x_{2,t} + \cdots + \beta_k x_{k,t} + \varepsilon_t, \qquad (5.1)$$

where y is the variable to be forecast and $x_1, \dots, x_k$ are the k predictor variables. Each of the predictor variables must be numerical. The coefficients $\beta_1, \dots, \beta_k$ measure the effect of each predictor after taking into account the effects of all the other predictors in the model. Thus, the coefficients measure the *marginal effects* of the predictor variables.

Example: US consumption expenditure Figure 5.4 shows additional predictors that may be useful for forecasting US consumption expenditure. These are quarterly percentage changes in industrial production and personal savings, and quarterly changes in the unemployment rate (as this is already a percentage). Building a multiple linear regression model can potentially generate more accurate forecasts as we expect consumption expenditure to not only depend on personal income but on other predictors as well.

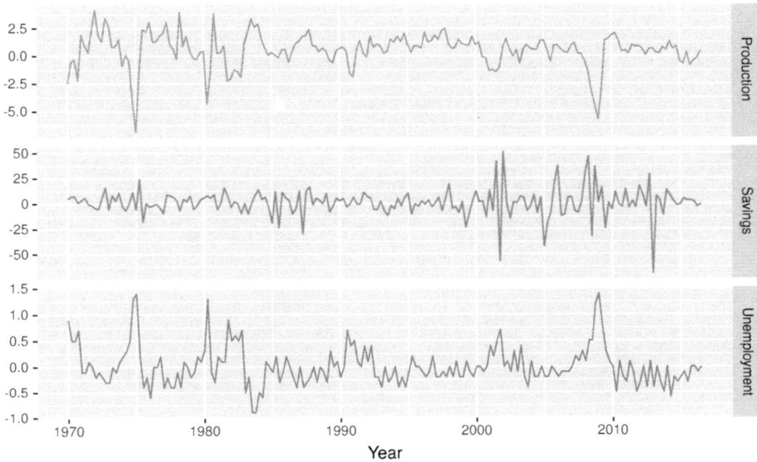

Figure 5.4: Quarterly percentage changes in industrial production and personal savings and quarterly changes in the unemployment rate for the US over the period 1970Q1-2016Q3.

Figure 5.5 is a scatterplot matrix of five variables. The first column shows the relationships between the forecast variable (consumption) and each of the predictors. The scatterplots show positive relationships with income and industrial production, and negative relationships with savings and unemployment. The strength of these relationships are shown by the correlation coefficients across the first row. The remaining scatterplots and correlation coefficients show the relationships between the predictors.

```
uschange %>%
  as.data.frame() %>%
  GGally::ggpairs()
```

Assumptions

When we use a linear regression model, we are implicitly making some assumptions about the variables in Equation (5.1).

First, we assume that the model is a reasonable approximation to reality; that is, the relationship between the forecast variable and the predictor variables satisfies this linear equation.

Second, we make the following assumptions about the errors $(\varepsilon_1, \dots, \varepsilon_T)$:

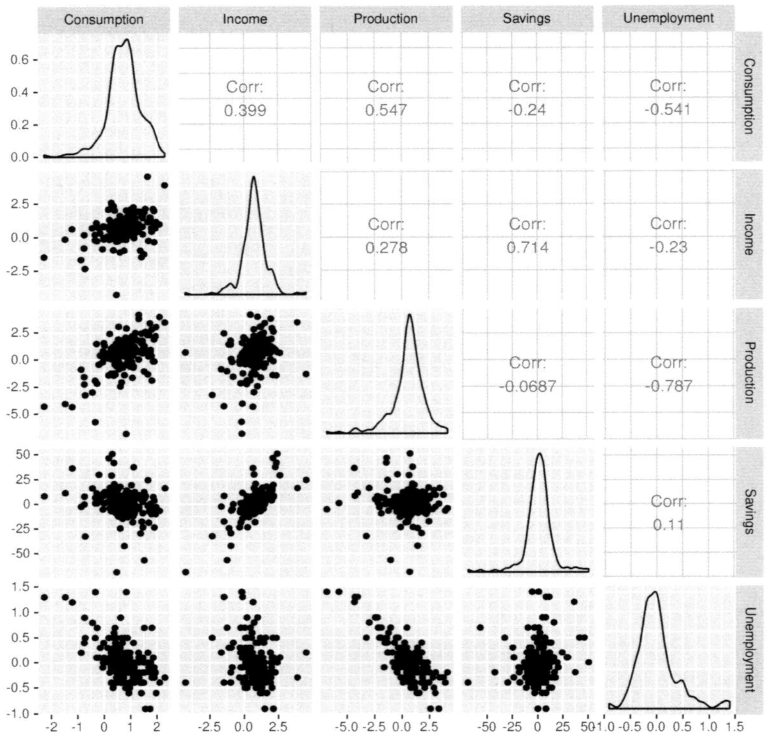

Figure 5.5: A scatterplot matrix of US consumption expenditure and the four predictors.

- they have mean zero; otherwise the forecasts will be systematically biased.
- they are not autocorrelated; otherwise the forecasts will be inefficient, as there is more information in the data that can be exploited.
- they are unrelated to the predictor variables; otherwise there would be more information that should be included in the systematic part of the model.

It is also useful to have the errors being normally distributed with a constant variance σ^2 in order to easily produce prediction intervals.

Another important assumption in the linear regression model is that each predictor x is not a random variable. If we were performing a controlled experiment in a laboratory, we could control the values of each x (so they would not be random) and observe the resulting values of y. With observational data (including most data in business and economics), it is not possible to control the value of x, we simply observe it. Hence we make this an assumption.

5.2 Least squares estimation

In practice, of course, we have a collection of observations but we do not know the values of the coefficients $\beta_0, \beta_1, \dots, \beta_k$. These need to be estimated from the data.

The least squares principle provides a way of choosing the coefficients effectively by minimizing the sum of the squared errors. That is, we choose the values of $\beta_0, \beta_1, \dots, \beta_k$ that minimize

$$\sum_{t=1}^{T} \varepsilon_t^2 = \sum_{t=1}^{T} (y_t - \beta_0 - \beta_1 x_{1,t} - \beta_2 x_{2,t} - \cdots - \beta_k x_{k,t})^2.$$

This is called **least squares** estimation because it gives the least value for the sum of squared errors. Finding the best estimates of the coefficients is often called "fitting" the model to the data, or sometimes "learning" or "training" the model. The line shown in Figure 5.3 was obtained in this way.

When we refer to the *estimated* coefficients, we will use the notation $\hat{\beta}_0, \dots, \hat{\beta}_k$. The equations for these will be given in Section 5.7.

The `tslm()` function fits a linear regression model to time series data. It is very similar to the `lm()` function which is widely used for linear models, but `tslm()` provides additional facilities for handling time series.

Example: US consumption expenditure A multiple linear regression model for US consumption is

$$y_t = \beta_0 + \beta_1 x_{1,t} + \beta_2 x_{2,t} + \beta_3 x_{3,t} + \beta_4 x_{4,t} + \varepsilon_t,$$

where y is the percentage change in real personal consumption expenditure, x_1 is the percentage change in real personal disposable income, x_2 is the percentage change in industrial production, x_3 is the percentage change in personal savings and x_4 is the change in the unemployment rate.

The following output provides information about the fitted model. The first column of `Coefficients` gives an estimate of each β coefficient and the second column gives its standard error (i.e., the standard deviation which would be obtained from repeatedly estimating the β coefficients on similar data sets). The standard error gives a measure of the uncertainty in the estimated β coefficient.

```
fit.consMR <- tslm(
  Consumption ~ Income + Production + Unemployment + Savings,
  data=uschange)
summary(fit.consMR)
#>
#> Call:
#> tslm(formula = Consumption ~ Income + Production +
#>     Unemployment + Savings, data = uschange)
#>
#> Residuals:
#>     Min      1Q  Median      3Q     Max
#> -0.8830 -0.1764 -0.0368  0.1525  1.2055
#>
#> Coefficients:
#>              Estimate Std. Error t value Pr(>|t|)
#> (Intercept)   0.26729    0.03721    7.18  1.7e-11 ***
#> Income        0.71448    0.04219   16.93  < 2e-16 ***
#> Production    0.04589    0.02588    1.77    0.078 .
#> Unemployment -0.20477    0.10550   -1.94    0.054 .
#> Savings      -0.04527    0.00278  -16.29  < 2e-16 ***
#> ---
#> Signif. codes:
#> 0 '***' 0.001 '**' 0.01 '*' 0.05 '.' 0.1 ' ' 1
#>
#> Residual standard error: 0.329 on 182 degrees of freedom
#> Multiple R-squared:  0.754,  Adjusted R-squared:  0.749
#> F-statistic:  139 on 4 and 182 DF,  p-value: <2e-16
```

For forecasting purposes, the final two columns are of limited interest. The "t value" is the ratio of an estimated β coefficient to its standard error and the last column gives the p-value: the probability of the estimated β coefficient being as large as it is if there was no real relationship between consumption and the corresponding predictor. This is useful when studying the effect of each predictor, but is not particularly useful for forecasting.

Fitted values

Predictions of y can be obtained by using the estimated coefficients in the regression equation and setting the error term to zero. In general we write,

$$\hat{y}_t = \hat{\beta}_0 + \hat{\beta}_1 x_{1,t} + \hat{\beta}_2 x_{2,t} + \cdots + \hat{\beta}_k x_{k,t}.$$

Plugging in the values of $x_{1,t}, \ldots, x_{k,t}$ for $t = 1, \ldots, T$ returns predictions of y_t within the training-sample, referred to as *fitted values*. Note that these are predictions of the data used to estimate the model, not genuine forecasts of future values of y.

The following plots show the actual values compared to the fitted values for the percentage change in the US consumption expenditure series. The time plot in Figure 5.6 shows that the fitted values follow the actual data fairly closely. This is verified by the strong positive relationship shown by the scatterplot in Figure 5.7.

```
autoplot(uschange[,'Consumption'], series="Data") +
  autolayer(fitted(fit.consMR), series="Fitted") +
  xlab("Year") + ylab("") +
  ggtitle("Percent change in US consumption expenditure") +
  guides(colour=guide_legend(title=" "))
```

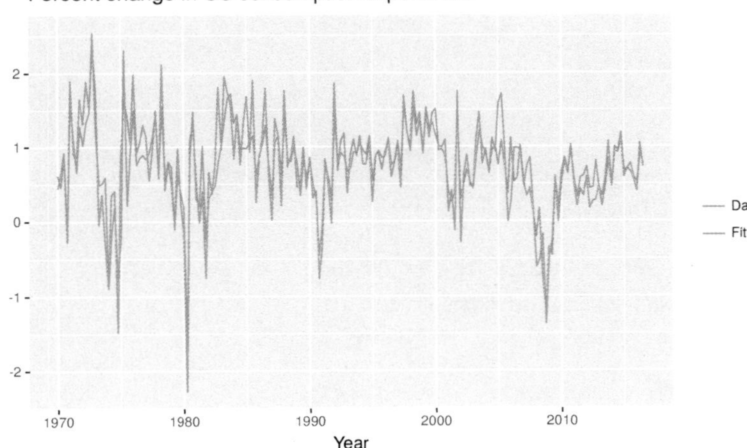

Figure 5.6: Time plot of actual US consumption expenditure and predicted US consumption expenditure.

```
cbind(Data = uschange[,"Consumption"],
      Fitted = fitted(fit.consMR)) %>%
  as.data.frame() %>%
  ggplot(aes(x=Data, y=Fitted)) +
    geom_point() +
    xlab("Fitted (predicted values)") +
    ylab("Data (actual values)") +
    ggtitle("Percent change in US consumption expenditure") +
    geom_abline(intercept=0, slope=1)
```

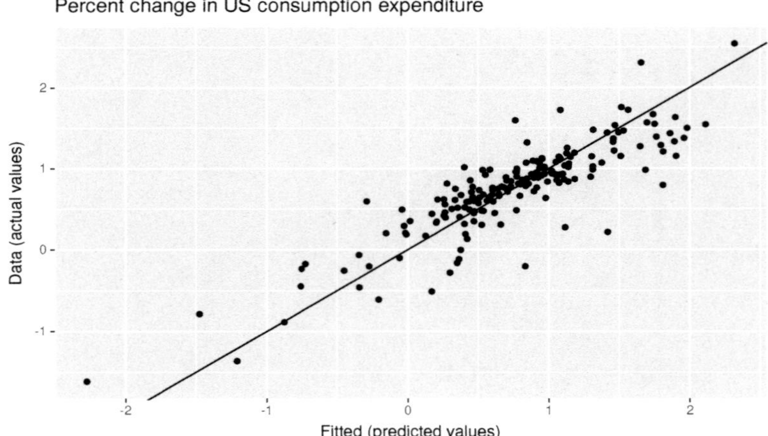

Figure 5.7: Actual US consumption expenditure plotted against predicted US consumption expenditure.

Goodness-of-fit

A common way to summarise how well a linear regression model fits the data is via the coefficient of determination, or R^2. This can be calculated as the square of the correlation between the observed y values and the predicted $\hat{y}$ values. Alternatively, it can also be calculated as,

$$R^2 = \frac{\sum(\hat{y}_t - \bar{y})^2}{\sum(y_t - \bar{y})^2},$$

where the summations are over all observations. Thus, it reflects the proportion of variation in the forecast variable that is accounted for (or explained) by the regression model.

In simple linear regression, the value of R^2 is also equal to the square of the correlation between y and x (provided an intercept has been included).

If the predictions are close to the actual values, we would expect R^2 to be close to 1. On the other hand, if the predictions are unrelated to the actual values, then $R^2 = 0$ (again, assuming there is an intercept). In all cases, R^2 lies between 0 and 1.

The R^2 value is used frequently, though often incorrectly, in forecasting. The value of R^2 will never decrease when adding an extra predictor to the model and this can lead to over-fitting. There are no set rules for what is a good R^2 value, and typical values of R^2 depend on the type of data used. Validating a model's forecasting performance on the test data is much better than measuring the R^2 value on the training data.

Example: US consumption expenditure Figure 5.7 plots the actual consumption expenditure values versus the fitted values. The correlation between these variables is $r = 0.868$ hence $R^2 = 0.754$ (shown in the output above). In this case model does an excellent job as it explains 75.4% of the variation in the consumption data. Compare that to the R^2 value of 0.16 obtained from the simple regression with the same data set in Section 5.1. Adding the three extra predictors has allowed a lot more of the variation in the consumption data to be explained.

Standard error of the regression

Another measure of how well the model has fitted the data is the standard deviation of the residuals, which is often known as the "residual standard error". This is shown in the above output with the value 0.329.

It is calculated using

$$\hat{\sigma}_e = \sqrt{\frac{1}{T-k-1}\sum_{t=1}^{T} e_t^2}, \tag{5.2}$$

where k is the number of predictors in the model. Notice that we divide by $T-k-1$ because we have estimated $k+1$ parameters (the intercept and a coefficient for each predictor variable) in computing the residuals.

The standard error is related to the size of the average error that the model produces. We can compare this error to the sample mean of y or with the standard deviation of y to gain some perspective on the accuracy of the model.

The standard error will be used when generating prediction intervals, discussed in Section 5.6.

5.3 Evaluating the regression model

The differences between the observed y values and the corresponding fitted $\hat{y}$ values are the training-set errors or "residuals" defined as,

$$\begin{aligned} e_t &= y_t - \hat{y}_t \\ &= y_t - \hat{\beta}_0 - \hat{\beta}_1 x_{1,t} - \hat{\beta}_2 x_{2,t} - \cdots - \hat{\beta}_k x_{k,t} \end{aligned}$$

for $t = 1,\dots,T$. Each residual is the unpredictable component of the associated observation.

The residuals have some useful properties including the following two:

$$\sum_{t=1}^{T} e_t = 0 \quad \text{and} \quad \sum_{t=1}^{T} x_{k,t} e_t = 0 \qquad \text{for all } k.$$

As a result of these properties, it is clear that the average of the residuals is zero, and that the correlation between the residuals and the observations for the predictor variable is also zero. (This is not necessarily true when the intercept is omitted from the model.)

After selecting the regression variables and fitting a regression model, it is necessary to plot the residuals to check that the assumptions of the model have been satisfied. There are a series of plots that should be produced in order to check different aspects of the fitted model and the underlying assumptions. We will now discuss each of them in turn.

ACF plot of residuals

With time series data, it is highly likely that the value of a variable observed in the current time period will be similar to its value in the previous period, or even the period before that, and so on. Therefore when fitting a regression model to time series data, it is very common to find autocorrelation in the residuals. In this case, the estimated model violates the assumption of no autocorrelation in the errors, and our forecasts may be inefficient — there is some information left over which should be accounted for in the model in order to obtain better forecasts. The forecasts from a model with autocorrelated errors are still unbiased, and so are not "wrong", but they will usually have larger prediction intervals than they need to. Therefore we should always look at an ACF plot of the residuals.

Another useful test of autocorrelation in the residuals designed to take account for the regression model is the **Breusch-Godfrey** test, also referred to as the LM (Lagrange Multiplier) test for serial correlation. It is used to test the joint hypothesis that there is no autocorrelation in the residuals up to a certain specified order. A small p-value indicates there is significant autocorrelation remaining in the residuals.

The Breusch-Godfrey test is similar to the Ljung-Box test, but it is specifically designed for use with regression models.

Histogram of residuals

It is always a good idea to check whether the residuals are normally distributed. As we explained earlier, this is not essential for forecasting, but it does make the calculation of prediction intervals much easier.

Example Using the `checkresiduals()` function introduced in Section 3.3, we can obtain all the useful residual diagnostics mentioned above.

```
checkresiduals(fit.consMR)
```

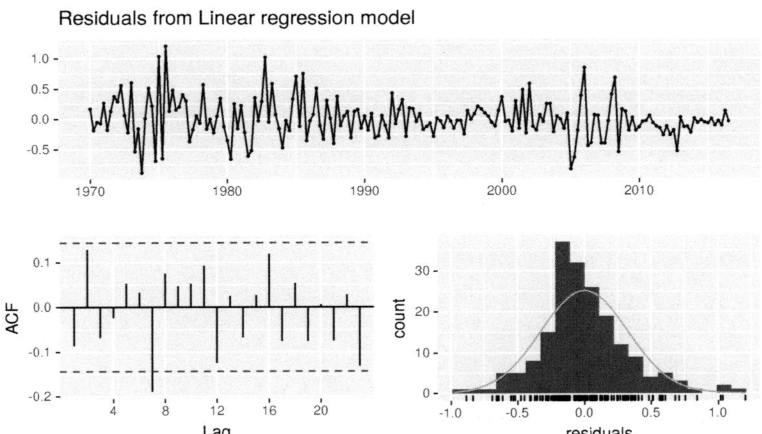

Figure 5.8: Analysing the residuals from a regression model for US quarterly consumption.

```
#>
#>  Breusch-Godfrey test for serial correlation of
#>  order up to 8
#>
#> data:  Residuals from Linear regression model
#> LM test = 15, df = 8, p-value = 0.06
```

Figure 5.8 shows a time plot, the ACF and the histogram of the residuals from the multiple regression model fitted to the US quarterly consumption data, as well as the Breusch-Godfrey test for jointly testing up to 8th order autocorrelation. (The `checkresiduals()` function will use the Breusch-Godfrey test for regression models, but the Ljung-Box test otherwise.)

The time plot shows some changing variation over time, but is otherwise relatively unremarkable. This heteroscedasticity will potentially make the prediction interval coverage inaccurate.

The histogram shows that the residuals seem to be slightly skewed, which may also affect the coverage probability of the prediction intervals.

The autocorrelation plot shows a significant spike at lag 7, but it is not quite enough for the Breusch-Godfrey to be significant at the 5% level. In any case, the autocorrelation is not particularly large, and at lag 7 it is unlikely to have any noticeable impact on the forecasts or the prediction intervals. In Chapter 9 we discuss dynamic regression models used for better capturing information left in the residuals.

Residual plots against predictors

We would expect the residuals to be randomly scattered without showing any systematic patterns. A simple and quick way to check this is to examine scatterplots of the residuals against each of the predictor variables. If these scatterplots show a pattern, then the relationship may be nonlinear and the model will need to be modified accordingly. See Section 5.8 for a discussion of nonlinear regression.

It is also necessary to plot the residuals against any predictors that are *not* in the model. If any of these show a pattern, then the corresponding predictor may need to be added to the model (possibly in a nonlinear form).

Example The residuals from the multiple regression model for forecasting US consumption plotted against each predictor in Figure 5.9 seem to be randomly scattered. Therefore we are satisfied with these in this case.

```
df <- as.data.frame(uschange)
df[,"Residuals"]  <- as.numeric(residuals(fit.consMR))
p1 <- ggplot(df, aes(x=Income, y=Residuals)) +
  geom_point()
p2 <- ggplot(df, aes(x=Production, y=Residuals)) +
  geom_point()
p3 <- ggplot(df, aes(x=Savings, y=Residuals)) +
  geom_point()
p4 <- ggplot(df, aes(x=Unemployment, y=Residuals)) +
  geom_point()
gridExtra::grid.arrange(p1, p2, p3, p4, nrow=2)
```

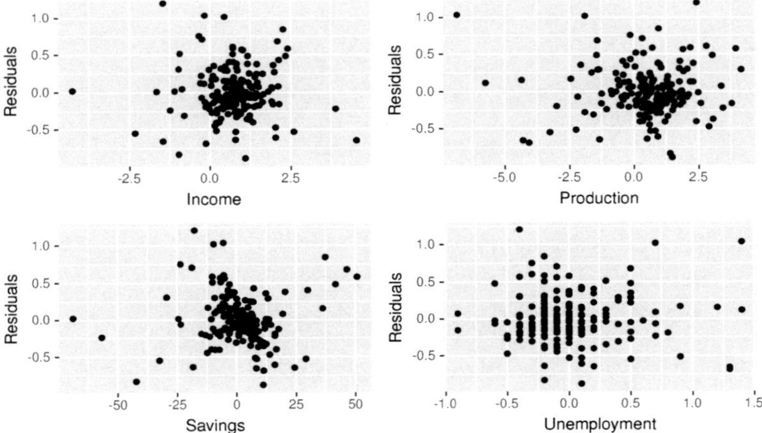

Figure 5.9: Scatterplots of residuals versus each predictor.

Residual plots against fitted values

A plot of the residuals against the fitted values should also show no pattern. If a pattern is observed, there may be "heteroscedasticity" in the errors which means that the variance of the residuals may not be constant. If this problem occurs, a transformation of the forecast variable such as a logarithm or square root may be required (see Section 3.2.)

Example Continuing the previous example, Figure 5.10 shows the residuals plotted against the fitted values. The random scatter suggests the errors are homoscedastic.

```
cbind(Fitted = fitted(fit.consMR),
      Residuals=residuals(fit.consMR)) %>%
  as.data.frame() %>%
  ggplot(aes(x=Fitted, y=Residuals)) + geom_point()
```

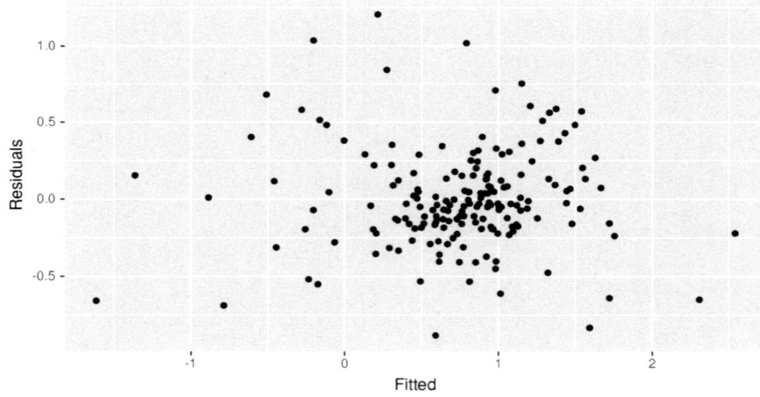

Figure 5.10: Scatterplots of residuals versus fitted values.

Outliers and influential observations

Observations that take extreme values compared to the majority of the data are called **outliers**. Observations that have a large influence on the estimated coefficients of a regression model are called **influential observations**. Usually, influential observations are also outliers that are extreme in the x direction.

There are formal methods for detecting outliers and influential observations that are beyond the scope of this textbook. As we suggested at the beginning of Chapter 2, becoming familiar with your data prior to performing any analysis is of vital importance. A scatter plot of y against each x is always a useful starting point in regression analysis, and often helps to identify unusual observations.

One source of outliers is incorrect data entry. Simple descriptive statistics of your data can identify minima and maxima that are not sensible. If such an observation is identified, and it has been recorded incorrectly, it should be corrected or removed from the sample immediately.

Outliers also occur when some observations are simply different. In this case it may not be wise for these observations to be removed. If an observation has been identified as a likely outlier, it is important to study it and analyse the possible reasons behind it. The decision to remove or retain an observation can be a challenging one (especially when outliers are influential observations). It is wise to report results both with and without the removal of such observations.

Example Figure 5.11 highlights the effect of a single outlier when regressing US consumption on income (the example introduced in Section 5.1). In the left panel the outlier is only extreme in the direction of y, as the percentage change in consumption has been incorrectly recorded as -4%. The red line is the regression line fitted to the data which includes the outlier, compared to the black line which is the line fitted to the data without the outlier. In the right panel the outlier now is also extreme in the direction of x with the 4% decrease in consumption corresponding to a 6% increase in income. In this case the outlier is extremely influential as the red line now deviates substantially from the black line.

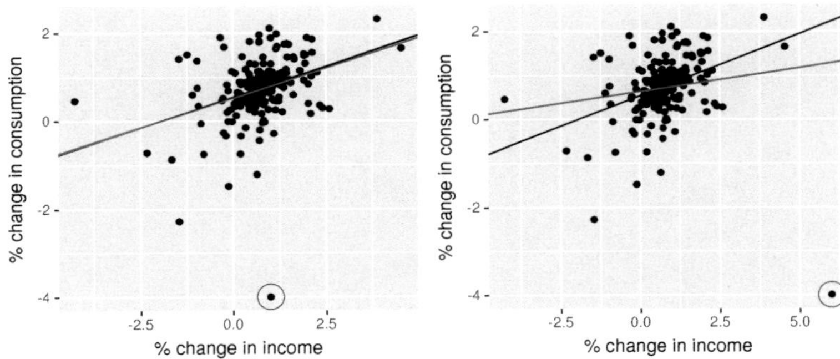

Figure 5.11: The effect of outliers and influential observations on regression

Spurious regression

More often than not, time series data are "non-stationary"; that is, the values of the time series do not fluctuate around a constant mean or with a constant variance. We will deal with time series stationarity in more detail in Chapter 8, but here we need to address the effect that non-stationary data can have on regression models.

For example, consider the two variables plotted in Figure 5.12. These appear to be related simply because they both trend upwards in the same manner. However, air passenger traffic in Australia has nothing to do with rice production in Guinea.

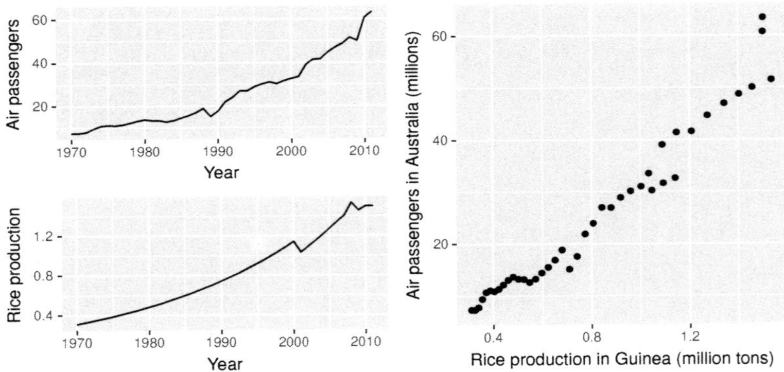

Figure 5.12: Trending time series data can appear to be related, as shown in this example where air passengers in Australia are regressed against rice production in Guinea.

Regressing non-stationary time series can lead to spurious regressions. The output of regressing Australian air passengers on rice production in Guinea is shown in Figure 5.13. High R^2 and high residual autocorrelation can be signs of spurious regression. Notice these features in the output below. We discuss the issues surrounding non-stationary data and spurious regressions in more detail in Chapter 9.

Cases of spurious regression might appear to give reasonable short-term forecasts, but they will generally not continue to work into the future.

```
aussies <- window(ausair, end=2011)
fit <- tslm(aussies ~ guinearice)
summary(fit)
#>
#> Call:
#> tslm(formula = aussies ~ guinearice)
#>
#> Residuals:
#>     Min      1Q Median      3Q     Max
#> -5.945 -1.892 -0.327  1.862 10.421
#>
#> Coefficients:
#>             Estimate Std. Error t value Pr(>|t|)
#> (Intercept)    -7.49       1.20   -6.23  2.3e-07 ***
#> guinearice     40.29       1.34   30.13  < 2e-16 ***
#> ---
#> Signif. codes:
#> 0 '***' 0.001 '**' 0.01 '*' 0.05 '.' 0.1 ' ' 1
#>
#> Residual standard error: 3.24 on 40 degrees of freedom
#> Multiple R-squared:  0.958,  Adjusted R-squared:  0.957
#> F-statistic:  908 on 1 and 40 DF,  p-value: <2e-16
```

```
checkresiduals(fit)
```

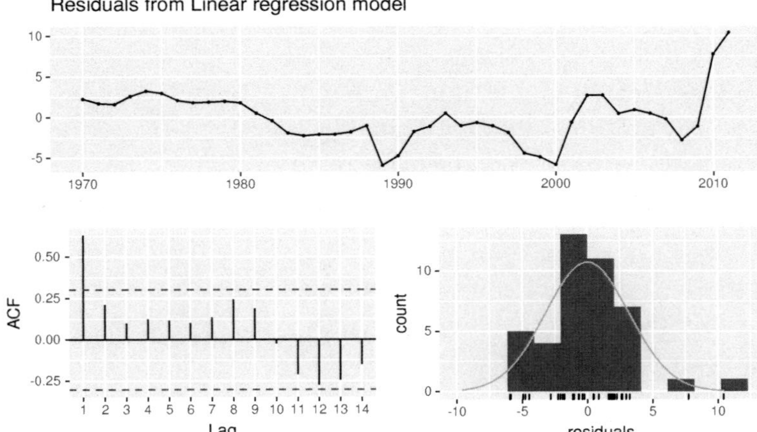

Figure 5.13: Residuals from a spurious regression.

```
#>
#>  Breusch-Godfrey test for serial correlation of
#>  order up to 8
#>
#> data:  Residuals from Linear regression model
#> LM test = 29, df = 8, p-value = 3e-04
```

5.4 Some useful predictors

There are several very useful predictors that occur frequently when using regression for time series data.

Trend

It is very common for time series data to be trending. A linear trend can be modelled by simply using $x_{1,t} = t$ as a predictor,

$$y_t = \beta_0 + \beta_1 t + \varepsilon_t,$$

where $t = 1,\dots,T$. A trend variable can be specified in the `tslm()` function using the `trend` predictor. In Section 5.8 we discuss how we can also model a nonlinear trends.

Dummy variables

So far, we have assumed that each predictor takes numerical values. But what about when a predictor is a categorical variable taking only two values (e.g., "yes" and "no")? Such a variable might arise, for example, when forecasting daily sales and you want to take account of whether the day is a **public holiday** or not. So the predictor takes value "yes" on a public holiday, and "no" otherwise.

This situation can still be handled within the framework of multiple regression models by creating a "dummy variable" which takes value 1 corresponding to "yes" and 0 corresponding to "no". A dummy variable is also known as an "indicator variable".

A dummy variable can also be used to account for an **outlier** in the data. Rather than omit the outlier, a dummy variable removes its effect. In this case, the dummy variable takes value 1 for that observation and 0 everywhere else. An example is the case where a special event has occurred. For example when forecasting tourist arrivals to Brazil, we will need to account for the effect of the Rio de Janeiro summer Olympics in 2016.

If there are more than two categories, then the variable can be coded using several dummy variables (one fewer than the total number of categories). `tslm()` will automatically handle this case if you specify a factor variable as a predictor. There is usually no need to manually create the corresponding dummy variables.

Seasonal dummy variables

Suppose that we are forecasting daily data and we want to account for the day of the week as a predictor. Then the following dummy variables can be created.

	$d_{1,t}$	$d_{2,t}$	$d_{3,t}$	$d_{4,t}$	$d_{5,t}$	$d_{6,t}$
Monday	1	0	0	0	0	0
Tuesday	0	1	0	0	0	0
Wednesday	0	0	1	0	0	0
Thursday	0	0	0	1	0	0
Friday	0	0	0	0	1	0
Saturday	0	0	0	0	0	1
Sunday	0	0	0	0	0	0
Monday	1	0	0	0	0	0
⋮	⋮	⋮	⋮	⋮	⋮	⋮

Notice that only six dummy variables are needed to code seven categories. That is because the seventh category (in this case Sunday) is captured by the intercept, and is specified when the dummy variables are all set to zero.

Many beginners will try to add a seventh dummy variable for the seventh category. This is known as the "dummy variable trap", because it will cause the regression to fail. There will be one too many parameters to estimate when an intercept is also included. The general rule is to use one fewer dummy variables than categories. So for quarterly data, use three dummy variables; for monthly data, use 11 dummy variables; and for daily data, use six dummy variables, and so on.

The interpretation of each of the coefficients associated with the dummy variables is that it is *a measure of the effect of that category relative to the omitted category*. In the above example, the coefficient of $d_{1,t}$ associated with Monday will measure the effect of Monday on the forecast variable compared to the effect of Sunday. An example of interpreting estimated dummy variable coefficients capturing the quarterly seasonality of Australian beer production follows.

The `tslm()` function will automatically handle this situation if you specify the predictor `season`.

Example: Australian quarterly beer production Recall the Australian quarterly beer production data shown again in Figure 5.14.

```
beer2 <- window(ausbeer, start=1992)
autoplot(beer2) + xlab("Year") + ylab("Megalitres")
```

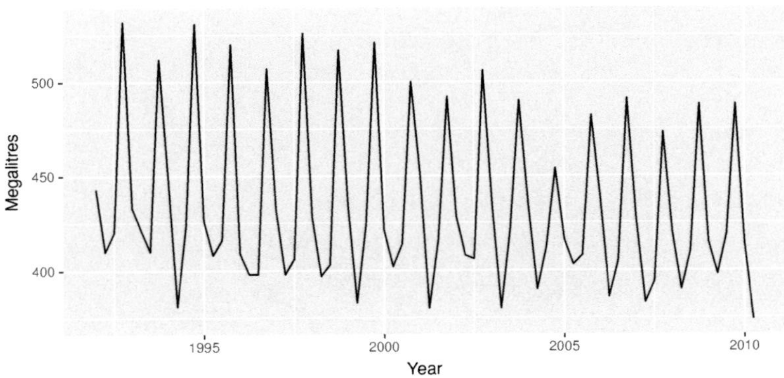

Figure 5.14: Australian quarterly beer production.

We want to forecast the value of future beer production. We can model this data using a regression model with a linear trend and quarterly dummy variables,

$$y_t = \beta_0 + \beta_1 t + \beta_2 d_{2,t} + \beta_3 d_{3,t} + \beta_4 d_{4,t} + \varepsilon_t,$$

where $d_{i,t} = 1$ if t is in quarter i and 0 otherwise. The first quarter variable has been omitted, so the coefficients associated with the other quarters are measures of the difference between those quarters and the first quarter.

```
fit.beer <- tslm(beer2 ~ trend + season)
summary(fit.beer)
#>
#> Call:
#> tslm(formula = beer2 ~ trend + season)
#>
#> Residuals:
#>     Min      1Q Median      3Q     Max
#> -42.90  -7.60  -0.46   7.99  21.79
#>
#> Coefficients:
#>             Estimate Std. Error t value Pr(>|t|)
#> (Intercept) 441.8004     3.7335  118.33  < 2e-16 ***
#> trend        -0.3403     0.0666   -5.11  2.7e-06 ***
#> season2     -34.6597     3.9683   -8.73  9.1e-13 ***
#> season3     -17.8216     4.0225   -4.43  3.4e-05 ***
#> season4      72.7964     4.0230   18.09  < 2e-16 ***
#> ---
#> Signif. codes:
#> 0 '***' 0.001 '**' 0.01 '*' 0.05 '.' 0.1 ' ' 1
#>
#> Residual standard error: 12.2 on 69 degrees of freedom
#> Multiple R-squared:  0.924,  Adjusted R-squared:  0.92
#> F-statistic:  211 on 4 and 69 DF,  p-value: <2e-16
```

Note that `trend` and `season` are not objects in the R workspace; they are created automatically by `tslm()` when specified in this way.

There is an average downward trend of -0.34 megalitres per quarter. On average, the second quarter has production of 34.7 megalitres lower than the first quarter, the third quarter has production of 17.8 megalitres lower than the first quarter, and the fourth quarter has production of 72.8 megalitres higher than the first quarter.

```
autoplot(beer2, series="Data") +
  autolayer(fitted(fit.beer), series="Fitted") +
  xlab("Year") + ylab("Megalitres") +
  ggtitle("Quarterly Beer Production")
```

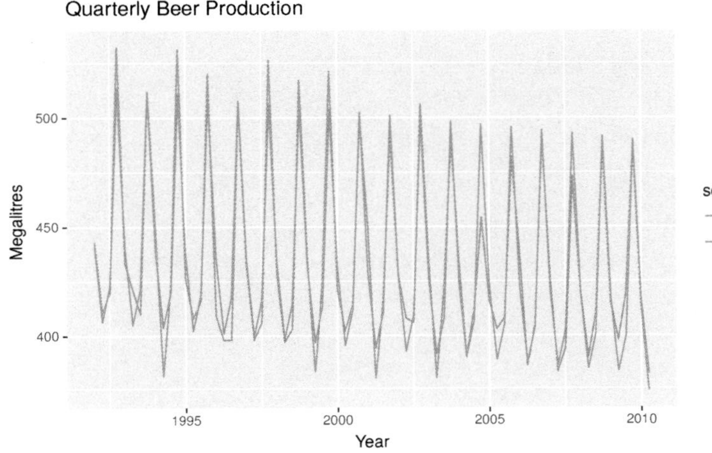

Figure 5.15: Time plot of beer production and predicted beer production.

```
cbind(Data=beer2, Fitted=fitted(fit.beer)) %>%
  as.data.frame() %>%
  ggplot(aes(x = Data, y = Fitted,
             colour = as.factor(cycle(beer2)))) +
    geom_point() +
    ylab("Fitted") + xlab("Actual values") +
    ggtitle("Quarterly beer production") +
    scale_colour_brewer(palette="Dark2", name="Quarter") +
    geom_abline(intercept=0, slope=1)
```

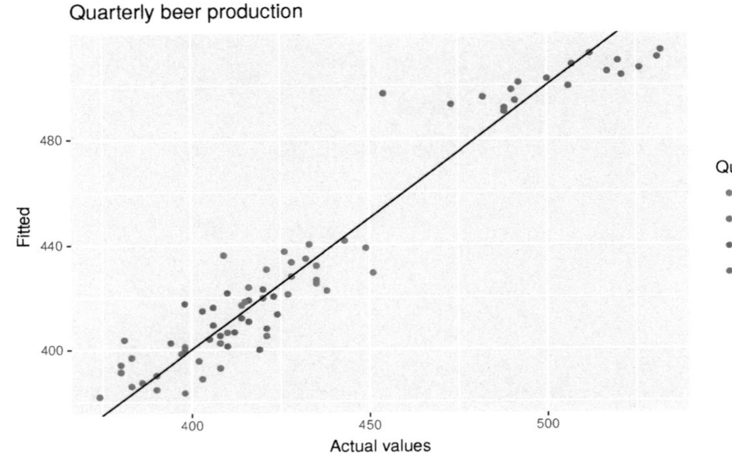

Figure 5.16: Actual beer production plotted against predicted beer production.

Intervention variables

It is often necessary to model interventions that may have affected the variable to be forecast. For example, competitor activity, advertising expenditure, industrial action, and so on, can all have an effect.

When the effect lasts only for one period, we use a "spike" variable. This is a dummy variable that takes value one in the period of the intervention and zero elsewhere. A spike variable is equivalent to a dummy variable for handling an outlier.

Other interventions have an immediate and permanent effect. If an intervention causes a level shift (i.e., the value of the series changes suddenly and permanently from the time of intervention), then we use a "step" variable. A step variable takes value zero before the intervention and one from the time of intervention onward.

Another form of permanent effect is a change of slope. Here the intervention is handled using a piecewise linear trend; a trend that bends at the time of intervention and hence is nonlinear. We will discuss this in Section 5.8.

Trading days

The number of trading days in a month can vary considerably and can have a substantial effect on sales data. To allow for this, the number of trading days in each month can be included as a predictor.

For monthly or quarterly data, the `bizdays()` function will compute the number of trading days in each period.

An alternative that allows for the effects of different days of the week has the following predictors:

$$\begin{aligned}
x_1 &= \text{number of Mondays in month;} \\
x_2 &= \text{number of Tuesdays in month;} \\
&\vdots \\
x_7 &= \text{number of Sundays in month.}
\end{aligned}$$

Distributed lags

It is often useful to include advertising expenditure as a predictor. However, since the effect of advertising can last beyond the actual campaign, we need to include lagged values of advertising expenditure. Thus, the following predictors may be used.

$$\begin{aligned} x_1 &= \text{advertising for previous month;} \\ x_2 &= \text{advertising for two months previously;} \\ &\vdots \\ x_m &= \text{advertising for } m \text{ months previously.} \end{aligned}$$

It is common to require the coefficients to decrease as the lag increases, although this is beyond the scope of this book.

Easter

Easter differs from most holidays because it is not held on the same date each year, and its effect can last for several days. In this case, a dummy variable can be used with value one where the holiday falls in the particular time period and zero otherwise.

With monthly data, if Easter falls in March then the dummy variable takes value 1 in March, and if it falls in April the dummy variable takes value 1 in April. When Easter starts in March and finishes in April, the dummy variable is split proportionally between months.

The `easter()` function will compute the dummy variable for you.

Fourier series

An alternative to using seasonal dummy variables, especially for long seasonal periods, is to use Fourier terms. Jean-Baptiste Fourier was a French mathematician, born in the 1700s, who showed that a series of sine and cosine terms of the right frequencies can approximate any periodic function. We can use them for seasonal patterns.

If m is the seasonal period, then the first few Fourier terms are given by

$$x_{1,t} = \sin\left(\tfrac{2\pi t}{m}\right), x_{2,t} = \cos\left(\tfrac{2\pi t}{m}\right), x_{3,t} = \sin\left(\tfrac{4\pi t}{m}\right),$$

$$x_{4,t} = \cos\left(\tfrac{4\pi t}{m}\right), x_{5,t} = \sin\left(\tfrac{6\pi t}{m}\right), x_{6,t} = \cos\left(\tfrac{6\pi t}{m}\right),$$

and so on. If we have monthly seasonality, and we use the first 11 of these predictor variables, then we will get exactly the same forecasts as using 11 dummy variables.

With Fourier terms, we often need fewer predictors than with dummy variables, especially when m is large. This makes them useful for weekly data, for example, where $m \approx 52$. For short seasonal periods (e.g., quarterly data), there is little advantage in using Fourier terms over seasonal dummy variables.

These Fourier terms are produced using the `fourier()` function. For example, the Australian beer data can be modelled like this.

```
fourier.beer <- tslm(beer2 ~ trend + fourier(beer2, K=2))
summary(fourier.beer)
#>
#> Call:
#> tslm(formula = beer2 ~ trend + fourier(beer2, K = 2))
#>
#> Residuals:
#>     Min      1Q Median      3Q     Max
#> -42.90  -7.60  -0.46   7.99  21.79
#>
#> Coefficients:
#>                          Estimate Std. Error t value
#> (Intercept)              446.8792     2.8732  155.53
#> trend                     -0.3403     0.0666   -5.11
#> fourier(beer2, K = 2)S1-4  8.9108     2.0112    4.43
#> fourier(beer2, K = 2)C1-4 53.7281     2.0112   26.71
#> fourier(beer2, K = 2)C2-4 13.9896     1.4226    9.83
#>                          Pr(>|t|)
#> (Intercept)               < 2e-16 ***
#> trend                     2.7e-06 ***
#> fourier(beer2, K = 2)S1-4 3.4e-05 ***
#> fourier(beer2, K = 2)C1-4  < 2e-16 ***
#> fourier(beer2, K = 2)C2-4 9.3e-15 ***
#> ---
#> Signif. codes:
#> 0 '***' 0.001 '**' 0.01 '*' 0.05 '.' 0.1 ' ' 1
#>
#> Residual standard error: 12.2 on 69 degrees of freedom
#> Multiple R-squared:  0.924,  Adjusted R-squared:  0.92
#> F-statistic:  211 on 4 and 69 DF,  p-value: <2e-16
```

The first argument to `fourier()` allows it to identify the seasonal period m and the length of the predictors to return. The second argument `K` specifies how many pairs of sin and cos terms to include. The maximum allowed is $K = m/2$ where m is the seasonal period. Because we have used the maximum here, the results are identical to those obtained when using seasonal dummy variables.

If only the first two Fourier terms are used ($x_{1,t}$ and $x_{2,t}$), the seasonal pattern will follow a simple sine wave. A regression model containing Fourier terms is often called a **harmonic regression** because the successive Fourier terms represent harmonics of the first two Fourier terms.

5.5 Selecting predictors

When there are many possible predictors, we need some strategy for selecting the best predictors to use in a regression model.

A common approach that is *not recommended* is to plot the forecast variable against a particular predictor and if there is no noticeable relationship, drop that predictor from the model. This is invalid because it is not always possible to see the relationship from a scatterplot, especially when the effects of other predictors have not been accounted for.

Another common approach which is also invalid is to do a multiple linear regression on all the predictors and disregard all variables whose p-values are greater than 0.05. To start with, statistical significance does not always indicate predictive value. Even if forecasting is not the goal, this is not a good strategy because the p-values can be misleading when two or more predictors are correlated with each other (see Section 5.9).

Instead, we will use a measure of predictive accuracy. Five such measures are introduced in this section. They can be calculated using the `CV()` function, here applied to the model for US consumption:

```
CV(fit.consMR)
#>        CV       AIC      AICc       BIC     AdjR2
#>    0.1163 -409.2980 -408.8314 -389.9114    0.7486
```

We compare these values against the corresponding values from other models. For the CV, AIC, AICc and BIC measures, we want to find the model with the lowest value; for Adjusted R^2, we seek the model with the highest value.

Adjusted R^2

Computer output for a regression will always give the R^2 value, discussed in Section 5.1. However, it is not a good measure of the predictive ability of a model. Imagine a model which produces forecasts that are exactly 20% of the actual values. In that case, the R^2 value would be 1 (indicating perfect correlation), but the forecasts are not close to the actual values.

In addition, R^2 does not allow for "degrees of freedom". Adding *any* variable tends to increase the value of R^2, even if that variable is irrelevant. For these reasons, forecasters should not use R^2 to determine whether a model will give good predictions, as it will lead to overfitting.

An equivalent idea is to select the model which gives the minimum sum of squared errors (SSE), given by

$$\text{SSE} = \sum_{t=1}^{T} e_t^2.$$

Minimizing the SSE is equivalent to maximizing R^2 and will always choose the model with the most variables, and so is not a valid way of selecting predictors.

An alternative which is designed to overcome these problems is the adjusted R^2 (also called "R-bar-squared"):

$$\bar{R}^2 = 1 - (1 - R^2)\frac{T-1}{T-k-1},$$

where T is the number of observations and k is the number of predictors. This is an improvement on R^2, as it will no longer increase with each added predictor. Using this measure, the best model will be the one with the largest value of $\bar{R}^2$. Maximizing $\bar{R}^2$ is equivalent to minimizing the standard error $\hat{\sigma}_e$ given in Equation (5.2).

Maximizing $\bar{R}^2$ works quite well as a method of selecting predictors, although it does tend to err on the side of selecting too many predictors.

Cross-validation

Time series cross-validation was introduced in Section 3.4 as a general tool for determining the predictive ability of a model. For regression models, it is also possible to use classical leave-one-out cross-validation to selection predictors (Bergmeir, Hyndman, and Koo 2018). This is faster and makes more efficient use of the data. The procedure uses the following steps:

1. Remove observation t from the data set, and fit the model using the remaining data. Then compute the error ($e_t^* = y_t - \hat{y}_t$) for the omitted observation. (This is not the same as the residual because the tth observation was not used in estimating the value of $\hat{y}_t$.)
2. Repeat step 1 for $t = 1, \dots, T$.
3. Compute the MSE from $e_1^*, \dots, e_T^*$. We shall call this the **CV**.

Although this looks like a time-consuming procedure, there are very fast methods of calculating CV, so that it takes no longer than fitting one model to the full data set. The equation for computing CV efficiently is given in Section 5.7. Under this criterion, the best model is the one with the smallest value of CV.

Akaike's Information Criterion

A closely-related method is Akaike's Information Criterion, which we define as

$$\text{AIC} = T \log\left(\frac{\text{SSE}}{T}\right) + 2(k+2),$$

where T is the number of observations used for estimation and k is the number of predictors in the model. Different computer packages use slightly different definitions for the AIC, although they should all lead to the same model being selected. The $k+2$ part of the equation occurs because there are $k+2$ parameters in the model: the k coefficients for the predictors, the intercept and the variance of the residuals. The idea here is to penalize the fit of the model (SSE) with the number of parameters that need to be estimated.

The model with the minimum value of the AIC is often the best model for forecasting. For large values of T, minimizing the AIC is equivalent to minimizing the CV value.

Corrected Akaike's Information Criterion

For small values of T, the AIC tends to select too many predictors, and so a bias-corrected version of the AIC has been developed,

$$\text{AIC}_{\text{c}} = \text{AIC} + \frac{2(k+2)(k+3)}{T-k-3}.$$

As with the AIC, the AICc should be minimized.

Schwarz's Bayesian Information Criterion

A related measure is Schwarz's Bayesian Information Criterion (usually abbreviated to BIC, SBIC or SC):

$$\text{BIC} = T\log\left(\frac{\text{SSE}}{T}\right) + (k+2)\log(T).$$

As with the AIC, minimizing the BIC is intended to give the best model. The model chosen by the BIC is either the same as that chosen by the AIC, or one with fewer terms. This is because the BIC penalizes the number of parameters more heavily than the AIC. For large values of T, minimizing BIC is similar to leave-v-out cross-validation when $v = T[1 - 1/(\log(T) - 1)]$.

Which measure should we use?

While $\bar{R}^2$ is very widely used, and has been around longer than the other measures, its tendency to select too many predictor variables makes it less suitable for forecasting.

Many statisticians like to use the BIC because it has the feature that if there is a true underlying model, the BIC will select that model given enough data. However, in reality, there is rarely, if ever, a true underlying model, and even if there was a true underlying model, selecting that model will not necessarily give the best forecasts (because the parameter estimates may not be accurate).

Consequently, we recommend that one of the AICc, AIC, or CV statistics be used, each of which has forecasting as their objective. If the value of T is large enough, they will all lead to the same model. In most of the examples in this book, we use the AICc value to select the forecasting model.

Example: US consumption In the multiple regression example for forecasting US consumption we considered four predictors. With four predictors, there are $2^4 = 16$ possible models. Now we can check if all four predictors are actually useful, or whether we can drop one or more of them. All 16 models were fitted and the results are summarised in Table 5.1. A "1" indicates that the predictor was included in the model, and a "0" means that the predictor was not included in the model. Hence the first row shows the measures of predictive accuracy for a model including all four predictors.

The results have been sorted according to the AICc. Therefore the best models are given at the top of the table, and the worst at the bottom of the table.

Income	Production	Savings	Unemployment	CV	AIC	AICc	BIC	AdjR2
1	1	1	1	0.116	-409.3	-408.8	-389.9	0.749
1	0	1	1	0.116	-408.1	-407.8	-391.9	0.746
1	1	1	0	0.118	-407.5	-407.1	-391.3	0.745
1	0	1	0	0.129	-388.7	-388.5	-375.8	0.716
1	1	0	1	0.278	-243.2	-242.8	-227.0	0.386
1	0	0	1	0.283	-237.9	-237.7	-225.0	0.365
1	1	0	0	0.289	-236.1	-235.9	-223.2	0.359
0	1	1	1	0.293	-234.4	-234.0	-218.2	0.356
0	1	1	0	0.300	-228.9	-228.7	-216.0	0.334
0	1	0	1	0.303	-226.3	-226.1	-213.4	0.324
0	0	1	1	0.306	-224.6	-224.4	-211.7	0.318
0	1	0	0	0.314	-219.6	-219.5	-209.9	0.296
0	0	0	1	0.314	-217.7	-217.5	-208.0	0.288
1	0	0	0	0.372	-185.4	-185.3	-175.7	0.154
0	0	1	0	0.414	-164.1	-164.0	-154.4	0.052
0	0	0	0	0.432	-155.1	-155.0	-148.6	0.000

Table 5.1: All 16 possible models for forecasting US consumption with 4 predictors.

The best model contains all four predictors. However, a closer look at the results reveals some interesting features. There is clear separation between the models in the first four rows and the ones below. This indicates that Income and Savings are both more important variables than Production and Unemployment. Also, the first two rows have almost identical values of CV, AIC and AICc. So we could possibly drop the Production variable and get very similar forecasts. Note that Production and Unemployment are highly (negatively) correlated, as shown in Figure 5.5, so most of the predictive information in Production is also contained in the Unemployment variable.

Best subset regression

Where possible, all potential regression models should be fitted (as was done in the example above) and the best model should be selected based on one of the measures discussed. This is known as "best subsets" regression or "all possible subsets" regression.

Stepwise regression

If there are a large number of predictors, it is not possible to fit all possible models. For example, 40 predictors leads to $2^{40} > 1$ trillion possible models! Consequently, a strategy is required to limit the number of models to be explored.

An approach that works quite well is *backwards stepwise regression*:

- Start with the model containing all potential predictors.
- Remove one predictor at a time. Keep the model if it improves the measure of predictive accuracy.
- Iterate until no further improvement.

If the number of potential predictors is too large, then the backwards stepwise regression will not work and *forward stepwise regression* can be used instead. This procedure starts with a model that includes only the intercept. Predictors are added one at a time, and the one that most improves the measure of predictive accuracy is retained in the model. The procedure is repeated until no further improvement can be achieved.

Alternatively for either the backward or forward direction, a starting model can be one that includes a subset of potential predictors. In this case, an extra step needs to be included. For the backwards procedure we should also consider adding a predictor with each step, and for the forward procedure we should also consider dropping a predictor with each step. These are referred to as *hybrid* procedures.

It is important to realise that any stepwise approach is not guaranteed to lead to the best possible model, but it almost always leads to a good model. For further details see James et al. (2014).

Beware of inference after selecting predictors

We do not discuss statistical inference of the predictors in this book (e.g., looking at p-values associated with each predictor). If you do wish to look at the statistical significance of the predictors, beware that *any* procedure involving selecting predictors first will invalidate the assumptions behind the p-values. The procedures we recommend for selecting predictors are helpful when the model is used for forecasting; they are not helpful if you wish to study the effect of any predictor on the forecast variable.

5.6 Forecasting with regression

Recall that predictions of y can be obtained using

$$\hat{y}_t = \hat{\beta}_0 + \hat{\beta}_1 x_{1,t} + \hat{\beta}_2 x_{2,t} + \cdots + \hat{\beta}_k x_{k,t},$$

which comprises the estimated coefficients and ignores the error in the regression equation. Plugging in the values of the predictor variables $x_{1,t},\dots,x_{k,t}$ for $t = 1,\dots,T$ returned the fitted (training-sample) values of y. What we are interested in here, however, is forecasting *future* values of y.

Ex-ante versus ex-post forecasts

When using regression models for time series data, we need to distinguish between the different types of forecasts that can be produced, depending on what is assumed to be known when the forecasts are computed.

Ex-ante forecasts are those that are made using only the information that is available in advance. For example, ex-ante forecasts for the percentage change in US consumption for quarters following the end of the sample, should only use information that was available *up to and including* 2016 Q3. These are genuine forecasts, made in advance using whatever information is available at the time. Therefore in order to generate ex-ante forecasts, the model requires forecasts of the predictors. To obtain these we can use one of the simple methods introduced in Section 3.1 or more sophisticated pure time series approaches that follow in Chapters 7 and 8. Alternatively, forecasts from some other source, such as a government agency, may be available and can be used.

Ex-post forecasts are those that are made using later information on the predictors. For example, ex-post forecasts of consumption may use the actual observations of the predictors, once these have been observed. These are not genuine forecasts, but are useful for studying the behaviour of forecasting models.

The model from which ex-post forecasts are produced should not be estimated using data from the forecast period. That is, ex-post forecasts can assume knowledge of the predictor variables (the x variables), but should not assume knowledge of the data that are to be forecast (the y variable).

A comparative evaluation of ex-ante forecasts and ex-post forecasts can help to separate out the sources of forecast uncertainty. This will show whether forecast errors have arisen due to poor forecasts of the predictor or due to a poor forecasting model.

Example: Australian quarterly beer production Normally, we cannot use actual future values of the predictor variables when producing ex-ante forecasts because their values will not be known in advance. However, the special predictors introduced in Section 5.4 are all known in advance, as they are based on calendar variables (e.g., seasonal dummy variables or public holiday indicators) or deterministic functions of time (e.g. time trend). In such cases, there is no difference between ex-ante and ex-post forecasts.

```
beer2 <- window(ausbeer, start=1992)
fit.beer <- tslm(beer2 ~ trend + season)
fcast <- forecast(fit.beer)
autoplot(fcast) +
  ggtitle("Forecasts of beer production using regression") +
  xlab("Year") + ylab("megalitres")
```

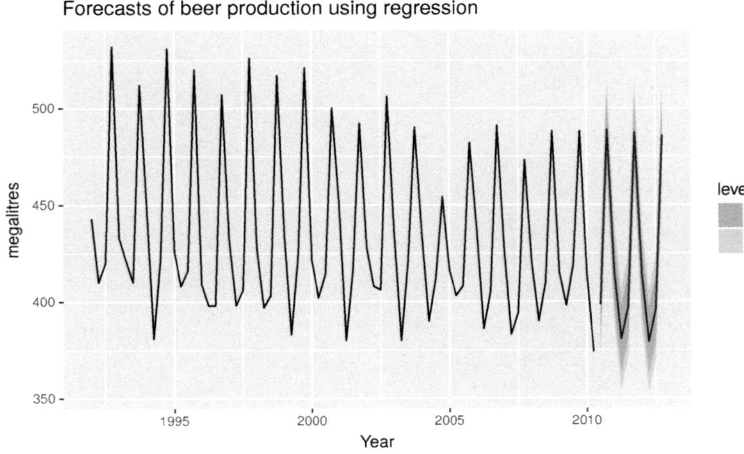

Figure 5.17: Forecasts from the regression model for beer production. The dark shaded region shows 80% prediction intervals and the light shaded region shows 95% prediction intervals.

Scenario based forecasting

In this setting, the forecaster assumes possible scenarios for the predictor variables that are of interest. For example, a US policy maker may be interested in comparing the predicted change in consumption when there is a constant growth of 1% and 0.5% respectively for income and savings with no change in the employment rate, versus a respective decline of 1% and 0.5%, for each of the four quarters following the end of the sample. The resulting forecasts are calculated below and shown in Figure 5.18. We should note that prediction intervals for scenario based forecasts do not include the uncertainty associated with the future values of the predictor variables. They assume that the values of the predictors are known in advance.

```
fit.consBest <- tslm(
  Consumption ~ Income + Savings + Unemployment,
  data = uschange)
h <- 4
newdata <- data.frame(
    Income = c(1, 1, 1, 1),
    Savings = c(0.5, 0.5, 0.5, 0.5),
    Unemployment = c(0, 0, 0, 0))
fcast.up <- forecast(fit.consBest, newdata = newdata)
newdata <- data.frame(
    Income = rep(-1, h),
    Savings = rep(-0.5, h),
    Unemployment = rep(0, h))
fcast.down <- forecast(fit.consBest, newdata = newdata)
```

```
autoplot(uschange[, 1]) +
  ylab("% change in US consumption") +
  autolayer(fcast.up, PI = TRUE, series = "increase") +
  autolayer(fcast.down, PI = TRUE, series = "decrease") +
  guides(colour = guide_legend(title = "Scenario"))
```

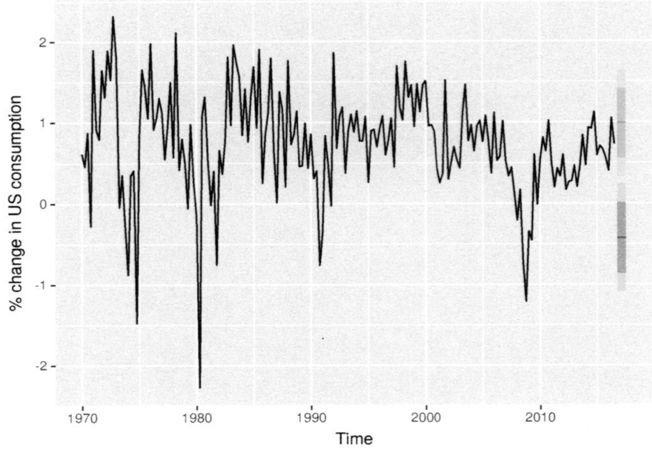

Figure 5.18: Forecasting percentage changes in personal consumption expenditure for the US under scenario based forecasting.

Building a predictive regression model

The great advantage of regression models is that they can be used to capture important relationships between the forecast variable of interest and the predictor variables. A major challenge however, is that in order to generate ex-ante forecasts, the model requires future values of each predictor. If scenario based forecasting is of interest then these models are extremely useful. However, if ex-ante forecasting is the main focus, obtaining forecasts of the predictors can be very challenging (in many cases generating forecasts for the predictor variables can be more challenging than forecasting directly the forecast variable without using predictors).

An alternative formulation is to use as predictors their lagged values. Assuming that we are interested in generating a h-step ahead forecast we write

$$y_{t+h} = \beta_0 + \beta_1 x_{1,t} + \cdots + \beta_k x_{k,t} + \varepsilon_{t+h}$$

for $h = 1, 2 \ldots$. The predictor set is formed by values of the xs that are observed h time periods prior to observing y. Therefore when the estimated model is projected into the future, i.e., beyond the end of the sample T, all predictor values are available.

Including lagged values of the predictors does not only make the model operational for easily generating forecasts, it also makes it intuitively appealing. For example, the effect of a policy change with the aim of increasing production may not have an instantaneous effect on consumption expenditure. It is most likely that this will happen with a lagging effect. We touched upon this in Section 5.4 when briefly introducing distributed lags as predictors. Several directions for generalising regression models to better incorporate the rich dynamics observed in time series are discussed in Section 9.

Prediction intervals

With each forecast for the change in consumption in Figure 5.18, 95% and 80% prediction intervals are also included. The general formulation of how to calculate prediction intervals for multiple regression models is presented in Section 5.7. As this involves some advanced matrix algebra we present here the case for calculating prediction intervals for a simple regression, where a forecast can be generated using the equation,

$$\hat{y} = \hat{\beta}_0 + \hat{\beta}_1 x.$$

Assuming that the regression errors are normally distributed, an approximate 95% prediction interval associated with this forecast is given by

$$\hat{y} \pm 1.96\hat{\sigma}_e\sqrt{1 + \frac{1}{T} + \frac{(x - \bar{x})^2}{(T-1)s_x^2}}, \tag{5.3}$$

where T is the total number of observations, $\bar{x}$ is the mean of the observed x values, s_x is the standard deviation of the observed x values and $\hat{\sigma}_e$ is the standard error of the regression given by Equation (5.2). Similarly, an 80% prediction interval can be obtained by replacing 1.96 by 1.28. Other prediction intervals can be obtained by replacing the 1.96 with the appropriate value given in Table 3.1. If R is used to obtain prediction intervals, more exact calculations are obtained (especially for small values of T) than what is given by Equation (5.3).

Equation (5.3) shows that the prediction interval is wider when x is far from $\bar{x}$. That is, we are more certain about our forecasts when considering values of the predictor variable close to its sample mean.

Example The estimated simple regression line in the US consumption example is

$$\hat{y}_t = 0.55 + 0.28x_t.$$

Assuming that for the next four quarters, personal income will increase by its historical mean value of $\bar{x} = 0.72\%$, consumption is forecast to increase by 1.95% and the corresponding 95% and 80% prediction intervals are $[0.69, 3.21]$ and $[1.13, 2.77]$ respectively (calculated using R). If we assume an extreme increase of 5% in income, then the prediction intervals are considerably wider as shown in Figure 5.19.

```
fit.cons <- tslm(Consumption ~ Income, data = uschange)
h <- 4
fcast.ave <- forecast(fit.cons,
  newdata = data.frame(
    Income = rep(mean(uschange[,"Income"]), h)))
fcast.up <- forecast(fit.cons,
  newdata = data.frame(Income = rep(5, h)))
autoplot(uschange[, "Consumption"]) +
  ylab("% change in US consumption") +
  autolayer(fcast.ave, series = "Average increase",
    PI = TRUE) +
  autolayer(fcast.up, series = "Extreme increase",
    PI = TRUE) +
  guides(colour = guide_legend(title = "Scenario"))
```

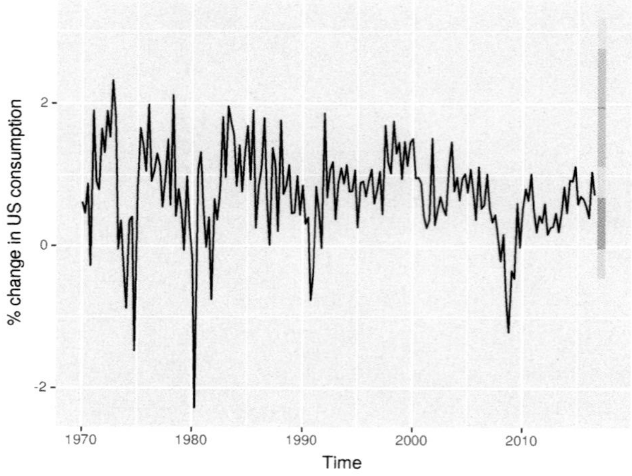

Figure 5.19: Prediction intervals if income is increased by its historical mean of 0.72% versus an extreme increase of 5%.

5.7 Matrix formulation

Warning: this is a more advanced, optional section and assumes knowledge of matrix algebra.

Recall that multiple regression model can be written as

$$y_t = \beta_0 + \beta_1 x_{1,t} + \beta_2 x_{2,t} + \cdots + \beta_k x_{k,t} + \varepsilon_t$$

where ε_t has mean zero and variance σ^2. This expresses the relationship between a single value of the forecast variable and the predictors.

It can be convenient to write this in matrix form where all the values of the forecast variable are given in a single equation. Let $\boldsymbol{y} = (y_1, \dots, y_T)'$, $\boldsymbol{\varepsilon} = (\varepsilon_1, \dots, \varepsilon_T)'$, $\boldsymbol{\beta} = (\beta_0, \dots, \beta_k)'$ and

$$\boldsymbol{X} = \begin{bmatrix} 1 & x_{1,1} & x_{2,1} & \dots & x_{k,1} \\ 1 & x_{1,2} & x_{2,2} & \dots & x_{k,2} \\ \vdots & \vdots & \vdots & & \vdots \\ 1 & x_{1,T} & x_{2,T} & \dots & x_{k,T} \end{bmatrix}.$$

Then

$$\boldsymbol{y} = \boldsymbol{X}\boldsymbol{\beta} + \boldsymbol{\varepsilon}.$$

where $\boldsymbol{\varepsilon}$ has mean $\boldsymbol{0}$ and variance $\sigma^2\boldsymbol{I}$. Note that the $\boldsymbol{X}$ matrix has T rows reflecting the number of observations and $k+1$ columns reflecting the intercept which is represented by the column of ones plus the number of predictors.

Least squares estimation

Least squares estimation is performed by minimizing the expression $\boldsymbol{\varepsilon}'\boldsymbol{\varepsilon} = (\boldsymbol{y} - \boldsymbol{X}\boldsymbol{\beta})'(\boldsymbol{y} - \boldsymbol{X}\boldsymbol{\beta})$. It can be shown that this is minimized when $\boldsymbol{\beta}$ takes the value

$$\hat{\boldsymbol{\beta}} = (\boldsymbol{X}'\boldsymbol{X})^{-1}\boldsymbol{X}'\boldsymbol{y}$$

This is sometimes known as the "normal equation". The estimated coefficients require the inversion of the matrix $\boldsymbol{X}'\boldsymbol{X}$. If $\boldsymbol{X}$ is not of full column rank then matrix $\boldsymbol{X}'\boldsymbol{X}$ is singular and the model cannot be estimated. This will occur, for example, if you fall for the "dummy variable trap", i.e., having the same number of dummy variables as there are categories of a categorical predictor, as discussed in Section 5.4.

The residual variance is estimated using

$$\hat{\sigma}_e^2 = \frac{1}{T-k-1}(\boldsymbol{y} - \boldsymbol{X}\hat{\boldsymbol{\beta}})'(\boldsymbol{y} - \boldsymbol{X}\hat{\boldsymbol{\beta}}).$$

Fitted values and cross-validation

The normal equation shows that the fitted values can be calculated using

$$\hat{\boldsymbol{y}} = \boldsymbol{X}\hat{\boldsymbol{\beta}} = \boldsymbol{X}(\boldsymbol{X}'\boldsymbol{X})^{-1}\boldsymbol{X}'\boldsymbol{y} = \boldsymbol{H}\boldsymbol{y},$$

where $\boldsymbol{H} = \boldsymbol{X}(\boldsymbol{X}'\boldsymbol{X})^{-1}\boldsymbol{X}'$ is known as the "hat-matrix" because it is used to compute $\hat{\boldsymbol{y}}$ ("y-hat").

If the diagonal values of $\boldsymbol{H}$ are denoted by $h_1, \dots, h_T$, then the cross-validation statistic can be computed using

$$\text{CV} = \frac{1}{T}\sum_{t=1}^{T}[e_t/(1-h_t)]^2,$$

where e_t is the residual obtained from fitting the model to all T observations. Thus, it is not necessary to actually fit T separate models when computing the CV statistic.

Forecasts and prediction intervals

Let $\boldsymbol{x}^*$ be a row vector containing the values of the predictors (in the same format as $\boldsymbol{X}$) for which we want to generate a forecast . Then the forecast is given by

$$\hat{y} = \boldsymbol{x}^*\hat{\boldsymbol{\beta}} = \boldsymbol{x}^*(\boldsymbol{X}'\boldsymbol{X})^{-1}\boldsymbol{X}'\boldsymbol{Y}$$

and its estimated variance is given by

$$\hat{\sigma}_e^2\left[1 + \boldsymbol{x}^*(\boldsymbol{X}'\boldsymbol{X})^{-1}(\boldsymbol{x}^*)'\right].$$

A 95% prediction interval can be calculated (assuming normally distributed errors) as

$$\hat{y} \pm 1.96\hat{\sigma}_e\sqrt{1 + \boldsymbol{x}^*(\boldsymbol{X}'\boldsymbol{X})^{-1}(\boldsymbol{x}^*)'}.$$

This takes into account the uncertainty due to the error term ε and the uncertainty in the coefficient estimates. However, it ignores any errors in $\boldsymbol{x}^*$. Thus, if the future values of the predictors are uncertain, then the prediction interval calculated using this expression will be too narrow.

5.8 Nonlinear regression

Although the linear relationship assumed so far in this chapter is often adequate, there are many cases in which a nonlinear functional form is more suitable. To keep things simple in this section we assume that we only have one predictor x.

The simplest way of modelling a nonlinear relationship is to transform the forecast variable y and/or the predictor variable x before estimating a regression model. While this provides a non-linear functional form, the model is still linear in the parameters. The most commonly used transformation is the (natural) logarithm (see Section 3.2).

A **log-log** functional form is specified as

$$\log y = \beta_0 + \beta_1 \log x + \varepsilon.$$

In this model, the slope β_1 can be interpreted as an elasticity: β_1 is the average percentage change in y resulting from a 1% increase in x. Other useful forms can also be specified. The **log-linear** form is specified by only transforming the forecast variable and the **linear-log** form is obtained by transforming the predictor.

Recall that in order to perform a logarithmic transformation to a variable, all of its observed values must be greater than zero. In the case that variable x contains zeros, we use the transformation $\log(x+1)$; i.e., we add one to the value of the variable and then take logarithms. This has a similar effect to taking logarithms but avoids the problem of zeros. It also has the neat side-effect of zeros on the original scale remaining zeros on the transformed scale.

There are cases for which simply transforming the data will not be adequate and a more general specification may be required. Then the model we use is

$$y = f(x) + \varepsilon$$

where f is a nonlinear function. In standard (linear) regression, $f(x) = \beta_0 + \beta_1 x$. In the specification of nonlinear regression that follows, we allow f to be a more flexible nonlinear function of x, compared to simply a logarithmic or other transformation.

One of the simplest specifications is to make f **piecewise linear**. That is, we introduce points where the slope of f can change. These points are called **knots**. This can be achieved by letting $x_{1,t} = x$ and introducing variable $x_{2,t}$ such that

$$x_{2,t} = (x-c)_+ = \begin{cases} 0 & x < c \\ (x-c) & x \geq c \end{cases}$$

The notation $(x-c)_+$ means the value $x-c$ if it is positive and 0 otherwise. This forces the slope to bend at point c. Additional bends can be included in the relationship by adding further variables of the above form.

An example of this follows by considering $x = t$ and fitting a piecewise linear trend to a time series.

Piecewise linear relationships constructed in this way are a special case of **regression splines**. In general, a linear regression spline is obtained using

$$x_1 = x \quad x_2 = (x-c_1)_+ \quad \dots \quad x_k = (x-c_{k-1})_+$$

where $c_1, \dots, c_{k-1}$ are the knots (the points at which the line can bend). Selecting the number of knots $(k-1)$ and where they should be positioned can be difficult and somewhat arbitrary. Some automatic knot selection algorithms are available in some software, but are not yet widely used.

A smoother result can be obtained using piecewise cubics rather than piecewise lines. These are constrained to be continuous (they join up) and smooth (so that there are no sudden changes of direction, as we see with piecewise linear splines). In general, a cubic regression spline is written as

$$x_1 = x \quad x_2 = x^2 \quad x_3 = x^3 \quad x_4 = (x-c_1)_+ \quad \dots \quad x_k = (x-c_{k-3})_+.$$

Cubic splines usually give a better fit to the data. However, forecasting values of y when x is outside the range of the historical data becomes very unreliable.

Forecasting with a nonlinear trend

In Section 5.4 fitting a linear trend to a time series by setting $x = t$ was introduced. The simplest way of fitting a nonlinear trend is using quadratic or higher order trends obtained by specifying

$$x_{1,t} = t, \quad x_{2,t} = t^2, \quad \ldots.$$

However, it is not recommended that quadratic or higher order trends be used in forecasting. When they are extrapolated, the resulting forecasts are often very unrealistic.

A better approach is to use the piecewise specification introduced above and fit a piecewise linear trend which bends at some point in time. We can think of this as a nonlinear trend constructed of linear pieces. If the trend bends at time τ, then it can be specified by simply replacing $x = t$ and $c = \tau$ above such that we include the predictors,

$$x_{1,t} = t$$

$$x_{2,t} = (t-\tau)_+ = \begin{cases} 0 & t < \tau \\ (t-\tau) & t \geq \tau \end{cases}$$

in the model. If the associated coefficients of $x_{1,t}$ and $x_{2,t}$ are β_1 and β_2, then β_1 gives the slope of the trend before time τ, while the slope of the line after time τ is given by $\beta_1 + \beta_2$. Additional bends can be included in the relationship by adding further variables of the form $(t-\tau)_+$ where τ is the "knot" or point in time at which the line should bend.

Example: Boston marathon winning times The top panel of Figure 5.20 shows the Boston marathon winning times (in minutes) since it started in 1897. The time series shows a general downward trend as the winning times have been improving over the years. The bottom panel shows the residuals from fitting a linear trend to the data. The plot shows an obvious nonlinear pattern which has not been captured by the linear trend. There is also some heteroscedasticity, with decreasing variation over time.

Fitting an exponential trend (equivalent to a log-linear regression) to the data can be achieved by transforming the y variable so that the model to be fitted is,

$$\log y_t = \beta_0 + \beta_1 t + \varepsilon_t.$$

This also addresses the heteroscedasticity. The fitted exponential trend and forecasts are shown in Figure 5.21. Although the exponential trend does not seem to fit the data much better

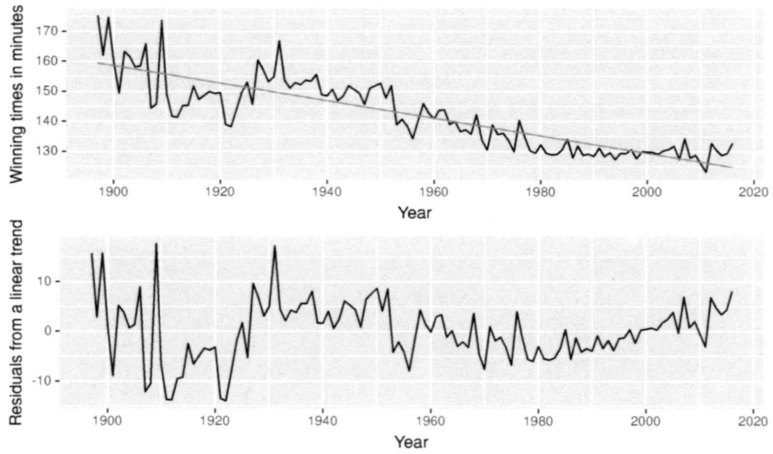

Figure 5.20: Fitting a linear trend to the Boston marathon winning times is inadequate

than the linear trend, it gives a more sensible projection in that the winning times will decrease in the future but at a decaying rate rather than a fixed linear rate.

The plot of winning times reveals three very different periods. There is a lot of volatility in the winning times up to about 1940, with the winning times decreasing overall but with significant increases during the 1920s. After 1940 there is a near-linear decrease in times, followed by a flattening out after the 1980s, with the suggestion of an upturn towards the end of the sample. To account for these changes, we specify the years 1940 and 1980 as knots. We should warn here that subjective identification of knots can lead to over-fitting, which can be detrimental to the forecast performance of a model, and should be performed with caution.

```
h <- 10
fit.lin <- tslm(marathon ~ trend)
fcasts.lin <- forecast(fit.lin, h = h)
fit.exp <- tslm(marathon ~ trend, lambda = 0)
fcasts.exp <- forecast(fit.exp, h = h)

t <- time(marathon)
t.break1 <- 1940
t.break2 <- 1980
tb1 <- ts(pmax(0, t - t.break1), start = 1897)
tb2 <- ts(pmax(0, t - t.break2), start = 1897)

fit.pw <- tslm(marathon ~ t + tb1 + tb2)
t.new <- t[length(t)] + seq(h)
tb1.new <- tb1[length(tb1)] + seq(h)
```

```
tb2.new <- tb2[length(tb2)] + seq(h)

newdata <- cbind(t=t.new, tb1=tb1.new, tb2=tb2.new) %>%
  as.data.frame()
fcasts.pw <- forecast(fit.pw, newdata = newdata)

fit.spline <- tslm(marathon ~ t + I(t^2) + I(t^3) +
  I(tb1^3) + I(tb2^3))
fcasts.spl <- forecast(fit.spline, newdata = newdata)

autoplot(marathon) +
  autolayer(fitted(fit.lin), series = "Linear") +
  autolayer(fitted(fit.exp), series = "Exponential") +
  autolayer(fitted(fit.pw), series = "Piecewise") +
  autolayer(fitted(fit.spline), series = "Cubic Spline") +
  autolayer(fcasts.pw, series="Piecewise") +
  autolayer(fcasts.lin, series="Linear", PI=FALSE) +
  autolayer(fcasts.exp, series="Exponential", PI=FALSE) +
  autolayer(fcasts.spl, series="Cubic Spline", PI=FALSE) +
  xlab("Year") + ylab("Winning times in minutes") +
  ggtitle("Boston Marathon") +
  guides(colour = guide_legend(title = " "))
```

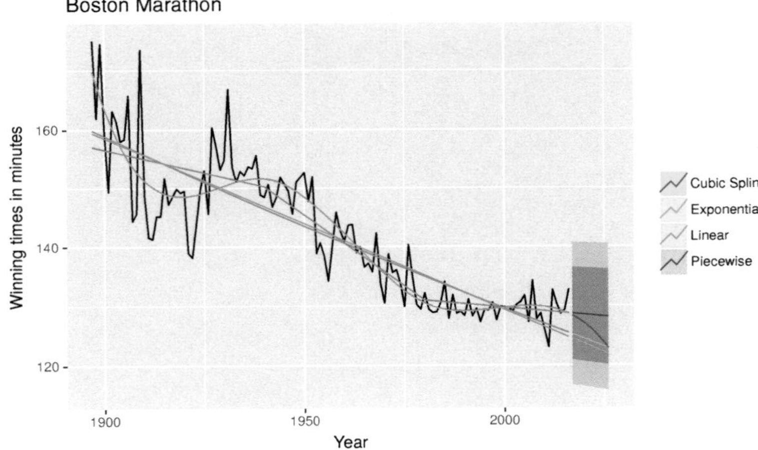

Figure 5.21: Projecting forecasts from a linear, exponential, piecewise linear trends and a cubic spline for the Boston marathon winning times

Figure 5.21 above shows the fitted lines and forecasts from linear, exponential, piecewise linear, and cubic spline trends. The best forecasts appear to come from the piecewise linear trend, while the cubic spline gives the best fit to the historical data but poor forecasts.

There is an alternative formulation of cubic splines (called **natural cubic smoothing splines**) that imposes some constraints, so the spline function is linear at the end, which usually gives much better forecasts without compromising the fit. In Figure 5.22, we have used the `splinef()` function to produce the cubic spline forecasts. This uses many more knots than we used in Figure 5.21, but the coefficients are constrained to prevent over-fitting, and the curve is linear at both ends. This has the added advantage that knot selection is not subjective. We have also used a log transformation (`lambda=0`) to handle the heteroscedasticity.

```
marathon %>%
  splinef(lambda=0) %>%
  autoplot()
```

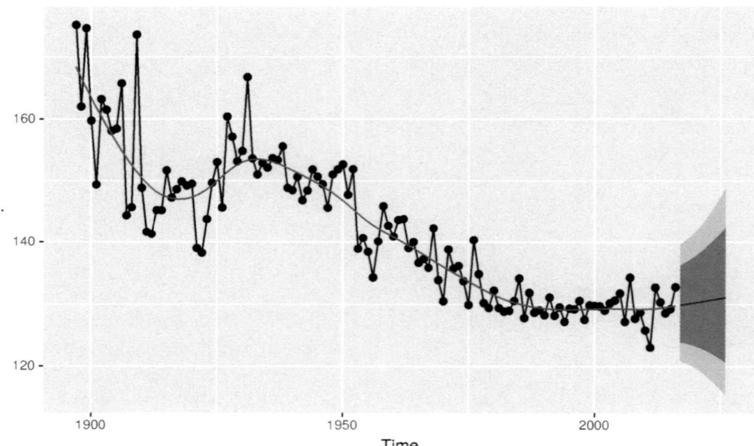

Figure 5.22: Natural cubic smoothing splines applied to the marathon data. The forecasts are a linear projection of the trend at the end of the observed data.

The residuals plotted in Figure 5.23 show that this model has captured the trend well, although there is some heteroscedasity remaining. The wide prediction interval associated with the forecasts reflects the volatility observed in the historical winning times.

```
marathon %>%
  splinef(lambda=0) %>%
  checkresiduals()
```

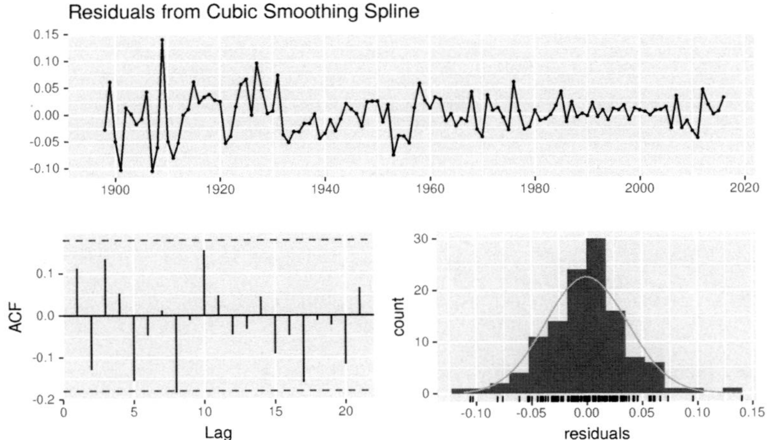

Figure 5.23: Residuals from the cublic spline trend.

5.9 Correlation, causation and forecasting

Correlation is not causation

It is important not to confuse correlation with causation, or causation with forecasting. A variable x may be useful for forecasting a variable y, but that does not mean x is causing y. It is possible that x *is* causing y, but it may be that y is causing x, or that the relationship between them is more complicated than simple causality.

For example, it is possible to model the number of drownings at a beach resort each month with the number of ice-creams sold in the same period. The model can give reasonable forecasts, not because ice-creams cause drownings, but because people eat more ice-creams on hot days when they are also more likely to go swimming. So the two variables (ice-cream sales and drownings) are correlated, but one is not causing the other. They are both caused by a third variable (temperature).

Similarly, it is possible to forecast if it will rain in the afternoon by observing the number of cyclists on the road in the morning. When there are fewer cyclists than usual, it is more likely to rain later in the day. The model can give reasonable forecasts, not because cyclists prevent rain, but because people are more likely to cycle when the published weather forecast is for a dry day. In this case, there is a causal relationship, but in the opposite direction to our forecasting model. The number of cyclists falls because there is rain forecast. That is, x (rainfall) is affecting y (cyclists).

It is important to understand that correlations are useful for forecasting, even when there is no causal relationship between the two variables, or when the correlation runs in the opposite direction to the model.

However, often a better model is possible if a causal mechanism can be determined. A better model for drownings will probably include temperatures and visitor numbers and exclude ice-cream sales. A good forecasting model for rainfall will not include cyclists, but it will include atmospheric observations from the previous few days.

Confounded predictors

A related issue involves confounding variables. Suppose we are forecasting monthly sales of a company for 2012, using data from 2000–2011. In January 2008, a new competitor came into the market and started taking some market share. At the same time, the economy began to decline. In your forecasting model, you include both competitor activity (measured using advertising time on a local television station) and the health of the economy (measured using GDP). It will not be possible to separate the effects of these two predictors because they are correlated. We say that two variables are **confounded** when their effects on the forecast variable cannot be separated. Any pair of correlated predictors will have some level of confounding, but we would not normally describe them as confounded unless there was a relatively high level of correlation between them.

Confounding is not really a problem for forecasting, as we can still compute forecasts without needing to separate out the effects of the predictors. However, it becomes a problem with scenario forecasting as the scenarios should take account of the relationships between predictors. It is also a problem if some historical analysis of the contributions of various predictors is required.

Multicollinearity and forecasting

A closely related issue is **multicollinearity**, which occurs when similar information is provided by two or more of the predictor variables in a multiple regression.

It can occur when two predictors are highly correlated with each other (that is, they have a correlation coefficient close to +1 or -1). In this case, knowing the value of one of the variables tells you a lot about the value of the other variable. Hence, they are providing similar information. For example, foot size can be used to predict height, but including the size of both left and right feet in the same model is not going to make the forecasts any better, although it won't make them worse either.

Multicollinearity can also occur when a linear combination of predictors is highly correlated with another linear combination of predictors. In this case, knowing the value of the first group of predictors tells you a lot about the value of the second group of predictors. Hence, they are providing similar information.

An example of this problem is the dummy variable trap discussed in Section 5.4. Suppose you have quarterly data and use four dummy variables, d_1, d_2, d_3 and d_4. Then $d_4 = 1 - d_1 - d_2 - d_3$, so there is perfect correlation between d_4 and $d_1 + d_2 + d_3$.

In the case of perfect correlation (i.e., a correlation of +1 or -1, such as in the dummy variable trap), it is not possible to estimate the regression model.

If there is high correlation (close to but not equal to +1 or -1), then the estimation of the regression coefficients is computationally difficult. In fact, some software (notably Microsoft Excel) may give highly inaccurate estimates of the coefficients. Most reputable statistical software will use algorithms to limit the effect of multicollinearity on the coefficient estimates, but you do need to be careful. The major software packages such as R, SPSS, SAS and Stata all use estimation algorithms to avoid the problem as much as possible.

When multicollinearity is present, the uncertainty associated with individual regression coefficients will be large. This is because they are difficult to estimate. Consequently, statistical tests (e.g., t-tests) on regression coefficients are unreliable.

(In forecasting we are rarely interested in such tests.) Also, it will not be possible to make accurate statements about the contribution of each separate predictor to the forecast.

Forecasts will be unreliable if the values of the future predictors are outside the range of the historical values of the predictors. For example, suppose you have fitted a regression model with predictors x_1 and x_2 which are highly correlated with each other, and suppose that the values of x_1 in the fitting data ranged between 0 and 100. Then forecasts based on $x_1 > 100$ or $x_1 < 0$ will be unreliable. It is always a little dangerous when future values of the predictors lie much outside the historical range, but it is especially problematic when multicollinearity is present.

Note that if you are using good statistical software, if you are not interested in the specific contributions of each predictor, and if the future values of your predictor variables are within their historical ranges, there is nothing to worry about — multicollinearity is not a problem except when there is perfect correlation.

5.10 Exercises

1. Daily electricity demand for Victoria, Australia, during 2014 is contained in `elecdaily`. The data for the first 20 days can be obtained as follows.

   ```
   daily20 <- head(elecdaily,20)
   ```

   a. Plot the data and find the regression model for Demand with temperature as an explanatory variable. Why is there a positive relationship?

   b. Produce a residual plot. Is the model adequate? Are there any outliers or influential observations?

   c. Use the model to forecast the electricity demand that you would expect for the next day if the maximum temperature was 15° and compare it with the forecast if the with maximum temperature was 35°. Do you believe these forecasts?

d. Give prediction intervals for your forecasts. The following R code will get you started:

```
autoplot(daily20, facets=TRUE)
daily20 %>%
  as.data.frame() %>%
  ggplot(aes(x=Temperature, y=Demand)) +
  geom_point() +
  geom_smooth(method="lm", se=FALSE)
fit <- tslm(Demand ~ Temperature, data=daily20)
checkresiduals(fit)
forecast(fit, newdata=data.frame(Temperature=c(15,35)))
```

e. Plot Demand vs Temperature for all of the available data in `elecdaily`. What does this say about your model?

2. Data set `mens400` contains the winning times (in seconds) for the men's 400 meters final in each Olympic Games from 1896 to 2016.

   a. Plot the winning time against the year. Describe the main features of the plot.
   b. Fit a regression line to the data. Obviously the winning times have been decreasing, but at what *average* rate per year?
   c. Plot the residuals against the year. What does this indicate about the suitability of the fitted line?
   d. Predict the winning time for the men's 400 meters final in the 2020 Olympics. Give a prediction interval for your forecasts. What assumptions have you made in these calculations?

3. Type `easter(ausbeer)` and interpret what you see.

4. An elasticity coefficient is the ratio of the percentage change in the forecast variable (y) to the percentage change in the predictor variable (x). Mathematically, the elasticity is defined as $(dy/dx) \times (x/y)$. Consider the log-log model,

$$\log y = \beta_0 + \beta_1 \log x + \varepsilon.$$

   Express y as a function of x and show that the coefficient β_1 is the elasticity coefficient.

5. The data set `fancy` concerns the monthly sales figures of a shop which opened in January 1987 and sells gifts, souvenirs, and novelties. The shop is situated on the wharf at a beach

resort town in Queensland, Australia. The sales volume varies with the seasonal population of tourists. There is a large influx of visitors to the town at Christmas and for the local surfing festival, held every March since 1988. Over time, the shop has expanded its premises, range of products, and staff.

a. Produce a time plot of the data and describe the patterns in the graph. Identify any unusual or unexpected fluctuations in the time series.
b. Explain why it is necessary to take logarithms of these data before fitting a model.
c. Use R to fit a regression model to the logarithms of these sales data with a linear trend, seasonal dummies and a "surfing festival" dummy variable.
d. Plot the residuals against time and against the fitted values. Do these plots reveal any problems with the model?
e. Do boxplots of the residuals for each month. Does this reveal any problems with the model?
f. What do the values of the coefficients tell you about each variable?
g. What does the Breusch-Godfrey test tell you about your model?
h. Regardless of your answers to the above questions, use your regression model to predict the monthly sales for 1994, 1995, and 1996. Produce prediction intervals for each of your forecasts.
i. Transform your predictions and intervals to obtain predictions and intervals for the raw data.
j. How could you improve these predictions by modifying the model?

6. The `gasoline` series consists of weekly data for supplies of US finished motor gasoline product, from 2 February 1991 to 20 January 2017. The units are in "million barrels per day". Consider only the data to the end of 2004.

   a. Fit a harmonic regression with trend to the data. Experiment with changing the number Fourier terms. Plot the observed gasoline and fitted values and comment on what you see.

b. Select the appropriate number of Fourier terms to include by minimizing the AICc or CV value.

c. Check the residuals of the final model using the `checkresiduals()` function. Even though the residuals fail the correlation tests, the results are probably not severe enough to make much difference to the forecasts and prediction intervals. (Note that the correlations are relatively small, even though they are significant.)

d. To forecast using harmonic regression, you will need to generate the future values of the Fourier terms. This can be done as follows.

```
fc <- forecast(fit, newdata=data.frame(fourier(x,K,h)))
```

where `fit` is the fitted model using `tslm()`, `K` is the number of Fourier terms used in creating `fit`, and `h` is the forecast horizon required.

Forecast the next year of data.

e. Plot the forecasts along with the actual data for 2005. What do you find?

7. Data set `huron` gives the water level of Lake Huron in feet from 1875–1972.

    a. Plot the data and comment on its features.
    b. Fit a linear regression and compare this to a piecewise linear trend model with a knot at 1915.
    c. Generate forecasts from these two models for the period upto 1980 and comment on these.

8. *(For advanced readers following on from Section 5.7).*

    Using matrix notation it was shown that if $\boldsymbol{y} = \boldsymbol{X}\boldsymbol{\beta} + \boldsymbol{\varepsilon}$, where $\boldsymbol{e}$ has mean $\boldsymbol{0}$ and variance matrix $\sigma^2\boldsymbol{I}$, the estimated coefficients are given by $\hat{\boldsymbol{\beta}} = (\boldsymbol{X}'\boldsymbol{X})^{-1}\boldsymbol{X}'\boldsymbol{y}$ and a forecast is given by $\hat{y} = \boldsymbol{x}^*\hat{\boldsymbol{\beta}} = \boldsymbol{x}^*(\boldsymbol{X}'\boldsymbol{X})^{-1}\boldsymbol{X}'\boldsymbol{y}$ where $\boldsymbol{x}^*$ is a row vector containing the values of the regressors for the forecast (in the same format as $\boldsymbol{X}$), and the forecast variance is given by $var(\hat{y}) = \sigma^2\left[1 + \boldsymbol{x}^*(\boldsymbol{X}'\boldsymbol{X})^{-1}(\boldsymbol{x}^*)'\right]$.

Consider the simple time trend model where $y_t = \beta_0 + \beta_1 t$. Using the following results,

$$\sum_{t=1}^{T} t = \frac{1}{2}T(T+1), \quad \sum_{t=1}^{T} t^2 = \frac{1}{6}T(T+1)(2T+1)$$

derive the following expressions:

a. $\boldsymbol{X}'\boldsymbol{X} = \frac{1}{6}\begin{bmatrix} 6T & 3T(T+1) \\ 3T(T+1) & T(T+1)(2T+1) \end{bmatrix}$

b. $(\boldsymbol{X}'\boldsymbol{X})^{-1} = \frac{2}{T(T^2-1)}\begin{bmatrix} (T+1)(2T+1) & -3(T+1) \\ -3(T+1) & 6 \end{bmatrix}$

c. $\hat{\beta}_0 = \frac{2}{T(T-1)}\left[(2T+1)\sum_{t=1}^{T} y_t - 3\sum_{t=1}^{T} t y_t\right]$

$$\hat{\beta}_1 = \frac{6}{T(T^2-1)}\left[2\sum_{t=1}^{T} t y_t - (T+1)\sum_{t=1}^{T} y_t\right]$$

d. $\text{Var}(\hat{y}_t) = \hat{\sigma}^2\left[1 + \frac{2}{T(T-1)}\left(1 - 4T - 6h + 6\frac{(T+h)^2}{T+1}\right)\right]$

5.11 Further reading

There are countless books on regression analysis, but few with a focus on regression for time series and forecasting.

- A good general and modern book on regression is Sheather (2009).
- Another general regression text full of excellent practical advice is Harrell (2015).
- Ord, Fildes, and Kourentzes (2017) provides a practical coverage of regression models for time series in Chapters 7–9, with a strong emphasis on forecasting.

Chapter 6

Time series decomposition

Time series data can exhibit a variety of patterns, and it is often helpful to split a time series into several components, each representing an underlying pattern category.

In Section 2.3 we discussed three types of time series patterns: trend, seasonality and cycles. When we decompose a time series into components, we usually combine the trend and cycle into a single **trend-cycle** component (sometimes called the **trend** for simplicity). Thus we think of a time series as comprising three components: a trend-cycle component, a seasonal component, and a remainder component (containing anything else in the time series).

In this chapter, we consider some common methods for extracting these components from a time series. Often this is done to help improve understanding of the time series, but it can also be used to improve forecast accuracy.

6.1 Time series components

If we assume an additive decomposition, then we can write

$$y_t = S_t + T_t + R_t,$$

where y_t is the data, S_t is the seasonal component, T_t is the trend-cycle component, and R_t is the remainder component, all at period t. Alternatively, a multiplicative decomposition would be written as

$$y_t = S_t \times T_t \times R_t.$$

The additive decomposition is the most appropriate if the magnitude of the seasonal fluctuations, or the variation around the trend-cycle, does not vary with the level of the time series. When the variation in the seasonal pattern, or the variation around the trend-cycle, appears to be proportional to the level of the time series, then a multiplicative decomposition is more appropriate. Multiplicative decompositions are common with economic time series.

An alternative to using a multiplicative decomposition is to first transform the data until the variation in the series appears to be stable over time, then use an additive decomposition. When a log transformation has been used, this is equivalent to using a multiplicative decomposition because

$$y_t = S_t \times T_t \times R_t \quad \text{is equivalent to} \quad \log y_t = \log S_t + \log T_t + \log R_t.$$

Electrical equipment manufacturing

We will look at several methods for obtaining the components S_t, T_t and R_t later in this chapter, but first, it is helpful to see an example. We will decompose the new orders index for electrical equipment shown in Figure 6.1. The data show the number of new orders for electrical equipment (computer, electronic and optical products) in the Euro area (16 countries). The data have been adjusted by working days and normalized so that a value of 100 corresponds to 2005.

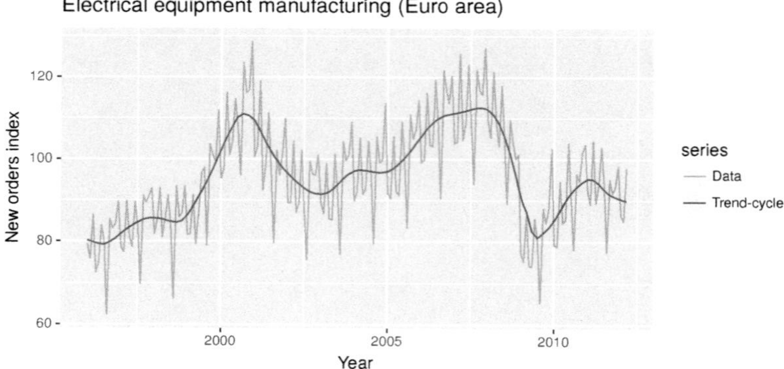

Figure 6.1: Electrical equipment orders: the trend-cycle component (red) and the raw data (grey).

Figure 6.1 shows the trend-cycle component, T_t, in red and the original data, y_t, in grey. The trend-cycle shows the overall movement in the series, ignoring the seasonality and any small random fluctuations.

Figure 6.2 shows an additive decomposition of these data. The method used for estimating components in this example is STL, which is discussed in Section 6.6.

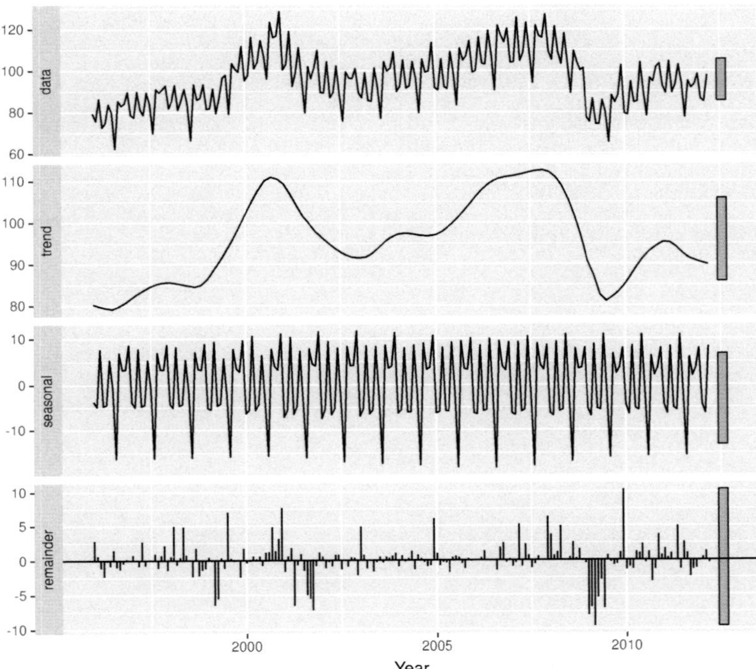

Figure 6.2: The electrical equipment orders (top) and its three additive components.

The three components are shown separately in the bottom three panels of Figure 6.2. These components can be added together to reconstruct the data shown in the top panel. Notice that the seasonal component changes very slowly over time, so that any two consecutive years have very similar patterns, but years far apart may have different seasonal patterns. The remainder component shown in the bottom panel is what is left over when the seasonal and trend-cycle components have been subtracted from the data.

The grey bars to the right of each panel show the relative scales of the components. Each grey bar represents the same length but because the plots are on different scales, the bars vary in size. The large grey bar in the bottom panel shows that the variation in the remainder component is small compared to the variation in the data, which has a bar about one quarter the size. If we shrunk the bottom three panels until their bars became the same size as that in the data panel, then all the panels would be on the same scale.

Seasonally adjusted data

If the seasonal component is removed from the original data, the resulting values are the "seasonally adjusted" data. For an additive decomposition, the seasonally adjusted data are given by $y_t - S_t$, and for multiplicative data, the seasonally adjusted values are obtained using y_t/S_t.

Figure 6.3 shows the seasonally adjusted electrical equipment orders.

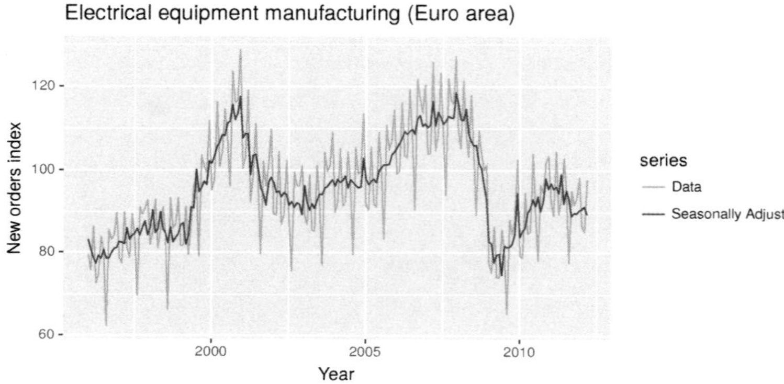

Figure 6.3: Seasonally adjusted electrical equipment orders (blue) and the original data (grey).

If the variation due to seasonality is not of primary interest, the seasonally adjusted series can be useful. For example, monthly unemployment data are usually seasonally adjusted in order to highlight variation due to the underlying state of the economy rather than the seasonal variation. An increase in unemployment due to school leavers seeking work is seasonal variation, while an increase in unemployment due to an economic recession is non-seasonal. Most economic analysts who study unemployment data are more interested in the non-seasonal variation. Consequently, employment data (and many other economic series) are usually seasonally adjusted.

Seasonally adjusted series contain the remainder component as well as the trend-cycle. Therefore, they are not "smooth", and "downturns" or "upturns" can be misleading. If the purpose is to look for turning points in a series, and interpret any changes in direction, then it is better to use the trend-cycle component rather than the seasonally adjusted data.

6.2 Moving averages

The classical method of time series decomposition originated in the 1920s and was widely used until the 1950s. It still forms the basis of many time series decomposition methods, so it is important to understand how it works. The first step in a classical decomposition is to use a moving average method to estimate the trend-cycle, so we begin by discussing moving averages.

Moving average smoothing

A moving average of order m can be written as

$$\hat{T}_t = \frac{1}{m} \sum_{j=-k}^{k} y_{t+j}, \tag{6.1}$$

where $m = 2k + 1$. That is, the estimate of the trend-cycle at time t is obtained by averaging values of the time series within k periods of t. Observations that are nearby in time are also likely to be close in value. Therefore, the average eliminates some of the randomness in the data, leaving a smooth trend-cycle component. We call this an m-**MA**, meaning a moving average of order m.

```
autoplot(elecsales) + xlab("Year") + ylab("GWh") +
  ggtitle("Annual electricity sales: South Australia")
```

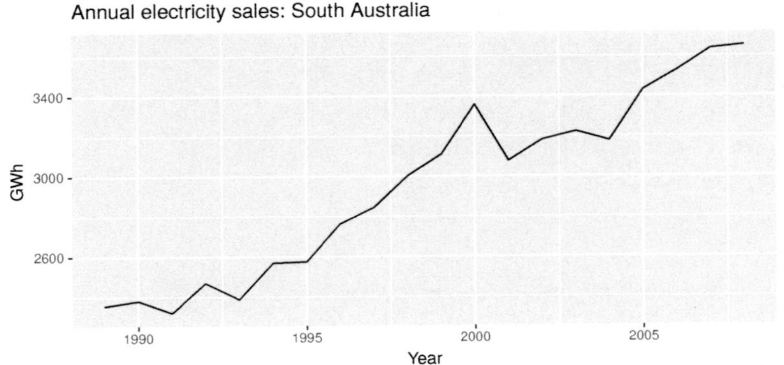

Figure 6.4: Residential electricity sales (excluding hot water) for South Australia: 1989–2008.

For example, consider Figure 6.4 which shows the volume of electricity sold to residential customers in South Australia each year from 1989 to 2008 (hot water sales have been excluded). The data are also shown in Table 6.1.

Year	Sales (GWh)	5-MA
1989	2354.34	
1990	2379.71	
1991	2318.52	2381.53
1992	2468.99	2424.56
1993	2386.09	2463.76
1994	2569.47	2552.60
1995	2575.72	2627.70
1996	2762.72	2750.62
1997	2844.50	2858.35
1998	3000.70	3014.70
1999	3108.10	3077.30
2000	3357.50	3144.52
2001	3075.70	3188.70
2002	3180.60	3202.32
2003	3221.60	3216.94
2004	3176.20	3307.30
2005	3430.60	3398.75
2006	3527.48	3485.43
2007	3637.89	
2008	3655.00	

Table 6.1: Annual electricity sales to residential customers in South Australia. 1989–2008.

In the second column of this table, a moving average of order 5 is shown, providing an estimate of the trend-cycle. The first value in this column is the average of the first five observations (1989–1993); the second value in the 5-MA column is the average of the values for 1990–1994; and so on. Each value in the 5-MA column is the average of the observations in the five year window centred on the corresponding year. In the notation of Equation (6.1), column 5-MA contains the values of $\hat{T}_t$ with $k = 2$ and $m = 2k + 1 = 5$. This is easily computed using

```
ma(elecsales, 5)
```

There are no values for either the first two years or the last two years, because we do not have two observations on either side. Later we will use more sophisticated methods of trend-cycle estimation which do allow estimates near the endpoints.

To see what the trend-cycle estimate looks like, we plot it along with the original data in Figure 6.5.

```
autoplot(elecsales, series="Data") +
  autolayer(ma(elecsales,5), series="5-MA") +
  xlab("Year") + ylab("GWh") +
  ggtitle("Annual electricity sales: South Australia") +
  scale_colour_manual(values=c("Data"="grey50","5-MA"="red"),
                      breaks=c("Data","5-MA"))
```

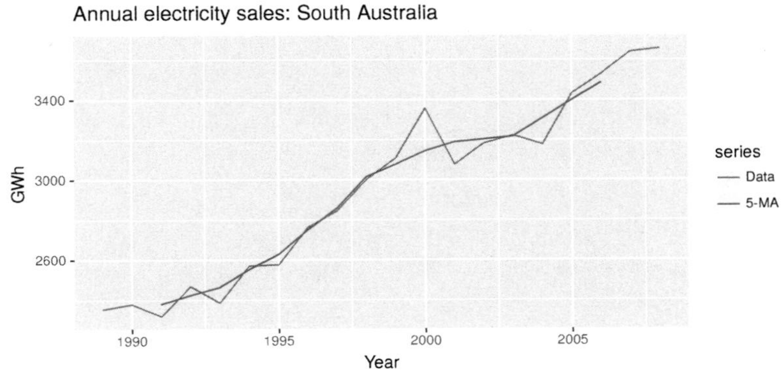

Figure 6.5: Residential electricity sales (black) along with the 5-MA estimate of the trend-cycle (red).

Notice that the trend-cycle (in red) is smoother than the original data and captures the main movement of the time series without all of the minor fluctuations. The order of the moving average determines the smoothness of the trend-cycle estimate. In general, a larger order means a smoother curve. Figure 6.6 shows the effect of changing the order of the moving average for the residential electricity sales data.

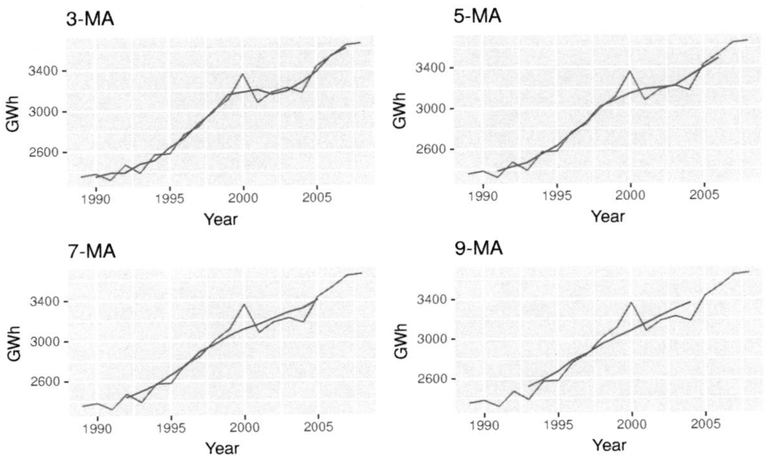

Figure 6.6: Different moving averages applied to the residential electricity sales data.

Simple moving averages such as these are usually of an odd order (e.g., 3, 5, 7, etc.). This is so they are symmetric: in a moving average of order $m = 2k + 1$, the middle observation, and k observations on either side, are averaged. But if m was even, it would no longer be symmetric.

Moving averages of moving averages

It is possible to apply a moving average to a moving average. One reason for doing this is to make an even-order moving average symmetric.

For example, we might take a moving average of order 4, and then apply another moving average of order 2 to the results. In the following table, this has been done for the first few years of the Australian quarterly beer production data.

```
beer2 <- window(ausbeer,start=1992)
ma4 <- ma(beer2, order=4, centre=FALSE)
ma2x4 <- ma(beer2, order=4, centre=TRUE)
```

Year	Quarter	Observation	4-MA	2x4-MA
1992	Q1	443		
1992	Q2	410	451.25	
1992	Q3	420	448.75	450.00
1992	Q4	532	451.50	450.12
1993	Q1	433	449.00	450.25
1993	Q2	421	444.00	446.50
1993	Q3	410	448.00	446.00
1993	Q4	512	438.00	443.00
1994	Q1	449	441.25	439.62
1994	Q2	381	446.00	443.62
1994	Q3	423	440.25	443.12
1994	Q4	531	447.00	443.62
1995	Q1	426	445.25	446.12
1995	Q2	408	442.50	443.88
1995	Q3	416	438.25	440.38
1995	Q4	520	435.75	437.00
1996	Q1	409	431.25	433.50
1996	Q2	398	428.00	429.62
1996	Q3	398	433.75	430.88
1996	Q4	507	433.75	433.75

Table 6.2: A moving average of order 4 applied to the quarterly beer data, followed by a moving average of order 2.

The notation "2×4-MA" in the last column means a 4-MA followed by a 2-MA. The values in the last column are obtained by taking a moving average of order 2 of the values in the previous column. For example, the first two values in the 4-MA column are 451.25=(443+410+420+532)/4 and 448.75=(410+420+532+433)/4. The first value in the 2x4-MA column is the average of these two: 450.00=(451.25+448.75)/2.

When a 2-MA follows a moving average of an even order (such as 4), it is called a "centred moving average of order 4". This is because the results are now symmetric. To see that this is the case, we can write the 2×4-MA as follows:

$$\begin{aligned}\hat{T}_t &= \frac{1}{2}\Big[\frac{1}{4}(y_{t-2} + y_{t-1} + y_t + y_{t+1}) + \frac{1}{4}(y_{t-1} + y_t + y_{t+1} + y_{t+2})\Big] \\ &= \frac{1}{8}y_{t-2} + \frac{1}{4}y_{t-1} + \frac{1}{4}y_t + \frac{1}{4}y_{t+1} + \frac{1}{8}y_{t+2}.\end{aligned}$$

It is now a weighted average of observations that is symmetric.

Other combinations of moving averages are also possible. For example, a 3×3-MA is often used, and consists of a moving average of order 3 followed by another moving average of order 3. In general, an even order MA should be followed by an even order MA to make it symmetric. Similarly, an odd order MA should be followed by an odd order MA.

Estimating the trend-cycle with seasonal data

The most common use of centred moving averages is for estimating the trend-cycle from seasonal data. Consider the 2×4-MA:

$$\hat{T}_t = \frac{1}{8}y_{t-2} + \frac{1}{4}y_{t-1} + \frac{1}{4}y_t + \frac{1}{4}y_{t+1} + \frac{1}{8}y_{t+2}.$$

When applied to quarterly data, each quarter of the year is given equal weight as the first and last terms apply to the same quarter in consecutive years. Consequently, the seasonal variation will be averaged out and the resulting values of $\hat{T}_t$ will have little or no seasonal variation remaining. A similar effect would be obtained using a 2×8-MA or a 2×12-MA to quarterly data.

In general, a $2 \times m$-MA is equivalent to a weighted moving average of order $m + 1$ where all observations take the weight $1/m$, except for the first and last terms which take weights

$1/(2m)$. So, if the seasonal period is even and of order m, we use a $2 \times m$-MA to estimate the trend-cycle. If the seasonal period is odd and of order m, we use a m-MA to estimate the trend-cycle. For example, a 2×12-MA can be used to estimate the trend-cycle of monthly data and a 7-MA can be used to estimate the trend-cycle of daily data with a weekly seasonality.

Other choices for the order of the MA will usually result in trend-cycle estimates being contaminated by the seasonality in the data.

Example: Electrical equipment manufacturing

```
autoplot(elecequip, series="Data") +
  autolayer(ma(elecequip, 12), series="12-MA") +
  xlab("Year") + ylab("New orders index") +
  ggtitle("Electrical equipment manufacturing (Euro area)") +
  scale_colour_manual(values=c("Data"="grey","12-MA"="red"),
                      breaks=c("Data","12-MA"))
```

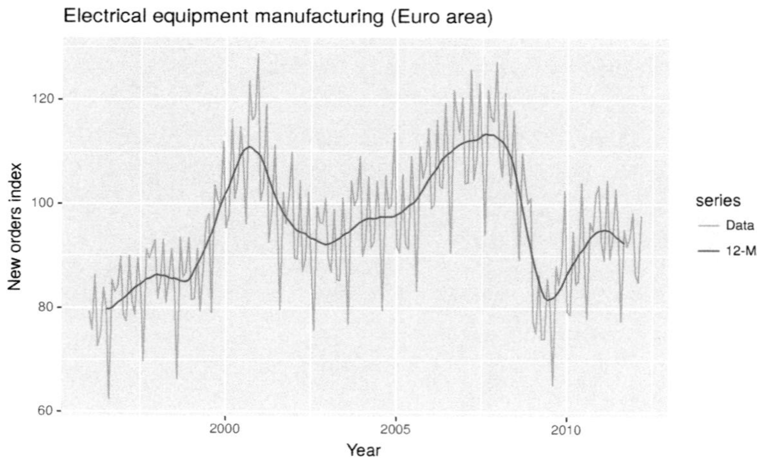

Figure 6.7: A 2x12-MA applied to the electrical equipment orders index.

Figure 6.7 shows a 2×12-MA applied to the electrical equipment orders index. Notice that the smooth line shows no seasonality; it is almost the same as the trend-cycle shown in Figure 6.1, which was estimated using a much more sophisticated method than a moving average. Any other choice for the order of the moving average (except for 24, 36, etc.) would have resulted in a smooth line that showed some seasonal fluctuations.

Weighted moving averages

Combinations of moving averages result in weighted moving averages. For example, the 2×4-MA discussed above is equivalent to a weighted 5-MA with weights given by $\left[\frac{1}{8}, \frac{1}{4}, \frac{1}{4}, \frac{1}{4}, \frac{1}{8}\right]$. In general, a weighted m-MA can be written as

$$\hat{T}_t = \sum_{j=-k}^{k} a_j y_{t+j},$$

where $k = (m-1)/2$, and the weights are given by $[a_{-k}, \dots, a_k]$. It is important that the weights all sum to one and that they are symmetric so that $a_j = a_{-j}$. The simple m-MA is a special case where all of the weights are equal to $1/m$.

A major advantage of weighted moving averages is that they yield a smoother estimate of the trend-cycle. Instead of observations entering and leaving the calculation at full weight, their weights slowly increase and then slowly decrease, resulting in a smoother curve.

6.3 Classical decomposition

The classical decomposition method originated in the 1920s. It is a relatively simple procedure, and forms the starting point for most other methods of time series decomposition. There are two forms of classical decomposition: an additive decomposition and a multiplicative decomposition. These are described below for a time series with seasonal period m (e.g., $m = 4$ for quarterly data, $m = 12$ for monthly data, $m = 7$ for daily data with a weekly pattern).

In classical decomposition, we assume that the seasonal component is constant from year to year. For multiplicative seasonality, the m values that form the seasonal component are sometimes called the "seasonal indices".

Additive decomposition

Step 1 If m is an even number, compute the trend-cycle component $\hat{T}_t$ using a $2 \times m$-MA. If m is an odd number, compute the trend-cycle component $\hat{T}_t$ using an m-MA.

Step 2 Calculate the detrended series: $y_t - \hat{T}_t$.

Step 3 To estimate the seasonal component for each season, simply average the detrended values for that season. For example, with monthly data, the seasonal component for March is the average of all the detrended March values in the data. These seasonal component values are then adjusted to ensure that they add to zero. The seasonal component is obtained by stringing together these values for each year of data. This gives $\hat{S}_t$.

Step 4 The remainder component is calculated by subtracting the estimated seasonal and trend-cycle components: $\hat{R}_t = y_t - \hat{T}_t - \hat{S}_t$.

Multiplicative decomposition

A classical multiplicative decomposition is very similar, except that the subtractions are replaced by divisions.

Step 1 If m is an even number, compute the trend-cycle component $\hat{T}_t$ using a $2 \times m$-MA. If m is an odd number, compute the trend-cycle component $\hat{T}_t$ using an m-MA.

Step 2 Calculate the detrended series: $y_t/\hat{T}_t$.

Step 3 To estimate the seasonal component for each season, simply average the detrended values for that season. For example, with monthly data, the seasonal index for March is the average of all the detrended March values in the data. These seasonal indexes are then adjusted to ensure that they add to m. The seasonal component is obtained by stringing together all of the seasonal indices for each year of data. This gives $\hat{S}_t$.

Step 4 The remainder component is calculated by dividing out the estimated seasonal and trend-cycle components: $\hat{R}_t = y_t/(\hat{T}_t\hat{S}_t)$.

Figure 6.8 shows a classical decomposition of the electrical equipment index. Compare this decomposition with that shown in Figure 6.1. The run of large negative remainder values in 2009 suggests that there is some "leakage" of the trend-cycle component into the remainder component. The trend-cycle estimate has over-smoothed the drop in the data, and the corresponding remainder values have been affected by the poor trend-cycle estimate.

```
elecequip %>% decompose(type="multiplicative") %>%
  autoplot() + xlab("Year") +
  ggtitle("Classical multiplicative decomposition
    of electrical equipment index")
```

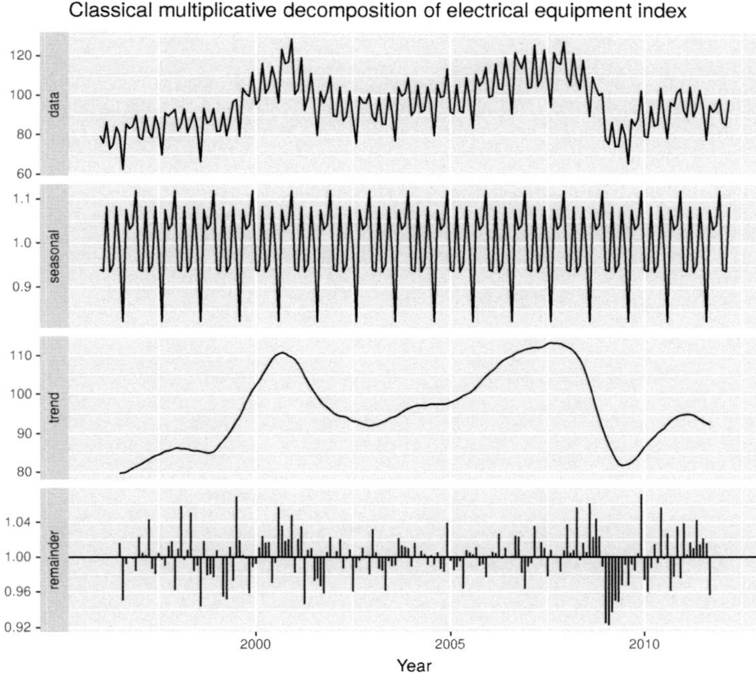

Figure 6.8: A classical multiplicative decomposition of the new orders index for electrical equipment.

Comments on classical decomposition

While classical decomposition is still widely used, it is not recommended, as there are now several much better methods. Some of the problems with classical decomposition are summarised below.

- The estimate of the trend-cycle is unavailable for the first few and last few observations. For example, if $m = 12$, there is no trend-cycle estimate for the first six or the last six observations. Consequently, there is also no estimate of the remainder component for the same time periods.
- The trend-cycle estimate tends to over-smooth rapid rises and falls in the data (as seen in the above example).
- Classical decomposition methods assume that the seasonal component repeats from year to year. For many series, this

is a reasonable assumption, but for some longer series it is not. For example, electricity demand patterns have changed over time as air conditioning has become more widespread. Specifically, in many locations, the seasonal usage pattern from several decades ago had its maximum demand in winter (due to heating), while the current seasonal pattern has its maximum demand in summer (due to air conditioning). The classical decomposition methods are unable to capture these seasonal changes over time.

- Occasionally, the values of the time series in a small number of periods may be particularly unusual. For example, the monthly air passenger traffic may be affected by an industrial dispute, making the traffic during the dispute very different from usual. The classical method is not robust to these kinds of unusual values.

6.4 X11 decomposition

Another popular method for decomposing quarterly and monthly data is the X11 method which originated in the US Census Bureau and Statistics Canada.

This method is based on classical decomposition, but includes many extra steps and features in order to overcome the drawbacks of classical decomposition that were discussed in the previous section. In particular, trend-cycle estimates are available for all observations including the end points, and the seasonal component is allowed to vary slowly over time. X11 also has some sophisticated methods for handling trading day variation, holiday effects and the effects of known predictors. It handles both additive and multiplicative decomposition. The process is entirely automatic and tends to be highly robust to outliers and level shifts in the time series.

The details of the X11 method are described in Dagum and Bianconcini (2016). Here we will only demonstrate how to use the automatic procedure in R.

The X11 method is available using the `seas()` function from the **seasonal** package[1] for R.

[1] `https://cran.r-project.org/package=seasonal`

```
library(seasonal)
elecequip %>% seas(x11="") -> fit
autoplot(fit) +
  ggtitle("X11 decomposition of electrical equipment index")
```

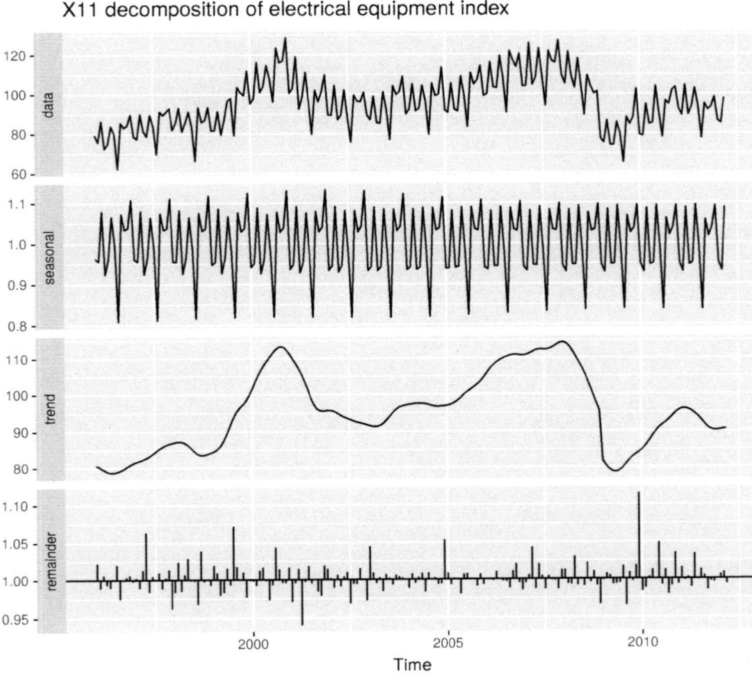

Figure 6.9: An X11 decomposition of the new orders index for electrical equipment.

Compare this decomposition with the STL decomposition shown in Figure 6.1 and the classical decomposition shown in Figure 6.8. The X11 trend-cycle has captured the sudden fall in the data in early 2009 better than either of the other two methods, and the unusual observation at the end of 2009 is now more clearly seen in the remainder component.

Given the output from the `seas()` function, `seasonal()` will extract the seasonal component, `trendcycle()` will extract the trend-cycle component, `remainder()` will extract the remainder component, and `seasadj()` will compute the seasonally adjusted time series.

For example, Figure 6.10 shows the trend-cycle component and the seasonally adjusted data, along with the original data.

```
autoplot(elecequip, series="Data") +
  autolayer(trendcycle(fit), series="Trend") +
  autolayer(seasadj(fit), series="Seasonally Adjusted") +
  xlab("Year") + ylab("New orders index") +
  ggtitle("Electrical equipment manufacturing (Euro area)") +
  scale_colour_manual(values=c("gray","blue","red"),
             breaks=c("Data","Seasonally Adjusted","Trend"))
```

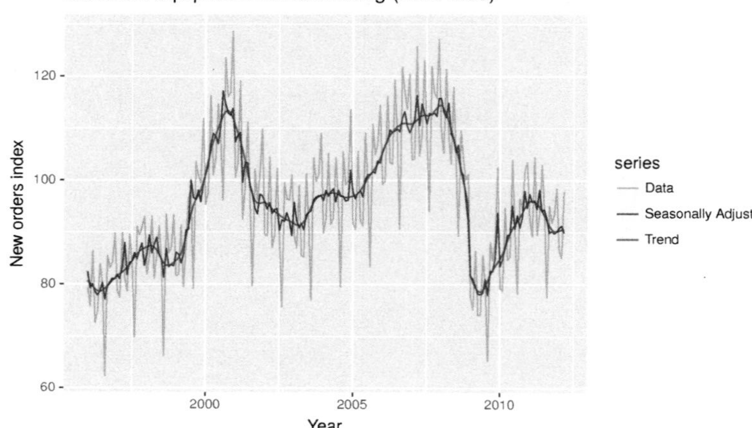

Figure 6.10: Electrical equipment orders: the original data (grey), the trend-cycle component (red) and the seasonally adjusted data (blue).

It can be useful to use seasonal plots and seasonal sub-series plots of the seasonal component. These help us to visualize the variation in the seasonal component over time. Figure 6.11 shows a seasonal sub-series plot of the seasonal component from Figure 6.9. In this case, there are only very small changes over time.

```
fit %>% seasonal() %>% ggsubseriesplot() + ylab("Seasonal")
```

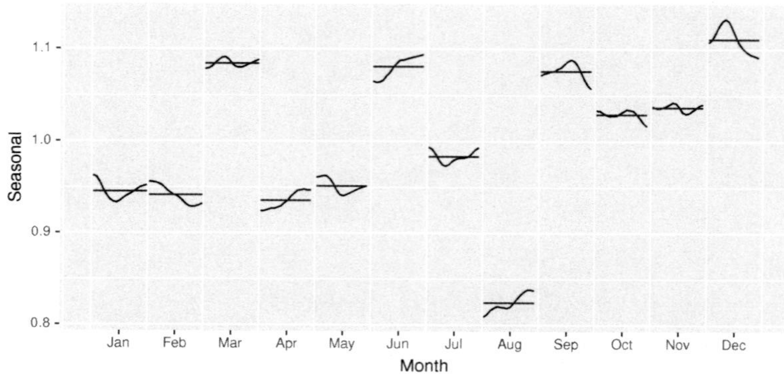

Figure 6.11: Seasonal sub-series plot of the seasonal component from the X11 decomposition of the new orders index for electrical equipment.

6.5 SEATS decomposition

"SEATS" stands for "Seasonal Extraction in ARIMA Time Series" (ARIMA models are discussed in Chapter 8). This procedure was developed at the Bank of Spain, and is now widely used by government agencies around the world. The procedure works only with quarterly and monthly data. So seasonality of other kinds, such as daily data, or hourly data, or weekly data, require an alternative approach.

The details are beyond the scope of this book. However, a complete discussion of the method is available in Dagum and Bianconcini (2016). Here we will only demonstrate how to use it via the **seasonal** package.

```
library(seasonal)
elecequip %>% seas() %>%
autoplot() +
  ggtitle("SEATS decomposition of electrical equipment index")
```

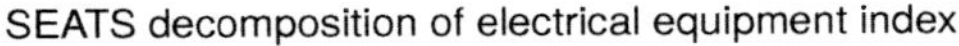

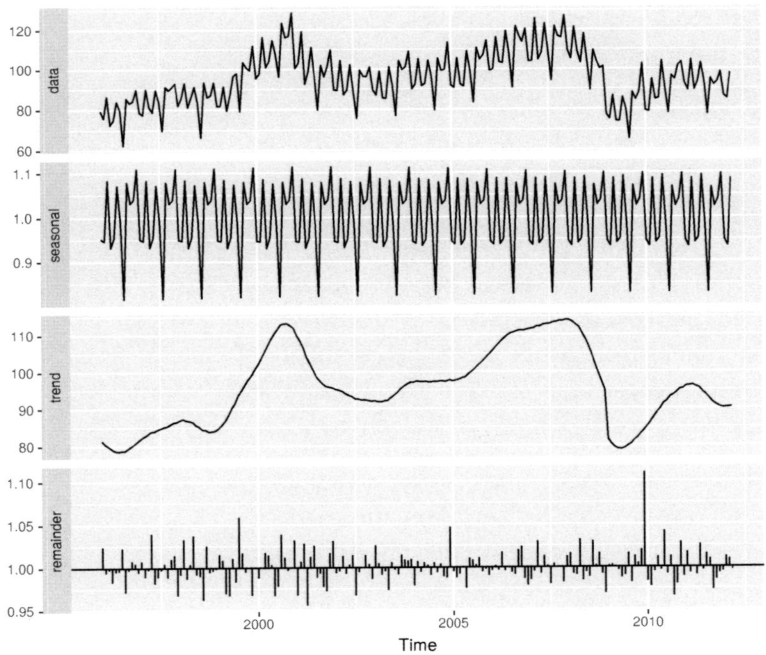

Figure 6.12: A SEATS decomposition of the new orders index for electrical equipment.

The result is quite similar to the X11 decomposition shown in Figure 6.9.

As with the X11 method, we can use the `seasonal()`, `trend-cycle()` and `remainder()` functions to extract the individual components, and `seasadj()` to compute the seasonally adjusted time series.

The **seasonal** package has many options for handling variations of X11 and SEATS. See the package website[2] for a detailed introduction to the options and features available.

[2] `http://www.seasonal.website/seasonal.html`

6.6 STL decomposition

STL is a very versatile and robust method for decomposing time series. STL is an acronym for "Seasonal and Trend decomposition using Loess", while Loess is a method for estimating nonlinear relationships. The STL method was developed by Cleveland et al. (1990).

STL has several advantages over the classical, SEATS and X11 decomposition methods:

- Unlike SEATS and X11, STL will handle any type of seasonality, not only monthly and quarterly data.
- The seasonal component is allowed to change over time, and the rate of change can be controlled by the user.
- The smoothness of the trend-cycle can also be controlled by the user.
- It can be robust to outliers (i.e., the user can specify a robust decomposition), so that occasional unusual observations will not affect the estimates of the trend-cycle and seasonal components. They will, however, affect the remainder component.

On the other hand, STL has some disadvantages. In particular, it does not handle trading day or calendar variation automatically, and it only provides facilities for additive decompositions.

It is possible to obtain a multiplicative decomposition by first taking logs of the data, then back-transforming the components. Decompositions between additive and multiplicative can be obtained using a Box-Cox transformation of the data with $0 < \lambda < 1$. A value of $\lambda = 0$ corresponds to the multiplicative decomposition while $\lambda = 1$ is equivalent to an additive decomposition.

The best way to begin learning how to use STL is to see some examples and experiment with the settings. Figure 6.2 showed an example of STL applied to the electrical equipment orders data. Figure 6.13 shows an alternative STL decomposition where the trend-cycle is more flexible, the seasonal component does not change over time, and the robust option has been used. Here, it is more obvious that there has been a downturn at the end of the series, and that the orders in 2009 were unusually low (corresponding to some large negative values in the remainder component).

```
elecequip %>%
  stl(t.window=13, s.window="periodic", robust=TRUE) %>%
  autoplot()
```

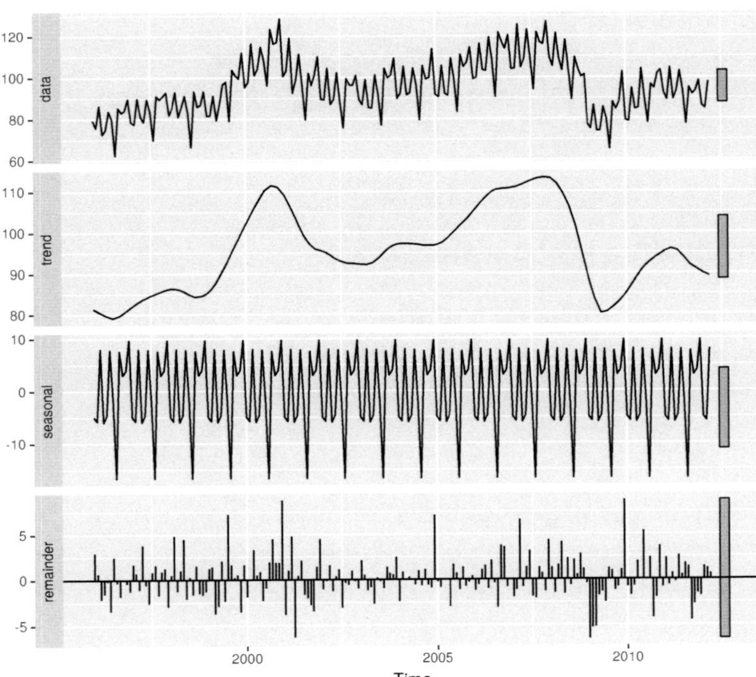

Figure 6.13: The electrical equipment orders (top) and its three additive components obtained from a robust STL decomposition with flexible trend-cycle and fixed seasonality.

The two main parameters to be chosen when using STL are the trend-cycle window (`t.window`) and the seasonal window (`s.window`). These control how rapidly the trend-cycle and seasonal components can change. Smaller values allow for more rapid changes. Both `t.window` and `s.window` should be odd numbers and refer to the number of consecutive years to be used when estimating the trend-cycle and seasonal components respectively. The user must specify `s.window` as there is no default. Setting it to be infinite is equivalent to forcing the seasonal component to be periodic (i.e., identical across years). Specifying `t.window` is optional, and a default value will be used if it is omitted.

The `mstl()` function provides a convenient automated STL decomposition using `s.window=13`, and `t.window` also chosen automatically. This usually gives a good balance between overfitting the seasonality and allowing it to slowly change over time. But, as with any automated procedure, the default settings will need adjusting for some time series.

As with the other decomposition methods discussed in this book, to obtain the separate components plotted in Figure 6.8, use the `seasonal()` function for the seasonal component, the `trendcycle()` function for trend-cycle component, and the `remainder()` function for the remainder component. The `seasadj()` function can be used to compute the seasonally adjusted series.

6.7 Measuring strength of trend and seasonality

A time series decomposition can be used to measure the strength of trend and seasonality in a time series (Wang, Smith, and Hyndman 2006). Recall that the decomposition is written as

$$y_t = T_t + S_t + R_t,$$

where T_t is the smoothed trend component, S_t is the seasonal component and R_t is a remainder component. For strongly trended data, the seasonally adjusted data should have much more variation than the remainder component. Therefore $\text{Var}(R_t)/\text{Var}(T_t + R_t)$ should be relatively small. But for data with little or no trend, the two variances should be approximately the same. So we define the strength of trend as:

$$F_T = \max\left(0, 1 - \frac{\text{Var}(R_t)}{\text{Var}(T_t + R_t)}\right).$$

This will give a measure of the strength of the trend between 0 and 1. Because the variance of the remainder might occasionally be even larger than the variance of the seasonally adjusted data, we set the minimal possible value of F_T equal to zero.

The strength of seasonality is defined similarly, but with respect to the detrended data rather than the seasonally adjusted data:

$$F_S = \max\left(0, 1 - \frac{\text{Var}(R_t)}{\text{Var}(S_t + R_t)}\right).$$

A series with seasonal strength F_S close to 0 exhibits almost no seasonality, while a series with strong seasonality will have F_S close to 1 because $\text{Var}(R_t)$ will be much smaller than $\text{Var}(S_t + R_t)$.

These measures can be useful, for example, when there you have a large collection of time series, and you need to find the series with the most trend or the most seasonality.

6.8 Forecasting with decomposition

While decomposition is primarily useful for studying time series data, and exploring historical changes over time, it can also be used in forecasting.

Assuming an additive decomposition, the decomposed time series can be written as

$$y_t = \hat{S}_t + \hat{A}_t,$$

where $\hat{A}_t = \hat{T}_t + \hat{R}_t$ is the seasonally adjusted component. Or, if a multiplicative decomposition has been used, we can write

$$y_t = \hat{S}_t\hat{A}_t,$$

where $\hat{A}_t = \hat{T}_t\hat{R}_t$.

To forecast a decomposed time series, we forecast the seasonal component, $\hat{S}_t$, and the seasonally adjusted component $\hat{A}_t$, separately. It is usually assumed that the seasonal component is unchanging, or changing extremely slowly, so it is forecast by simply taking the last year of the estimated component. In other words, a seasonal naïve method is used for the seasonal component.

To forecast the seasonally adjusted component, any non-seasonal forecasting method may be used. For example, a random walk with drift model, or Holt's method (discussed in the next chapter), or a non-seasonal ARIMA model (discussed in Chapter 8), may be used.

Example: Electrical equipment manufacturing

```
fit <- stl(elecequip, t.window=13, s.window="periodic",
  robust=TRUE)
fit %>% seasadj() %>% naive() %>%
  autoplot() + ylab("New orders index") +
  ggtitle("Naive forecasts of seasonally adjusted data")
```

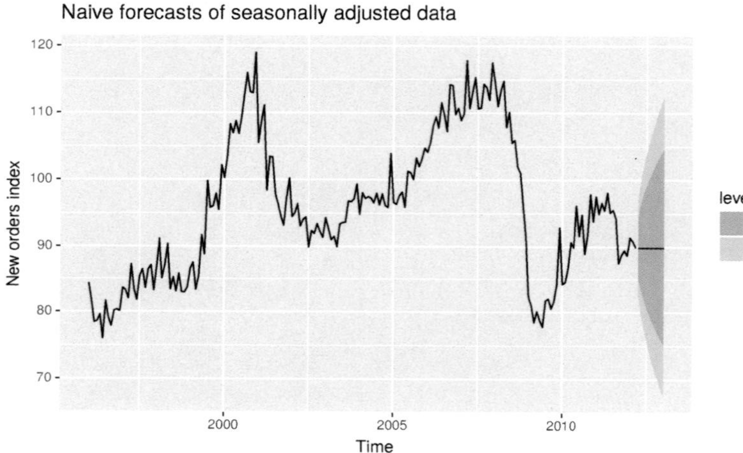

Figure 6.14: Naïve forecasts of the seasonally adjusted data obtained from an STL decomposition of the electrical equipment orders data.

Figure 6.14 shows naïve forecasts of the seasonally adjusted electrical equipment orders data. These are then "reseasonalized" by adding in the seasonal naïve forecasts of the seasonal component.

This is made easy with the `forecast()` function applied to the `stl` object. You need to specify the method being used on the seasonally adjusted data, and the function will do the reseasonalizing for you. The resulting forecasts of the original data are shown in Figure 6.15.

```
fit %>% forecast(method="naive") %>%
  autoplot() + ylab("New orders index")
```

The prediction intervals shown in this graph are constructed in the same way as the point forecasts. That is, the upper and lower limits of the prediction intervals on the seasonally adjusted data are "reseasonalized" by adding in the forecasts of

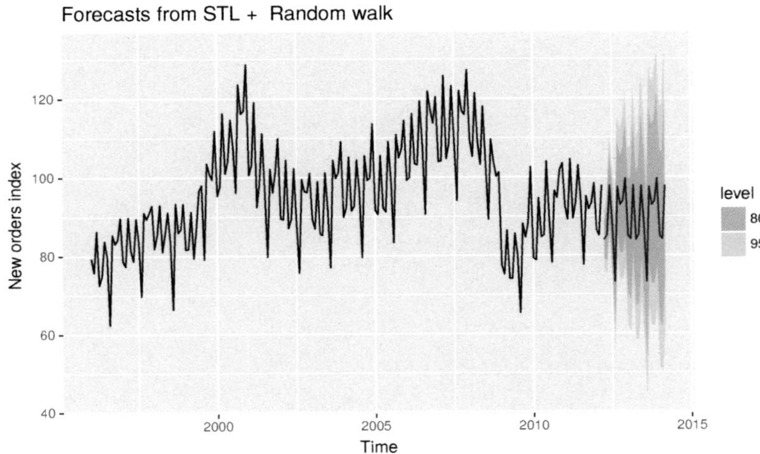

Figure 6.15: Forecasts of the electrical equipment orders data based on a naïve forecast of the seasonally adjusted data and a seasonal naïve forecast of the seasonal component, after an STL decomposition of the data.

the seasonal component. In this calculation, the uncertainty in the forecasts of the seasonal component has been ignored. The rationale for this choice is that the uncertainty in the seasonal component is much smaller than that for the seasonally adjusted data, and so it is a reasonable approximation to ignore it.

A short-cut approach is to use the `stlf()` function. The following code will decompose the time series using STL, forecast the seasonally adjusted series, and return reseasonalize the forecasts.

```
fcast <- stlf(elecequip, method='naive')
```

The `stlf()` function uses `mstl()` to carry out the decomposition, so there are default values for `s.window` and `t.window`.

As well as the naïve method, several other possible forecasting methods are available with `stlf()`, as described in the corresponding help file. If `method` is not specified, it will use the ETS approach (discussed in the next chapter) applied to the seasonally adjusted series. This usually produces quite good forecasts for seasonal time series, and some companies use it routinely for all their operational forecasts.

6.9 Exercises

1. Show that a 3 × 5 MA is equivalent to a 7-term weighted moving average with weights of 0.067, 0.133, 0.200, 0.200, 0.200, 0.133, and 0.067.

2. The `plastics` data set consists of the monthly sales (in thousands) of product A for a plastics manufacturer for five years.

   a. Plot the time series of sales of product A. Can you identify seasonal fluctuations and/or a trend-cycle?
   b. Use a classical multiplicative decomposition to calculate the trend-cycle and seasonal indices.
   c. Do the results support the graphical interpretation from part a?
   d. Compute and plot the seasonally adjusted data.
   e. Change one observation to be an outlier (e.g., add 500 to one observation), and recompute the seasonally adjusted data. What is the effect of the outlier?
   f. Does it make any difference if the outlier is near the end rather than in the middle of the time series?

3. Recall your retail time series data (from Exercise 3 in Section 2.10). Decompose the series using X11. Does it reveal any outliers, or unusual features that you had not noticed previously?

4. Figures 6.16 and 6.17 shows the result of decomposing the number of persons in the civilian labor force in Australia each month from February 1978 to August 1995.

   a. Write about 3–5 sentences describing the results of the decomposition. Pay particular attention to the scales of the graphs in making your interpretation.
   b. Is the recession of 1991/1992 visible in the estimated components?

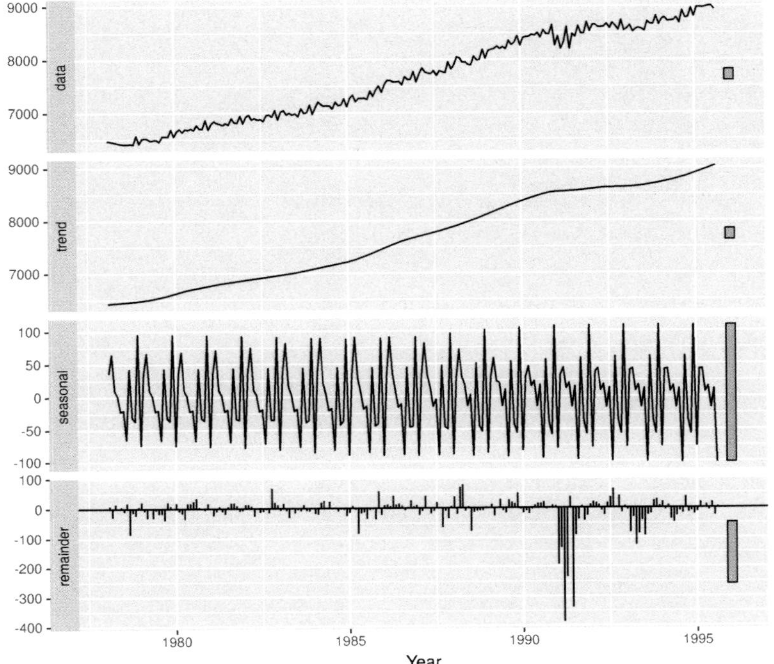

Figure 6.16: Decomposition of the number of persons in the civilian labor force in Australia each month from February 1978 to August 1995.

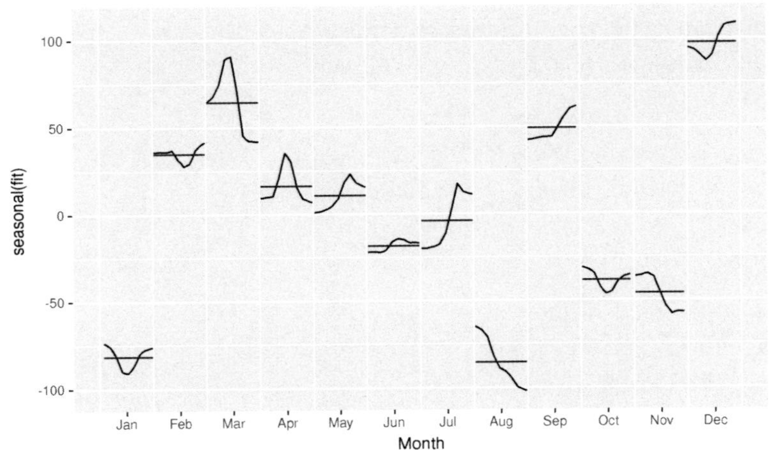

Figure 6.17: Seasonal component from the decomposition shown in the previous figure.

5. This exercise uses the `cangas` data (monthly Canadian gas production in billions of cubic metres, January 1960 – February 2005).

    a. Plot the data using `autoplot()`, `ggsubseriesplot()` and `ggseasonplot()` to look at the effect of the changing seasonality over time. What do you think is causing it to change so much?
    b. Do an STL decomposition of the data. You will need to choose `s.window` to allow for the changing shape of the seasonal component.
    c. Compare the results with those obtained using SEATS and X11. How are they different?

6. We will use the `bricksq` data (Australian quarterly clay brick production. 1956–1994) for this exercise.

    a. Use an STL decomposition to calculate the trend-cycle and seasonal indices. (Experiment with having fixed or changing seasonality.)
    b. Compute and plot the seasonally adjusted data.
    c. Use a naïve method to produce forecasts of the seasonally adjusted data.
    d. Use `stlf()` to reseasonalize the results, giving forecasts for the original data.
    e. Do the residuals look uncorrelated?
    f. Repeat with a robust STL decomposition. Does it make much difference?
    g. Compare forecasts from `stlf()` with those from `snaive()`, using a test set comprising the last 2 years of data. Which is better?

7. Use `stlf()` to produce forecasts of the `writing` series with either `method="naive"` or `method="rwdrift"`, whichever is most appropriate. Use the `lambda` argument if you think a Box-Cox transformation is required.

8. Use `stlf()` to produce forecasts of the `fancy` series with either `method="naive"` or `method="rwdrift"`, whichever is most appropriate. Use the `lambda` argument if you think a Box-Cox transformation is required.

6.10 Further reading

- A detailed modern discussion of SEATS and X11 decomposition methods is provided by Dagum and Bianconcini (2016).
- Cleveland et al. (1990) introduced STL, and still provides the best description of the algorithm.
- For a discussion of forecasting using STL, see Theodosiou (2011).

Chapter 7

Exponential smoothing

Exponential smoothing was proposed in the late 1950s (Brown 1959; Holt 1957; Winters 1960), and has motivated some of the most successful forecasting methods. Forecasts produced using exponential smoothing methods are weighted averages of past observations, with the weights decaying exponentially as the observations get older. In other words, the more recent the observation the higher the associated weight. This framework generates reliable forecasts quickly and for a wide range of time series, which is a great advantage and of major importance to applications in industry.

This chapter is divided into two parts. In the first part (Sections 7.1–7.4) we present the mechanics of the most important exponential smoothing methods, and their application in forecasting time series with various characteristics. This helps us develop an intuition to how these methods work. In this setting, selecting and using a forecasting method may appear to be somewhat ad hoc. The selection of the method is generally based on recognising key components of the time series (trend and seasonal) and the way in which these enter the smoothing method (e.g., in an additive, damped or multiplicative manner).

In the second part of the chapter (Sections 7.5–7.7) we present the statistical models that underlie exponential smoothing methods. These models generate identical point forecasts to the methods discussed in the first part of the chapter, but also generate prediction intervals. Furthermore, this statistical framework allows for genuine model selection between competing models.

7.1 Simple exponential smoothing

The simplest of the exponentially smoothing methods is naturally called **simple exponential smoothing** (SES)[1]. This method is suitable for forecasting data with no clear trend or seasonal pattern. For example, the data in Figure 7.1 do not display any clear trending behaviour or any seasonality. (There is a rise in the last few years, which might suggest a trend. We will consider whether a trended method would be better for this series later in this chapter.) We have already considered the naïve and the average as possible methods for forecasting such data (Section 3.1).

[1] In some books it is called "single exponential smoothing".

```
oildata <- window(oil, start=1996)
autoplot(oildata) +
  ylab("Oil (millions of tonnes)") + xlab("Year")
```

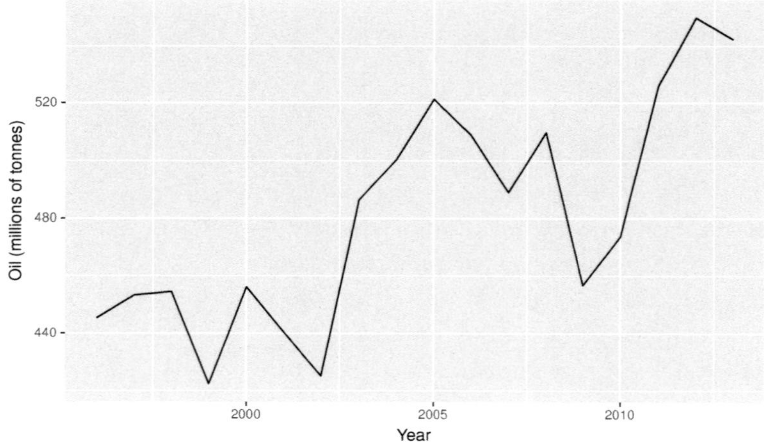

Figure 7.1: Oil production in Saudi Arabia from 1980 to 2013.

Using the naïve method, all forecasts for the future are equal to the last observed value of the series,

$$\hat{y}_{T+h|T} = y_T,$$

for $h = 1, 2, \ldots$. Hence, the naïve method assumes that the most recent observation is the only important one, and all previous observations provide no information for the future. This can be thought of as a weighted average where all of the weight is given to the last observation.

Using the average method, all future forecasts are equal to a simple average of the observed data,

$$\hat{y}_{T+h|T} = \frac{1}{T}\sum_{t=1}^{T} y_t,$$

for $h = 1, 2, \ldots$. Hence, the average method assumes that all observations are of equal importance, and gives them equal weights when generating forecasts.

We often want something between these two extremes. For example, it may be sensible to attach larger weights to more recent observations than to observations from the distant past. This is exactly the concept behind simple exponential smoothing. Forecasts are calculated using weighted averages, where the weights decrease exponentially as observations come from further in the past — the smallest weights are associated with the oldest observations:

$$\hat{y}_{T+1|T} = \alpha y_T + \alpha(1-\alpha)y_{T-1} + \alpha(1-\alpha)^2 y_{T-2} + \cdots, \qquad (7.1)$$

where $0 \le \alpha \le 1$ is the smoothing parameter. The one-step-ahead forecast for time $T + 1$ is a weighted average of all of the observations in the series $y_1, \ldots, y_T$. The rate at which the weights decrease is controlled by the parameter α.

The table below shows the weights attached to observations for four different values of α when forecasting using simple exponential smoothing. Note that the sum of the weights even for a small value of α will be approximately one for any reasonable sample size.

	$\alpha = 0.2$	$\alpha = 0.4$	$\alpha = 0.6$	$\alpha = 0.8$
y_T	0.2000	0.4000	0.6000	0.8000
y_{T-1}	0.1600	0.2400	0.2400	0.1600
y_{T-2}	0.1280	0.1440	0.0960	0.0320
y_{T-3}	0.1024	0.0864	0.0384	0.0064
y_{T-4}	0.0819	0.0518	0.0154	0.0013
y_{T-5}	0.0655	0.0311	0.0061	0.0003

For any α between 0 and 1, the weights attached to the observations decrease exponentially as we go back in time, hence the name "exponential smoothing". If α is small (i.e., close to 0), more weight is given to observations from the more distant past. If α is large (i.e., close to 1), more weight is given to the more recent observations. For the extreme case where $\alpha = 1$, $\hat{y}_{T+1|T} = y_T$, and the forecasts are equal to the naïve forecasts.

We present two equivalent forms of simple exponential smoothing, each of which leads to the forecast Equation (7.1).

Weighted average form

The forecast at time $T+1$ is equal to a weighted average between the most recent observation y_T and the previous forecast $\hat{y}_{T|T-1}$:

$$\hat{y}_{T+1|t} = \alpha y_T + (1-\alpha)\hat{y}_{T|T-1},$$

where $0 \leq \alpha \leq 1$ is the smoothing parameter. Similarly, we can write the fitted values as

$$\hat{y}_{t+1|t} = \alpha y_t + (1-\alpha)\hat{y}_{t|t-1},$$

for $t = 1,\dots,T$. (Recall that fitted values are simply one-step forecasts of the training data.)

The process has to start somewhere, so we let the first fitted value at time 1 be denoted by ℓ_0 (which we will have to estimate). Then

$$\begin{aligned}
\hat{y}_{2|1} &= \alpha y_1 + (1-\alpha)\ell_0 \\
\hat{y}_{3|2} &= \alpha y_2 + (1-\alpha)\hat{y}_{2|1} \\
\hat{y}_{4|3} &= \alpha y_3 + (1-\alpha)\hat{y}_{3|2} \\
&\vdots \\
\hat{y}_{T|T-1} &= \alpha y_{T-1} + (1-\alpha)\hat{y}_{T-1|T-2} \\
\hat{y}_{T+1|T} &= \alpha y_T + (1-\alpha)\hat{y}_{T|T-1}.
\end{aligned}$$

Substituting each equation into the following equation, we obtain

$$\begin{aligned}
\hat{y}_{3|2} &= \alpha y_2 + (1-\alpha)[\alpha y_1 + (1-\alpha)\ell_0] \\
&= \alpha y_2 + \alpha(1-\alpha) y_1 + (1-\alpha)^2 \ell_0 \\
\hat{y}_{4|3} &= \alpha y_3 + (1-\alpha)[\alpha y_2 + \alpha(1-\alpha) y_1 + (1-\alpha)^2 \ell_0] \\
&= \alpha y_3 + \alpha(1-\alpha) y_2 + \alpha(1-\alpha)^2 y_1 + (1-\alpha)^3 \ell_0 \\
&\vdots \\
\hat{y}_{T+1|T} &= \sum_{j=0}^{T-1} \alpha(1-\alpha)^j y_{T-j} + (1-\alpha)^T \ell_0.
\end{aligned}$$

The last term becomes tiny for large T. So, the weighted average form leads to the same forecast Equation (7.1).

Component form

An alternative representation is the component form. For simple exponential smoothing, the only component included is the level, ℓ_t. (Other methods which are considered later in this chapter may also include a trend b_t and a seasonal component s_t.) Component form representations of exponential smoothing methods comprise a forecast equation and a smoothing equation for each of the components included in the method. The component form of simple exponential smoothing is given by:

$$\begin{aligned}
\text{Forecast equation} \qquad & \hat{y}_{t+h|t} = \ell_t \\
\text{Smoothing equation} \qquad & \ell_t = \alpha y_t + (1-\alpha)\ell_{t-1},
\end{aligned}$$

where ℓ_t is the level (or the smoothed value) of the series at time t. Setting $h = 1$ gives the fitted values, while setting $t = T$ gives the true forecasts beyond the training data.

The forecast equation shows that the forecast value at time $t+1$ is the estimated level at time t. The smoothing equation for the level (usually referred to as the level equation) gives the estimated level of the series at each period t.

If we replace ℓ_t with $\hat{y}_{t+1|t}$ and ℓ_{t-1} with $\hat{y}_{t|t-1}$ in the smoothing equation, we will recover the weighted average form of simple exponential smoothing.

The component form of simple exponential smoothing is not particularly useful, but it will be the easiest form to use when we start adding other components.

Flat forecasts

Simple exponential smoothing has a "flat" forecast function:

$$\hat{y}_{T+h|T} = \hat{y}_{T+1|T} = \ell_T, \qquad h = 2, 3, \dots.$$

That is, all forecasts take the same value, equal to the last level component. Remember that these forecasts will only be suitable if the time series has no trend or seasonal component.

Optimization

The application of every exponential smoothing method requires the smoothing parameters and the initial values to be chosen. In particular, for simple exponential smoothing, we need to select the values of α and ℓ_0. All forecasts can be computed from the data once we know those values. For the methods that follow there is usually more than one smoothing parameter and more than one initial component to be chosen.

In some cases, the smoothing parameters may be chosen in a subjective manner — the forecaster specifies the value of the smoothing parameters based on previous experience. However, a more reliable and objective way to obtain values for the unknown parameters is to estimate them from the observed data.

In Section 5.2, we estimated the coefficients of a regression model by minimizing the sum of the squared residuals (usually known as SSE or "sum of squared errors"). Similarly, the unknown parameters and the initial values for any exponential smoothing method can be estimated by minimizing the SSE. The residuals are specified as $e_t = y_t - \hat{y}_{t|t-1}$ for $t = 1, \dots, T$. Hence, we find the values of the unknown parameters and the initial values that minimize

$$\text{SSE} = \sum_{t=1}^{T} (y_t - \hat{y}_{t|t-1})^2 = \sum_{t=1}^{T} e_t^2.$$

Unlike the regression case (where we have formulas which return the values of the regression coefficients that minimize the SSE), this involves a non-linear minimization problem, and we need to use an optimization tool to solve it.

Example: Oil production

In this example, simple exponential smoothing is applied to forecast oil production in Saudi Arabia.

```
oildata <- window(oil, start=1996)
# Estimate parameters
fc <- ses(oildata, h=5)
# Accuracy of one-step-ahead training errors: period 1-12
round(accuracy(fc),2)
#>                ME  RMSE   MAE MPE MAPE MASE  ACF1
#> Training set 6.4 28.12 22.26 1.1 4.61 0.93 -0.03
```

This gives parameter estimates $\hat{\alpha} = 0.83$ and $\hat{\ell}_0 = 446.6$, obtained by minimizing SSE over periods $t = 1, 2, \dots, 12$, subject to the restriction that $0 \le \alpha \le 1$.

In Table 7.1 we demonstrate the calculation using these parameters. The second last column shows the estimated level for times $t = 0$ to $t = 12$; the last few rows of the last column show the forecasts for $h = 1, 2, 3$.

The black line in Figure 7.2 is a plot of the data, which shows a changing level over time.

```
autoplot(fc) +
  autolayer(fitted(fc), series="Fitted") +
  ylab("Oil (millions of tonnes)") + xlab("Year")
```

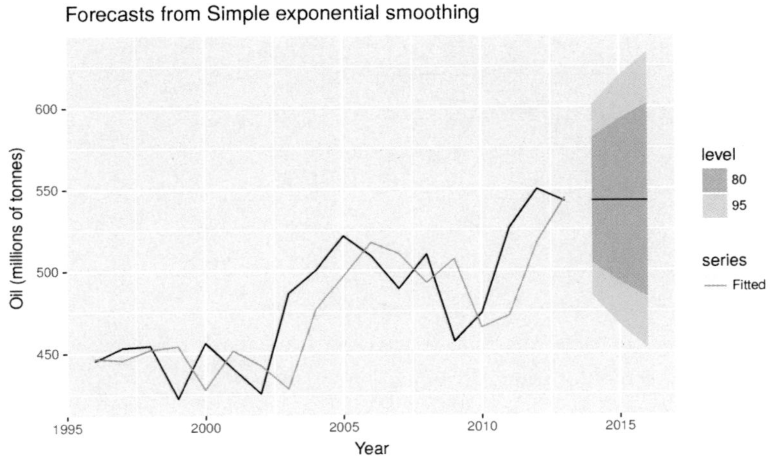

Figure 7.2: Simple exponential smoothing applied to oil production in Saudi Arabia (1996–2013).

The forecasts for the period 2014–2016 are plotted in Figure 7.2. Also plotted are one-step-ahead fitted values alongside the data over the period 1996–2013. The large value of α in this

Year	Time	Observation	Level	Forecast
	t	y_t	ℓ_t	$\hat{y}_{t+1\|t}$
1995	0		446.59	
1996	1	445.36	445.57	446.59
1997	2	453.20	451.93	445.57
1998	3	454.41	454.00	451.93
1999	4	422.38	427.63	454.00
2000	5	456.04	451.32	427.63
2001	6	440.39	442.20	451.32
2002	7	425.19	428.02	442.20
2003	8	486.21	476.54	428.02
2004	9	500.43	496.46	476.54
2005	10	521.28	517.15	496.46
2006	11	508.95	510.31	517.15
2007	12	488.89	492.45	510.31
2008	13	509.87	506.98	492.45
2009	14	456.72	465.07	506.98
2010	15	473.82	472.36	465.07
2011	16	525.95	517.05	472.36
2012	17	549.83	544.39	517.05
2013	18	542.34	542.68	544.39
	h			$\hat{y}_{T+h\|T}$
2014	1			542.68
2015	2			542.68
2016	3			542.68

Table 7.1: Forecasting the total oil production in millions of tonnes for Saudi Arabia using simple exponential smoothing.

example is reflected in the large adjustment that takes place in the estimated level ℓ_t at each time. A smaller value of α would lead to smaller changes over time, and so the series of fitted values would be smoother.

The prediction intervals shown here are calculated using the methods described in Section 7.5. The prediction intervals show that there is considerable uncertainty in the future values of oil production over the three-year forecast period. So interpreting the point forecasts without accounting for the large uncertainty can be very misleading.

7.2 Trend methods

Holt's linear trend method

Holt (1957) extended simple exponential smoothing to allow the forecasting of data with a trend. This method involves a forecast equation and two smoothing equations (one for the level and one for the trend):

$$\begin{aligned}
\text{Forecast equation} \quad & \hat{y}_{t+h|t} = \ell_t + hb_t \\
\text{Level equation} \quad & \ell_t = \alpha y_t + (1-\alpha)(\ell_{t-1} + b_{t-1}) \\
\text{Trend equation} \quad & b_t = \beta^*(\ell_t - \ell_{t-1}) + (1-\beta^*)b_{t-1},
\end{aligned}$$

where ℓ_t denotes an estimate of the level of the series at time t, b_t denotes an estimate of the trend (slope) of the series at time t, α is the smoothing parameter for the level, $0 \le \alpha \le 1$, and β^* is the smoothing parameter for the trend, $0 \le \beta^* \le 1$. (We denote this as β^* instead of β for reasons that will be explained in Section 7.5.)

As with simple exponential smoothing, the level equation here shows that ℓ_t is a weighted average of observation y_t and the one-step-ahead training forecast for time t, here given by $\ell_{t-1}+b_{t-1}$. The trend equation shows that b_t is a weighted average of the estimated trend at time t based on $\ell_t - \ell_{t-1}$ and b_{t-1}, the previous estimate of the trend.

The forecast function is no longer flat but trending. The h-step-ahead forecast is equal to the last estimated level plus h times the last estimated trend value. Hence the forecasts are a linear function of h.

Example: Air Passengers

```
air <- window(ausair, start=1990)
fc <- holt(air, h=5)
```

In Table 7.2 we demonstrate the application of Holt's method to annual passenger numbers for Australian airlines. The smoothing parameters, α and β^*, and the initial values ℓ_0 and b_0 are estimated by minimizing the SSE for the one-step training errors as in Section 7.1.

Year	Time	Observation	Level	Slope	Forecast
	t	y_t	ℓ_t	b_t	$\hat{y}_{t\|t-1}$
1989	0		15.57	2.102	
1990	1	17.55	17.57	2.102	17.67
1991	2	21.86	21.49	2.102	19.68
1992	3	23.89	23.84	2.102	23.59
1993	4	26.93	26.76	2.102	25.94
1994	5	26.89	27.22	2.102	28.86
1995	6	28.83	28.92	2.102	29.33
1996	7	30.08	30.24	2.102	31.02
1997	8	30.95	31.19	2.102	32.34
1998	9	30.19	30.71	2.101	33.29
1999	10	31.58	31.79	2.101	32.81
2000	11	32.58	32.80	2.101	33.89
2001	12	33.48	33.72	2.101	34.90
2002	13	39.02	38.48	2.101	35.82
2003	14	41.39	41.25	2.101	40.58
2004	15	41.60	41.89	2.101	43.35
2005	16	44.66	44.54	2.101	44.00
2006	17	46.95	46.90	2.101	46.65
2007	18	48.73	48.78	2.101	49.00
2008	19	51.49	51.38	2.101	50.88
2009	20	50.03	50.61	2.101	53.49
2010	21	60.64	59.30	2.102	52.72
2011	22	63.36	63.03	2.102	61.40
2012	23	66.36	66.15	2.102	65.13
2013	24	68.20	68.21	2.102	68.25
2014	25	68.12	68.49	2.102	70.31
2015	26	69.78	69.92	2.102	70.60
2016	27	72.60	72.50	2.102	72.02
	h				$\hat{y}_{t+h\|t}$
	1				74.60
	2				76.70
	3				78.80
	4				80.91
	5				83.01

Table 7.2: Applying Holt's linear method with $\alpha = 0.8321$ and $\beta^* = 0.0001$ to Australian air passenger data (millions of passengers).

The very small value of β^* means that the slope hardly changes over time.

Damped trend methods

The forecasts generated by Holt's linear method display a constant trend (increasing or decreasing) indefinitely into the future. Empirical evidence indicates that these methods tend to over-forecast, especially for longer forecast horizons. Motivated by this observation, Gardner and McKenzie (1985) introduced a parameter that "dampens" the trend to a flat line some time in the future. Methods that include a damped trend have proven to be very successful, and are arguably the most popular individual methods when forecasts are required automatically for many series.

In conjunction with the smoothing parameters α and β^* (with values between 0 and 1 as in Holt's method), this method also includes a damping parameter $0 < \phi < 1$:

$$\begin{aligned}\hat{y}_{t+h|t} &= \ell_t + (\phi + \phi^2 + \cdots + \phi^h)b_t \\ \ell_t &= \alpha y_t + (1-\alpha)(\ell_{t-1} + \phi b_{t-1}) \\ b_t &= \beta^*(\ell_t - \ell_{t-1}) + (1-\beta^*)\phi b_{t-1}.\end{aligned}$$

If $\phi = 1$, the method is identical to Holt's linear method. For values between 0 and 1, ϕ dampens the trend so that it approaches a constant some time in the future. In fact, the forecasts converge to $\ell_T + \phi b_T/(1-\phi)$ as $h \to \infty$ for any value $0 < \phi < 1$. This means that short-run forecasts are trended while long-run forecasts are constant.

In practice, ϕ is rarely less than 0.8 as the damping has a very strong effect for smaller values. Values of ϕ close to 1 will mean that a damped model is not able to be distinguished from a non-damped model. For these reasons, we usually restrict ϕ to a minimum of 0.8 and a maximum of 0.98.

Example: Air Passengers (continued)

Figure 7.3 shows the forecasts for years 2017–2031 generated from Holt's linear trend method and the damped trend method.

```
fc <- holt(air, h=15)
fc2 <- holt(air, damped=TRUE, phi = 0.9, h=15)
autoplot(air) +
  autolayer(fc, series="Holt's method", PI=FALSE) +
  autolayer(fc2, series="Damped Holt's method", PI=FALSE) +
  ggtitle("Forecasts from Holt's method") + xlab("Year") +
  ylab("Air passengers in Australia (millions)") +
  guides(colour=guide_legend(title="Forecast"))
```

We have set the damping parameter to a relatively low number ($\phi = 0.90$) to exaggerate the effect of damping for comparison. Usually, we would estimate ϕ along with the other parameters. We have also used a rather large forecast horizon ($h = 15$) to highlight the difference between a damped trend and a linear

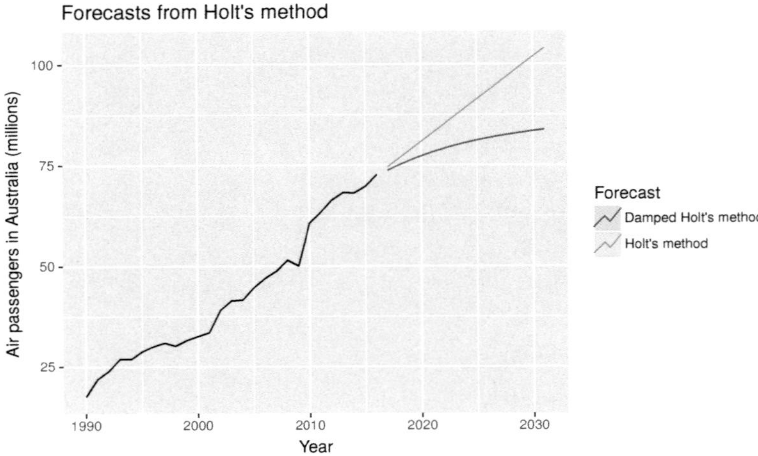

Figure 7.3: Forecasting total annual passengers of air carriers registered in Australia (millions of passengers, 1990–2016). For the damped trend method, $\phi = 0.90$.

trend. In practice, we would not normally want to forecast so many years ahead with only 27 years of data.

Example: Sheep in Asia

In this example, we compare the forecasting performance of the three exponential smoothing methods that we have considered so far in forecasting the sheep livestock population in Asia. The data spans the period 1970–2007 and is shown in Figure 7.4.

```
autoplot(livestock) +
  xlab("Year") + ylab("Livestock, sheep in Asia (millions)")
```

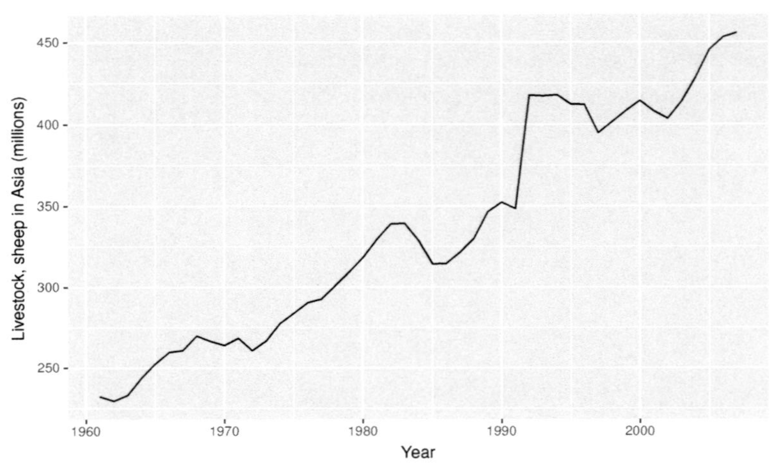

Figure 7.4: Annual sheep livestock numbers in Asia (in million head)

We will use time series cross-validation to compare the one-step forecast accuracy of the three methods.

```
e1 <- tsCV(livestock, ses, h=1)
e2 <- tsCV(livestock, holt, h=1)
e3 <- tsCV(livestock, holt, damped=TRUE, h=1)
# Compare MSE:
mean(e1^2, na.rm=TRUE)
#> [1] 178.3
mean(e2^2, na.rm=TRUE)
#> [1] 173.4
mean(e3^2, na.rm=TRUE)
#> [1] 162.6
# Compare MAE:
mean(abs(e1), na.rm=TRUE)
#> [1] 8.532
mean(abs(e2), na.rm=TRUE)
#> [1] 8.803
mean(abs(e3), na.rm=TRUE)
#> [1] 8.024
```

Damped Holt's method is best whether you compare MAE or MSE values. So we will proceed with using the damped Holt's method and apply it to the whole data set to get forecasts for future years.

```
fc <- holt(livestock, damped=TRUE)
# Estimated parameters:
fc[["model"]]
#> Damped Holt's method
#>
#> Call:
#>  holt(y = livestock, damped = TRUE)
#>
#>   Smoothing parameters:
#>     alpha = 0.9999
#>     beta  = 3e-04
#>     phi   = 0.9798
#>
#>   Initial states:
#>     l = 223.35
#>     b = 6.9046
#>
#>   sigma:  12.84
#>
#>   AIC  AICc   BIC
#> 427.6 429.7 438.7
```

The smoothing parameter for the slope is estimated to be essentially zero, indicating that the trend is not changing over time. The value of α is very close to one, showing that the level reacts strongly to each new observation.

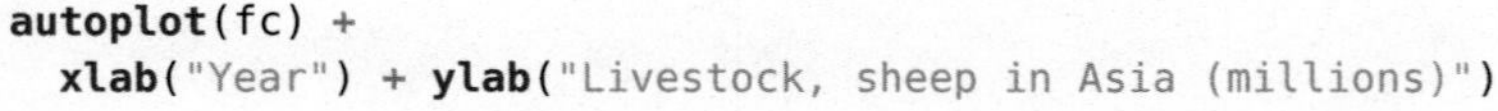

```
autoplot(fc) +
  xlab("Year") + ylab("Livestock, sheep in Asia (millions)")
```

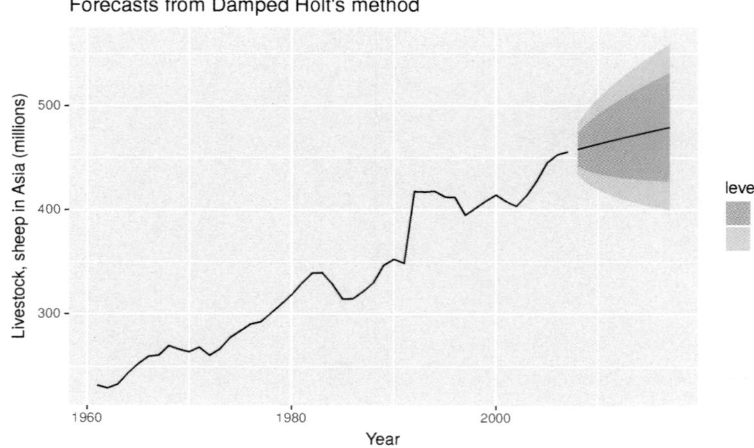

Figure 7.5: Forecasting livestock, sheep in Asia: comparing forecasting performance of non-seasonal method.

The resulting forecasts look sensible with increasing trend, and relatively wide prediction intervals reflecting the variation in the historical data. The prediction intervals are calculated using the methods described in Section 7.5.

In this example, the process of selecting a method was relatively easy as both MSE and MAE comparisons suggested the same method (damped Holt's). However, sometimes different accuracy measures will suggest different forecasting methods, and then a decision is required as to which forecasting method we prefer to use. As forecasting tasks can vary by many dimensions (length of forecast horizon, size of test set, forecast error measures, frequency of data, etc.), it is unlikely that one method will be better than all others for all forecasting scenarios. What we require from a forecasting method are consistently sensible forecasts, and these should be frequently evaluated against the task at hand.

7.3 Holt-Winters' seasonal method

Holt (1957) and Winters (1960) extended Holt's method to capture seasonality. The Holt-Winters seasonal method comprises the forecast equation and three smoothing equations — one for the level ℓ_t, one for the trend b_t, and one for the seasonal component s_t, with corresponding smoothing parameters α, β^* and γ. We use m to denote the frequency of the seasonality, i.e., the number of seasons in a year. For example, for quarterly data $m = 4$, and for monthly data $m = 12$.

There are two variations to this method that differ in the nature of the seasonal component. The additive method is preferred when the seasonal variations are roughly constant through the series, while the multiplicative method is preferred when the seasonal variations are changing proportional to the level of the series. With the additive method, the seasonal component is expressed in absolute terms in the scale of the observed series, and in the level equation the series is seasonally adjusted by subtracting the seasonal component. Within each year, the seasonal component will add up to approximately zero. With the multiplicative method, the seasonal component is expressed in relative terms (percentages), and the series is seasonally adjusted by dividing through by the seasonal component. Within each year, the seasonal component will sum up to approximately m.

Holt-Winters' additive method

The component form for the additive method is:

$$\begin{aligned}
\hat{y}_{t+h|t} &= \ell_t + hb_t + s_{t+h-m(k+1)} \\
\ell_t &= \alpha(y_t - s_{t-m}) + (1-\alpha)(\ell_{t-1} + b_{t-1}) \\
b_t &= \beta^*(\ell_t - \ell_{t-1}) + (1-\beta^*)b_{t-1} \\
s_t &= \gamma(y_t - \ell_{t-1} - b_{t-1}) + (1-\gamma)s_{t-m},
\end{aligned}$$

where k is the integer part of $(h-1)/m$, which ensures that the estimates of the seasonal indices used for forecasting come from the final year of the sample. The level equation shows a weighted average between the seasonally adjusted observation $(y_t - s_{t-m})$ and the non-seasonal forecast $(\ell_{t-1} + b_{t-1})$ for time t. The trend equation is identical to Holt's linear method. The seasonal equation shows a weighted average between the current seasonal index, $(y_t - \ell_{t-1} - b_{t-1})$, and the seasonal index of the same season last year (i.e., m time periods ago).

The equation for the seasonal component is often expressed as

$$s_t = \gamma^*(y_t - \ell_t) + (1-\gamma^*)s_{t-m}.$$

If we substitute ℓ_t from the smoothing equation for the level of the component form above, we get

$$s_t = \gamma^*(1-\alpha)(y_t - \ell_{t-1} - b_{t-1}) + [1 - \gamma^*(1-\alpha)]s_{t-m},$$

which is identical to the smoothing equation for the seasonal component we specify here, with $\gamma = \gamma^*(1-\alpha)$. The usual parameter restriction is $0 \le \gamma^* \le 1$, which translates to $0 \le \gamma \le 1-\alpha$.

Holt-Winters' multiplicative method

The component form for the multiplicative method is:

$$\begin{aligned}
\hat{y}_{t+h|t} &= (\ell_t + hb_t)s_{t+h-m(k+1)} \\
\ell_t &= \alpha\frac{y_t}{s_{t-m}} + (1-\alpha)(\ell_{t-1} + b_{t-1}) \\
b_t &= \beta^*(\ell_t - \ell_{t-1}) + (1-\beta^*)b_{t-1} \\
s_t &= \gamma\frac{y_t}{(\ell_{t-1} + b_{t-1})} + (1-\gamma)s_{t-m}
\end{aligned}$$

Example: International tourist visitor nights in Australia

We apply Holt-Winters' method with both additive and multiplicative seasonality to forecast quarterly visitor nights in Australia spent by international tourists. Figure 7.6 shows the data from 2005, and the forecasts for 2016–2017. The data show an obvious seasonal pattern, with peaks observed in the March quarter of each year, corresponding to the Australian summer.

```
aust <- window(austourists,start=2005)
fit1 <- hw(aust,seasonal="additive")
fit2 <- hw(aust,seasonal="multiplicative")
autoplot(aust) +
  autolayer(fit1, series="HW additive forecasts", PI=FALSE) +
  autolayer(fit2, series="HW multiplicative forecasts",
    PI=FALSE) +
  xlab("Year") +
  ylab("Visitor nights (millions)") +
  ggtitle("International visitors nights in Australia") +
  guides(colour=guide_legend(title="Forecast"))
```

The applications of both methods (with additive and multiplicative seasonality) are presented in Tables 7.3 and 7.4 respectively. Because both methods have exactly the same number of parameters to estimate, we can compare the training RMSE from both

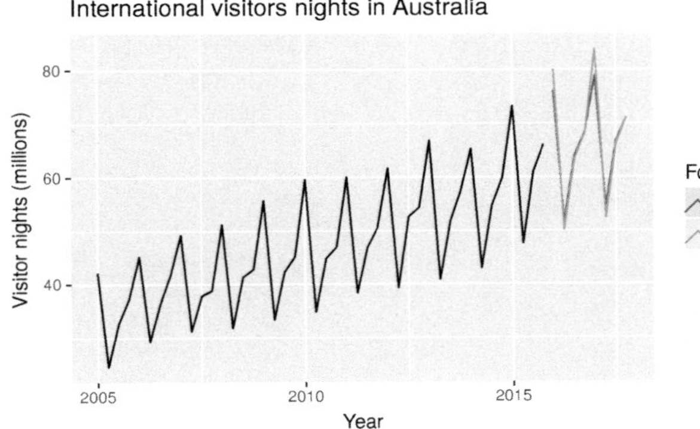

Figure 7.6: Forecasting international visitor nights in Australia using the Holt-Winters method with both additive and multiplicative seasonality.

	t	y_t	ℓ_t	b_t	s_t	$\hat{y}_t$
2004 Q1	-3				9.70	
2004 Q2	-2				-9.31	
2004 Q3	-1				-1.69	
2004 Q4	0		32.26	0.70	1.31	
2005 Q1	1	42.21	32.82	0.70	9.50	42.66
2005 Q2	2	24.65	33.66	0.70	-9.13	24.21
2005 Q3	3	32.67	34.36	0.70	-1.69	32.67
2005 Q4	4	37.26	35.33	0.70	1.69	36.37
	⋮	⋮	⋮	⋮	⋮	⋮
2015 Q1	41	73.26	59.96	0.70	12.18	69.05
2015 Q2	42	47.70	60.69	0.70	-13.02	47.59
2015 Q3	43	61.10	61.96	0.70	-1.35	59.24
2015 Q4	44	66.06	63.22	0.70	2.35	64.22
	h					$\hat{y}_{T+h\|T}$
2016 Q1	1					76.10
2016 Q2	2					51.60
2016 Q3	3					63.97
2016 Q4	4					68.37
2017 Q1	5					78.90
2017 Q2	6					54.41
2017 Q3	7					66.77
2017 Q4	8					71.18

Table 7.3: Applying Holt-Winters' method with additive seasonality for forecasting international visitor nights in Australia. Notice that the additive seasonal component sums to approximately zero. The smoothing parameters and initial estimates for the components have been estimated by minimizing RMSE ($\alpha = 0.306$, $\beta^* = 0.0003$, $\gamma = 0.426$ and RMSE= 1.763).

models. In this case, the method with multiplicative seasonality fits the data best. This was to be expected, as the time plot shows that the seasonal variation in the data increases as the level of the series increases. This is also reflected in the two sets of forecasts; the forecasts generated by the method with the multiplicative seasonality display larger and increasing seasonal variation as the level of the forecasts increases compared to the forecasts generated by the method with additive seasonality.

	t	y_t	ℓ_t	b_t	s_t	$\hat{y}_t$
2004 Q1	-3				1.24	
2004 Q2	-2				0.77	
2004 Q3	-1				0.96	
2004 Q4	0		32.49	0.70	1.02	
2005 Q1	1	42.21	33.51	0.71	1.24	41.29
2005 Q2	2	24.65	33.24	0.68	0.77	26.36
2005 Q3	3	32.67	33.94	0.68	0.96	32.62
2005 Q4	4	37.26	35.40	0.70	1.02	35.44
	⋮	⋮	⋮	⋮	⋮	⋮
2015 Q1	41	73.26	58.57	0.66	1.24	72.59
2015 Q2	42	47.70	60.42	0.69	0.77	45.62
2015 Q3	43	61.10	62.17	0.72	0.96	58.77
2015 Q4	44	66.06	63.62	0.75	1.02	64.38
	h					$\hat{y}_{T+h\|T}$
2016 Q1	1					80.09
2016 Q2	2					50.15
2016 Q3	3					63.34
2016 Q4	4					68.18
2017 Q1	5					83.80
2017 Q2	6					52.45
2017 Q3	7					66.21
2017 Q4	8					71.23

Table 7.4: Applying Holt-Winters' method with multiplicative seasonality for forecasting international visitor nights in Australia. Notice that the multiplicative seasonal component sums to approximately $m = 4$. The smoothing parameters and initial estimates for the components have been estimated by minimizing RMSE ($\alpha = 0.441$, $\beta^* = 0.030$, $\gamma = 0.002$ and RMSE= 1.576).

The estimated states for both models are plotted in Figure 7.7. The small value of γ for the multiplicative model means that the seasonal component hardly changes over time. The small value of β^* for the additive model means the slope component hardly changes over time (check the vertical scale). The increasing size of the seasonal component for the additive model suggests that the model is less appropriate than the multiplicative model.

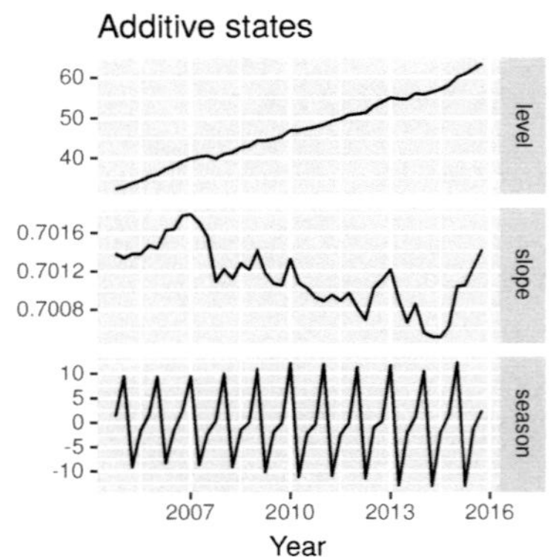

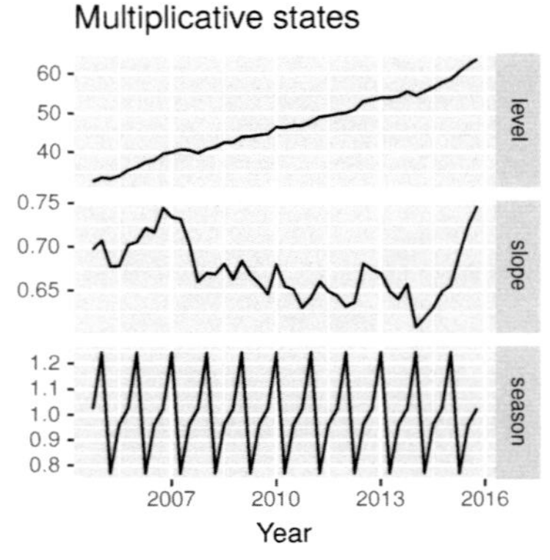

Figure 7.7: Estimated components for the Holt-Winters method with additive and multiplicative seasonal components.

Holt-Winters' damped method

Damping is possible with both additive and multiplicative Holt-Winters' methods. A method that often provides accurate and robust forecasts for seasonal data is the Holt-Winters method with a damped trend and multiplicative seasonality:

$$\begin{aligned}
\hat{y}_{t+h|t} &= \left[\ell_t + (\phi + \phi^2 + \cdots + \phi^h)b_t\right]s_{t+h-m(k+1)}. \\
\ell_t &= \alpha(y_t/s_{t-m}) + (1-\alpha)(\ell_{t-1} + \phi b_{t-1}) \\
b_t &= \beta^*(\ell_t - \ell_{t-1}) + (1-\beta^*)\phi b_{t-1} \\
s_t &= \gamma \frac{y_t}{(\ell_{t-1} + \phi b_{t-1})} + (1-\gamma)s_{t-m}.
\end{aligned}$$

```
hw(y, damped=TRUE, seasonal="multiplicative")
```

Example: Holt-Winters method with daily data

The Holt-Winters method can also be used for daily type of data, where the seasonal period is $m = 7$, and the appropriate unit of time for h is in days. Here, we generate daily forecasts for the last five weeks for the `hyndsight` data, which contains the daily pageviews on the Hyndsight blog for one year starting April 30, 2014.

```
fc <- hw(subset(hyndsight,end=length(hyndsight)-35),
         damped = TRUE, seasonal="multiplicative", h=35)
autoplot(hyndsight) +
  autolayer(fc, series="HW multi damped", PI=FALSE)+
  guides(colour=guide_legend(title="Daily forecasts"))
```

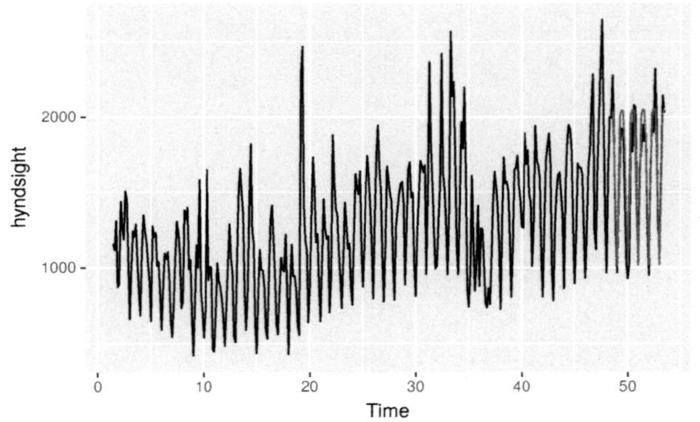

Figure 7.8: Forecasts of daily pageviews on the Hyndsight blog.

Clearly the model has identified the weekly seasonal pattern and the increasing trend at the end of the data, and the forecasts are a close match to the test data.

7.4 A taxonomy of exponential smoothing methods

Exponential smoothing methods are not restricted to those we have presented so far. By considering variations in the combinations of the trend and seasonal components, nine exponential smoothing methods are possible, listed in Table 7.5. Each method is labelled by a pair of letters (T,S) defining the type of 'Trend' and 'Seasonal' components. For example, (A,M) is the method with an additive trend and multiplicative seasonality; (A_d,N) is the method with damped trend and no seasonality; and so on.

Trend Component	**Seasonal Component**		
	N (None)	A (Additive)	M (Multiplicative)
N (None)	(N,N)	(N,A)	(N,M)
A (Additive)	(A,N)	(A,A)	(A,M)
A_d (Additive damped)	(A_d,N)	(A_d,A)	(A_d,M)

Table 7.5: A two-way classification of exponential smoothing methods.

Some of these methods we have already seen using other names:

Short hand	Method
(N,N)	Simple exponential smoothing
(A,N)	Holt's linear method
(A_d,N)	Additive damped trend method
(A,A)	Additive Holt-Winters' method
(A,M)	Multiplicative Holt-Winters' method
(A_d,M)	Holt-Winters' damped method

This type of classification was first proposed by Pegels (1969), who also included a method with a multiplicative trend. It was later extended by Gardner (1985) to include methods with an additive damped trend and by Taylor (2003) to include methods with a multiplicative damped trend. We do not consider the multiplicative trend methods in this book as they tend to produce poor forecasts. See Hyndman, Koehler, Ord, et al. (2008) for a more thorough discussion of all exponential smoothing methods.

Table 7.6 gives the recursive formulas for applying the nine exponential smoothing methods in Table 7.5. Each cell includes the forecast equation for generating h-step-ahead forecasts, and the smoothing equations for applying the method.

Trend	Seasonal N	Seasonal A	Seasonal M
N	$\hat{y}_{t+h\|t} = \ell_t$ $\ell_t = \alpha y_t + (1-\alpha)\ell_{t-1}$	$\hat{y}_{t+h\|t} = \ell_t + s_{t+h-m(k+1)}$ $\ell_t = \alpha(y_t - s_{t-m}) + (1-\alpha)\ell_{t-1}$ $s_t = \gamma(y_t - \ell_{t-1}) + (1-\gamma)s_{t-m}$	$\hat{y}_{t+h\|t} = \ell_t s_{t+h-m(k+1)}$ $\ell_t = \alpha(y_t/s_{t-m}) + (1-\alpha)\ell_{t-1}$ $s_t = \gamma(y_t/\ell_{t-1}) + (1-\gamma)s_{t-m}$
A	$\hat{y}_{t+h\|t} = \ell_t + hb_t$ $\ell_t = \alpha y_t + (1-\alpha)(\ell_{t-1} + b_{t-1})$ $b_t = \beta^*(\ell_t - \ell_{t-1}) + (1-\beta^*)b_{t-1}$	$\hat{y}_{t+h\|t} = \ell_t + hb_t + s_{t+h-m(k+1)}$ $\ell_t = \alpha(y_t - s_{t-m}) + (1-\alpha)(\ell_{t-1} + b_{t-1})$ $b_t = \beta^*(\ell_t - \ell_{t-1}) + (1-\beta^*)b_{t-1}$ $s_t = \gamma(y_t - \ell_{t-1} - b_{t-1}) + (1-\gamma)s_{t-m}$	$\hat{y}_{t+h\|t} = (\ell_t + hb_t)s_{t+h-m(k+1)}$ $\ell_t = \alpha(y_t/s_{t-m}) + (1-\alpha)(\ell_{t-1} + b_{t-1})$ $b_t = \beta^*(\ell_t - \ell_{t-1}) + (1-\beta^*)b_{t-1}$ $s_t = \gamma(y_t/(\ell_{t-1} + b_{t-1})) + (1-\gamma)s_{t-m}$
A_d	$\hat{y}_{t+h\|t} = \ell_t + \phi_h b_t$ $\ell_t = \alpha y_t + (1-\alpha)(\ell_{t-1} + \phi b_{t-1})$ $b_t = \beta^*(\ell_t - \ell_{t-1}) + (1-\beta^*)\phi b_{t-1}$	$\hat{y}_{t+h\|t} = \ell_t + \phi_h b_t + s_{t+h-m(k+1)}$ $\ell_t = \alpha(y_t - s_{t-m}) + (1-\alpha)(\ell_{t-1} + \phi b_{t-1})$ $b_t = \beta^*(\ell_t - \ell_{t-1}) + (1-\beta^*)\phi b_{t-1}$ $s_t = \gamma(y_t - \ell_{t-1} - \phi b_{t-1}) + (1-\gamma)s_{t-m}$	$\hat{y}_{t+h\|t} = (\ell_t + \phi_h b_t)s_{t+h-m(k+1)}$ $\ell_t = \alpha(y_t/s_{t-m}) + (1-\alpha)(\ell_{t-1} + \phi b_{t-1})$ $b_t = \beta^*(\ell_t - \ell_{t-1}) + (1-\beta^*)\phi b_{t-1}$ $s_t = \gamma(y_t/(\ell_{t-1} + \phi b_{t-1})) + (1-\gamma)s_{t-m}$

Table 7.6: Formulas for recursive calculations and point forecasts. In each case, ℓ_t denotes the series level at time t, b_t denotes the slope at time t, s_t denotes the seasonal component of the series at time t, and m denotes the number of seasons in a year; α, β^*, γ and ϕ are smoothing parameters, $\phi_h = \phi + \phi^2 + \cdots + \phi^h$, and k is the integer part of $(h-1)/m$.

7.5 Innovations state space models for exponential smoothing

In the rest of this chapter, we study the statistical models that underlie the exponential smoothing methods we have considered so far. The exponential smoothing methods presented in Table 7.6 are algorithms which generate point forecasts. The statistical models in this section generate the same point forecasts, but can also generate prediction (or forecast) intervals. A statistical model is a stochastic (or random) data generating process that can produce an entire forecast distribution. We will also describe how to using the model selection criteria introduced in Chapter 5 to choose the model in an objective manner.

Each model consists of a measurement equation that describes the observed data, and some state equations that describe how the unobserved components or states (level, trend, seasonal) change over time. Hence, these are referred to as **state space models**.

For each method there exist two models: one with additive errors and one with multiplicative errors. The point forecasts produced by the models are identical if they use the same smoothing parameter values. They will, however, generate different prediction intervals.

To distinguish between a model with additive errors and one with multiplicative errors (and also to distinguish the models from the methods), we add a third letter to the classification of Table 7.5. We label each state space model as ETS($\cdot,\cdot,\cdot$) for (Error, Trend, Seasonal). This label can also be thought of as ExponenTial Smoothing. Using the same notation as in Table 7.5, the possibilities for each component are: Error = {A,M}, Trend = {N,A,A$_d$} and Seasonal = {N,A,M}.

ETS(A,N,N): simple exponential smoothing with additive errors

Recall the component form of simple exponential smoothing:

$$\begin{aligned} \text{Forecast equation} \qquad & \hat{y}_{t+1|t} = \ell_t \\ \text{Smoothing equation} \qquad & \ell_t = \alpha y_t + (1-\alpha)\ell_{t-1}, \end{aligned}$$

If we re-arrange the smoothing equation for the level, we get the "error correction" form:

$$\begin{aligned} \ell_t &= \ell_{t-1} + \alpha(y_t - \ell_{t-1}) \\ &= \ell_{t-1} + \alpha e_t \end{aligned}$$

where $e_t = y_t - \ell_{t-1} = y_t - \hat{y}_{t|t-1}$ is the residual at time t.

The training data errors lead to the adjustment of the estimated level throughout the smoothing process for $t = 1,\dots,T$. For example, if the error at time t is negative, then $y_t < \hat{y}_{t|t-1}$ and so the level at time $t-1$ has been over-estimated. The new level ℓ_t is then the previous level ℓ_{t-1} adjusted downwards. The closer α is to one, the "rougher" the estimate of the level (large adjustments take place). The smaller the α, the "smoother" the level (small adjustments take place).

We can also write $y_t = \ell_{t-1} + e_t$, so that each observation can be represented by the previous level plus an error. To make this into an innovations state space model, all we need to do is specify the probability distribution for e_t. For a model with additive errors, we assume that residuals (the one-step training errors) e_t are normally distributed white noise with mean 0 and variance σ^2. A short-hand notation for this is $e_t = \varepsilon_t \sim \text{NID}(0,\sigma^2)$; NID stands for "normally and independently distributed".

Then the equations of the model can be written as

$$y_t = \ell_{t-1} + \varepsilon_t \tag{7.2}$$
$$\ell_t = \ell_{t-1} + \alpha\varepsilon_t. \tag{7.3}$$

We refer to (7.2) as the *measurement* (or observation) equation and (7.3) as the *state* (or transition) equation. These two equations, together with the statistical distribution of the errors, form a fully specified statistical model. Specifically, these constitute an innovations state space model underlying simple exponential smoothing.

The term "innovations" comes from the fact that all equations use the same random error process, ε_t. For the same reason, this formulation is also referred to as a "single source of error" model. There are alternative multiple source of error formulations which we do not present here.

The measurement equation shows the relationship between the observations and the unobserved states. In this case, observation y_t is a linear function of the level ℓ_{t-1}, the predictable part of y_t, and the error ε_t, the unpredictable part of y_t. For other innovations state space models, this relationship may be nonlinear.

The state equation shows the evolution of the state through time. The influence of the smoothing parameter α is the same as for the methods discussed earlier. For example, α governs the amount of change in successive levels: high values of α allow rapid changes in the level; low values of α lead to smooth changes. If $\alpha = 0$, the level of the series does not change over time; if $\alpha = 1$, the model reduces to a random walk model, $y_t = y_{t-1} + \varepsilon_t$. (See Section 8.1 for a discussion of this model.)

ETS(M,N,N): simple exponential smoothing with multiplicative errors

In a similar fashion, we can specify models with multiplicative errors by writing the one-step-ahead training errors as relative errors:

$$\varepsilon_t = \frac{y_t - \hat{y}_{t|t-1}}{\hat{y}_{t|t-1}}$$

where $\varepsilon_t \sim \text{NID}(0, \sigma^2)$. Substituting $\hat{y}_{t|t-1} = \ell_{t-1}$ gives $y_t = \ell_{t-1} + \ell_{t-1}\varepsilon_t$ and $e_t = y_t - \hat{y}_{t|t-1} = \ell_{t-1}\varepsilon_t$.

Then we can write the multiplicative form of the state space model as

$$\begin{aligned} y_t &= \ell_{t-1}(1 + \varepsilon_t) \\ \ell_t &= \ell_{t-1}(1 + \alpha\varepsilon_t). \end{aligned}$$

ETS(A,A,N): Holt's linear method with additive errors

For this model, we assume that the one-step-ahead training errors are given by $\varepsilon_t = y_t - \ell_{t-1} - b_{t-1} \sim \text{NID}(0, \sigma^2)$. Substituting this into the error correction equations for Holt's linear method we obtain

$$\begin{aligned} y_t &= \ell_{t-1} + b_{t-1} + \varepsilon_t \\ \ell_t &= \ell_{t-1} + b_{t-1} + \alpha\varepsilon_t \\ b_t &= b_{t-1} + \beta\varepsilon_t, \end{aligned}$$

where, for simplicity, we have set $\beta = \alpha\beta^*$.

ETS(M,A,N): Holt's linear method with multiplicative errors

Specifying one-step-ahead training errors as relative errors such that

$$\varepsilon_t = \frac{y_t - (\ell_{t-1} + b_{t-1})}{(\ell_{t-1} + b_{t-1})}$$

and following an approach similar to that used above, the innovations state space model underlying Holt's linear method with multiplicative errors is specified as

$$\begin{aligned} y_t &= (\ell_{t-1} + b_{t-1})(1 + \varepsilon_t) \\ \ell_t &= (\ell_{t-1} + b_{t-1})(1 + \alpha\varepsilon_t) \\ b_t &= b_{t-1} + \beta(\ell_{t-1} + b_{t-1})\varepsilon_t \end{aligned}$$

where again $\beta = \alpha\beta^*$ and $\varepsilon_t \sim \text{NID}(0, \sigma^2)$.

Other ETS models

In a similar fashion, we can write an innovations state space model for each of the exponential smoothing methods of Table 7.6. Table 7.7 presents the equations for all of the models in the ETS framework.

ADDITIVE ERROR MODELS

Trend	**Seasonal** N	A	M
N	$y_t = \ell_{t-1} + \varepsilon_t$ $\ell_t = \ell_{t-1} + \alpha\varepsilon_t$	$y_t = \ell_{t-1} + s_{t-m} + \varepsilon_t$ $\ell_t = \ell_{t-1} + \alpha\varepsilon_t$ $s_t = s_{t-m} + \gamma\varepsilon_t$	$y_t = \ell_{t-1}s_{t-m} + \varepsilon_t$ $\ell_t = \ell_{t-1} + \alpha\varepsilon_t/s_{t-m}$ $s_t = s_{t-m} + \gamma\varepsilon_t/\ell_{t-1}$
A	$y_t = \ell_{t-1} + b_{t-1} + \varepsilon_t$ $\ell_t = \ell_{t-1} + b_{t-1} + \alpha\varepsilon_t$ $b_t = b_{t-1} + \beta\varepsilon_t$	$y_t = \ell_{t-1} + b_{t-1} + s_{t-m} + \varepsilon_t$ $\ell_t = \ell_{t-1} + b_{t-1} + \alpha\varepsilon_t$ $b_t = b_{t-1} + \beta\varepsilon_t$ $s_t = s_{t-m} + \gamma\varepsilon_t$	$y_t = (\ell_{t-1} + b_{t-1})s_{t-m} + \varepsilon_t$ $\ell_t = \ell_{t-1} + b_{t-1} + \alpha\varepsilon_t/s_{t-m}$ $b_t = b_{t-1} + \beta\varepsilon_t/s_{t-m}$ $s_t = s_{t-m} + \gamma\varepsilon_t/(\ell_{t-1} + b_{t-1})$
A$_d$	$y_t = \ell_{t-1} + \phi b_{t-1} + \varepsilon_t$ $\ell_t = \ell_{t-1} + \phi b_{t-1} + \alpha\varepsilon_t$ $b_t = \phi b_{t-1} + \beta\varepsilon_t$	$y_t = \ell_{t-1} + \phi b_{t-1} + s_{t-m} + \varepsilon_t$ $\ell_t = \ell_{t-1} + \phi b_{t-1} + \alpha\varepsilon_t$ $b_t = \phi b_{t-1} + \beta\varepsilon_t$ $s_t = s_{t-m} + \gamma\varepsilon_t$	$y_t = (\ell_{t-1} + \phi b_{t-1})s_{t-m} + \varepsilon_t$ $\ell_t = \ell_{t-1} + \phi b_{t-1} + \alpha\varepsilon_t/s_{t-m}$ $b_t = \phi b_{t-1} + \beta\varepsilon_t/s_{t-m}$ $s_t = s_{t-m} + \gamma\varepsilon_t/(\ell_{t-1} + \phi b_{t-1})$

MULTIPLICATIVE ERROR MODELS

Trend	**Seasonal** N	A	M
N	$y_t = \ell_{t-1}(1 + \varepsilon_t)$ $\ell_t = \ell_{t-1}(1 + \alpha\varepsilon_t)$	$y_t = (\ell_{t-1} + s_{t-m})(1 + \varepsilon_t)$ $\ell_t = \ell_{t-1} + \alpha(\ell_{t-1} + s_{t-m})\varepsilon_t$ $s_t = s_{t-m} + \gamma(\ell_{t-1} + s_{t-m})\varepsilon_t$	$y_t = \ell_{t-1}s_{t-m}(1 + \varepsilon_t)$ $\ell_t = \ell_{t-1}(1 + \alpha\varepsilon_t)$ $s_t = s_{t-m}(1 + \gamma\varepsilon_t)$
A	$y_t = (\ell_{t-1} + b_{t-1})(1 + \varepsilon_t)$ $\ell_t = (\ell_{t-1} + b_{t-1})(1 + \alpha\varepsilon_t)$ $b_t = b_{t-1} + \beta(\ell_{t-1} + b_{t-1})\varepsilon_t$	$y_t = (\ell_{t-1} + b_{t-1} + s_{t-m})(1 + \varepsilon_t)$ $\ell_t = \ell_{t-1} + b_{t-1} + \alpha(\ell_{t-1} + b_{t-1} + s_{t-m})\varepsilon_t$ $b_t = b_{t-1} + \beta(\ell_{t-1} + b_{t-1} + s_{t-m})\varepsilon_t$ $s_t = s_{t-m} + \gamma(\ell_{t-1} + b_{t-1} + s_{t-m})\varepsilon_t$	$y_t = (\ell_{t-1} + b_{t-1})s_{t-m}(1 + \varepsilon_t)$ $\ell_t = (\ell_{t-1} + b_{t-1})(1 + \alpha\varepsilon_t)$ $b_t = b_{t-1} + \beta(\ell_{t-1} + b_{t-1})\varepsilon_t$ $s_t = s_{t-m}(1 + \gamma\varepsilon_t)$
A$_d$	$y_t = (\ell_{t-1} + \phi b_{t-1})(1 + \varepsilon_t)$ $\ell_t = (\ell_{t-1} + \phi b_{t-1})(1 + \alpha\varepsilon_t)$ $b_t = \phi b_{t-1} + \beta(\ell_{t-1} + \phi b_{t-1})\varepsilon_t$	$y_t = (\ell_{t-1} + \phi b_{t-1} + s_{t-m})(1 + \varepsilon_t)$ $\ell_t = \ell_{t-1} + \phi b_{t-1} + \alpha(\ell_{t-1} + \phi b_{t-1} + s_{t-m})\varepsilon_t$ $b_t = \phi b_{t-1} + \beta(\ell_{t-1} + \phi b_{t-1} + s_{t-m})\varepsilon_t$ $s_t = s_{t-m} + \gamma(\ell_{t-1} + \phi b_{t-1} + s_{t-m})\varepsilon_t$	$y_t = (\ell_{t-1} + \phi b_{t-1})s_{t-m}(1 + \varepsilon_t)$ $\ell_t = (\ell_{t-1} + \phi b_{t-1})(1 + \alpha\varepsilon_t)$ $b_t = \phi b_{t-1} + \beta(\ell_{t-1} + \phi b_{t-1})\varepsilon_t$ $s_t = s_{t-m}(1 + \gamma\varepsilon_t)$

Table 7.7: State space equations for each of the models in the ETS framework.

7.6 Estimation and model selection

Estimating ETS models

An alternative to estimating the parameters by minimizing the sum of squared errors is to maximize the "likelihood". The likelihood is the probability of the data arising from the specified model. Thus, a large likelihood is associated with a good model. For an additive error model, maximizing the likelihood gives the same results as minimizing the sum of squared errors. However, different results will be obtained for multiplicative error models. In this section, we will estimate the smoothing parameters α, β, γ and ϕ, and the initial states ℓ_0, b_0, $s_0, s_{-1}, \dots, s_{-m+1}$, by maximizing the likelihood.

The possible values that the smoothing parameters can take are restricted. Traditionally, the parameters have been constrained to lie between 0 and 1 so that the equations can be interpreted as weighted averages. That is, $0 < \alpha, \beta^*, \gamma^*, \phi < 1$. For the state space models, we have set $\beta = \alpha\beta^*$ and $\gamma = (1-\alpha)\gamma^*$. Therefore, the traditional restrictions translate to $0 < \alpha < 1$, $0 < \beta < \alpha$ and $0 < \gamma < 1 - \alpha$. In practice, the damping parameter ϕ is usually constrained further to prevent numerical difficulties in estimating the model. In R, it is restricted so that $0.8 < \phi < 0.98$.

Another way to view the parameters is through a consideration of the mathematical properties of the state space models. The parameters are constrained in order to prevent observations in the distant past having a continuing effect on current forecasts. This leads to some *admissibility* constraints on the parameters, which are usually (but not always) less restrictive than the traditional constraints region (Hyndman, Koehler, Ord, et al. 2008, Ch10). For example, for the ETS(A,N,N) model, the traditional parameter region is $0 < \alpha < 1$ but the admissible region is $0 < \alpha < 2$. For the ETS(A,A,N) model, the traditional parameter region is $0 < \alpha < 1$ and $0 < \beta < \alpha$ but the admissible region is $0 < \alpha < 2$ and $0 < \beta < 4 - 2\alpha$.

Model selection

A great advantage of the ETS statistical framework is that information criteria can be used for model selection. The AIC, AIC_c and BIC, introduced in Section 5.5, can be used here to determine which of the ETS models is most appropriate for a given time series.

For ETS models, Akaike's Information Criterion (AIC) is defined as

$$\text{AIC} = -2\log(L) + 2k,$$

where L is the likelihood of the model and k is the total number of parameters and initial states that have been estimated (including the residual variance).

The AIC corrected for small sample bias (AIC_c) is defined as

$$\text{AIC}_\text{c} = \text{AIC} + \frac{k(k+1)}{T-k-1},$$

and the Bayesian Information Criterion (BIC) is

$$\text{BIC} = \text{AIC} + k[\log(T) - 2].$$

Three of the combinations of (Error, Trend, Seasonal) can lead to numerical difficulties. Specifically, the models that can cause such instabilities are ETS(A,N,M), ETS(A,A,M), and ETS(A,A_d,M), due to division by values potentially close to zero in the state equations. We normally do not consider these particular combinations when selecting a model.

Models with multiplicative errors are useful when the data are strictly positive, but are not numerically stable when the data contain zeros or negative values. Therefore, multiplicative error models will not be considered if the time series is not strictly positive. In that case, only the six fully additive models will be applied.

The `ets()` function in R

The models can be estimated in R using the `ets()` function in the **forecast** package. Unlike the `ses()`, `holt()` and `hw()` functions, the `ets()` function does not produce forecasts. Rather, it estimates the model parameters and returns information about the fitted model. By default it uses the AICc to select an appropriate model, although other information criteria can be selected.

The R code below shows the most important arguments that this function can take, and their default values. If only the time series is specified, and all other arguments are left at their default values, then an appropriate model will be selected automatically. We explain the arguments below. See the help file for a more complete description.

```
ets(y, model="ZZZ", damped=NULL, alpha=NULL, beta=NULL,
    gamma=NULL, phi=NULL, lambda=NULL, biasadj=FALSE,
    additive.only=FALSE, restrict=TRUE,
    allow.multiplicative.trend=FALSE)
```

`y` The time series to be forecast.

`model` A three-letter code indicating the model to be estimated using the ETS classification and notation. The possible inputs are "N" for none, "A" for additive, "M" for multiplicative, or "Z" for automatic selection. If any of the inputs is left as "Z", then this component is selected according to the information criterion. The default value of `ZZZ` ensures that all components are selected using the information criterion.

`damped` If `damped=TRUE`, then a damped trend will be used (either A or M). If `damped=FALSE`, then a non-damped trend will used. If `damped=NULL` (the default), then either a damped or a non-damped trend will be selected, depending on which model has the smallest value for the information criterion.

`alpha`, `beta`, `gamma`, `phi` The values of the smoothing parameters can be specified using these arguments. If they are set to `NULL` (the default setting for each of them), the parameters are estimated.

`lambda` Box-Cox transformation parameter. It will be ignored if `lambda=NULL` (the default value). Otherwise, the time series will be transformed before the model is estimated. When `lambda` is not `NULL`, `additive.only` is set to `TRUE`.

`biasadj` If `TRUE` and `lambda` is not `NULL`, then the back-transformed fitted values and forecasts will be bias-adjusted.

`additive.only` Only models with additive components will be considered if `additive.only=TRUE`. Otherwise, all models will be considered.

`restrict` If `restrict=TRUE` (the default), the models that cause numerical difficulties are not considered in model selection.

`allow.multiplicative.trend` Multiplicative trend models are also available, but not covered in this book. Set this argument to `TRUE` to allow these models to be considered.

Working with `ets` objects

The `ets()` function will return an object of class `ets`. There are many R functions designed to make working with `ets` objects easy. A few of them are described below.

`coef()` returns all fitted parameters.

`accuracy()` returns accuracy measures computed on the training data.

`summary()` prints some summary information about the fitted model.

`autoplot()` and `plot()` produce time plots of the components.

`residuals()` returns residuals from the estimated model.

`fitted()` returns one-step forecasts for the training data.

simulate() will simulate future sample paths from the fitted model.

forecast() computes point forecasts and prediction intervals, as described in the next section.

Example: International tourist visitor nights in Australia

We now employ the ETS statistical framework to forecast tourist visitor nights in Australia by international arrivals over the period 2016–2019. We let the `ets()` function select the model by minimizing the AICc.

```
aust <- window(austourists, start=2005)
fit <- ets(aust)
summary(fit)
#> ETS(M,A,M)
#>
#> Call:
#>  ets(y = aust)
#>
#>   Smoothing parameters:
#>     alpha = 0.1908
#>     beta  = 0.0392
#>     gamma = 2e-04
#>
#>   Initial states:
#>     l = 32.3679
#>     b = 0.9281
#>     s = 1.022 0.9628 0.7683 1.247
#>
#>   sigma:  0.0383
#>
#>   AIC  AICc   BIC
#> 224.9 230.2 240.9
#>
#> Training set error measures:
#>                    ME  RMSE  MAE     MPE  MAPE   MASE
#> Training set 0.04837 1.671 1.25 -0.1846 2.693 0.4095
#>                 ACF1
#> Training set 0.2006
```

The model selected is ETS(M,A,M):

$$
\begin{aligned}
y_t &= (\ell_{t-1} + b_{t-1})s_{t-m}(1 + \varepsilon_t) \\
\ell_t &= (\ell_{t-1} + b_{t-1})(1 + \alpha\varepsilon_t) \\
b_t &= b_{t-1} + \beta(\ell_{t-1} + b_{t_1})\varepsilon_t \\
s_t &= s_{t-m}(1 + \gamma\varepsilon_t).
\end{aligned}
$$

The parameter estimates are $\hat{\alpha} = 0.1908$, $\hat{\beta} = 0.03919$, and $\hat{\gamma} = 0.0001917$. The output also returns the estimates for the initial states ℓ_0, b_0, s_0, s_{-1}, s_{-2} and s_{-3}. Compare these with the values obtained for the equivalent Holt-Winters method with multiplicative seasonality presented in Table 7.4. The ETS(M,A,M) model will give different point forecasts to the multiplicative Holt-Winters' method, because the parameters have been estimated differently. With the `ets()` function, the default estimation method is maximum likelihood rather than minimum sum of squares.

Figure 7.9 shows the states over time, while Figure 7.11 shows point forecasts and prediction intervals generated from the model. The small values of β and γ mean that the slope and seasonal components change very little over time. The narrow prediction intervals indicate that the series is relatively easy to forecast due to the strong trend and seasonality.

```
autoplot(fit)
```

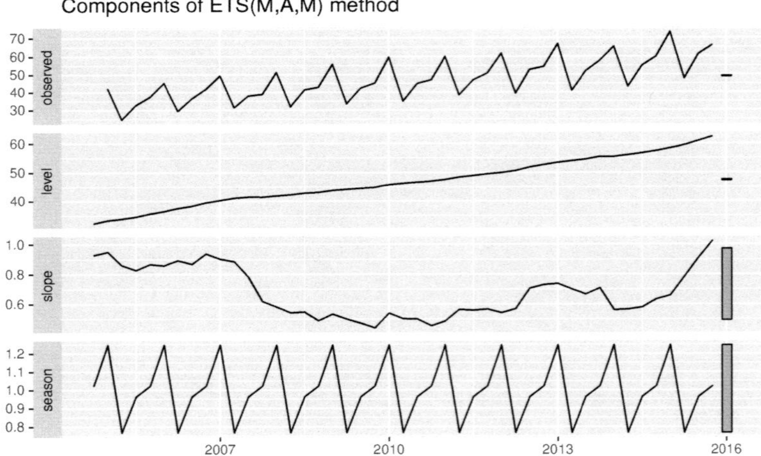

Figure 7.9: Graphical representation of the estimated states over time.

Because this model has multiplicative errors, the residuals are not equivalent to the one-step training errors. The residuals are given by $\hat{\varepsilon}_t$, while the one-step training errors are defined as $y_t - \hat{y}_{t|t-1}$. We can obtain both using the `residuals()` function.

```
cbind('Residuals' = residuals(fit),
      'Forecast errors' = residuals(fit,type='response')) %>%
  autoplot(facet=TRUE) + xlab("Year") + ylab("")
```

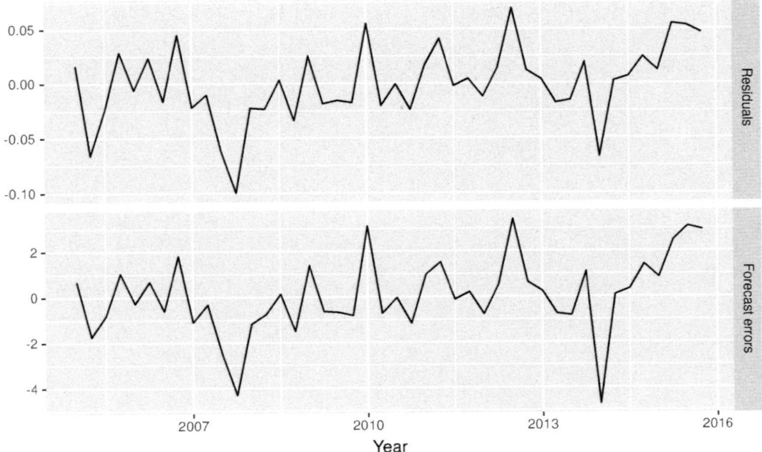

Figure 7.10: Residuals and one-step forecast errors from the ETS(M,A,M) model.

The `type` argument is used in the `residuals()` function to distinguish between residuals and forecast errors. The default is `type='innovation'` which gives regular residuals.

7.7 Forecasting with ETS models

Point forecasts are obtained from the models by iterating the equations for $t = T+1,\dots,T+h$ and setting all $\varepsilon_t = 0$ for $t > T$.

For example, for model ETS(M,A,N), $y_{T+1} = (\ell_T + b_T)(1+\varepsilon_{T+1})$. Therefore $\hat{y}_{T+1|T} = \ell_T + b_T$. Similarly,

$$\begin{aligned} y_{T+2} &= (\ell_{T+1} + b_{T+1})(1+\varepsilon_{T+1}) \\ &= \left[(\ell_T + b_T)(1+\alpha\varepsilon_{T+1}) + b_T + \beta(\ell_T + b_T)\varepsilon_{T+1}\right](1+\varepsilon_{T+1}). \end{aligned}$$

Therefore, $\hat{y}_{T+2|T} = \ell_T + 2b_T$, and so on. These forecasts are identical to the forecasts from Holt's linear method, and also to those from model ETS(A,A,N). Thus, the point forecasts obtained from the method and from the two models that underlie the method are identical (assuming that the same parameter values are used).

ETS point forecasts are equal to the medians of the forecast distributions. For models with only additive components, the forecast distributions are normal, so the medians and means are equal. For ETS models with multiplicative errors, or with multiplicative seasonality, the point forecasts will not be equal to the means of the forecast distributions.

To obtain forecasts from an ETS model, we use the `forecast()` function.

```
fit %>% forecast(h=8) %>%
  autoplot() +
  ylab("International visitor night in Australia (millions)")
```

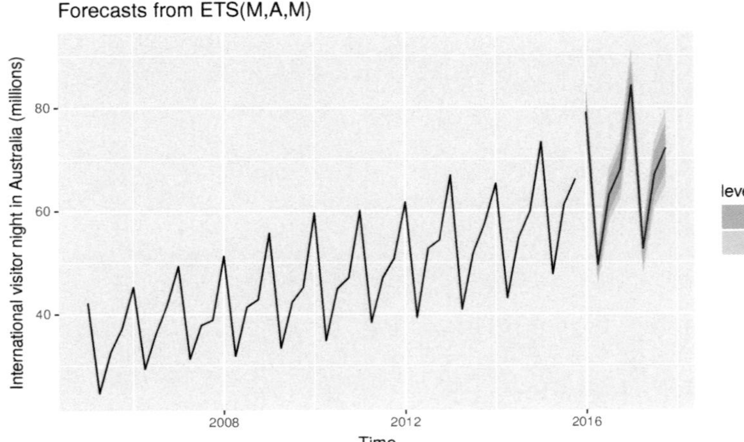

Figure 7.11: Forecasting international visitor nights in Australia using an ETS(M,A,M) model.

Prediction intervals

A big advantage of the models is that prediction intervals can also be generated — something that cannot be done using the methods. The prediction intervals will differ between models with additive and multiplicative methods.

For most ETS models, a prediction interval can be written as

$$\hat{y}_{T+h|T} \pm c\sigma_h$$

where c depends on the coverage probability, and σ_h^2 is the forecast variance. Values for c were given in Table 3.1. For ETS models, formulas for σ_h^2 can be complicated; the details are given in Chapter 6 of Hyndman, Koehler, Ord, et al. (2008). In Table 7.8 we give the formulas for the additive ETS models, which are the simplest.

For a few ETS models, there are no known formulas for prediction intervals. In these cases, the `forecast()` function uses simulated future sample paths and computes prediction intervals from the percentiles of these simulated future paths.

Model	Forecast variance: σ_h^2
(A,N,N)	$\sigma_h^2 = \sigma^2\Big[1 + \alpha^2(h-1)\Big]$
(A,A,N)	$\sigma_h^2 = \sigma^2\Big[1 + (h-1)\big\{\alpha^2 + \alpha\beta h + \frac{1}{6}\beta^2 h(2h-1)\big\}\Big]$
(A,A$_d$,N)	$\sigma_h^2 = \sigma^2\Big[1 + \alpha^2(h-1) + \frac{\beta\phi h}{(1-\phi)^2}\{2\alpha(1-\phi) + \beta\phi\} - \frac{\beta\phi(1-\phi^h)}{(1-\phi)^2(1-\phi^2)}\big\{2\alpha(1-\phi^2) + \beta\phi(1+2\phi-\phi^h)\big\}\Big]$
(A,N,A)	$\sigma_h^2 = \sigma^2\Big[1 + \alpha^2(h-1) + \gamma k(2\alpha + \gamma)\Big]$
(A,A,A)	$\sigma_h^2 = \sigma^2\Big[1 + (h-1)\big\{\alpha^2 + \alpha\beta h + \frac{1}{6}\beta^2 h(2h-1)\big\} + \gamma k\big\{2\alpha + \gamma + \beta m(k+1)\big\}\Big]$
(A,A$_d$,A)	$\sigma_h^2 = \sigma^2\Big[1 + \alpha^2(h-1) + \gamma k(2\alpha + \gamma) + \frac{\beta\phi h}{(1-\phi)^2}\{2\alpha(1-\phi) + \beta\phi\} - \frac{\beta\phi(1-\phi^h)}{(1-\phi)^2(1-\phi^2)}\big\{2\alpha(1-\phi^2) + \beta\phi(1+2\phi-\phi^h)\big\} + \frac{2\beta\gamma\phi}{(1-\phi)(1-\phi^m)}\big\{k(1-\phi^m) - \phi^m(1-\phi^{mk})\big\}\Big]$

Table 7.8: Forecast variance expressions for each additive state space model, where σ^2 is the residual variance, m is the seasonal period, and k is the integer part of $(h-1)/m$ (i.e., the number of complete years in the forecast period prior to time $T+h$).

Using `forecast()`

The R code below shows the possible arguments that this function takes when applied to an ETS model. We explain each of the arguments in what follows.

```
forecast(object, h=ifelse(object$m>1, 2*object$m, 10),
level=c(80,95), fan=FALSE, simulate=FALSE, bootstrap=FALSE,
npaths=5000, PI=TRUE, lambda=object$lambda, biasadj=NULL, ...)
```

`object` The object returned by the `ets()` function.

`h` The forecast horizon — the number of periods to be forecast.

`level` The confidence level for the prediction intervals.

`fan` If `fan=TRUE`, `level=seq(50,99,by=1)`. This is suitable for fan plots.

`simulate` If `simulate=TRUE`, prediction intervals are produced by simulation rather than using algebraic formulas. Simulation will also be used (even if `simulate=FALSE`) where there are no algebraic formulas available for the particular model.

bootstrap If `bootstrap=TRUE` and `simulate=TRUE`, then the simulated prediction intervals use re-sampled errors rather than normally distributed errors.

npaths The number of sample paths used in computing simulated prediction intervals.

PI If `PI=TRUE`, then prediction intervals are produced; otherwise only point forecasts are calculated.

lambda The Box-Cox transformation parameter. This is ignored if `lambda=NULL`. Otherwise, the forecasts are back-transformed via an inverse Box-Cox transformation.

biasadj If `lambda` is not `NULL`, the backtransformed forecasts (and prediction intervals) are bias-adjusted.

7.8 Exercises

1. Consider the `pigs` series — the number of pigs slaughtered in Victoria each month.

   a. Use the `ses()` function in R to find the optimal values of α and ℓ_0, and generate forecasts for the next four months.
   b. Compute a 95% prediction interval for the first forecast using $\hat{y}\pm1.96s$ where s is the standard deviation of the residuals. Compare your interval with the interval produced by R.

2. Write your own function to implement simple exponential smoothing. The function should take arguments `y` (the time series), `alpha` (the smoothing parameter α) and `level` (the initial level ℓ_0). It should return the forecast of the next observation in the series. Does it give the same forecast as `ses()`?

3. Modify your function from the previous exercise to return the sum of squared errors rather than the forecast of the next observation. Then use the `optim()` function to find the optimal values of α and ℓ_0. Do you get the same values as the `ses()` function?

4. Combine your previous two functions to produce a function which both finds the optimal values of α and ℓ_0, and produces a forecast of the next observation in the series.

5. Data set `books` contains the daily sales of paperback and hardcover books at the same store. The task is to forecast the next four days' sales for paperback and hardcover books.

    a. Plot the series and discuss the main features of the data.
    b. Use the `ses()` function to forecast each series, and plot the forecasts.
    c. Compute the RMSE values for the training data in each case.

6. a. Now apply Holt's linear method to the `paperback` and `hardback` series and compute four-day forecasts in each case.
    b. Compare the RMSE measures of Holt's method for the two series to those of simple exponential smoothing in the previous question. (Remember that Holt's method is using one more parameter than SES.) Discuss the merits of the two forecasting methods for these data sets.
    c. Compare the forecasts for the two series using both methods. Which do you think is best?
    d. Calculate a 95% prediction interval for the first forecast for each series, using the RMSE values and assuming normal errors. Compare your intervals with those produced using `ses` and `holt`.

7. For this exercise use data set `eggs`, the price of a dozen eggs in the United States from 1900–1993. Experiment with the various options in the `holt()` function to see how much the forecasts change with damped trend, or with a Box-Cox transformation. Try to develop an intuition of what each argument is doing to the forecasts.

    [Hint: use `h=100` when calling `holt()` so you can clearly see the differences between the various options when plotting the forecasts.]

    Which model gives the best RMSE?

8. Recall your retail time series data (from Exercise 3 in Section 2.10).

    a. Why is multiplicative seasonality necessary for this series?
    b. Apply Holt-Winters' multiplicative method to the data. Experiment with making the trend damped.

c. Compare the RMSE of the one-step forecasts from the two methods. Which do you prefer?
d. Check that the residuals from the best method look like white noise.
e. Now find the test set RMSE, while training the model to the end of 2010. Can you beat the seasonal naïve approach from Exercise 7 in Section 3.7?

9. For the same retail data, try an STL decomposition applied to the Box-Cox transformed series, followed by ETS on the seasonally adjusted data. How does that compare with your best previous forecasts on the test set?

10. For this exercise use data set `ukcars`, the quarterly UK passenger vehicle production data from 1977Q1–2005Q1.

    a. Plot the data and describe the main features of the series.
    b. Decompose the series using STL and obtain the seasonally adjusted data.
    c. Forecast the next two years of the series using an additive damped trend method applied to the seasonally adjusted data. (This can be done in one step using `stlf()` with arguments `etsmodel="AAN", damped=TRUE`.)
    d. Forecast the next two years of the series using Holt's linear method applied to the seasonally adjusted data (as before but with `damped=FALSE`).
    e. Now use `ets()` to choose a seasonal model for the data.
    f. Compare the RMSE of the ETS model with the RMSE of the models you obtained using STL decompositions. Which gives the better in-sample fits?
    g. Compare the forecasts from the three approaches? Which seems most reasonable?
    h. Check the residuals of your preferred model.

11. For this exercise use data set `visitors`, the monthly Australian short-term overseas visitors data, May 1985–April 2005.

    a. Make a time plot of your data and describe the main features of the series.
    b. Split your data into a training set and a test set comprising the last two years of available data. Forecast the test set using Holt-Winters' multiplicative method.

c. Why is multiplicative seasonality necessary here?
d. Forecast the two-year test set using each of the following methods:
   i) an ETS model;
   ii) an additive ETS model applied to a Box-Cox transformed series;
   iii) a seasonal naïve method;
   iv) an STL decomposition applied to the Box-Cox transformed data followed by an ETS model applied to the seasonally adjusted (transformed) data.
e. Which method gives the best forecasts? Does it pass the residual tests?
f. Compare the same four methods using time series cross-validation with the `tsCV()` function instead of using a training and test set. Do you come to the same conclusions?

12. The `fets()` function below returns ETS forecasts.

```
fets <- function(y, h) {
  forecast(ets(y), h = h)
}
```

   a. Apply `tsCV()` for a forecast horizon of $h = 4$, for both ETS and seasonal naïve methods to the `qcement` data, (Hint: use the newly created `fets()` and the existing `snaive()` functions as your forecast function arguments.)
   b. Compute the MSE of the resulting 4-step-ahead errors. (Hint: make sure you remove missing values.) Why are there missing values? Comment on which forecasts are more accurate. Is this what you expected?

13. Compare `ets()`, `snaive()` and `stlf()` on the following six time series. For `stlf()`, you might need to use a Box-Cox transformation. Use a test set of three years to decide what gives the best forecasts. `ausbeer`, `bricksq`, `dole`, `a10`, `h02`, `usmelec`.

14. a. Use `ets()` on the following series:

   `bicoal`, `chicken`, `dole`, `usdeaths`, `lynx`, `ibmclose`, `eggs`.

   Does it always give good forecasts?

b. Find an example where it does not work well. Can you figure out why?

15. Show that the point forecasts from an ETS(M,A,M) model are the same as those obtained using Holt-Winters' multiplicative method.

16. Show that the forecast variance for an ETS(A,N,N) model is given by
$$\sigma^2\Big[1+\alpha^2(h-1)\Big].$$

17. Write down 95% prediction intervals for an ETS(A,N,N) model as a function of ℓ_T, α, h and σ, assuming Gaussian errors.

7.9 Further reading

- Two articles by Ev Gardner (Gardner 1985, 2006) provide a great overview of the history of exponential smoothing, and its many variations.
- A full book treatment of the subject providing the mathematical details is given by Hyndman, Koehler, Ord, et al. (2008).

Chapter 8

ARIMA models

ARIMA models provide another approach to time series forecasting. Exponential smoothing and ARIMA models are the two most widely-used approaches to time series forecasting, and provide complementary approaches to the problem. While exponential smoothing models are based on a description of the trend and seasonality in the data, ARIMA models aim to describe the autocorrelations in the data.

Before we introduce ARIMA models, we must first discuss the concept of stationarity and the technique of differencing time series.

8.1 Stationarity and differencing

A stationary time series is one whose properties do not depend on the time at which the series is observed.[1] Thus, time series with trends, or with seasonality, are not stationary — the trend and seasonality will affect the value of the time series at different times. On the other hand, a white noise series is stationary — it does not matter when you observe it, it should look much the same at any point in time.

[1] More precisely, if $\{y_t\}$ is a **stationary** time series, then for all s, the distribution of $(y_t, \dots, y_{t+s})$ does not depend on t.

Some cases can be confusing — a time series with cyclic behaviour (but with no trend or seasonality) is stationary. This is because the cycles are not of a fixed length, so before we observe the series we cannot be sure where the peaks and troughs of the cycles will be.

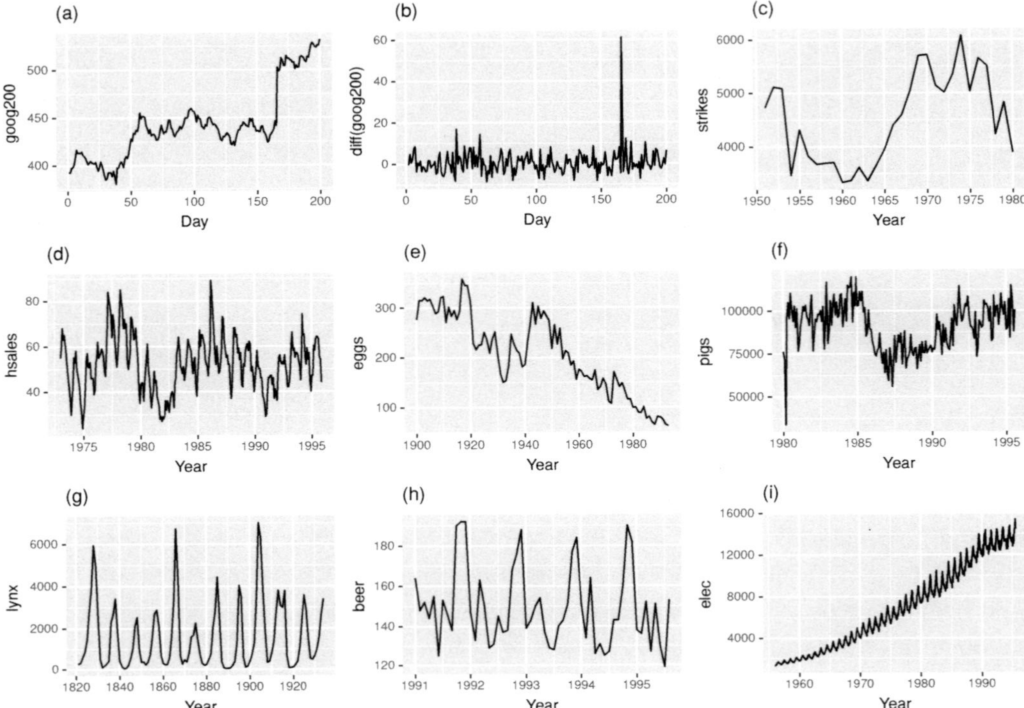

Figure 8.1: Which of these series are stationary? (a) Google stock price for 200 consecutive days; (b) Daily change in the Google stock price for 200 consecutive days; (c) Annual number of strikes in the US; (d) Monthly sales of new one-family houses sold in the US; (e) Annual price of a dozen eggs in the US (constant dollars); (f) Monthly total of pigs slaughtered in Victoria, Australia; (g) Annual total of lynx trapped in the McKenzie River district of north-west Canada; (h) Monthly Australian beer production; (i) Monthly Australian electricity production.

In general, a stationary time series will have no predictable patterns in the long-term. Time plots will show the series to be roughly horizontal (although some cyclic behaviour is possible), with constant variance.

Consider the nine series plotted in Figure 8.1. Which of these do you think are stationary?

Obvious seasonality rules out series (d), (h) and (i). Trends and changing levels rules out series (a), (c), (e), (f) and (i). Increasing variance also rules out (i). That leaves only (b) and (g) as stationary series.

At first glance, the strong cycles in series (g) might appear to make it non-stationary. But these cycles are aperiodic — they are caused when the lynx population becomes too large for the available feed, so that they stop breeding and the population falls to very low numbers, then the regeneration of their food sources allows the population to grow again, and so on. In the long-term, the timing of these cycles is not predictable. Hence the series is stationary.

Differencing

In Figure 8.1, note that the Google stock price was non-stationary in panel (a), but the daily changes were stationary in panel (b). This shows one way to make a non-stationary time series stationary — compute the differences between consecutive observations. This is known as **differencing**.

Transformations such as logarithms can help to stabilize the variance of a time series. Differencing can help stabilize the mean of a time series by removing changes in the level of a time series, and therefore eliminating (or reducing) trend and seasonality.

As well as looking at the time plot of the data, the ACF plot is also useful for identifying non-stationary time series. For a stationary time series, the ACF will drop to zero relatively quickly, while the ACF of non-stationary data decreases slowly. Also, for non-stationary data, the value of r_1 is often large and positive.

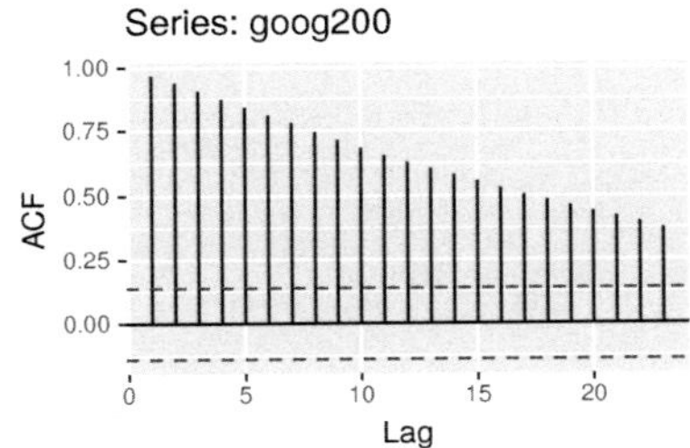

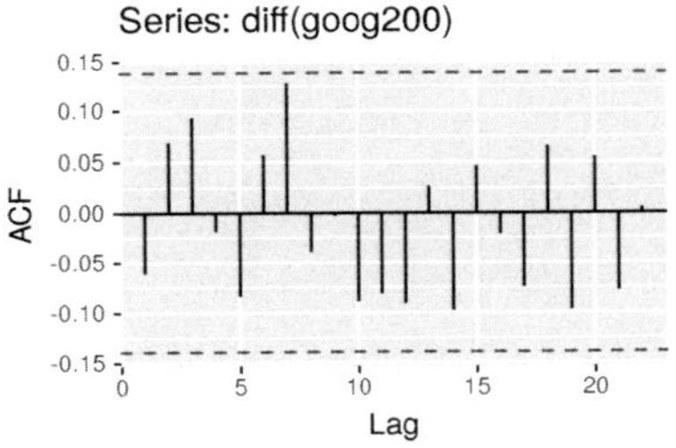

Figure 8.2: The ACF of the Google stock price (left) and of the daily changes in Google stock price (right).

```
Box.test(diff(goog200), lag=10, type="Ljung-Box")
#>
#>  Box-Ljung test
#>
#> data:  diff(goog200)
#> X-squared = 11, df = 10, p-value = 0.4
```

The ACF of the differenced Google stock price looks just like that of a white noise series. There are no autocorrelations lying outside the 95% limits, and the Ljung-Box Q^* statistic has a p-value of 0.355 (for $h = 10$). This suggests that the *daily change* in the Google stock price is essentially a random amount which is uncorrelated with that of previous days.

Random walk model

The differenced series is the *change* between consecutive observations in the original series, and can be written as

$$y'_t = y_t - y_{t-1}.$$

The differenced series will have only $T-1$ values, since it is not possible to calculate a difference y'_1 for the first observation.

When the differenced series is white noise, the model for the original series can be written as

$$y_t - y_{t-1} = \varepsilon_t,$$

where ε_t denotes white noise. Rearranging this leads to the "random walk" model

$$y_t = y_{t-1} + \varepsilon_t.$$

Random walk models are very widely used for non-stationary data, particularly financial and economic data. Random walks typically have:

- long periods of apparent trends up or down
- sudden and unpredictable changes in direction.

The forecasts from a random walk model are equal to the last observation, as future movements are unpredictable, and are equally likely to be up or down. Thus, the random walk model underpins naïve forecasts, first introduced in Section 3.1.

A closely related model allows the differences to have a non-zero mean. Then

$$y_t - y_{t-1} = c + \varepsilon_t \quad \text{or} \quad y_t = c + y_{t-1} + \varepsilon_t\,.$$

The value of c is the average of the changes between consecutive observations. If c is positive, then the average change is an increase in the value of y_t. Thus, y_t will tend to drift upwards. However, if c is negative, y_t will tend to drift downwards.

This is the model behind the drift method, also discussed in Section 3.1.

Second-order differencing

Occasionally the differenced data will not appear to be stationary and it may be necessary to difference the data a second time to obtain a stationary series:

$$\begin{aligned} y_t'' &= y_t' - y_{t-1}' \\ &= (y_t - y_{t-1}) - (y_{t-1} - y_{t-2}) \\ &= y_t - 2y_{t-1} + y_{t-2}. \end{aligned}$$

In this case, y_t'' will have $T-2$ values. Then, we would model the "change in the changes" of the original data. In practice, it is almost never necessary to go beyond second-order differences.

Seasonal differencing

A seasonal difference is the difference between an observation and the previous observation from the same season. So

$$y_t' = y_t - y_{t-m},$$

where $m =$ the number of seasons. These are also called "lag-m differences", as we subtract the observation after a lag of m periods.

If seasonally differenced data appear to be white noise, then an appropriate model for the original data is

$$y_t = y_{t-m} + \varepsilon_t.$$

Forecasts from this model are equal to the last observation from the relevant season. That is, this model gives seasonal naïve forecasts, introduced in Section 3.1.

The bottom panel in Figure 8.3 shows the seasonal differences of the logarithm of the monthly scripts for A10 (antidiabetic) drugs sold in Australia. The transformation and differencing have made the series look relatively stationary.

```
cbind("Sales ($million)" = a10,
      "Monthly log sales" = log(a10),
      "Annual change in log sales" = diff(log(a10),12)) %>%
  autoplot(facets=TRUE) +
    xlab("Year") + ylab("") +
    ggtitle("Antidiabetic drug sales")
```

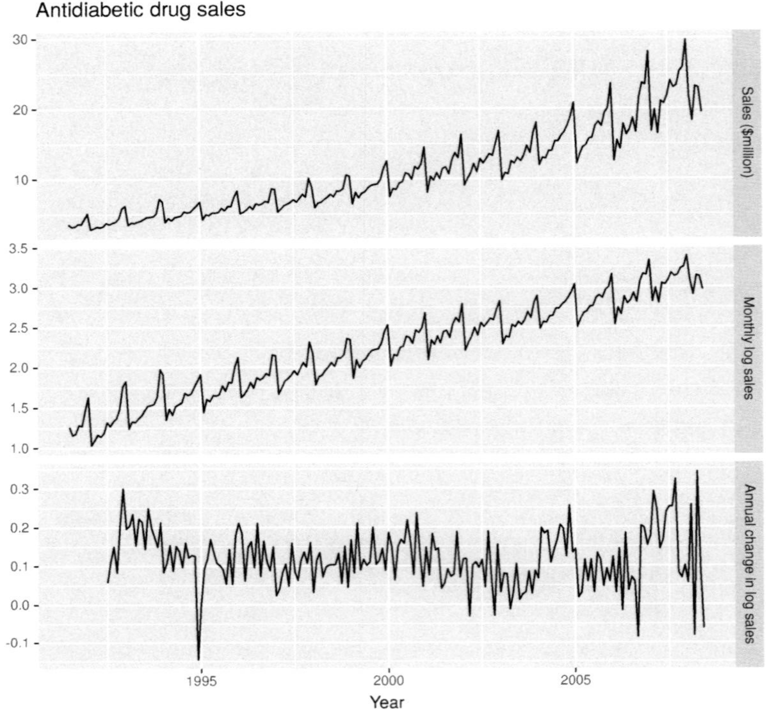

Figure 8.3: Logs and seasonal differences of the A10 (antidiabetic) sales data. The logarithms stabilize the variance, while the seasonal differences remove the seasonality and trend.

To distinguish seasonal differences from ordinary differences, we sometimes refer to ordinary differences as "first differences", meaning differences at lag 1.

Sometimes it is necessary to take both a seasonal difference and a first difference to obtain stationary data, as is shown in Figure 8.4. Here, the data are first transformed using logarithms (second panel), then seasonal differences are calculated (third panel). The data still seem somewhat non-stationary, and so a further lot of first differences are computed (bottom panel).

```
cbind("Billion kWh" = usmelec,
      "Logs" = log(usmelec),
      "Seasonally\n differenced logs" =
        diff(log(usmelec),12),
      "Doubly\n differenced logs" =
        diff(diff(log(usmelec),12),1)) %>%
  autoplot(facets=TRUE) +
    xlab("Year") + ylab("") +
    ggtitle("Monthly US net electricity generation")
```

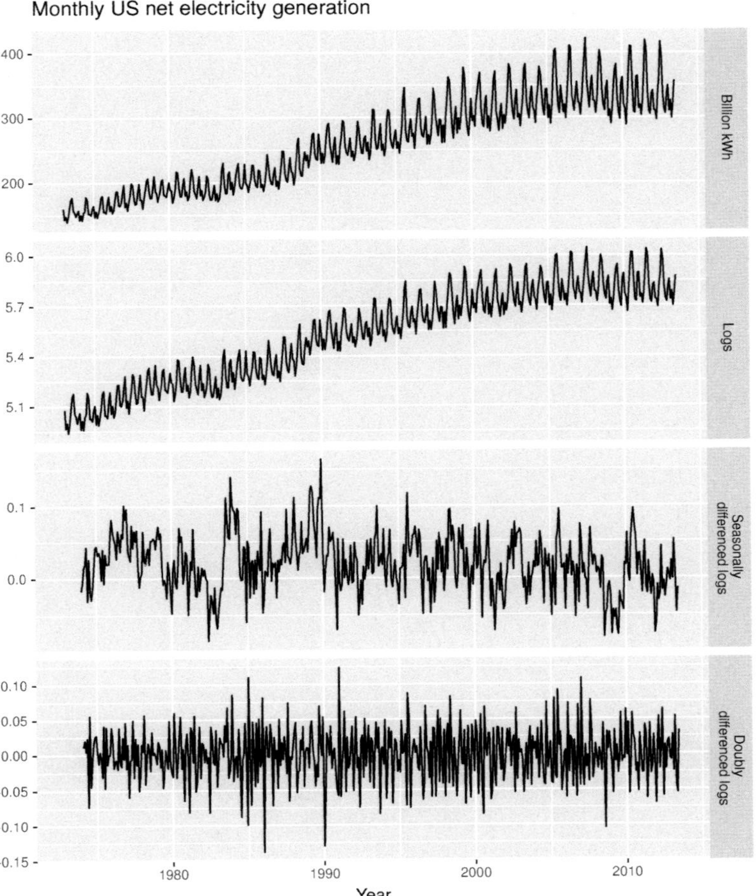

Figure 8.4: Top panel: US net electricity generation (billion kWh). Other panels show the same data after transforming and differencing.

There is a degree of subjectivity in selecting which differences to apply. The seasonally differenced data in Figure 8.3 do not show substantially different behaviour from the seasonally differenced data in Figure 8.4. In the latter case, we could have decided to stop with the seasonally differenced data, and not done an extra round of differencing. In the former case, we could have decided that the data were not sufficiently stationary and taken an extra round of differencing. Some formal tests for differencing are discussed below, but there are always some choices to be made in the modelling process, and different analysts may make different choices.

If $y'_t = y_t - y_{t-m}$ denotes a seasonally differenced series, then the twice-differenced series is

$$\begin{aligned} y''_t &= y'_t - y'_{t-1} \\ &= (y_t - y_{t-m}) - (y_{t-1} - y_{t-m-1}) \\ &= y_t - y_{t-1} - y_{t-m} + y_{t-m-1} \end{aligned}$$

When both seasonal and first differences are applied, it makes no difference which is done first—the result will be the same. However, if the data have a strong seasonal pattern, we recommend that seasonal differencing be done first, because the resulting series will sometimes be stationary and there will be no need for a further first difference. If first differencing is done first, there will still be seasonality present.

It is important that if differencing is used, the differences are interpretable. First differences are the change between one observation and the next. Seasonal differences are the change between one year to the next. Other lags are unlikely to make much interpretable sense and should be avoided.

Unit root tests

One way to determine more objectively whether differencing is required is to use a *unit root test*. These are statistical hypothesis tests of stationarity that are designed for determining whether differencing is required.

A number of different unit root tests are available, which are based on different assumptions and may lead to conflicting answers. In our analysis, we use the *Kwiatkowski-Phillips-Schmidt-Shin (KPSS) test* (Kwiatkowski et al. 1992). In this test, the null hypothesis is that the data are stationary, and we look for evidence that the null hypothesis is false. Consequently, small p-values (e.g., less than 0.05) suggest that differencing is required. The test can be computed using the `ur.kpss()` function from the **urca** package[2].

[2] `https://cran.r-project.org/package=urca`

For example, let us apply it to the Google stock price data.

```
library(urca)
goog %>% ur.kpss() %>% summary()
#>
#> #######################
#> # KPSS Unit Root Test #
#> #######################
#>
#> Test is of type: mu with 7 lags.
#>
#> Value of test-statistic is: 10.72
#>
#> Critical value for a significance level of:
#>                 10pct  5pct 2.5pct  1pct
#> critical values 0.347 0.463  0.574 0.739
```

The test statistic is much bigger than the 1% critical value, indicating that the null hypothesis is rejected. That is, the data are not stationary. We can difference the data, and apply the test again.

```
goog %>% diff() %>% ur.kpss() %>% summary()
#>
#> #######################
#> # KPSS Unit Root Test #
#> #######################
#>
#> Test is of type: mu with 7 lags.
#>
#> Value of test-statistic is: 0.0324
#>
#> Critical value for a significance level of:
#>                 10pct  5pct 2.5pct  1pct
#> critical values 0.347 0.463  0.574 0.739
```

This time, the test statistic is very small, and well within the range we would expect for stationary data. So we can conclude that the differenced data are stationary.

This process of using a sequence of KPSS tests to determine the appropriate number of first differences is carried out by the function `ndiffs()`.

```
ndiffs(goog)
#> [1] 1
```

As we saw from the KPSS tests above, one difference is required to make the `goog` data stationary.

A similar function for determining whether seasonal differencing is required is `nsdiffs()`, which uses the measure of seasonal strength introduced in Section 6.7 to determine the appropriate number of seasonal differences required. No seasonal differences are suggested if $F_S < 0.64$, otherwise one seasonal difference is suggested.

We can apply `nsdiffs()` to the logged US monthly electricity data.

```
usmelec %>% log() %>% nsdiffs()
#> [1] 1
usmelec %>% log() %>% diff(lag=12) %>% ndiffs()
#> [1] 1
```

Because `nsdiffs()` returns 1 (indicating one seasonal difference is required), we apply the `ndiffs()` function to the seasonally differenced data. These functions suggest we should do both a seasonal difference and a first difference.

8.2 Backshift notation

The backward shift operator B is a useful notational device when working with time series lags:

$$By_t = y_{t-1} \,.$$

(Some references use L for "lag" instead of B for "backshift".) In other words, B, operating on y_t, has the effect of shifting the data back one period. Two applications of B to y_t shifts the data back two periods:

$$B(By_t) = B^2 y_t = y_{t-2} \,.$$

For monthly data, if we wish to consider "the same month last year," the notation is $B^{12}y_t = y_{t-12}$.

The backward shift operator is convenient for describing the process of *differencing*. A first difference can be written as

$$y'_t = y_t - y_{t-1} = y_t - By_t = (1 - B)y_t \,.$$

Note that a first difference is represented by $(1 - B)$. Similarly, if second-order differences have to be computed, then:

$$y''_t = y_t - 2y_{t-1} + y_{t-2} = (1 - 2B + B^2)y_t = (1 - B)^2 y_t \,.$$

In general, a dth-order difference can be written as

$$(1-B)^d y_t.$$

Backshift notation is very useful when combining differences as the operator can be treated using ordinary algebraic rules. In particular, terms involving B can be multiplied together.

For example, a seasonal difference followed by a first difference can be written as

$$\begin{aligned}(1-B)(1-B^m)y_t &= (1-B-B^m+B^{m+1})y_t \\ &= y_t - y_{t-1} - y_{t-m} + y_{t-m-1},\end{aligned}$$

the same result we obtained earlier.

8.3 Autoregressive models

In a multiple regression model, we forecast the variable of interest using a linear combination of predictors. In an autoregression model, we forecast the variable of interest using a linear combination of *past values of the variable*. The term *auto*regression indicates that it is a regression of the variable against itself.

Thus, an autoregressive model of order p can be written as

$$y_t = c + \phi_1 y_{t-1} + \phi_2 y_{t-2} + \cdots + \phi_p y_{t-p} + \varepsilon_t,$$

where ε_t is white noise. This is like a multiple regression but with *lagged values* of y_t as predictors. We refer to this as an **AR(p) model**, an autoregressive model of order p.

Autoregressive models are remarkably flexible at handling a wide range of different time series patterns. The two series in Figure 8.5 show series from an AR(1) model and an AR(2) model. Changing the parameters $\phi_1,\dots,\phi_p$ results in different time series patterns. The variance of the error term ε_t will only change the scale of the series, not the patterns.

For an AR(1) model:

- when $\phi_1 = 0$, y_t is equivalent to white noise;
- when $\phi_1 = 1$ and $c = 0$, y_t is equivalent to a random walk;

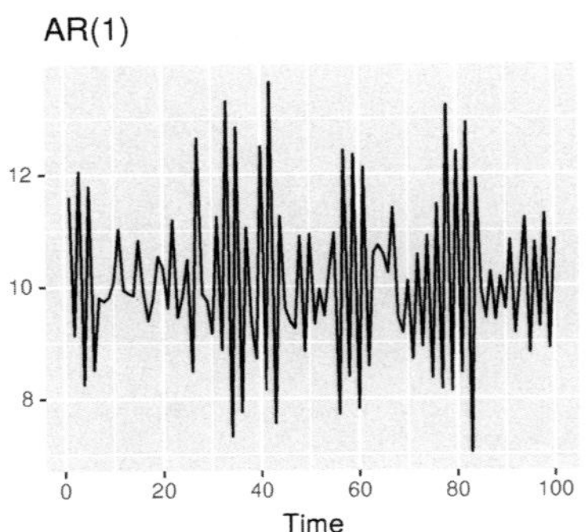

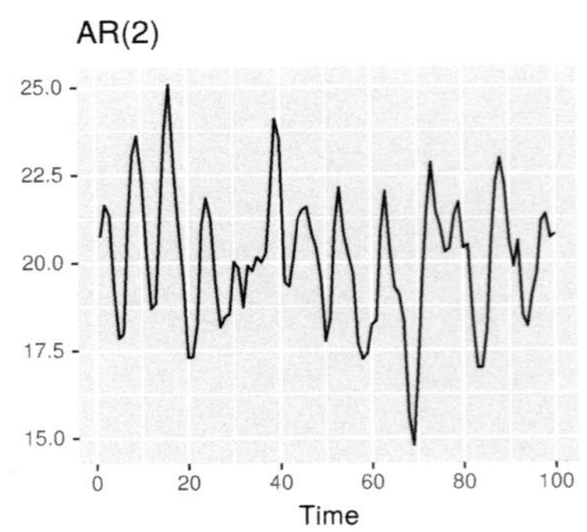

Figure 8.5: Two examples of data from autoregressive models with different parameters. Left: AR(1) with $y_t = 18 - 0.8y_{t-1} + \varepsilon_t$. Right: AR(2) with $y_t = 8 + 1.3y_{t-1} - 0.7y_{t-2} + \varepsilon_t$. In both cases, ε_t is normally distributed white noise with mean zero and variance one.

- when $\phi_1 = 1$ and $c \neq 0$, y_t is equivalent to a random walk with drift;
- when $\phi_1 < 0$, y_t tends to oscillate between positive and negative values;

We normally restrict autoregressive models to stationary data, in which case some constraints on the values of the parameters are required.

- For an AR(1) model: $-1 < \phi_1 < 1$.
- For an AR(2) model: $-1 < \phi_2 < 1$, $\phi_1 + \phi_2 < 1$,

When $p \geq 3$, the restrictions are much more complicated. R takes care of these restrictions when estimating a model.

8.4 Moving average models

Rather than using past values of the forecast variable in a regression, a moving average model uses past forecast errors in a regression-like model.

$$y_t = c + \varepsilon_t + \theta_1\varepsilon_{t-1} + \theta_2\varepsilon_{t-2} + \cdots + \theta_q\varepsilon_{t-q},$$

where ε_t is white noise. We refer to this as an **MA(q) model**, a moving average model of order q. Of course, we do not *observe* the values of ε_t, so it is not really a regression in the usual sense.

Notice that each value of y_t can be thought of as a weighted moving average of the past few forecast errors. However, moving average *models* should not be confused with the moving average *smoothing* we discussed in Chapter 6. A moving average model is used for forecasting future values, while moving

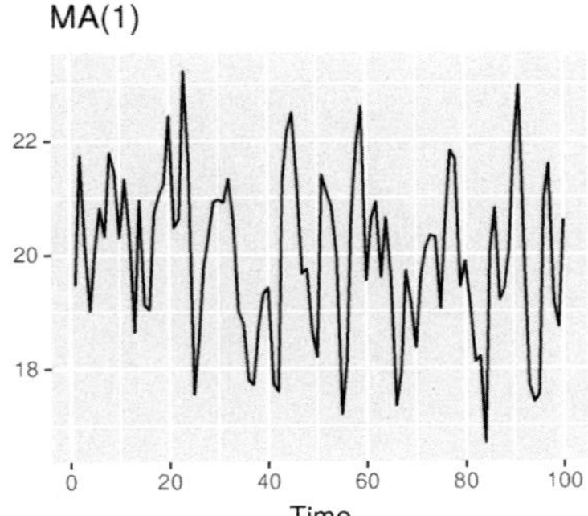

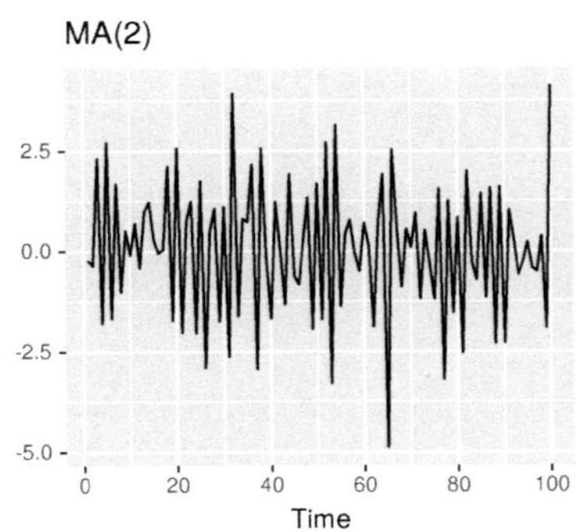

Figure 8.6: Two examples of data from moving average models with different parameters. Left: MA(1) with $y_t = 20 + \varepsilon_t + 0.8\varepsilon_{t-1}$. Right: MA(2) with $y_t = \varepsilon_t - \varepsilon_{t-1} + 0.8\varepsilon_{t-2}$. In both cases, ε_t is normally distributed white noise with mean zero and variance one.

average smoothing is used for estimating the trend-cycle of past values.

Figure 8.6 shows some data from an MA(1) model and an MA(2) model. Changing the parameters $\theta_1, \dots, \theta_q$ results in different time series patterns. As with autoregressive models, the variance of the error term ε_t will only change the scale of the series, not the patterns.

It is possible to write any stationary AR(p) model as an MA(∞) model. For example, using repeated substitution, we can demonstrate this for an AR(1) model:

$$\begin{aligned}
y_t &= \phi_1 y_{t-1} + \varepsilon_t \\
&= \phi_1(\phi_1 y_{t-2} + \varepsilon_{t-1}) + \varepsilon_t \\
&= \phi_1^2 y_{t-2} + \phi_1 \varepsilon_{t-1} + \varepsilon_t \\
&= \phi_1^3 y_{t-3} + \phi_1^2 \varepsilon_{t-2} + \phi_1 \varepsilon_{t-1} + \varepsilon_t \\
&\text{etc.}
\end{aligned}$$

Provided $-1 < \phi_1 < 1$, the value of ϕ_1^k will get smaller as k gets larger. So eventually we obtain

$$y_t = \varepsilon_t + \phi_1 \varepsilon_{t-1} + \phi_1^2 \varepsilon_{t-2} + \phi_1^3 \varepsilon_{t-3} + \cdots,$$

an MA(∞) process.

The reverse result holds if we impose some constraints on the MA parameters. Then the MA model is called **invertible**. That is, we can write any invertible MA(q) process as an AR(∞) process. Invertible models are not simply introduced to enable us to convert from MA models to AR models. They also have some desirable mathematical properties.

For example, consider the MA(1) process, $y_t = \varepsilon_t + \theta_1\varepsilon_{t-1}$. In its AR($\infty$) representation, the most recent error can be written as a linear function of current and past observations:

$$\varepsilon_t = \sum_{j=0}^{\infty}(-\theta)^j y_{t-j}.$$

When $|\theta| > 1$, the weights increase as lags increase, so the more distant the observations the greater their influence on the current error. When $|\theta| = 1$, the weights are constant in size, and the distant observations have the same influence as the recent observations. As neither of these situations make much sense, we require $|\theta| < 1$, so the most recent observations have higher weight than observations from the more distant past. Thus, the process is invertible when $|\theta| < 1$.

The invertibility constraints for other models are similar to the stationarity constraints.

- For an MA(1) model: $-1 < \theta_1 < 1$.
- For an MA(2) model: $-1 < \theta_2 < 1,\ \ \theta_2 + \theta_1 > -1,\ \ \theta_1 - \theta_2 < 1$.

More complicated conditions hold for $q \geq 3$. Again, R will take care of these constraints when estimating the models.

8.5 Non-seasonal ARIMA models

If we combine differencing with autoregression and a moving average model, we obtain a non-seasonal ARIMA model. ARIMA is an acronym for AutoRegressive Integrated Moving Average (in this context, "integration" is the reverse of differencing). The full model can be written as

$$y'_t = c + \phi_1 y'_{t-1} + \cdots + \phi_p y'_{t-p} + \theta_1\varepsilon_{t-1} + \cdots + \theta_q\varepsilon_{t-q} + \varepsilon_t, \qquad (8.1)$$

where y'_t is the differenced series (it may have been differenced more than once). The "predictors" on the right hand side include both lagged values of y_t and lagged errors. We call this an **ARIMA(p, d, q) model**, where

$p =$	order of the autoregressive part;
$d =$	degree of first differencing involved;
$q =$	order of the moving average part.

The same stationarity and invertibility conditions that are used for autoregressive and moving average models also apply to an ARIMA model.

Many of the models we have already discussed are special cases of the ARIMA model, as shown in Table 8.1.

White noise	ARIMA(0,0,0)
Random walk	ARIMA(0,1,0) with no constant
Random walk with drift	ARIMA(0,1,0) with a constant
Autoregression	ARIMA(p,0,0)
Moving average	ARIMA(0,0,q)

Table 8.1: Special cases of ARIMA models.

Once we start combining components in this way to form more complicated models, it is much easier to work with the backshift notation. For example, Equation (8.1) can be written in backshift notation as

$$\underset{\text{AR}(p)}{\underbrace{(1-\phi_1 B - \cdots - \phi_p B^p)}} \quad \underset{d\text{ differences}}{\underbrace{(1-B)^d y_t}} \quad = \quad c + \underset{\text{MA}(q)}{\underbrace{(1+\theta_1 B + \cdots + \theta_q B^q)\varepsilon_t}} \tag{8.2}$$

R uses a slightly different parametrization:

$$(1-\phi_1 B - \cdots - \phi_p B^p)(y'_t - \mu) = (1+\theta_1 B + \cdots + \theta_q B^q)\varepsilon_t,$$

where $y'_t = (1-B)^d y_t$ and μ is the mean of y'_t. To convert to the form given by (8.2), set $c = \mu(1-\phi_1 - \cdots - \phi_p)$.

Selecting appropriate values for p, d and q can be difficult. However, the `auto.arima()` function in R will do it for you automatically. In Section 8.7, we will learn how this function works, along with some methods for choosing these values yourself.

US consumption expenditure

Figure 8.7 shows quarterly percentage changes in US consumption expenditure. Although it is a quarterly series, there does not appear to be a seasonal pattern, so we will fit a non-seasonal ARIMA model.

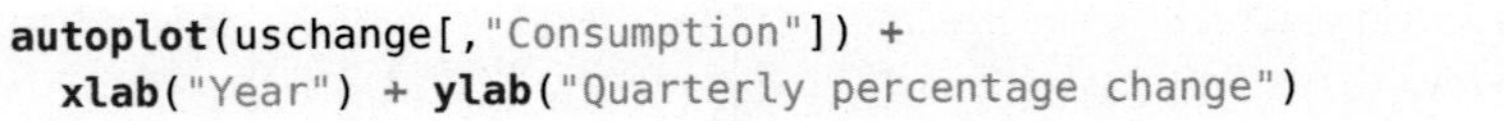

```
autoplot(uschange[,"Consumption"]) +
  xlab("Year") + ylab("Quarterly percentage change")
```

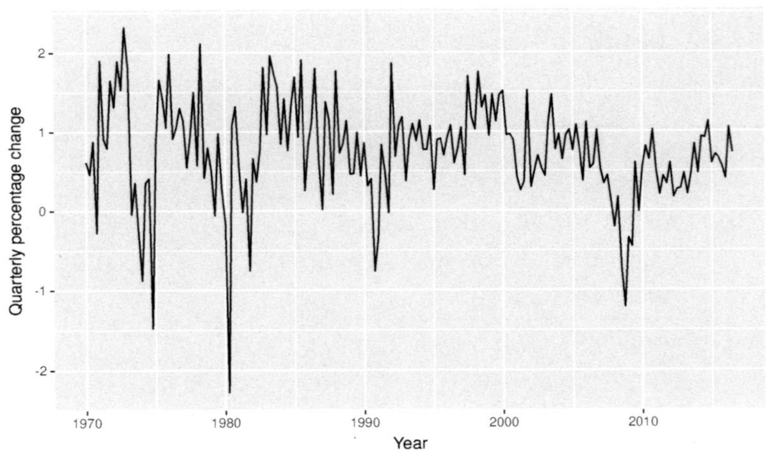

Figure 8.7: Quarterly percentage change in US consumption expenditure.

The following R code was used to select a model automatically.

```
(fit <- auto.arima(uschange[,"Consumption"]))
#> Series: uschange[, "Consumption"]
#> ARIMA(2,0,2) with non-zero mean
#>
#> Coefficients:
#>          ar1     ar2     ma1    ma2   mean
#>        1.391  -0.581  -1.180  0.558  0.746
#> s.e.   0.255   0.208   0.238  0.140  0.084
#>
#> sigma^2 estimated as 0.351:  log likelihood=-165.1
#> AIC=342.3   AICc=342.8   BIC=361.7
```

This is an ARIMA(2,0,2) model:

$$y_t = c + 1.391y_{t-1} - 0.581y_{t-2} - 1.180\varepsilon_{t-1} + 0.558\varepsilon_{t-2} + \varepsilon_t,$$

where $c = 0.746 \times (1 - 1.391 + 0.581) = 0.142$ and ε_t is white noise with a standard deviation of $0.593 = \sqrt{0.351}$. Forecasts from the model are shown in Figure 8.8.

```
fit %>% forecast(h=10) %>% autoplot(include=80)
```

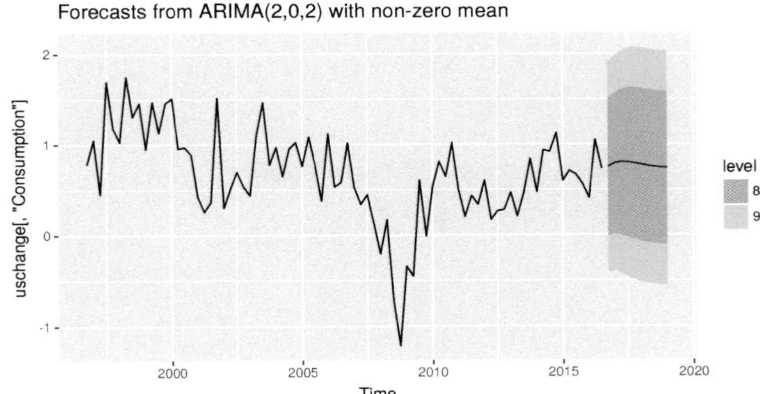

Figure 8.8: Forecasts of quarterly percentage changes in US consumption expenditure.

Understanding ARIMA models

The `auto.arima()` function is very useful, but anything automated can be a little dangerous, and it is worth understanding something of the behaviour of the models even when you rely on an automatic procedure to choose the model for you.

The constant c has an important effect on the long-term forecasts obtained from these models.

- If $c = 0$ and $d = 0$, the long-term forecasts will go to zero.
- If $c = 0$ and $d = 1$, the long-term forecasts will go to a non-zero constant.
- If $c = 0$ and $d = 2$, the long-term forecasts will follow a straight line.
- If $c \neq 0$ and $d = 0$, the long-term forecasts will go to the mean of the data.
- If $c \neq 0$ and $d = 1$, the long-term forecasts will follow a straight line.
- If $c \neq 0$ and $d = 2$, the long-term forecasts will follow a quadratic trend.

The value of d also has an effect on the prediction intervals — the higher the value of d, the more rapidly the prediction intervals increase in size. For $d = 0$, the long-term forecast standard deviation will go to the standard deviation of the historical data, so the prediction intervals will all be essentially the same.

This behaviour is seen in Figure 8.8 where $d = 0$ and $c \neq 0$. In this figure, the prediction intervals are almost the same for the last few forecast horizons, and the point forecasts are equal to the mean of the data.

The value of p is important if the data show cycles. To obtain cyclic forecasts, it is necessary to have $p \geq 2$, along with some additional conditions on the parameters. For an AR(2) model, cyclic behaviour occurs if $\phi_1^2 + 4\phi_2 < 0$. In that case, the average period of the cycles is [3]

$$\frac{2\pi}{\text{arc cos}(-\phi_1(1-\phi_2)/(4\phi_2))}.$$

[3] arc cos is the inverse cosine function. You should be able to find it on your calculator. It may be labelled acos or $\cos^{-1}$.

ACF and PACF plots

It is usually not possible to tell, simply from a time plot, what values of p and q are appropriate for the data. However, it is sometimes possible to use the ACF plot, and the closely related PACF plot, to determine appropriate values for p and q.

Recall that an ACF plot shows the autocorrelations which measure the relationship between y_t and y_{t-k} for different values of k. Now if y_t and y_{t-1} are correlated, then y_{t-1} and y_{t-2} must also be correlated. However, then y_t and y_{t-2} might be correlated, simply because they are both connected to y_{t-1}, rather than because of any new information contained in y_{t-2} that could be used in forecasting y_t.

To overcome this problem, we can use **partial autocorrelations**. These measure the relationship between y_t and y_{t-k} after removing the effects of lags $1, 2, 3, \dots, k-1$. So the first partial autocorrelation is identical to the first autocorrelation, because there is nothing between them to remove. Each partial autocorrelation can be estimated as the last coefficient in an autoregressive model. Specifically, α_k, the kth partial autocorrelation coefficient, is equal to the estimate of ϕ_k in an AR(k) model. In practice, there are more efficient algorithms for computing α_k than fitting all of these autoregressions, but they give the same results.

Figures 8.9 and 8.10 shows the ACF and PACF plots for the US consumption data shown in Figure 8.7. The partial autocorrelations have the same critical values of $\pm 1.96/\sqrt{T}$ as for ordinary autocorrelations, and these are typically shown on the plot as in Figure 8.9.

```
ggAcf(uschange[,"Consumption"],main="")
```

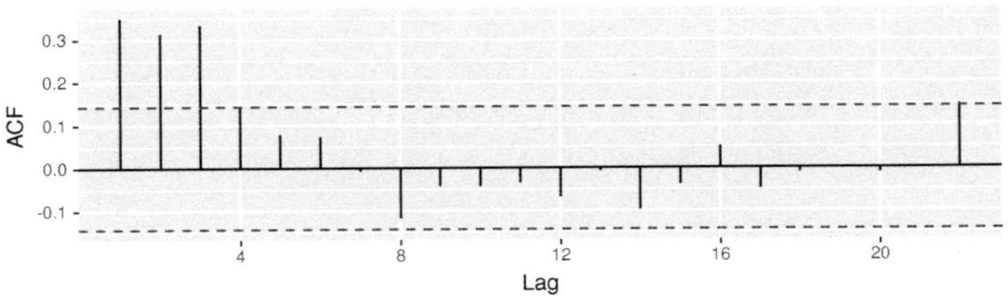

Figure 8.9: ACF of quarterly percentage change in US consumption.

```
ggPacf(uschange[,"Consumption"],main="")
```

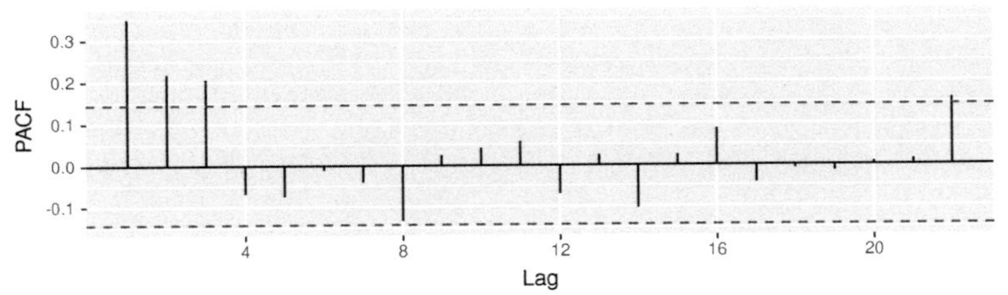

Figure 8.10: PACF of quarterly percentage change in US consumption.

If the data are from an ARIMA(p,d,0) or ARIMA(0,d,q) model, then the ACF and PACF plots can be helpful in determining the value of p or q.[4] If p and q are both positive, then the plots do not help in finding suitable values of p and q.

[4] A convenient way to produce a time plot, ACF plot and PACF plot in one command is to use the `ggtsdisplay()` function.

The data may follow an ARIMA(p,d,0) model if the ACF and PACF plots of the differenced data show the following patterns:

- the ACF is exponentially decaying or sinusoidal;
- there is a significant spike at lag p in the PACF, but none beyond lag p.

The data may follow an ARIMA(0,d,q) model if the ACF and PACF plots of the differenced data show the following patterns:

- the PACF is exponentially decaying or sinusoidal;
- there is a significant spike at lag q in the ACF, but none beyond lag q.

In Figure 8.9, we see that there are three spikes in the ACF, followed by an almost significant spike at lag 4. In the PACF, there are three significant spikes, and then no significant spikes thereafter (apart from one just outside the bounds at lag 22). We can ignore one significant spike in each plot if it is just outside the limits, and not in the first few lags. After all, the probability of a spike being significant by chance is about one in twenty, and we are plotting 22 spikes in each plot. The pattern in the first three spikes is what we would expect from an ARIMA(3,0,0), as the PACF tends to decrease. So in this case, the ACF and PACF lead us to think an ARIMA(3,0,0) model might be appropriate.

```
(fit2 <- Arima(uschange[,"Consumption"], order=c(3,0,0)))
#> Series: uschange[, "Consumption"]
#> ARIMA(3,0,0) with non-zero mean
#>
#> Coefficients:
#>          ar1    ar2    ar3   mean
#>        0.227  0.160  0.203  0.745
#> s.e.   0.071  0.072  0.071  0.103
#>
#> sigma^2 estimated as 0.349:  log likelihood=-165.2
#> AIC=340.3   AICc=340.7   BIC=356.5
```

This model is actually slightly better than the model identified by `auto.arima()` (with an AICc value of 340.67 compared to 342.75). The `auto.arima()` function did not find this model because it does not consider all possible models in its search. You can make it work harder by using the arguments `stepwise=FALSE` and `approximation=FALSE`:

```
(fit3 <- auto.arima(uschange[,"Consumption"], seasonal=FALSE,
  stepwise=FALSE, approximation=FALSE))
#> Series: uschange[, "Consumption"]
#> ARIMA(3,0,0) with non-zero mean
#>
#> Coefficients:
#>          ar1    ar2    ar3   mean
#>        0.227  0.160  0.203  0.745
#> s.e.   0.071  0.072  0.071  0.103
#>
#> sigma^2 estimated as 0.349:  log likelihood=-165.2
#> AIC=340.3   AICc=340.7   BIC=356.5
```

We also use the argument `seasonal=FALSE` to prevent it searching for seasonal ARIMA models; we will consider these models in Section 8.9.

This time, `auto.arima()` has found the same model that we guessed from the ACF and PACF plots. The forecasts from this ARIMA(3,0,0) model are almost identical to those shown in Figure 8.8 for the ARIMA(2,0,2) model, so we do not produce the plot here.

8.6 Estimation and order selection

Maximum likelihood estimation

Once the model order has been identified (i.e., the values of p, d and q), we need to estimate the parameters $c, \phi_1, \dots, \phi_p, \theta_1, \dots, \theta_q$. When R estimates the ARIMA model, it uses *maximum likelihood estimation* (MLE). This technique finds the values of the parameters which maximize the probability of obtaining the data that we have observed. For ARIMA models, MLE is very similar to the *least squares* estimates that would be obtained by minimizing

$$\sum_{t=1}^{T} \varepsilon_t^2.$$

(For the regression models considered in Chapter 5, MLE gives exactly the same parameter estimates as least squares estimation.) Note that ARIMA models are much more complicated to estimate than regression models, and different software will give slightly different answers as they use different methods of estimation, and different optimization algorithms.

In practice, R will report the value of the *log likelihood* of the data; that is, the logarithm of the probability of the observed data coming from the estimated model. For given values of p, d and q, R will try to maximize the log likelihood when finding parameter estimates.

Information Criteria

Akaike's Information Criterion (AIC), which was useful in selecting predictors for regression, is also useful for determining the order of an ARIMA model. It can be written as

$$\text{AIC} = -2\log(L) + 2(p+q+k+1),$$

where L is the likelihood of the data, $k = 1$ if $c \neq 0$ and $k = 0$ if $c = 0$. Note that the last term in parentheses is the number of parameters in the model (including σ^2, the variance of the residuals).

For ARIMA models, the corrected AIC can be written as

$$\text{AICc} = \text{AIC} + \frac{2(p+q+k+1)(p+q+k+2)}{T-p-q-k-2},$$

and the Bayesian Information Criterion can be written as

$$\text{BIC} = \text{AIC} + [\log(T) - 2](p + q + k + 1).$$

Good models are obtained by minimizing the AIC, AICc or BIC. Our preference is to use the AICc.

It is important to note that these information criteria tend not to be good guides to selecting the appropriate order of differencing (d) of a model, but only for selecting the values of p and q. This is because the differencing changes the data on which the likelihood is computed, making the AIC values between models with different orders of differencing not comparable. So we need to use some other approach to choose d, and then we can use the AICc to select p and q.

8.7 ARIMA modelling in R

How does `auto.arima()` work?

The `auto.arima()` function in R uses a variation of the Hyndman-Khandakar algorithm (Hyndman and Khandakar 2008), which combines unit root tests, minimization of the AICc and MLE to obtain an ARIMA model. The algorithm follows the steps shown on the following page. The arguments to `auto.arima()` provide for many variations on the algorithm. What is described here is the default behaviour.

The default procedure uses some approximations to speed up the search. These approximations can be avoided with the argument `approximation=FALSE`. It is possible that the minimum AICc model will not be found due to these approximations, or because of the use of a stepwise procedure. A much larger set of models will be searched if the argument `stepwise=FALSE` is used. See the help file for a full description of the arguments.

Choosing your own model

If you want to choose the model yourself, use the `Arima()` function in R. There is another function `arima()` in R which also fits an ARIMA model. However, it does not allow for the constant c unless $d = 0$, and it does not return everything required for other functions in the **forecast** package to work. Finally, it does not allow the estimated model to be applied

---

Hyndman-Khandakar algorithm for automatic ARIMA modelling

1. The number of differences d is determined using repeated KPSS tests.
2. The values of p and q are then chosen by minimizing the AICc after differencing the data d times. Rather than considering every possible combination of p and q, the algorithm uses a stepwise search to traverse the model space.
   (a) Four initial models are fitted:
   ARIMA$(0, d, 0)$,
   ARIMA$(2, d, 2)$,
   ARIMA$(1, d, 0)$,
   ARIMA$(0, d, 1)$.
   A constant is included unless $d = 2$. If $d \leq 1$, an additional model is also fitted:
   ARIMA$(0, d, 0)$ without a constant.
   (b) The best model (with the smallest AICc value) fitted in step (a) is set to be the "current model".
   (c) Variations on the current model are considered:
   - vary p and/or q from the current model by ± 1;
   - include/exclude c from the current model.

   The best model considered so far (either the current model, or one of these variations) becomes the new current model.
   (d) Repeat Step 2(b) until no lower AICc can be found.

---

to new data (which is useful for checking forecast accuracy). Consequently, it is recommended that `Arima()` be used instead.

Modelling procedure

When fitting an ARIMA model to a set of (non-seasonal) time series data, the following procedure provides a useful general approach.

1. Plot the data and identify any unusual observations.
2. If necessary, transform the data (using a Box-Cox transformation) to stabilize the variance.
3. If the data are non-stationary, take first differences of the data until the data are stationary.

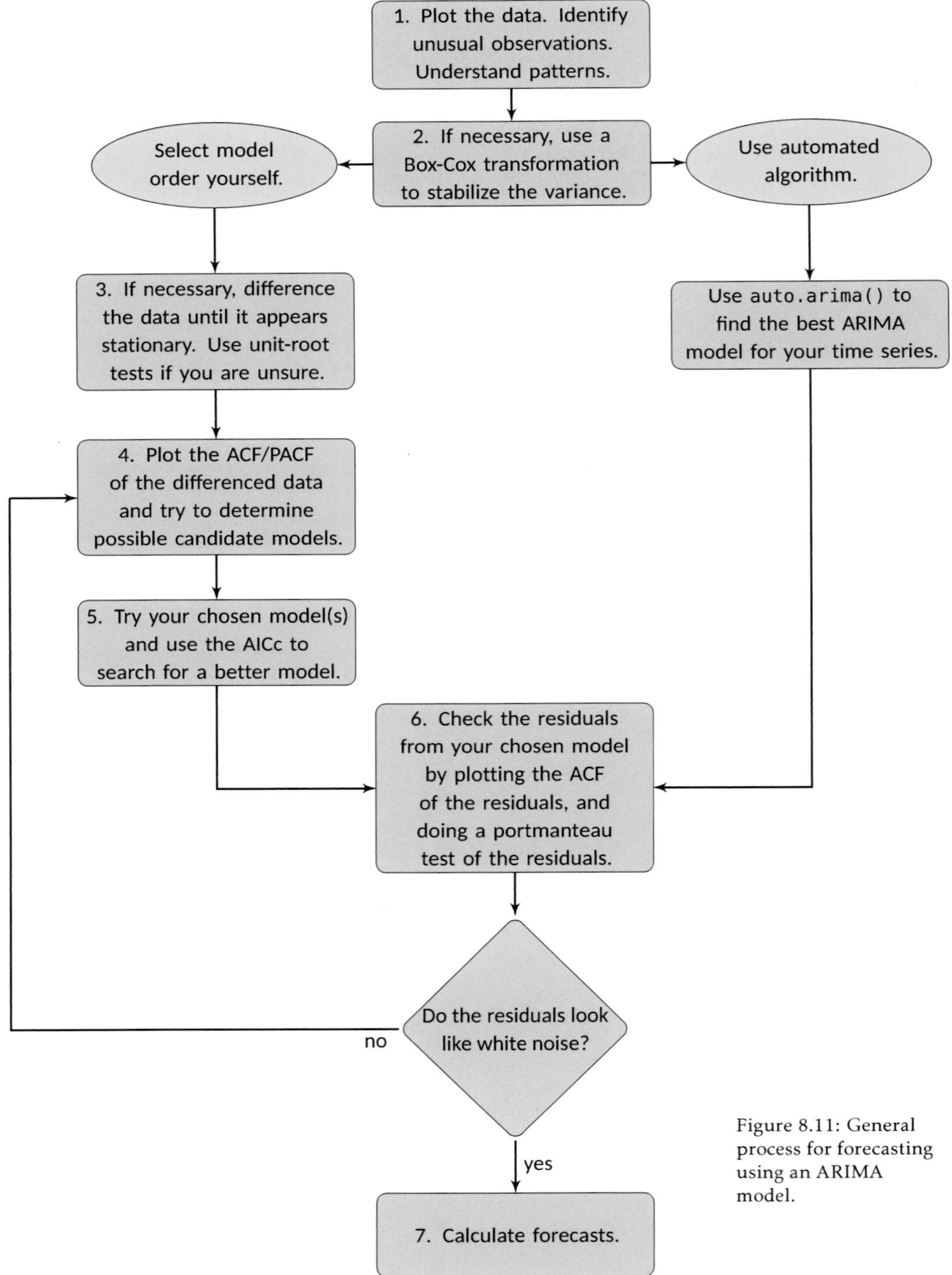

Figure 8.11: General process for forecasting using an ARIMA model.

4. Examine the ACF/PACF: Is an ARIMA($p, d, 0$) or ARIMA($0, d, q$) model appropriate?
5. Try your chosen model(s), and use the AICc to search for a better model.
6. Check the residuals from your chosen model by plotting the ACF of the residuals, and doing a portmanteau test of the residuals. If they do not look like white noise, try a modified model.
7. Once the residuals look like white noise, calculate forecasts.

The Hyndman-Khandakar algorithm only takes care of steps 3–5. So even if you use it, you will still need to take care of the other steps yourself.

The process is summarised in Figure 8.11.

Example: Seasonally adjusted electrical equipment orders

We will apply this procedure to the seasonally adjusted electrical equipment orders data shown in Figure 8.12.

```
elecequip %>% stl(s.window='periodic') %>% seasadj() -> eeadj
autoplot(eeadj)
```

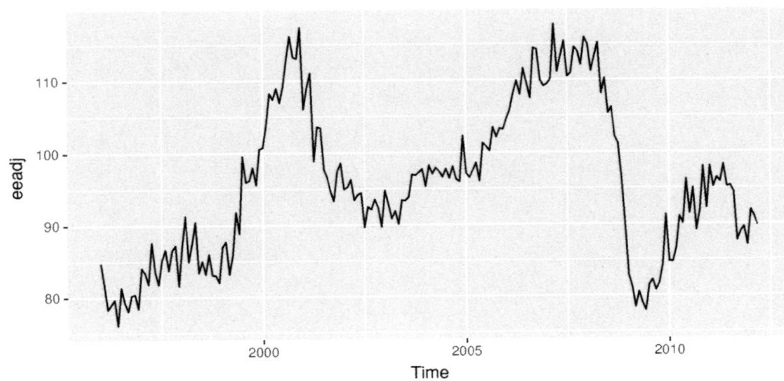

Figure 8.12: Seasonally adjusted electrical equipment orders index in the Euro area.

1. The time plot shows some sudden changes, particularly the big drop in 2008/2009. These changes are due to the global economic environment. Otherwise there is nothing unusual about the time plot and there appears to be no need to do any data adjustments.

2. There is no evidence of changing variance, so we will not do a Box-Cox transformation.

3. The data are clearly non-stationary, as the series wanders up and down for long periods. Consequently, we will take a first difference of the data. The differenced data are shown in Figure 8.13. These look stationary, and so we will not consider further differences.

```
eeadj %>% diff() %>% ggtsdisplay(main="")
```

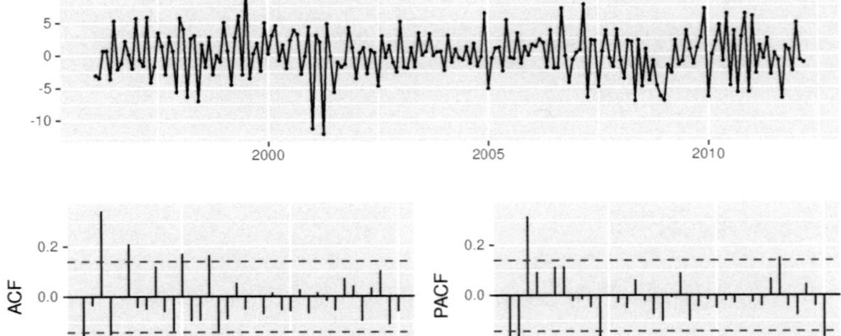

Figure 8.13: Time plot and ACF and PACF plots for the differenced seasonally adjusted electrical equipment data.

4. The PACF shown in Figure 8.13 is suggestive of an AR(3) model. So an initial candidate model is an ARIMA(3,1,0). There are no other obvious candidate models.

5. We fit an ARIMA(3,1,0) model along with variations including ARIMA(4,1,0), ARIMA(2,1,0), ARIMA(3,1,1), etc. Of these, the ARIMA(3,1,1) has a slightly smaller AICc value.

```
(fit <- Arima(eeadj, order=c(3,1,1)))
#> Series: eeadj
#> ARIMA(3,1,1)
#>
#> Coefficients:
#>          ar1    ar2    ar3     ma1
#>        0.004  0.092  0.370  -0.392
#> s.e.   0.220  0.098  0.067   0.243
#>
#> sigma^2 estimated as 9.58:  log likelihood=-492.7
#> AIC=995.4   AICc=995.7   BIC=1012
```

6. The ACF plot of the residuals from the ARIMA(3,1,1) model shows that all autocorrelations are within the threshold limits, indicating that the residuals are behaving like white noise. A portmanteau test returns a large p-value, also suggesting that the residuals are white noise.

```
checkresiduals(fit)
```

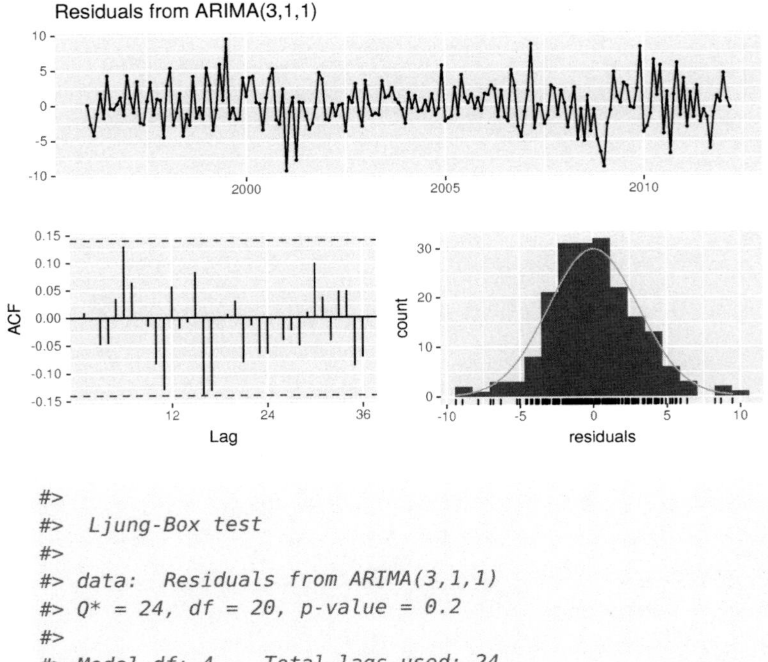

Figure 8.14: Residual plots for the ARIMA(3,1,1) model.

```
#>
#>  Ljung-Box test
#>
#> data:  Residuals from ARIMA(3,1,1)
#> Q* = 24, df = 20, p-value = 0.2
#>
#> Model df: 4.   Total lags used: 24
```

7. Forecasts from the chosen model are shown in Figure 8.15.

```
autoplot(forecast(fit))
```

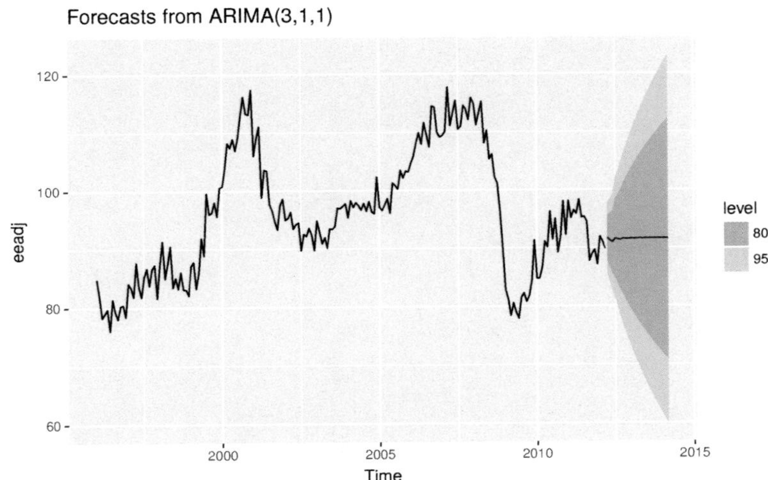

Figure 8.15: Forecasts for the seasonally adjusted electrical orders index.

If we had used the automated algorithm instead, we would have obtained an ARIMA(3,1,0) model using the default settings, but the ARIMA(3,1,1) model if we had set `approximation=FALSE`.

Understanding constants in R

A non-seasonal ARIMA model can be written as

$$(1-\phi_1 B-\cdots-\phi_p B^p)(1-B)^d y_t = c+(1+\theta_1 B+\cdots+\theta_q B^q)\varepsilon_t, \quad (8.3)$$

or equivalently as

$$(1-\phi_1 B-\cdots-\phi_p B^p)(1-B)^d (y_t-\mu t^d/d!) = (1+\theta_1 B+\cdots+\theta_q B^q)\varepsilon_t, \quad (8.4)$$

where $c=\mu(1-\phi_1-\cdots-\phi_p)$ and μ is the mean of $(1-B)^d y_t$. R uses the parametrization of Equation (8.4).

Thus, the inclusion of a constant in a non-stationary ARIMA model is equivalent to inducing a polynomial trend of order d in the forecast function. (If the constant is omitted, the forecast function includes a polynomial trend of order $d-1$.) When $d=0$, we have the special case that μ is the mean of y_t.

By default, the `Arima()` function sets $c=\mu=0$ when $d>0$ and provides an estimate of μ when $d=0$. It will be close to the sample mean of the time series, but usually not identical to it as the sample mean is not the maximum likelihood estimate when $p+q>0$.

The argument `include.mean` only has an effect when $d=0$ and is `TRUE` by default. Setting `include.mean=FALSE` will force $\mu=c=0$.

The argument `include.drift` allows $\mu\neq 0$ when $d=1$. For $d>1$, no constant is allowed as a quadratic or higher order trend is particularly dangerous when forecasting. The parameter μ is called the "drift" in the R output when $d=1$.

There is also an argument `include.constant` which, if `TRUE`, will set `include.mean=TRUE` if $d=0$ and `include.drift=TRUE` when $d=1$. If `include.constant=FALSE`, both `include.mean` and `include.drift` will be set to `FALSE`. If `include.constant` is used, the values of `include.mean=TRUE` and `include.drift=TRUE` are ignored.

The `auto.arima()` function automates the inclusion of a constant. By default, for $d = 0$ or $d = 1$, a constant will be included if it improves the AICc value; for $d > 1$ the constant is always omitted. If `allowdrift=FALSE` is specified, then the constant is only allowed when $d = 0$.

Plotting the characteristic roots

(This is a more advanced section and can be skipped if desired.)

We can re-write Equation (8.3) as

$$\phi(B)(1-B)^d y_t = c + \theta(B)\varepsilon_t$$

where $\phi(B) = (1 - \phi_1 B - \cdots - \phi_p B^p)$ is a pth order polynomial in B and $\theta(B) = (1 + \theta_1 B + \cdots + \theta_q B^q)$ is a qth order polynomial in B.

The stationarity conditions for the model are that the p complex roots of $\phi(B)$ lie outside the unit circle, and the invertibility conditions are that the q complex roots of $\theta(B)$ lie outside the unit circle. So we can see whether the model is close to invertibility or stationarity by a plot of the roots in relation to the complex unit circle.

It is easier to plot the inverse roots instead, as they should all lie *within* the unit circle. This is easily done in R. For the ARIMA(3,1,1) model fitted to the seasonally adjusted electrical equipment index, we obtain Figure 8.16.

```
autoplot(fit)
```

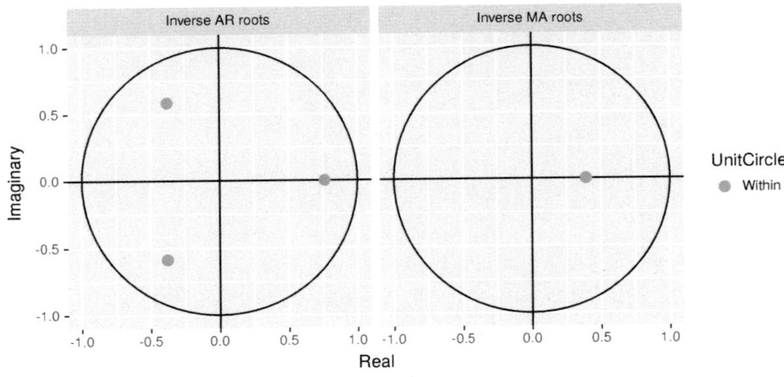

Figure 8.16: Inverse characteristic roots for the ARMA(3,1,1) model fitted to the seasonally adjusted electrical equipment index.

The three red dots in the left hand plot correspond to the roots of the polynomials $\phi(B)$, while the red dot in the right hand plot corresponds to the root of $\theta(B)$. They are all inside the unit circle, as we would expect because R ensures the fitted model is both stationary and invertible. Any roots close to the unit circle may be numerically unstable, and the corresponding model will not be good for forecasting.

The `Arima()` function will never return a model with inverse roots outside the unit circle. The `auto.arima()` function is even stricter, and will not select a model with roots close to the unit circle either.

8.8 Forecasting

Point forecasts

Although we have calculated forecasts from the ARIMA models in our examples, we have not yet explained how they are obtained. Point forecasts can be calculated using the following three steps.

1. Expand the ARIMA equation so that y_t is on the left hand side and all other terms are on the right.
2. Rewrite the equation by replacing t with $T+h$.
3. On the right hand side of the equation, replace future observations with their forecasts, future errors with zero, and past errors with the corresponding residuals.

Beginning with $h = 1$, these steps are then repeated for $h = 2,3,\ldots$ until all forecasts have been calculated.

The procedure is most easily understood via an example. We will illustrate it using the ARIMA(3,1,1) model fitted in the previous section. The model can be written as follows:

$$(1-\hat{\phi}_1 B-\hat{\phi}_2 B^2-\hat{\phi}_3 B^3)(1-B)y_t=(1+\hat{\theta}_1 B)\varepsilon_t,$$

where $\hat{\phi}_1 = 0.0044$, $\hat{\phi}_2 = 0.0916$, $\hat{\phi}_3 = 0.3698$ and $\hat{\theta}_1 = -0.3921$. Then we expand the left hand side to obtain

$$\left[1-(1+\hat{\phi}_1)B+(\hat{\phi}_1-\hat{\phi}_2)B^2+(\hat{\phi}_2-\hat{\phi}_3)B^3+\hat{\phi}_3 B^4\right]y_t=(1+\hat{\theta}_1 B)\varepsilon_t,$$

and applying the backshift operator gives

$$y_t-(1+\hat{\phi}_1)y_{t-1}+(\hat{\phi}_1-\hat{\phi}_2)y_{t-2}+(\hat{\phi}_2-\hat{\phi}_3)y_{t-3}+\hat{\phi}_3 y_{t-4}=\varepsilon_t+\hat{\theta}_1\varepsilon_{t-1}.$$

Finally, we move all terms other than y_t to the right hand side:

$$y_t = (1+\hat{\phi}_1)y_{t-1} - (\hat{\phi}_1 - \hat{\phi}_2)y_{t-2} - (\hat{\phi}_2 - \hat{\phi}_3)y_{t-3} - \hat{\phi}_3 y_{t-4} + \varepsilon_t + \hat{\theta}_1 \varepsilon_{t-1}. \tag{8.5}$$

This completes the first step. While the equation now looks like an ARIMA(4,0,1), it is still the same ARIMA(3,1,1) model we started with. It cannot be considered an ARIMA(4,0,1) because the coefficients do not satisfy the stationarity conditions.

For the second step, we replace t with $T+1$ in (8.5):

$$y_{T+1} = (1+\hat{\phi}_1)y_T - (\hat{\phi}_1 - \hat{\phi}_2)y_{T-1} - (\hat{\phi}_2 - \hat{\phi}_3)y_{T-2} - \hat{\phi}_3 y_{T-3} + \varepsilon_{T+1} + \hat{\theta}_1 \varepsilon_T.$$

Assuming we have observations up to time T, all values on the right hand side are known except for ε_{T+1}, which we replace with zero, and ε_T, which we replace with the last observed residual e_T:

$$\hat{y}_{T+1|T} = (1+\hat{\phi}_1)y_T - (\hat{\phi}_1 - \hat{\phi}_2)y_{T-1} - (\hat{\phi}_2 - \hat{\phi}_3)y_{T-2} - \hat{\phi}_3 y_{T-3} + \hat{\theta}_1 e_T.$$

A forecast of y_{T+2} is obtained by replacing t with $T+2$ in (8.5) . All values on the right hand side will be known at time T except y_{T+1} which we replace with $\hat{y}_{T+1|T}$, and ε_{T+2} and ε_{T+1}, both of which we replace with zero:

$$\hat{y}_{T+2|T} = (1+\hat{\phi}_1)\hat{y}_{T+1|T} - (\hat{\phi}_1 - \hat{\phi}_2)y_T - (\hat{\phi}_2 - \hat{\phi}_3)y_{T-1} - \hat{\phi}_3 y_{T-2}.$$

The process continues in this manner for all future time periods. In this way, any number of point forecasts can be obtained.

Prediction intervals

The calculation of ARIMA prediction intervals is more difficult, and the details are largely beyond the scope of this book. We will only give some simple examples.

The first prediction interval is easy to calculate. If $\hat{\sigma}$ is the standard deviation of the residuals, then a 95% prediction interval is given by $\hat{y}_{T+1|T} \pm 1.96\hat{\sigma}$. This result is true for all ARIMA models regardless of their parameters and orders.

Multi-step prediction intervals for ARIMA(0,0,q) models are relatively easy to calculate. We can write the model as

$$y_t = \varepsilon_t + \sum_{i=1}^{q} \theta_i \varepsilon_{t-i}.$$

Then, the estimated forecast variance can be written as

$$\hat{\sigma}_h = \hat{\sigma}^2 \left[1 + \sum_{i=1}^{h-1} \hat{\theta}_i^2 \right], \qquad \text{for } h = 2, 3, \dots,$$

and a 95% prediction interval is given by $\hat{y}_{T+h|T} \pm 1.96\sqrt{\hat{\sigma}_h}$.

In Section 8.4, we showed that an AR(1) model can be written as an MA(∞) model. Using this equivalence, the above result for MA(q) models can also be used to obtain prediction intervals for AR(1) models.

More general results, and other special cases of multi-step prediction intervals for an ARIMA(p,d,q) model, are given in more advanced textbooks such as Brockwell and Davis (2016).

The prediction intervals for ARIMA models are based on assumptions that the residuals are uncorrelated and normally distributed. If either of these assumptions does not hold, then the prediction intervals may be incorrect. For this reason, always plot the ACF and histogram of the residuals to check the assumptions before producing prediction intervals.

In general, prediction intervals from ARIMA models increase as the forecast horizon increases. For stationary models (i.e., with $d = 0$) they will converge, so that prediction intervals for long horizons are all essentially the same. For $d > 1$, the prediction intervals will continue to grow into the future.

As with most prediction interval calculations, ARIMA-based intervals tend to be too narrow. This occurs because only the variation in the errors has been accounted for. There is also variation in the parameter estimates, and in the model order, that has not been included in the calculation. In addition, the calculation assumes that the historical patterns that have been modelled will continue into the forecast period.

8.9 Seasonal ARIMA models

So far, we have restricted our attention to non-seasonal data and non-seasonal ARIMA models. However, ARIMA models are also capable of modelling a wide range of seasonal data.

A seasonal ARIMA model is formed by including additional seasonal terms in the ARIMA models we have seen so far. It is written as follows:

$$\text{ARIMA} \quad \underbrace{(p,d,q)}_{\substack{\uparrow \\ \text{Non-seasonal part} \\ \text{of the model}}} \quad \underbrace{(P,D,Q)_m}_{\substack{\uparrow \\ \text{Seasonal part} \\ \text{of the model}}}$$

where m = number of observations per year. We use uppercase notation for the seasonal parts of the model, and lowercase notation for the non-seasonal parts of the model.

The seasonal part of the model consists of terms that are very similar to the non-seasonal components of the model, but involve backshifts of the seasonal period. For example, an ARIMA$(1,1,1)(1,1,1)_4$ model (without a constant) is for quarterly data ($m = 4$), and can be written as

$$(1 - \phi_1 B)\,(1 - \Phi_1 B^4)(1 - B)(1 - B^4)y_t = (1 + \theta_1 B)\,(1 + \Theta_1 B^4)\varepsilon_t.$$

The additional seasonal terms are simply multiplied by the non-seasonal terms.

ACF/PACF

The seasonal part of an AR or MA model will be seen in the seasonal lags of the PACF and ACF. For example, an ARIMA$(0,0,0)(0,0,1)_{12}$ model will show:

- a spike at lag 12 in the ACF but no other significant spikes;
- exponential decay in the seasonal lags of the PACF (i.e., at lags 12, 24, 36, ...).

Similarly, an ARIMA$(0,0,0)(1,0,0)_{12}$ model will show:

- exponential decay in the seasonal lags of the ACF;
- a single significant spike at lag 12 in the PACF.

In considering the appropriate seasonal orders for a seasonal ARIMA model, restrict attention to the seasonal lags. and

The modelling procedure is almost the same as for non-seasonal data, except that we need to select seasonal AR and MA terms as well as the non-seasonal components of the model. The process is best illustrated via examples.

Example: European quarterly retail trade

We will describe the seasonal ARIMA modelling procedure using quarterly European retail trade data from 1996 to 2011. The data are plotted in Figure 8.17.

```
autoplot(euretail) + ylab("Retail index") + xlab("Year")
```

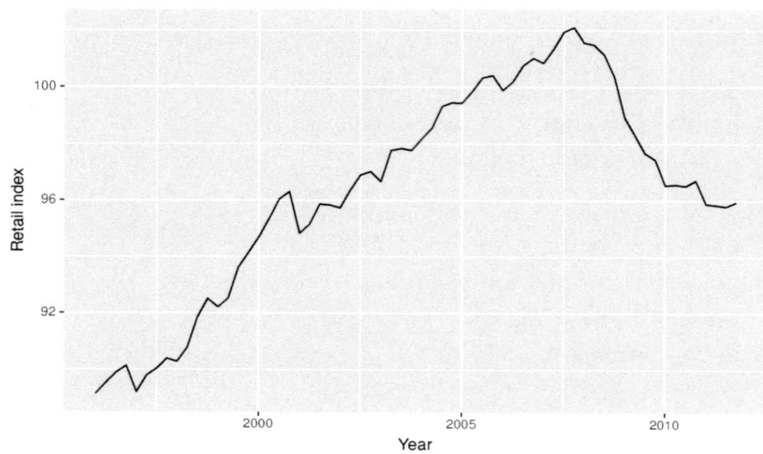

Figure 8.17: Quarterly retail trade index in the Euro area (17 countries), 1996–2011, covering wholesale and retail trade, and the repair of motor vehicles and motorcycles. (Index: 2005 = 100).

The data are clearly non-stationary, with some seasonality, so we will first take a seasonal difference. The seasonally differenced data are shown in Figure 8.18. These also appear to be non-stationary, so we take an additional first difference, shown in Figure 8.19.

```
euretail %>% diff(lag=4) %>% ggtsdisplay()
```

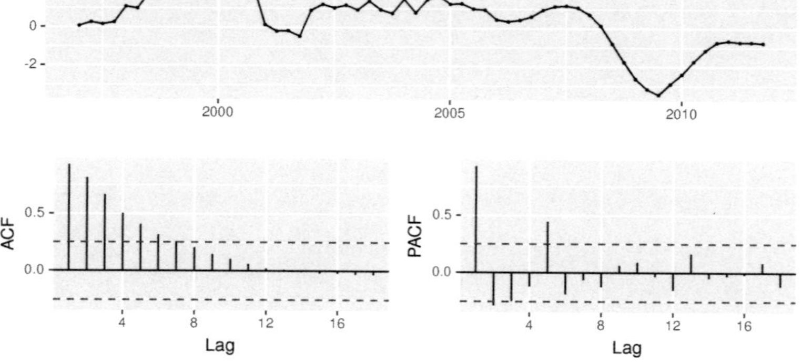

Figure 8.18: Seasonally differenced European retail trade index.

```
euretail %>% diff(lag=4) %>% diff() %>% ggtsdisplay()
```

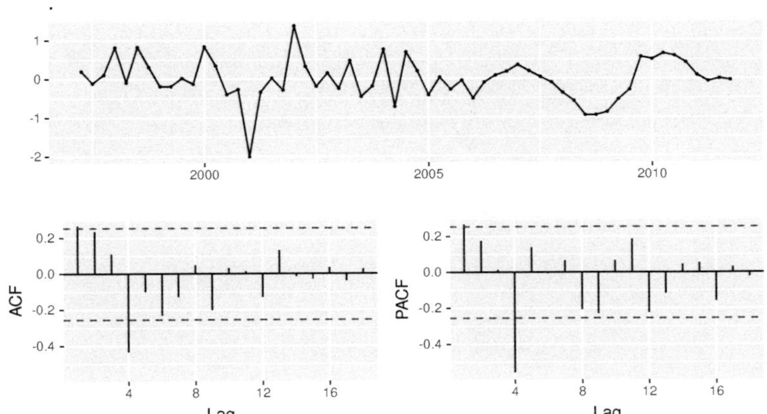

Figure 8.19: Double differenced European retail trade index.

Our aim now is to find an appropriate ARIMA model based on the ACF and PACF shown in Figure 8.19. The significant spike at lag 1 in the ACF suggests a non-seasonal MA(1) component, and the significant spike at lag 4 in the ACF suggests a seasonal MA(1) component. Consequently, we begin with an ARIMA(0,1,1)(0,1,1)$_4$ model, indicating a first and seasonal difference, and non-seasonal and seasonal MA(1) components. The residuals for the fitted model are shown in Figure 8.20. (By analogous logic applied to the PACF, we could also have started with an ARIMA(1,1,0)(1,1,0)$_4$ model.)

```
euretail %>%
  Arima(order=c(0,1,1), seasonal=c(0,1,1)) %>%
  residuals() %>% ggtsdisplay()
```

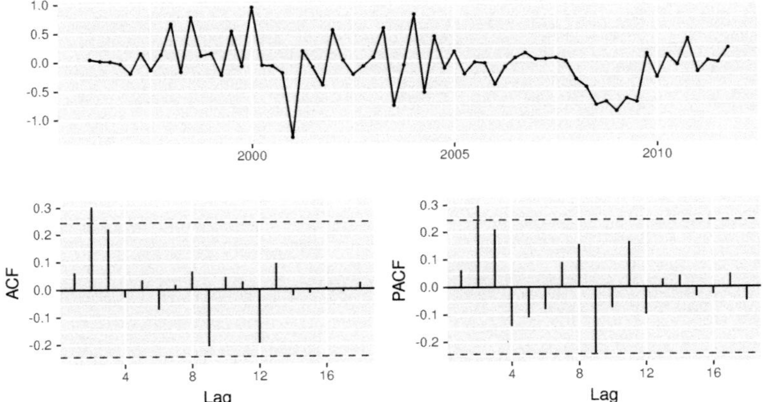

Figure 8.20: Residuals from the fitted ARIMA(0,1,1)(0,1,1)$_4$ model for the European retail trade index data.

Both the ACF and PACF show significant spikes at lag 2, and almost significant spikes at lag 3, indicating that some additional non-seasonal terms need to be included in the model. The AICc of the ARIMA(0,1,2)(0,1,1)$_4$ model is 74.36, while that for the ARIMA(0,1,3)(0,1,1)$_4$ model is 68.53. We tried other models with AR terms as well, but none that gave a smaller AICc value. Consequently, we choose the ARIMA(0,1,3)(0,1,1)$_4$ model. Its residuals are plotted in Figure 8.21. All the spikes are now within the significance limits, so the residuals appear to be white noise. The Ljung-Box test also shows that the residuals have no remaining autocorrelations.

```
fit3 <- Arima(euretail, order=c(0,1,3), seasonal=c(0,1,1))
checkresiduals(fit3)
```

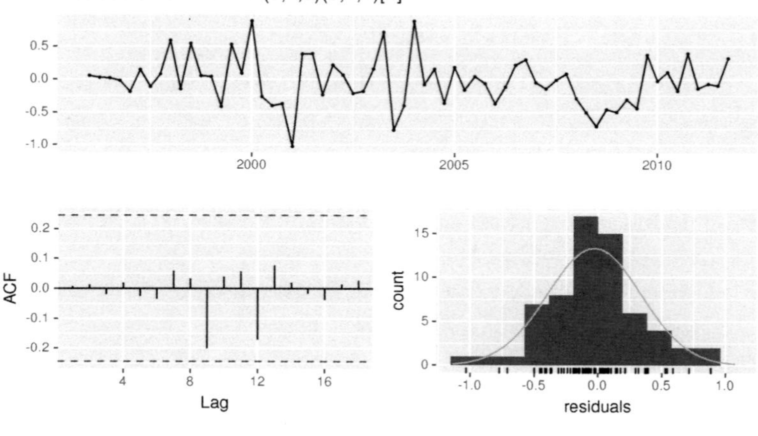

Figure 8.21: Residuals from the fitted ARIMA(0,1,3)(0,1,1)$_4$ model for the European retail trade index data.

```
#>
#>  Ljung-Box test
#>
#> data:  Residuals from ARIMA(0,1,3)(0,1,1)[4]
#> Q* = 0.51, df = 4, p-value = 1
#>
#> Model df: 4.   Total lags used: 8
```

Thus, we now have a seasonal ARIMA model that passes the required checks and is ready for forecasting. Forecasts from the model for the next three years are shown in Figure 8.22. The forecasts follow the recent trend in the data, because of the double differencing. The large and rapidly increasing prediction intervals show that the retail trade index could start increasing or decreasing at any time — while the point forecasts trend downwards, the prediction intervals allow for the data to trend upwards during the forecast period.

```
fit3 %>% forecast(h=12) %>% autoplot()
```

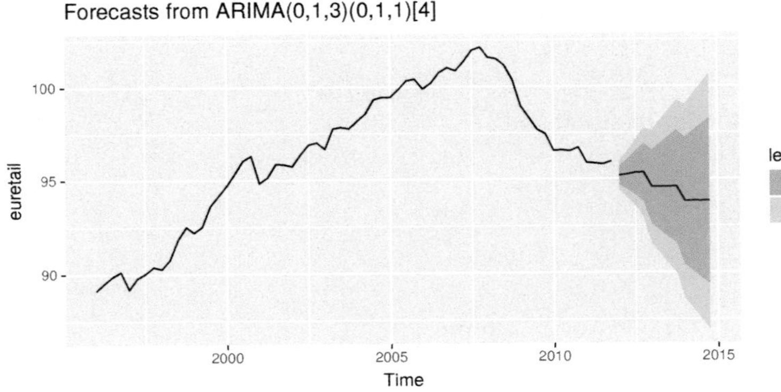

Figure 8.22: Forecasts of the European retail trade index data using the ARIMA(0,1,3)(0,1,1)$_4$ model. 80% and 95% prediction intervals are shown.

We could have used `auto.arima()` to do most of this work for us. It would have given the following result.

```
auto.arima(euretail)
#> Series: euretail
#> ARIMA(1,1,2)(0,1,1)[4]
#>
#> Coefficients:
#>          ar1     ma1    ma2    sma1
#>        0.736  -0.466  0.216  -0.843
#> s.e.   0.224   0.199  0.210   0.188
#>
#> sigma^2 estimated as 0.159:  log likelihood=-29.62
#> AIC=69.24   AICc=70.38   BIC=79.63
```

Notice that it has selected a different model (with a larger AICc value). `auto.arima()` takes some short-cuts in order to speed up the computation, and will not always give the best model. The short-cuts can be turned off, and then it will sometimes return a different model.

```
auto.arima(euretail, stepwise=FALSE, approximation=FALSE)
#> Series: euretail
#> ARIMA(0,1,3)(0,1,1)[4]
#>
#> Coefficients:
#>          ma1    ma2    ma3    sma1
#>        0.263  0.369  0.420  -0.664
#> s.e.   0.124  0.126  0.129   0.155
#>
```

```
#> sigma^2 estimated as 0.156:  log likelihood=-28.63
#> AIC=67.26   AICc=68.39   BIC=77.65
```

This time it returned the same model we had identified.

Example: Cortecosteroid drug sales in Australia

Our second example is more difficult. We will try to forecast monthly cortecosteroid drug sales in Australia. These are known as H02 drugs under the Anatomical Therapeutic Chemical classification scheme.

```
lh02 <- log(h02)
cbind("H02 sales (million scripts)" = h02,
      "Log H02 sales"=lh02) %>%
  autoplot(facets=TRUE) + xlab("Year") + ylab("")
```

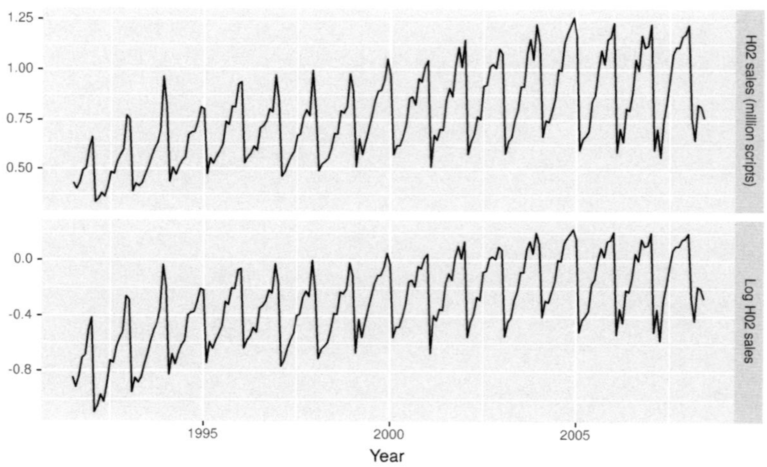

Figure 8.23: Cortecosteroid drug sales in Australia (in millions of scripts per month). Logged data shown in bottom panel.

Data from July 1991 to June 2008 are plotted in Figure 8.23. There is a small increase in the variance with the level, so we take logarithms to stabilize the variance.

The data are strongly seasonal and obviously non-stationary, so seasonal differencing will be used. The seasonally differenced data are shown in Figure 8.24. It is not clear at this point whether we should do another difference or not. We decide not to, but the choice is not obvious.

The last few observations appear to be different (more variable) from the earlier data. This may be due to the fact that data are sometimes revised when earlier sales are reported late.

```
lh02 %>% diff(lag=12) %>%
  ggtsdisplay(xlab="Year",
    main="Seasonally differenced H02 scripts")
```

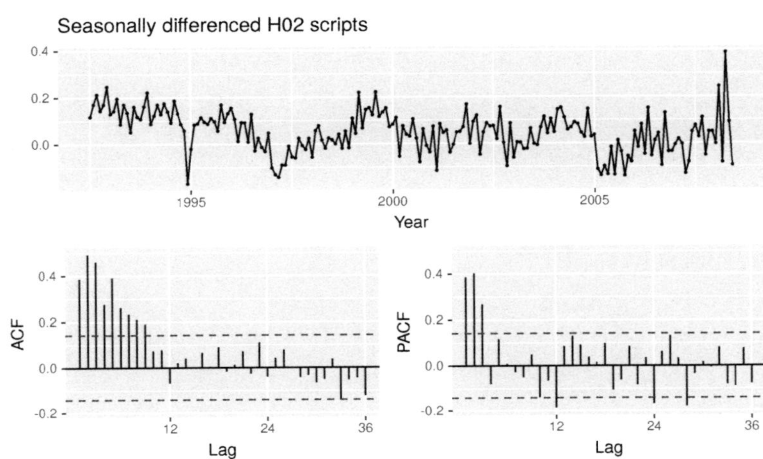

Figure 8.24: Seasonally differenced cortecosteroid drug sales in Australia (in millions of scripts per month).

In the plots of the seasonally differenced data, there are spikes in the PACF at lags 12 and 24, but nothing at seasonal lags in the ACF. This may be suggestive of a seasonal AR(2) term. In the non-seasonal lags, there are three significant spikes in the PACF, suggesting a possible AR(3) term. The pattern in the ACF is not indicative of any simple model.

Consequently, this initial analysis suggests that a possible model for these data is an ARIMA(3,0,0)(2,1,0)$_{12}$. We fit this model, along with some variations on it, and compute the AICc values shown in the following table.

Model	AICc
ARIMA(3,0,1)(0,1,2)$_{12}$	-485.5
ARIMA(3,0,1)(1,1,1)$_{12}$	-484.2
ARIMA(3,0,1)(0,1,1)$_{12}$	-483.7
ARIMA(3,0,1)(2,1,0)$_{12}$	-476.3
ARIMA(3,0,0)(2,1,0)$_{12}$	-475.1
ARIMA(3,0,2)(2,1,0)$_{12}$	-474.9
ARIMA(3,0,1)(1,1,0)$_{12}$	-463.4

Of these models, the best is the ARIMA(3,0,1)(0,1,2)$_{12}$ model (i.e., it has the smallest AICc value).

```
(fit <- Arima(h02, order=c(3,0,1), seasonal=c(0,1,2),
  lambda=0))
#> Series: h02
#> ARIMA(3,0,1)(0,1,2)[12]
#> Box Cox transformation: lambda= 0
#>
#> Coefficients:
#>          ar1     ar2     ar3     ma1     sma1     sma2
#>       -0.160   0.548   0.568   0.383   -0.522   -0.177
#> s.e.   0.164   0.088   0.094   0.190    0.086    0.087
#>
#> sigma^2 estimated as 0.00428:  log likelihood=250
#> AIC=-486.1   AICc=-485.5   BIC=-463.3
checkresiduals(fit, lag=36)
```

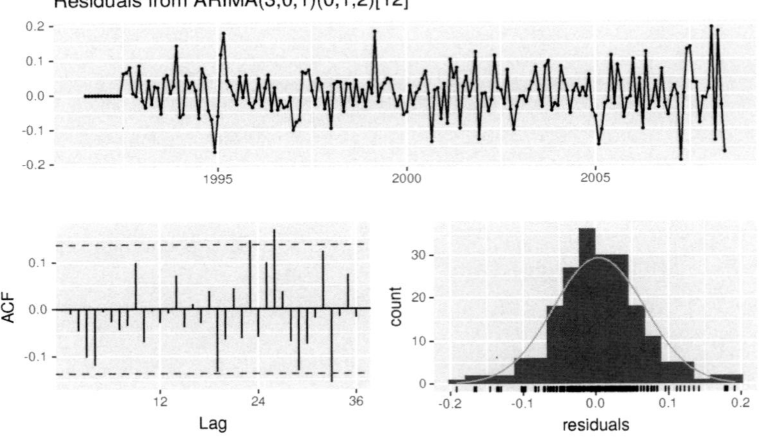

Figure 8.25: Residuals from the ARIMA$(3,0,1)(0,1,2)_{12}$ model applied to the H02 monthly script sales data.

```
#>
#>  Ljung-Box test
#>
#> data:  Residuals from ARIMA(3,0,1)(0,1,2)[12]
#> Q* = 51, df = 30, p-value = 0.01
#>
#> Model df: 6.   Total lags used: 36
```

The residuals from this model are shown in Figure 8.25. There are a few significant spikes in the ACF, and the model fails the Ljung-Box test. The model can still be used for forecasting, but the prediction intervals may not be accurate due to the correlated residuals.

Next we will try using the automatic ARIMA algorithm. Running `auto.arima()` with all arguments left at their default

Model	RMSE
ARIMA(3,0,1)(0,1,2)$_{12}$	0.0622
ARIMA(3,0,1)(1,1,1)$_{12}$	0.0630
ARIMA(2,1,4)(0,1,1)$_{12}$	0.0632
ARIMA(2,1,3)(0,1,1)$_{12}$	0.0634
ARIMA(3,0,3)(0,1,1)$_{12}$	0.0639
ARIMA(2,1,5)(0,1,1)$_{12}$	0.0640
ARIMA(3,0,1)(0,1,1)$_{12}$	0.0644
ARIMA(3,0,2)(0,1,1)$_{12}$	0.0644
ARIMA(3,0,2)(2,1,0)$_{12}$	0.0645
ARIMA(3,0,1)(2,1,0)$_{12}$	0.0646
ARIMA(4,0,2)(0,1,1)$_{12}$	0.0648
ARIMA(4,0,3)(0,1,1)$_{12}$	0.0648
ARIMA(3,0,0)(2,1,0)$_{12}$	0.0661
ARIMA(3,0,1)(1,1,0)$_{12}$	0.0679

Table 8.2: RMSE values for various ARIMA models applied to the H02 monthly script sales data.

values led to an ARIMA(2,1,3)(0,1,1)$_{12}$ model. However, the model still fails the Ljung-Box test. Sometimes it is just not possible to find a model that passes all of the tests.

Test set evaluation: We will compare some of the models fitted so far using a test set consisting of the last two years of data. Thus, we fit the models using data from July 1991 to June 2006, and forecast the script sales for July 2006 – June 2008. The results are summarised in the following table.

The models chosen manually and with `auto.arima()` are both in the top four models based on their RMSE values.

When models are compared using AICc values, it is important that all models have the same orders of differencing. However, when comparing models using a test set, it does not matter how the forecasts were produced — the comparisons are always valid. Consequently, in the table above, we can include some models with only seasonal differencing and some models with both first and seasonal differencing, while in the earlier table containing AICc values, we only compared models with seasonal differencing but no first differencing.

None of the models considered here pass all of the residual tests. In practice, we would normally use the best model we could find, even if it did not pass all of the tests.

Forecasts from the ARIMA(3,0,1)(0,1,2)$_{12}$ model (which has the lowest RMSE value on the test set, and the best AICc value amongst models with only seasonal differencing) are shown in Figure 8.26.

```
h02 %>%
  Arima(order=c(3,0,1), seasonal=c(0,1,2), lambda=0) %>%
  forecast() %>%
  autoplot() +
    ylab("H02 sales (million scripts)") + xlab("Year")
```

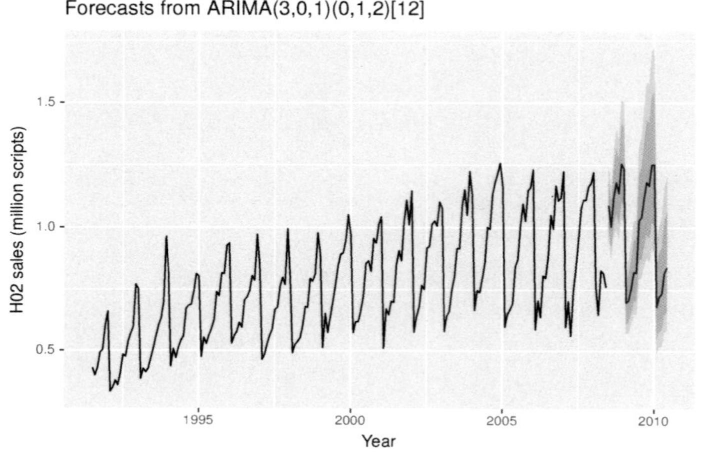

Figure 8.26: Forecasts from the ARIMA(3,0,1)(0,1,2)$_{12}$ model applied to the H02 monthly script sales data.

8.10 ARIMA vs ETS

It is a commonly held myth that ARIMA models are more general than exponential smoothing. While linear exponential smoothing models are all special cases of ARIMA models, the non-linear exponential smoothing models have no equivalent ARIMA counterparts. On the other hand, there are also many ARIMA models that have no exponential smoothing counterparts. In particular, all ETS models are non-stationary, while some ARIMA models are stationary.

The ETS models with seasonality or non-damped trend or both have two unit roots (i.e., they need two levels of differencing to make them stationary). All other ETS models have one unit root (they need one level of differencing to make them stationary).

ETS model	ARIMA model	Parameters
ETS(A,N,N)	ARIMA(0,1,1)	$\theta_1 = \alpha - 1$
ETS(A,A,N)	ARIMA(0,2,2)	$\theta_1 = \alpha + \beta - 2$
		$\theta_2 = 1 - \alpha$
ETS(A,A$_d$,N)	ARIMA(1,1,2)	$\phi_1 = \phi$
		$\theta_1 = \alpha + \phi\beta - 1 - \phi$
		$\theta_2 = (1 - \alpha)\phi$
ETS(A,N,A)	ARIMA$(0,1,m)(0,1,0)_m$	
ETS(A,A,A)	ARIMA$(0,1,m+1)(0,1,0)_m$	
ETS(A,A$_d$,A)	ARIMA$(0,1,m+1)(0,1,0)_m$	

Table 8.3: Equivalence relationships between ETS and ARIMA models.

Table 8.3 gives the equivalence relationships for the two classes of models. For the seasonal models, the ARIMA parameters have a large number of restrictions.

The AICc is useful for selecting between models in the same class. For example, we can use it to select an ARIMA model between candidate ARIMA models[5] or an ETS model between candidate ETS models. However, it cannot be used to compare between ETS and ARIMA models because they are in different model classes, and the likelihood is computed in different ways. The examples below demonstrate selecting between these classes of models.

[5] As already noted, comparing information criteria is only valid for ARIMA models of the same orders of differencing.

Example: Comparing `auto.arima()` and `ets()` on non-seasonal data

We can use time series cross-validation to compare an ARIMA model and an ETS model. The code below provides functions that return forecast objects from `auto.arima()` and `ets()` respectively.

```
fets <- function(x, h) {
  forecast(ets(x), h = h)
}
farima <- function(x, h) {
  forecast(auto.arima(x), h=h)
}
```

The returned objects can then be passed into `tsCV()`. Let's consider ARIMA models and ETS models for the `air` data as introduced in Section 7.2 where, `air <- window(ausair, start=1990)`.

```
# Compute CV errors for ETS as e1
e1 <- tsCV(air, fets, h=1)
# Compute CV errors for ARIMA as e2
e2 <- tsCV(air, farima, h=1)
# Find MSE of each model class
mean(e1^2, na.rm=TRUE)
#> [1] 7.864
mean(e2^2, na.rm=TRUE)
#> [1] 9.622
```

In this case the ets model has a lower tsCV statistic based on MSEs. Below we generate and plot forecasts for the next 5 years generated from an ETS model.

```
air %>% ets() %>% forecast() %>% autoplot()
```

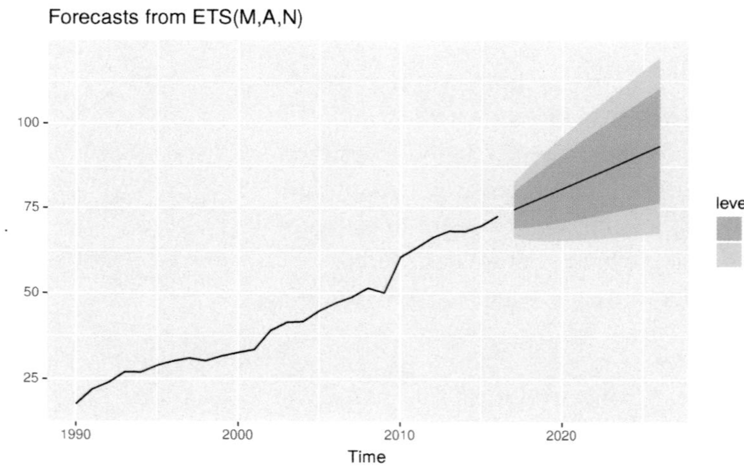

Figure 8.27: Forecasts from an ETS model fitted to monthly totals of air transport passengers in Australia.

Example: Comparing `auto.arima()` and `ets()` on seasonal data

In this case we want to compare seasonal ARIMA and ETS models applied to the quarterly cement production data `qcement`. Because the series is very long, we can afford to use a training and a test set rather than time series cross-validation. The advantage is that this is much faster. We create a training set from the beginning of 1988 to the end of 2007 and select an ARIMA and an ETS model using the `auto.arima()` and `ets()` functions.

```
# Consider the qcement data beginning in 1988
cement <- window(qcement, start=1988)
# Use 20 years of the data as the training set
train <- window(cement, end=c(2007,4))
```

The output below shows the ARIMA model selected and estimated by `auto.arima()`. The ARIMA model does well in capturing all the dynamics in the data as the residuals seem to be white noise.

```
(fit.arima <- auto.arima(train))

#> Series: train
#> ARIMA(2,0,0)(2,1,1)[4] with drift
#>
#> Coefficients:
#>          ar1    ar2    sar1     sar2     sma1  drift
#>        0.647  0.193  0.073  -0.240  -0.870  0.010
#> s.e.   0.116  0.118  0.160   0.139   0.162  0.003
#>
#> sigma^2 estimated as 0.0116:  log likelihood=61.45
#> AIC=-108.9   AICc=-107.2   BIC=-92.58
checkresiduals(fit.arima)
```

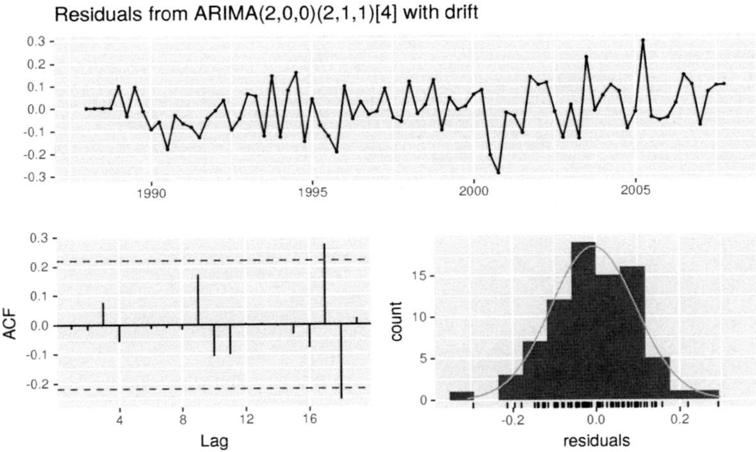

Figure 8.28: Residual diagnostic plots for the ARIMA model fitted to the quarterly cement production training data.

```
#>
#>  Ljung-Box test
#>
#> data:  Residuals from ARIMA(2,0,0)(2,1,1)[4] with drift
#> Q* = 3.5, df = 3, p-value = 0.3
#>
#> Model df: 6.   Total lags used: 9
```

The output below also shows the ETS model selected and estimated by `ets()`. This model also does well in capturing all the dynamics in the data, as the residuals similarly appear to be white noise.

```
(fit.ets <- ets(train))

#> ETS(M,N,M)
#>
#> Call:
#>  ets(y = train)
#>
#>   Smoothing parameters:
#>     alpha = 0.7341
#>     gamma = 1e-04
#>
#>   Initial states:
#>     l = 1.6439
#>     s = 1.031 1.044 1.01 0.9148
#>
#>   sigma:  0.0581
#>
#>      AIC     AICc      BIC
#> -2.1967 -0.6411 14.4775
checkresiduals(fit.ets)
```

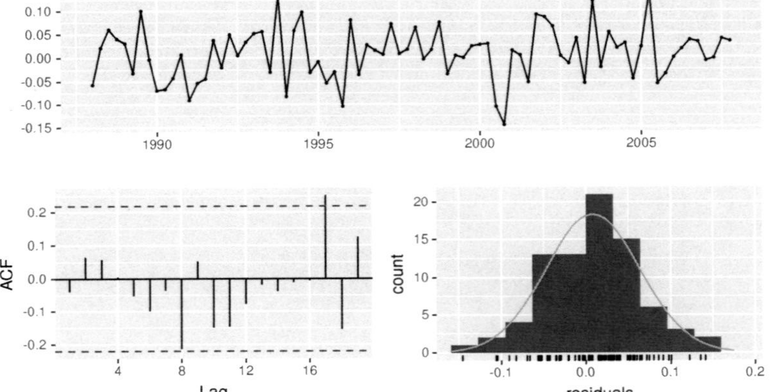

Figure 8.29: Residual diagnostic plots for the ETS model fitted to the quarterly cement production training data.

```
#>
#>  Ljung-Box test
#>
#> data:  Residuals from ETS(M,N,M)
#> Q* = 6.3, df = 3, p-value = 0.1
#>
#> Model df: 6.   Total lags used: 9
```

The output below evaluates the forecasting performance of the two competing models over the test set. In this case the ETS model seems to be the slightly more accurate model based on the test set RMSE, MAPE and MASE.

```
# Generate forecasts and compare accuracy over the test set
a1 <- fit.arima %>% forecast(h = 4*(2013-2007)+1) %>%
  accuracy(qcement)
a1[,c("RMSE","MAE","MAPE","MASE")]
#>                RMSE     MAE  MAPE   MASE
#> Training set 0.1006 0.07955 4.348 0.5435
#> Test set     0.1978 0.16749 7.653 1.1443
a2 <- fit.ets %>% forecast(h = 4*(2013-2007)+1) %>%
  accuracy(qcement)
a2[,c("RMSE","MAE","MAPE","MASE")]
#>                RMSE     MAE  MAPE   MASE
#> Training set 0.1022 0.07958 4.372 0.5437
#> Test set     0.1839 0.15395 6.986 1.0518
```

Notice that the ARIMA model fits the training data slightly better than the ETS model, but that the ETS model provides more accurate forecasts on the test set. A good fit to training data is never an indication that the model will forecast well.

Below we generate and plot forecasts from an ETS model for the next 3 years.

```
# Generate forecasts from an ETS model
cement %>% ets() %>% forecast(h=12) %>% autoplot()
```

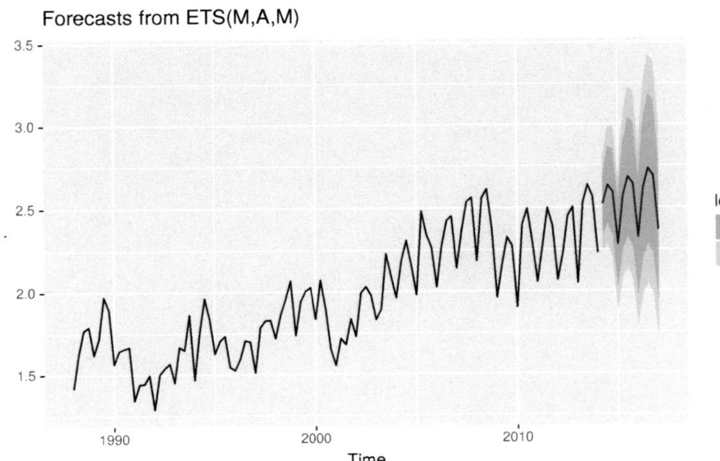

Figure 8.30: Forecasts from an ETS model fitted to all of the available quarterly cement production data.

8.11 Exercises

1. Figure 8.31 shows the ACFs for 36 random numbers, 360 random numbers and 1,000 random numbers.

   a. Explain the differences among these figures. Do they all indicate that the data are white noise?

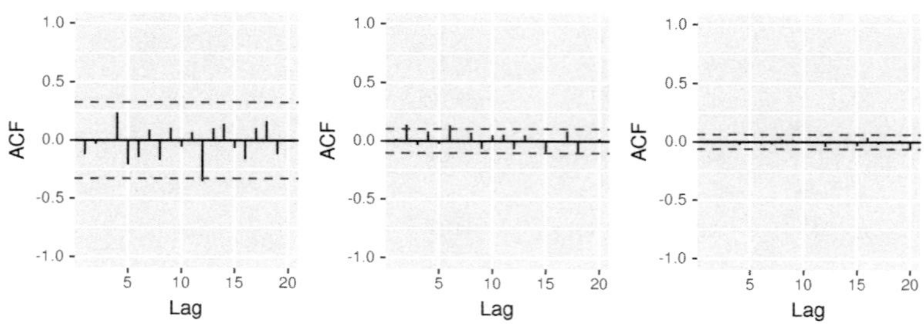

Figure 8.31: Left: ACF for a white noise series of 36 numbers. Middle: ACF for a white noise series of 360 numbers. Right: ACF for a white noise series of 1,000 numbers.

   b. Why are the critical values at different distances from the mean of zero? Why are the autocorrelations different in each figure when they each refer to white noise?

2. A classic example of a non-stationary series is the daily closing IBM stock price series (data set `ibmclose`). Use R to plot the daily closing prices for IBM stock and the ACF and PACF. Explain how each plot shows that the series is non-stationary and should be differenced.

3. For the following series, find an appropriate Box-Cox transformation and order of differencing in order to obtain stationary data.

   a. `usnetelec`
   b. `usgdp`
   c. `mcopper`
   d. `enplanements`
   e. `visitors`

4. For the `enplanements` data, write down the differences you chose above using backshift operator notation.

5. For your retail data (from Exercise 3 in Section 2.10), find the appropriate order of differencing (after transformation if necessary) to obtain stationary data.

6. Use R to simulate and plot some data from simple ARIMA models.

   a. Use the following R code to generate data from an AR(1) model with $\phi_1 = 0.6$ and $\sigma^2 = 1$. The process starts with $y_1 = 0$.

   ```
   y <- ts(numeric(100))
   e <- rnorm(100)
   for(i in 2:100)
     y[i] <- 0.6*y[i-1] + e[i]
   ```

   b. Produce a time plot for the series. How does the plot change as you change ϕ_1?

   c. Write your own code to generate data from an MA(1) model with $\theta_1 = 0.6$ and $\sigma^2 = 1$.

   d. Produce a time plot for the series. How does the plot change as you change θ_1?

   e. Generate data from an ARMA(1,1) model with $\phi_1 = 0.6$, $\theta_1 = 0.6$ and $\sigma^2 = 1$.

   f. Generate data from an AR(2) model with $\phi_1 = -0.8$, $\phi_2 = 0.3$ and $\sigma^2 = 1$. (Note that these parameters will give a non-stationary series.)

   g. Graph the latter two series and compare them.

7. Consider the number of women murdered each year (per 100,000 standard population) in the United States. (Data set `wmurders`).

   a. By studying appropriate graphs of the series in R, find an appropriate ARIMA(p,d,q) model for these data.
   b. Should you include a constant in the model? Explain.
   c. Write this model in terms of the backshift operator.
   d. Fit the model using R and examine the residuals. Is the model satisfactory?
   e. Forecast three times ahead. Check your forecasts by hand to make sure that you know how they have been calculated.
   f. Create a plot of the series with forecasts and prediction intervals for the next three periods shown.
   g. Does `auto.arima()` give the same model you have chosen? If not, which model do you think is better?

8. Consider the total international visitors to Australia (in millions) for the period 1980-2015. (Data set `austa`.)

    a. Use `auto.arima()` to find an appropriate ARIMA model. What model was selected. Check that the residuals look like white noise. Plot forecasts for the next 10 periods.
    b. Plot forecasts from an ARIMA(0,1,1) model with no drift and compare these to part a. Remove the MA term and plot again.
    c. Plot forecasts from an ARIMA(2,1,3) model with drift. Remove the constant and see what happens.
    d. Plot forecasts from an ARIMA(0,0,1) model with a constant. Remove the MA term and plot again.
    e. Plot forecasts from an ARIMA(0,2,1) model with no constant.

9. For the `usgdp` series:

    a. if necessary, find a suitable Box-Cox transformation for the data;
    b. fit a suitable ARIMA model to the transformed data using `auto.arima()`;
    c. try some other plausible models by experimenting with the orders chosen;
    d. choose what you think is the best model and check the residual diagnostics;
    e. produce forecasts of your fitted model. Do the forecasts look reasonable?
    f. compare the results with what you would obtain using `ets()` (with no transformation).

10. Consider `austourists`, the quarterly number of international tourists to Australia for the period 1999–2010. (Data set `austourists`.)

    a. Describe the time plot.
    b. What can you learn from the ACF graph?
    c. What can you learn from the PACF graph?
    d. Produce plots of the seasonally differenced data $(1 - B^4)Y_t$. What model do these graphs suggest?
    e. Does `auto.arima()` give the same model that you chose? If not, which model do you think is better?

f. Write the model in terms of the backshift operator, then without using the backshift operator.

11. Consider the total net generation of electricity (in billion kilowatt hours) by the U.S. electric industry (monthly for the period January 1973 – June 2013). (Data set `usmelec`.) In general there are two peaks per year: in mid-summer and mid-winter.

    a. Examine the 12-month moving average of this series to see what kind of trend is involved.
    b. Do the data need transforming? If so, find a suitable transformation.
    c. Are the data stationary? If not, find an appropriate differencing which yields stationary data.
    d. Identify a couple of ARIMA models that might be useful in describing the time series. Which of your models is the best according to their AIC values?
    e. Estimate the parameters of your best model and do diagnostic testing on the residuals. Do the residuals resemble white noise? If not, try to find another ARIMA model which fits better.
    f. Forecast the next 15 years of electricity generation by the U.S. electric industry. Get the latest figures from the EIA[6] to check the accuracy of your forecasts.
    g. Eventually, the prediction intervals are so wide that the forecasts are not particularly useful. How many years of forecasts do you think are sufficiently accurate to be usable?

[6] `https://bit.ly/usmelec`

12. For the `mcopper` data:

    a. if necessary, find a suitable Box-Cox transformation for the data;
    b. fit a suitable ARIMA model to the transformed data using `auto.arima()`;
    c. try some other plausible models by experimenting with the orders chosen;
    d. choose what you think is the best model and check the residual diagnostics;
    e. produce forecasts of your fitted model. Do the forecasts look reasonable?

f. compare the results with what you would obtain using `ets()` (with no transformation).

13. Choose one of the following seasonal time series: `hsales`, `auscafe`, `qauselec`, `qcement`, `qgas`.

    a. Do the data need transforming? If so, find a suitable transformation.
    b. Are the data stationary? If not, find an appropriate differencing which yields stationary data.
    c. Identify a couple of ARIMA models that might be useful in describing the time series. Which of your models is the best according to their AIC values?
    d. Estimate the parameters of your best model and do diagnostic testing on the residuals. Do the residuals resemble white noise? If not, try to find another ARIMA model which fits better.
    e. Forecast the next 24 months of data using your preferred model.
    f. Compare the forecasts obtained using `ets()`.

14. For the same time series you used in the previous exercise, try using a non-seasonal model applied to the seasonally adjusted data obtained from STL. The `stlf()` function will make the calculations easy (with `method="arima"`). Compare the forecasts with those obtained in the previous exercise. Which do you think is the best approach?

15. For your retail time series (Exercise 5 above):

    a. develop an appropriate seasonal ARIMA model;
    b. compare the forecasts with those you obtained in earlier chapters;
    c. Obtain up-to-date retail data from the ABS website[7] (Cat 8501.0, Table 11), and compare your forecasts with the actual numbers. How good were the forecasts from the various models?

[7] `https://bit.ly/absretail`

16. Consider the sheep population of England and Wales from 1867–1939 (data set `sheep`).

    a. Produce a time plot of the time series.

    b. Assume you decide to fit the following model:

    $$y_t = y_{t-1} + \phi_1(y_{t-1} - y_{t-2}) + \phi_2(y_{t-2} - y_{t-3}) + \phi_3(y_{t-3} - y_{t-4}) + \varepsilon_t,$$

where ε_t is a white noise series. What sort of ARIMA model is this (i.e., what are p, d, and q)?

c. By examining the ACF and PACF of the differenced data, explain why this model is appropriate.

d. The last five values of the series are given below:

Year	1935	1936	1937	1938	1939
Millions of sheep	1648	1665	1627	1791	1797

The estimated parameters are $\phi_1 = 0.42$, $\phi_2 = -0.20$, and $\phi_3 = -0.30$. Without using the `forecast` function, calculate forecasts for the next three years (1940–1942).

e. Now fit the model in R and obtain the forecasts using `forecast`. How are they different from yours? Why?

17. The annual bituminous coal production in the United States from 1920 to 1968 is in data set `bicoal`.

a. Produce a time plot of the data.

b. You decide to fit the following model to the series:

$$y_t = c + \phi_1 y_{t-1} + \phi_2 y_{t-2} + \phi_3 y_{t-3} + \phi_4 y_{t-4} + \varepsilon_t$$

where y_t is the coal production in year t and ε_t is a white noise series. What sort of ARIMA model is this (i.e., what are p, d, and q)?

c. Explain why this model was chosen using the ACF and PACF.

d. The last five values of the series are given below.

Year	1964	1965	1966	1967	1968
Millions of tons	467	512	534	552	545

The estimated parameters are $c = 162.00$, $\phi_1 = 0.83$, $\phi_2 = -0.34$, $\phi_3 = 0.55$, and $\phi_4 = -0.38$. Without using the `forecast` function, calculate forecasts for the next three years (1969–1971).

e. Now fit the model in R and obtain the forecasts from the same model. How are they different from yours? Why?

18. Before doing this exercise, you will need to install the **rdatamarket** package in R using

```
install.packages("rdatamarket")
```

a. Select a time series from Datamarket[8]. Then copy its short URL and import the data using

```
x <- ts(rdatamarket::dmseries("shorturl")[,1],
  start=??, frequency=??)
```

(Replace ?? with the appropriate values.)

b. Plot graphs of the data, and try to identify an appropriate ARIMA model.

c. Do residual diagnostic checking of your ARIMA model. Are the residuals white noise?

d. Use your chosen ARIMA model to forecast the next four years.

e. Now try to identify an appropriate ETS model.

f. Do residual diagnostic checking of your ETS model. Are the residuals white noise?

g. Use your chosen ETS model to forecast the next four years.

h. Which of the two models do you prefer?

[8] `https://bit.ly/datamarketfree`

8.12 Further reading

- The classic text which popularized ARIMA modelling was Box and Jenkins (1970). The most recent edition is Box, Jenkins, et al. (2015), and it is still an excellent reference for all things ARIMA.
- Brockwell and Davis (2016) provides a good introduction to the mathematical background to the models.
- Peña, Tiao, and Tsay (2001) describes some alternative automatic algorithms to the one used by `auto.arima()`.

Chapter 9

Dynamic regression models

The time series models in the previous two chapters allow for the inclusion of information from past observations of a series, but not for the inclusion of other information that may also be relevant. For example, the effects of holidays, competitor activity, changes in the law, the wider economy, or other external variables, may explain some of the historical variation and may lead to more accurate forecasts. On the other hand, the regression models in Chapter 5 allow for the inclusion of a lot of relevant information from predictor variables, but do not allow for the subtle time series dynamics that can be handled with ARIMA models. In this chapter, we consider how to extend ARIMA models in order to allow other information to be included in the models.

In Chapter 5 we considered regression models of the form

$$y_t = \beta_0 + \beta_1 x_{1,t} + \cdots + \beta_k x_{k,t} + \varepsilon_t,$$

where y_t is a linear function of the k predictor variables $(x_{1,t},\dots,x_{k,t})$, and ε_t is usually assumed to be an uncorrelated error term (i.e., it is white noise). We considered tests such as the Breusch-Godfrey test for assessing whether the resulting residuals were significantly correlated.

In this chapter, we will allow the errors from a regression to contain autocorrelation. To emphasise this change in perspective, we will replace ε_t with η_t in the equation. The error series η_t is assumed to follow an ARIMA model. For example, if η_t

follows an ARIMA(1,1,1) model, we can write

$$y_t = \beta_0 + \beta_1 x_{1,t} + \dots + \beta_k x_{k,t} + \eta_t,$$
$$(1 - \phi_1 B)(1 - B)\eta_t = (1 + \theta_1 B)\varepsilon_t,$$

where ε_t is a white noise series.

Notice that the model has two error terms here — the error from the regression model, which we denote by η_t, and the error from the ARIMA model, which we denote by ε_t. Only the ARIMA model errors are assumed to be white noise.

9.1 Estimation

When we estimate the parameters from the model, we need to minimise the sum of squared ε_t values. If we minimise the sum of squared η_t values instead (which is what would happen if we estimated the regression model ignoring the autocorrelations in the errors), then several problems arise.

1. The estimated coefficients $\hat{\beta}_0, \dots, \hat{\beta}_k$ are no longer the best estimates, as some information has been ignored in the calculation;
2. Any statistical tests associated with the model (e.g., t-tests on the coefficients) will be incorrect.
3. The AICc values of the fitted models are no longer a good guide as to which is the best model for forecasting.
4. In most cases, the p-values associated with the coefficients will be too small, and so some predictor variables will appear to be important when they are not. This is known as "spurious regression".

Minimising the sum of squared ε_t values avoids these problems. Alternatively, maximum likelihood estimation can be used; this will give very similar estimates of the coefficients.

An important consideration when estimating a regression with ARMA errors is that all of the variables in the model must first be stationary. Thus, we first have to check that y_t and all of the predictors $(x_{1,t}, \dots, x_{k,t})$ appear to be stationary. If we estimate the model when any of these are non-stationary, the estimated coefficients will not be consistent estimates (and therefore may not be meaningful). One exception to this is the case where non-stationary variables are co-integrated. If there exists a linear combination of the non-stationary y_t and the predictors that is stationary, then the estimated coefficients will be consistent.[1]

[1] Forecasting with cointegrated models is discussed by Harris and Sollis (2003).

We therefore first difference the non-stationary variables in the model. It is often desirable to maintain the form of the relationship between y_t and the predictors, and consequently it is common to difference all of the variables if any of them need differencing. The resulting model is then called a "model in differences", as distinct from a "model in levels", which is what is obtained when the original data are used without differencing.

If all of the variables in the model are stationary, then we only need to consider ARMA errors for the residuals. It is easy to see that a regression model with ARIMA errors is equivalent to a regression model in differences with ARMA errors. For example, if the above regression model with ARIMA(1,1,1) errors is differenced we obtain the model

$$\begin{aligned} y'_t &= \beta_1 x'_{1,t} + \cdots + \beta_k x'_{k,t} + \eta'_t, \\ (1 - \phi_1 B)\eta'_t &= (1 + \theta_1 B)\varepsilon_t, \end{aligned}$$

where $y'_t = y_t - y_{t-1}$, $x'_{t,i} = x_{t,i} - x_{t-1,i}$ and $\eta'_t = \eta_t - \eta_{t-1}$, which is a regression model in differences with ARMA errors.

9.2 Regression with ARIMA errors in R

The R function `Arima()` will fit a regression model with ARIMA errors if the argument `xreg` is used. The `order` argument specifies the order of the ARIMA error model. If differencing is specified, then the differencing is applied to all variables in the regression model before the model is estimated. For example, the R command

```
fit <- Arima(y, xreg=x, order=c(1,1,0))
```

will fit the model $y'_t = \beta_1 x'_t + \eta'_t$, where $\eta'_t = \phi_1 \eta'_{t-1} + \varepsilon_t$ is an AR(1) error. This is equivalent to the model

$$y_t = \beta_0 + \beta_1 x_t + \eta_t,$$

where η_t is an ARIMA(1,1,0) error. Notice that the constant term disappears due to the differencing. To include a constant in the differenced model, specify `include.drift=TRUE`.

The `auto.arima()` function will also handle regression terms via the `xreg` argument. The user must specify the predictor variables to include, but `auto.arima()` will select the best ARIMA model for the errors.

The AICc is calculated for the final model, and this value can be used to determine the best predictors. That is, the procedure should be repeated for all subsets of predictors to be considered, and the model with the lowest AICc value selected.

Example: US Personal Consumption and Income

Figure 9.1 shows the quarterly changes in personal consumption expenditure and personal disposable income from 1970 to 2016 Q3. We would like to forecast changes in expenditure based on changes in income. A change in income does not necessarily translate to an instant change in consumption (e.g., after the loss of a job, it may take a few months for expenses to be reduced to allow for the new circumstances). However, we will ignore this complexity in this example and try to measure the instantaneous effect of the average change of income on the average change of consumption expenditure.

```
autoplot(uschange[,1:2], facets=TRUE) +
  xlab("Year") + ylab("") +
  ggtitle("Quarterly changes in US consumption
    and personal income")
```

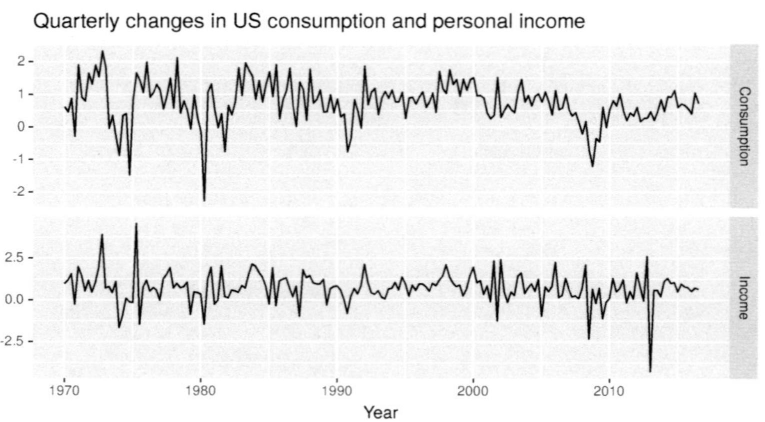

Figure 9.1: Percentage changes in quarterly personal consumption expenditure and personal disposable income for the USA, 1970 to 2016 Q3.

```
(fit <- auto.arima(uschange[,"Consumption"],
  xreg=uschange[,"Income"]))
#> Series: uschange[, "Consumption"]
#> Regression with ARIMA(1,0,2) errors
#>
#> Coefficients:
#>          ar1      ma1    ma2  intercept   xreg
#>        0.692  -0.576  0.198      0.599  0.203
#> s.e.   0.116   0.130  0.076      0.088  0.046
#>
#> sigma^2 estimated as 0.322:  log likelihood=-156.9
#> AIC=325.9   AICc=326.4   BIC=345.3
```

The data are clearly already stationary (as we are considering percentage changes rather than raw expenditure and income), so there is no need for any differencing. The fitted model is

$$
\begin{aligned}
y_t &= 0.60 + 0.20x_t + \eta_t, \\
\eta_t &= 0.69\eta_{t-1} + \varepsilon_t - 0.58\varepsilon_{t-1} + 0.20\varepsilon_{t-2}, \\
\varepsilon_t &\sim \text{NID}(0, 0.322).
\end{aligned}
$$

We can recover estimates of both the η_t and ε_t series using the `residuals()` function.

```
cbind("Regression Errors" = residuals(fit, type="regression"),
      "ARIMA errors" = residuals(fit, type="innovation")) %>%
  autoplot(facets=TRUE)
```

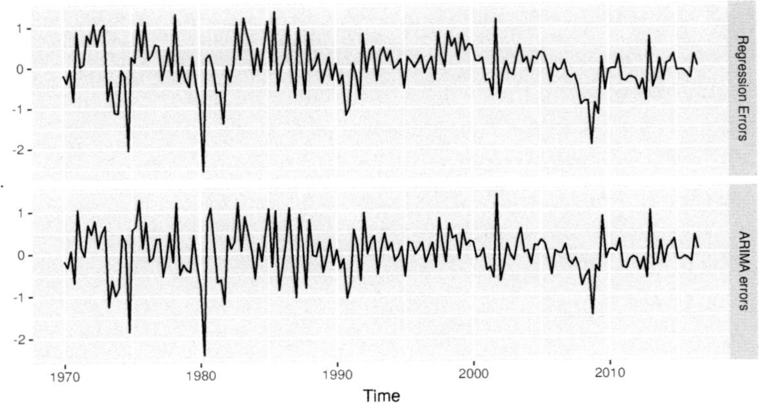

Figure 9.2: Regression errors (η_t) and ARIMA errors (ε_t) from the fitted model.

It is the ARIMA errors that should resemble a white noise series.

```
checkresiduals(fit)
```

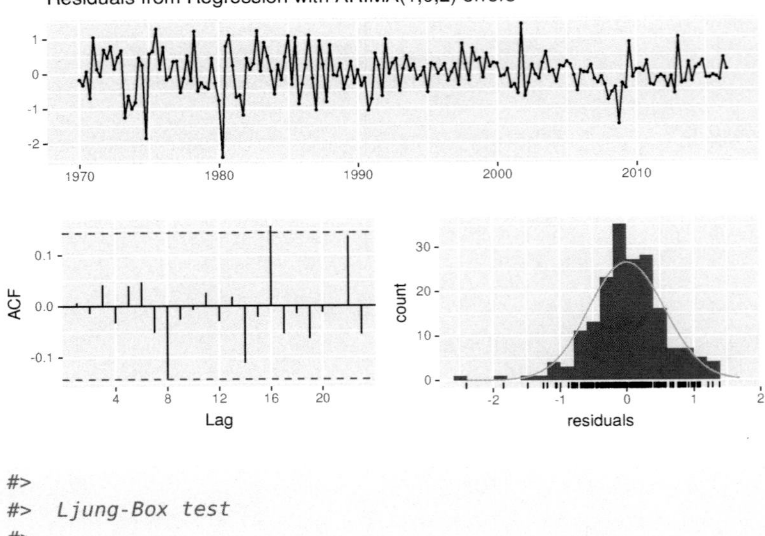

Figure 9.3: The residuals (i.e., the ARIMA errors) are not significantly different from white noise.

```
#>
#>  Ljung-Box test
#>
#> data:  Residuals from Regression with ARIMA(1,0,2) errors
#> Q* = 5.9, df = 3, p-value = 0.1
#>
#> Model df: 5.   Total lags used: 8
```

9.3 Forecasting

To forecast using a regression model with ARIMA errors, we need to forecast the regression part of the model and the ARIMA part of the model, and combine the results. As with ordinary regression models, in order to obtain forecasts we first need to forecast the predictors. When the predictors are known into the future (e.g., calendar-related variables such as time, day-of-week, etc.), this is straightforward. But when the predictors are themselves unknown, we must either model them separately, or use assumed future values for each predictor.

Example: US Personal Consumption and Income

We will calculate forecasts for the next eight quarters assuming that the future percentage changes in personal disposable income will be equal to the mean percentage change from the last forty years.

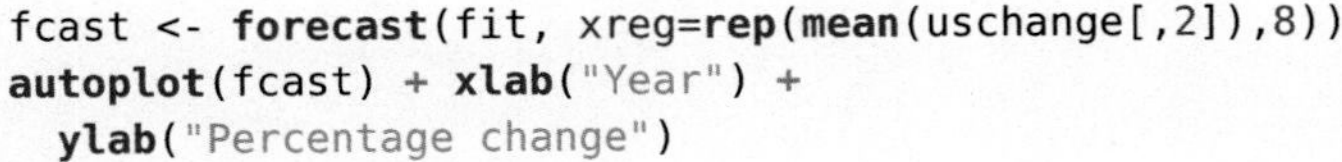

```
fcast <- forecast(fit, xreg=rep(mean(uschange[,2]),8))
autoplot(fcast) + xlab("Year") +
  ylab("Percentage change")
```

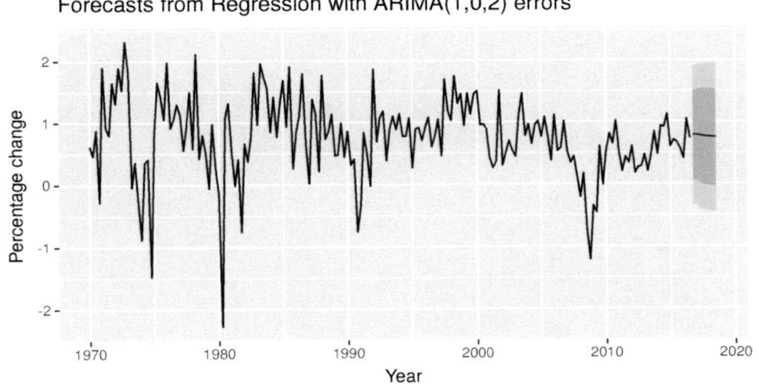

Figure 9.4: Forecasts obtained from regressing the percentage change in consumption expenditure on the percentage change in disposable income, with an ARIMA(1,0,2) error model.

The prediction intervals for this model are narrower than those for the model developed in Section 8.5 because we are now able to explain some of the variation in the data using the income predictor.

It is important to realise that the prediction intervals from regression models (with or without ARIMA errors) do not take into account the uncertainty in the forecasts of the predictors. So they should be interpreted as being conditional on the assumed (or estimated) future values of the predictor variables.

Example: Forecasting electricity demand

Daily electricity demand can be modelled as a function of temperature. As can be observed on an electricity bill, more electricity is used on cold days due to heating and hot days due to air conditioning. The higher demand on cold and hot days is reflected in the u-shape of Figure 9.5, where daily demand is plotted versus daily maximum temperature.

The data are stored as `elecdaily` including total daily demand, an indicator variable for workdays (a workday is represented with 1, and a non-workday is represented with 0), and daily maximum temperatures. Because there is weekly seasonality, the frequency has been set to 7. Figure 9.6 shows the time series of both daily demand and daily maximum temperatures. The plots highlight the need for both a non-linear and a dynamic model.

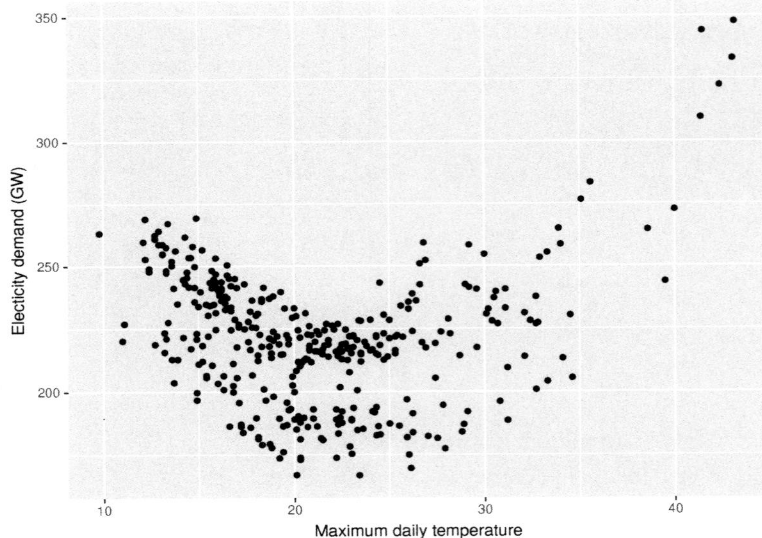

Figure 9.5: Daily electricity demand versus maximum daily temperature for the state of Victoria in Australia for 2014.

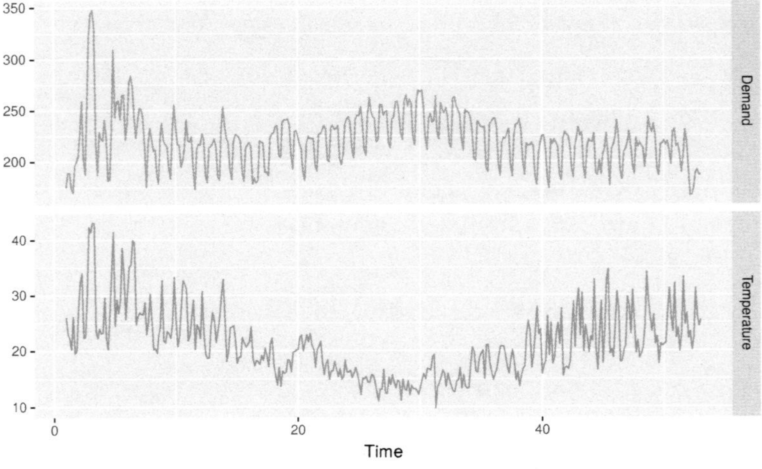

Figure 9.6: Daily electricity demand and maximum daily temperature for the state of Victoria in Australia for 2014.

In this example, we fit a quadratic regression model with ARMA errors using the auto.arima() function.

```
xreg <- cbind(MaxTemp = elecdaily[, "Temperature"],
              MaxTempSq = elecdaily[, "Temperature"]^2,
              Workday = elecdaily[, "WorkDay"])
fit <- auto.arima(elecdaily[, "Demand"], xreg = xreg)
checkresiduals(fit)
```

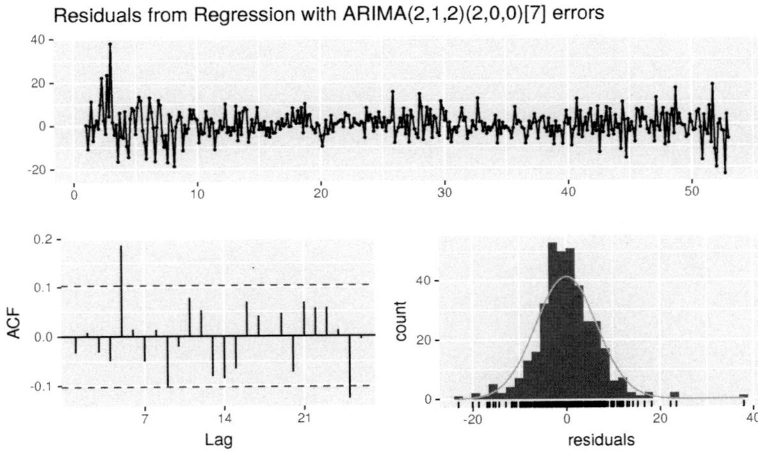

Figure 9.7: Residuals diagnostics for a dynamic regression model for daily electricity demand with workday and quadratic temperature effects.

```
#>
#>  Ljung-Box test
#>
#> data:  Residuals from Regression with
#>        ARIMA(2,1,2)(2,0,0)[7] errors
#> Q* = 28, df = 4, p-value = 1e-05
#>
#> Model df: 10.   Total lags used: 14
```

The model has some significant autocorrelation in the residuals, which means the prediction intervals may not provide accurate coverage. Also, the histogram of the residuals shows one positive outlier, which will also affect the coverage of the prediction intervals.

Using the estimated model we forecast 14 days ahead starting from Thursday 1 January 2015 (a non-work-day being a public holiday for New Years Day). In this case, we could obtain weather forecasts from the weather bureau for the next 14 days. But for the sake of illustration, we will use scenario based forecasting (as introduced in Section 5.6) where we set the temperature for the next 14 days to a constant 26 degrees.

```
fcast <- forecast(fit,
  xreg = cbind(rep(26,14), rep(26^2,14),
    c(0,1,0,0,1,1,1,1,1,0,0,1,1,1)))
autoplot(fcast) + ylab("Electicity demand (GW)")
```

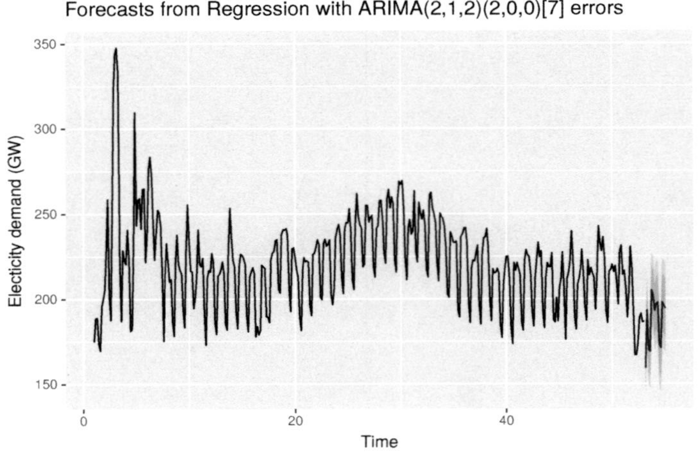

Figure 9.8: Forecasts from the dynamic regression model for daily electricity demand. All future temperatures have been set to 26 degrees, and the working day dummy variable has been set to known future values.

The point forecasts look reasonable for the first two weeks of 2015. The slow down in electricity demand at the end of 2014 (due to many people taking summer vacations) has caused the forecasts for the next two weeks to show similarly low demand values.

9.4 Stochastic and deterministic trends

There are two different ways of modelling a linear trend. A *deterministic trend* is obtained using the regression model

$$y_t = \beta_0 + \beta_1 t + \eta_t,$$

where η_t is an ARMA process. A *stochastic trend* is obtained using the model

$$y_t = \beta_0 + \beta_1 t + \eta_t,$$

where η_t is an ARIMA process with $d = 1$. In the latter case, we can difference both sides so that $y'_t = \beta_1 + \eta'_t$, where η'_t is an ARMA process. In other words,

$$y_t = y_{t-1} + \beta_1 + \eta'_t.$$

This is very similar to a random walk with drift (introduced in Section 8.1), but here the error term is an ARMA process rather than simply white noise.

Although these models appear quite similar (they only differ in the number of differences that need to be applied to η_t), their forecasting characteristics are quite different.

Example: International visitors to Australia

```
autoplot(austa) + xlab("Year") +
  ylab("millions of people") +
  ggtitle("Total annual international visitors to Australia")
```

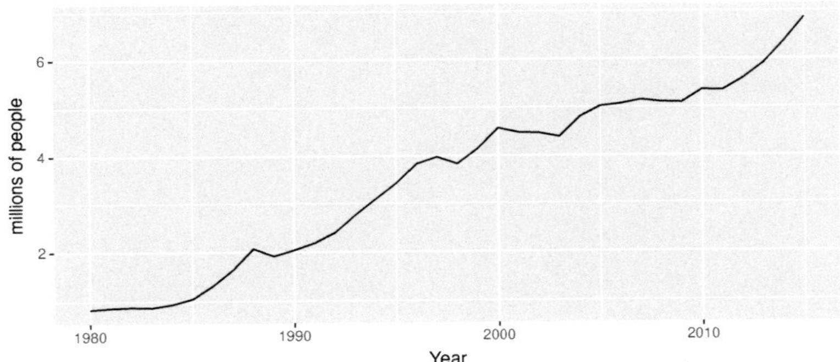

Figure 9.9: Annual international visitors to Australia, 1980–2015.

Figure 9.9 shows the total number of international visitors to Australia each year from 1980 to 2015. We will fit both a deterministic and a stochastic trend model to these data.

The deterministic trend model is obtained as follows:

```
trend <- seq_along(austa)
(fit1 <- auto.arima(austa, d=0, xreg=trend))
#> Series: austa
#> Regression with ARIMA(2,0,0) errors
#>
#> Coefficients:
#>          ar1      ar2  intercept    xreg
#>        1.113   -0.380      0.416   0.171
#> s.e.   0.160    0.158      0.190   0.009
#>
#> sigma^2 estimated as 0.0298:  log likelihood=13.6
#> AIC=-17.2   AICc=-15.2   BIC=-9.28
```

This model can be written as

$$
\begin{aligned}
y_t &= 0.42 + 0.17t + \eta_t \\
\eta_t &= 1.11\eta_{t-1} - 0.38\eta_{t-2} + \varepsilon_t \\
\varepsilon_t &\sim \text{NID}(0, 0.0298).
\end{aligned}
$$

The estimated growth in visitor numbers is 0.17 million people per year.

Alternatively, the stochastic trend model can be estimated.

```
(fit2 <- auto.arima(austa, d=1))
#> Series: austa
#> ARIMA(0,1,1) with drift
#>
#> Coefficients:
#>          ma1  drift
#>        0.301  0.173
#> s.e.   0.165  0.039
#>
#> sigma^2 estimated as 0.0338:  log likelihood=10.62
#> AIC=-15.24   AICc=-14.46   BIC=-10.57
```

This model can be written as $y_t - y_{t-1} = 0.17 + \eta'_t$, or equivalently

$$
\begin{aligned}
y_t &= y_0 + 0.17t + \eta_t \\
\eta_t &= \eta_{t-1} + 0.30\varepsilon_{t-1} + \varepsilon_t \\
\varepsilon_t &\sim \text{NID}(0, 0.0338).
\end{aligned}
$$

In this case, the estimated growth in visitor numbers is also 0.17 million people per year. Although the growth estimates are similar, the prediction intervals are not, as Figure 9.10 shows. In particular, stochastic trends have much wider prediction intervals because the errors are non-stationary.

```
fc1 <- forecast(fit1,
  xreg = data.frame(trend = length(austa) + 1:10))
fc2 <- forecast(fit2, h=10)
autoplot(austa) +
  autolayer(fc2, series="Stochastic trend") +
  autolayer(fc1, series="Deterministic trend") +
  ggtitle("Forecasts from trend models") +
  xlab("Year") + ylab("Visitors to Australia (millions)") +
  guides(colour=guide_legend(title="Forecast"))
```

There is an implicit assumption with deterministic trends that the slope of the trend is not going to change over time. On the other hand, stochastic trends can change, and the estimated growth is only assumed to be the average growth over the historical period, not necessarily the rate of growth that will be observed into the future. Consequently, it is safer to forecast with stochastic trends, especially for longer forecast horizons, as

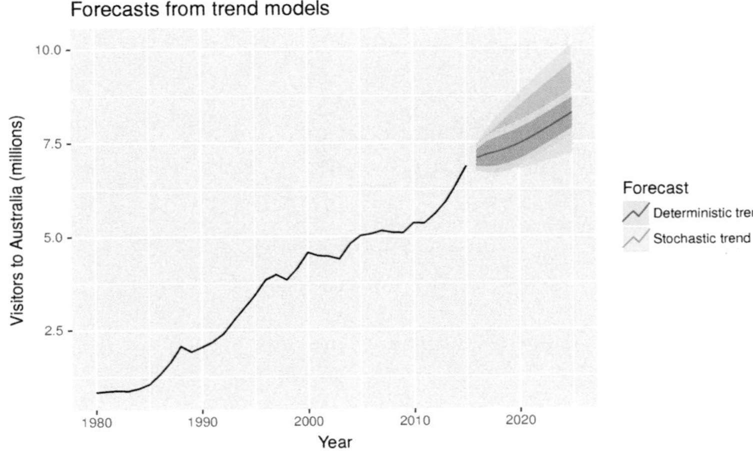

Figure 9.10: Forecasts of annual international visitors to Australia using a deterministic trend model and a stochastic trend model.

the prediction intervals allow for greater uncertainty in future growth.

9.5 Dynamic harmonic regression

When there are long seasonal periods, a dynamic regression with Fourier terms is often better than other models we have considered in this book.

For example, daily data can have annual seasonality of length 365, weekly data has seasonal period of approximately 52, while half-hourly data can have several seasonal periods, the shortest of which is the daily pattern of period 48.

Seasonal versions of ARIMA and ETS models are designed for shorter periods such as 12 for monthly data or 4 for quarterly data. The `ets()` function restricts seasonality to be a maximum period of 24 to allow hourly data but not data with a larger seasonal frequency. The problem is that there are $m-1$ parameters to be estimated for the initial seasonal states where m is the seasonal period. So for large m, the estimation becomes almost impossible.

The `Arima()` and `auto.arima()` functions will allow a seasonal period up to $m = 350$, but in practice will usually run out of memory whenever the seasonal period is more than about 200. In any case, seasonal differencing of very high order does not make a lot of sense — for daily data it involves comparing what happened today with what happened exactly a year ago and there is no constraint that the seasonal pattern is smooth.

So for such time series, we prefer a harmonic regression approach where the seasonal pattern is modelled using Fourier terms with short-term time series dynamics handled by an ARMA error.

The advantages of this approach are:

- it allows any length seasonality;
- for data with more than one seasonal period, Fourier terms of different frequencies can be included;
- the seasonal pattern is smooth for small values of K (but more wiggly seasonality can be handled by increasing K);
- the short-term dynamics are easily handled with a simple ARMA error.

The only real disadvantage (compared to a seasonal ARIMA model) is that the seasonality is assumed to be fixed — the seasonal pattern is not allowed to change over time. But in practice, seasonality is usually remarkably constant so this is not a big disadvantage except for very long time series.

Example: Australian eating out expenditure

In this example we demonstrate combining Fourier terms for capturing seasonality with ARIMA errors capturing other dynamics in the data. For simplicity, we will use an example with monthly data. The same modelling approach using weekly data is discussed in Section 12.1.

We use `auscafe`, the total monthly expenditure on cafes, restaurants and takeaway food services in Australia ($billion), starting in 2004 up to November 2016 and we forecast 24 months ahead. We vary the number of Fourier terms from 1 to 6 (which is equivalent to including seasonal dummies). Figure 9.11 shows the seasonal pattern projected forward as K increases. Notice that as K increases the Fourier terms capture and project a more "wiggly" seasonal pattern and simpler ARIMA models are required to capture other dynamics. The AICc value is minimized for $K = 5$, with a significant jump going from $K = 4$ to $K = 5$, hence the forecasts generated from this model would be the ones used.

```
cafe04 <- window(auscafe, start=2004)
plots <- list()
for (i in seq(6)) {
  fit <- auto.arima(cafe04, xreg = fourier(cafe04, K = i),
    seasonal = FALSE, lambda = 0)
  plots[[i]] <- autoplot(forecast(fit,
      xreg=fourier(cafe04, K=i, h=24))) +
    xlab(paste("K=",i,"   AICC=",round(fit[["aicc"]],2))) +
    ylab("") + ylim(1.5,4.7)
}
gridExtra::grid.arrange(
  plots[[1]],plots[[2]],plots[[3]],
  plots[[4]],plots[[5]],plots[[6]], nrow=3)
```

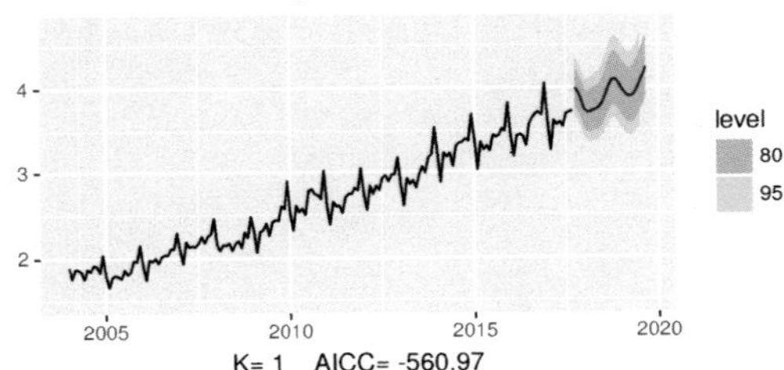

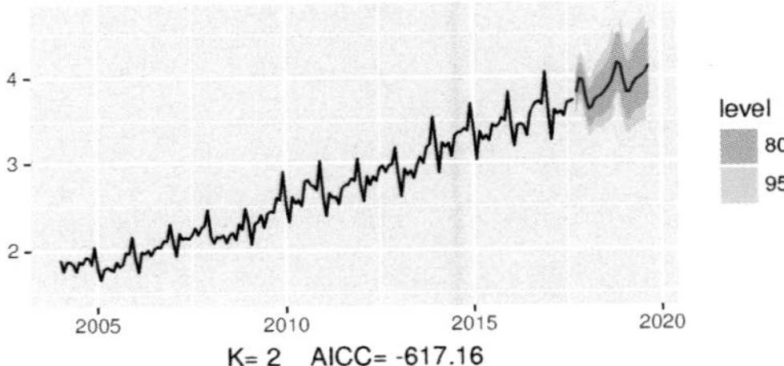

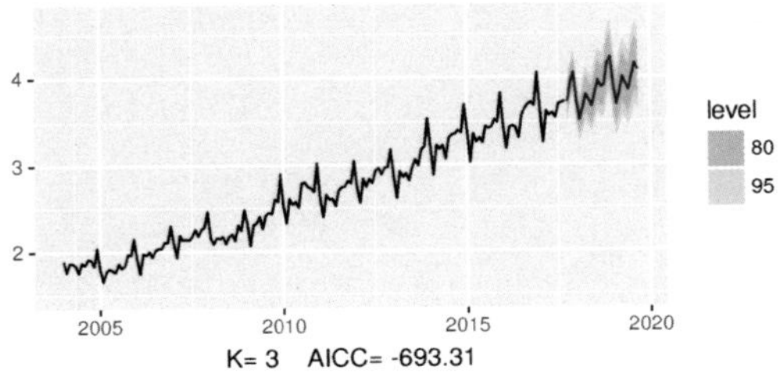

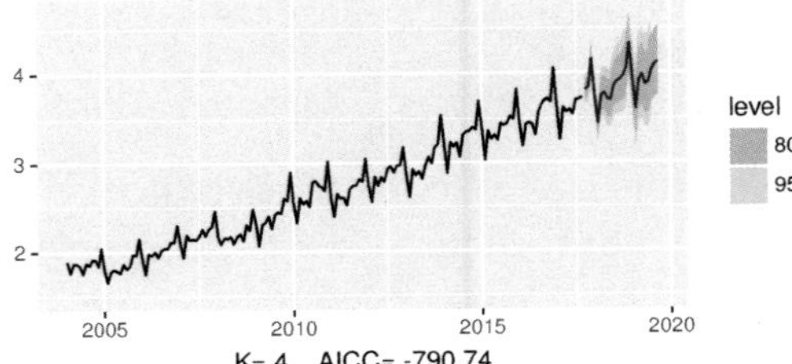

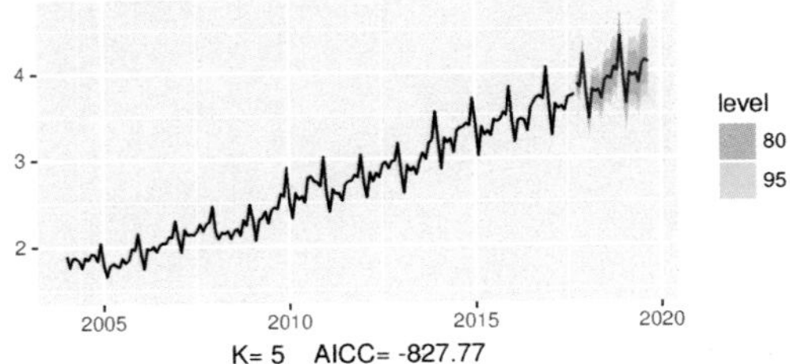

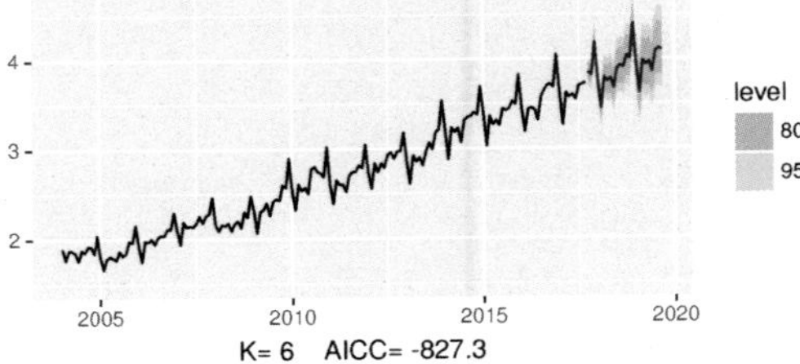

Figure 9.11: Using Fourier terms and ARIMA errors for forecasting monthly expenditure on eating out in Australia.

9.6 Lagged predictors

Sometimes, the impact of a predictor which is included in a regression model will not be simple and immediate. For example, an advertising campaign may impact sales for some time beyond the end of the campaign, and sales in one month will depend on the advertising expenditure in each of the past few months. Similarly, a change in a company's safety policy may reduce accidents immediately, but have a diminishing effect over time as employees take less care when they become familiar with the new working conditions.

In these situations, we need to allow for lagged effects of the predictor. Suppose that we have only one predictor in our model. Then a model which allows for lagged effects can be written as

$$y_t = \beta_0 + \gamma_0 x_t + \gamma_1 x_{t-1} + \cdots + \gamma_k x_{t-k} + \eta_t,$$

where η_t is an ARIMA process. The value of k can be selected using the AICc, along with the values of p and q for the ARIMA error.

Example: TV advertising and insurance quotations

A US insurance company advertises on national television in an attempt to increase the number of insurance quotations provided (and consequently the number of new policies). Figure 9.12 shows the number of quotations and the expenditure on television advertising for the company each month from January 2002 to April 2005.

```
autoplot(insurance, facets=TRUE) +
  xlab("Year") + ylab("") +
  ggtitle("Insurance advertising and quotations")
```

We will consider including advertising expenditure for up to four months; that is, the model may include advertising expenditure in the current month, and the three months before that. When comparing models, it is important that they all use the same training set. In the following code, we exclude the first three months in order to make fair comparisons.

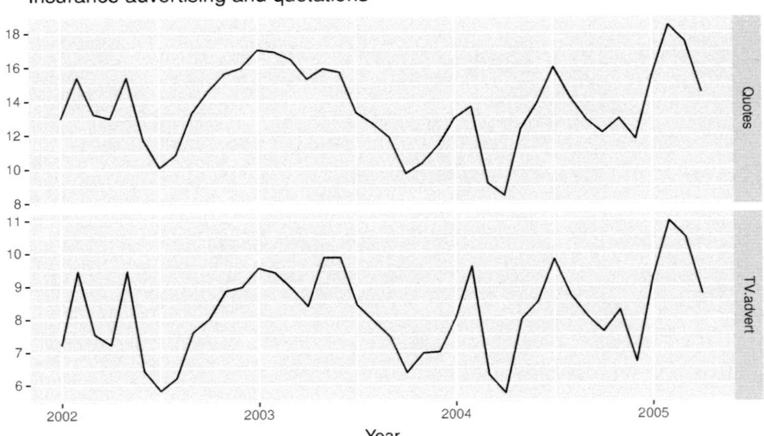

Figure 9.12: Numbers of insurance quotations provided per month and the expenditure on advertising per month.

```
# Lagged predictors. Test 0, 1, 2 or 3 lags.
Advert <- cbind(
    AdLag0 = insurance[,"TV.advert"],
    AdLag1 = stats::lag(insurance[,"TV.advert"],-1),
    AdLag2 = stats::lag(insurance[,"TV.advert"],-2),
    AdLag3 = stats::lag(insurance[,"TV.advert"],-3)) %>%
  head(NROW(insurance))

# Restrict data so models use same fitting period
fit1 <- auto.arima(insurance[4:40,1], xreg=Advert[4:40,1],
  stationary=TRUE)
fit2 <- auto.arima(insurance[4:40,1], xreg=Advert[4:40,1:2],
  stationary=TRUE)
fit3 <- auto.arima(insurance[4:40,1], xreg=Advert[4:40,1:3],
  stationary=TRUE)
fit4 <- auto.arima(insurance[4:40,1], xreg=Advert[4:40,1:4],
  stationary=TRUE)
```

Next we choose the optimal lag length for advertising based on the AICc.

```
c(fit1[["aicc"]],fit2[["aicc"]],fit3[["aicc"]],fit4[["aicc"]])
#> [1] 68.50 60.02 62.83 68.02
```

The best model (with the smallest AICc value) has two lagged predictors; that is, it includes advertising only in the current month and the previous month. So we now re-estimate that model, but using all the available data.

```
(fit <- auto.arima(insurance[,1], xreg=Advert[,1:2],
  stationary=TRUE))
#> Series: insurance[, 1]
#> Regression with ARIMA(3,0,0) errors
#>
#> Coefficients:
#>          ar1     ar2    ar3  intercept  AdLag0  AdLag1
#>        1.412  -0.932  0.359      2.039   1.256   0.162
#> s.e.   0.170   0.255  0.159      0.993   0.067   0.059
#>
#> sigma^2 estimated as 0.217:  log likelihood=-23.89
#> AIC=61.78   AICc=65.28   BIC=73.6
```

The chosen model has AR(3) errors. The model can be written as

$$y_t = 2.04 + 1.26x_t + 0.16x_{t-1} + \eta_t,$$

where y_t is the number of quotations provided in month t, x_t is the advertising expenditure in month t,

$$\eta_t = 1.41\eta_{t-1} - 0.93\eta_{t-2} + 0.36\eta_{t-3} + \varepsilon_t,$$

and ε_t is white noise.

We can calculate forecasts using this model if we assume future values for the advertising variable. If we set the future monthly advertising to 8 units, we get the forecasts in Figure 9.13.

```
fc8 <- forecast(fit, h=20,
  xreg=cbind(AdLag0 = rep(8,20),
             AdLag1 = c(Advert[40,1], rep(8,19))))
autoplot(fc8) + ylab("Quotes") +
  ggtitle("Forecast quotes with future advertising set to 8")
```

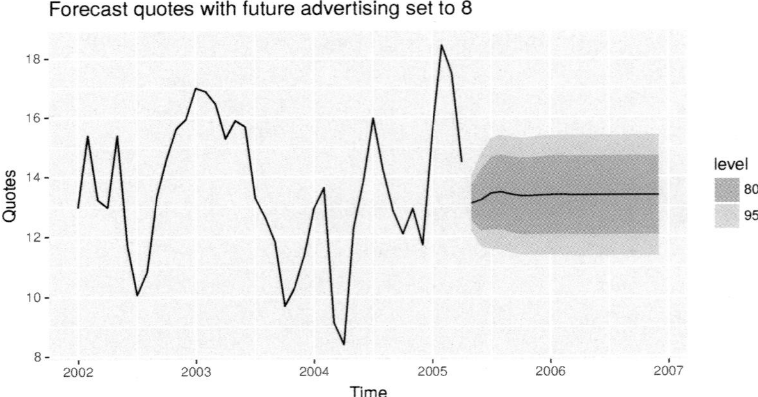

Figure 9.13: Forecasts of monthly insurance quotes, assuming that the future advertising expenditure is 8 units in each future month.

9.7 Exercises

1. Consider monthly sales and advertising data for an automotive parts company (data set `advert`).
   a. Plot the data using `autoplot`. Why is it useful to set `facets=TRUE`?
   b. Fit a standard regression model $y_t = a + bx_t + \eta_t$ where y_t denotes sales and x_t denotes advertising using the `tslm()` function.
   c. Show that the residuals have significant autocorrelation.
   d. What difference does it make you use the `Arima` function instead:

   ```
   Arima(advert[,"sales"], xreg=advert[,"advert"],
     order=c(0,0,0))
   ```

   e. Refit the model using `auto.arima()`. How much difference does the error model make to the estimated parameters? What ARIMA model for the errors is selected?
   f. Check the residuals of the fitted model.
   g. Assuming the advertising budget for the next six months is exactly 10 units per month, produce and plot sales forecasts with prediction intervals for the next six months.

2. This exercise uses data set `huron` giving the level of Lake Huron from 1875–1972.

   a. Fit a piecewise linear trend model to the Lake Huron data with a knot at 1920 and an ARMA error structure.
   b. Forecast the level for the next 30 years.

3. This exercise concerns `motel`: the total monthly takings from accommodation and the total room nights occupied at hotels, motels, and guest houses in Victoria, Australia, between January 1980 and June 1995. Total monthly takings are in thousands of Australian dollars; total room nights occupied are in thousands.

   a. Use the data to calculate the average cost of a night's accommodation in Victoria each month.
   b. Estimate the monthly CPI.
   c. Produce time series plots of both variables and explain why logarithms of both variables need to be taken before fitting any models.

d. Fit an appropriate regression model with ARIMA errors. Explain your reasoning in arriving at the final model.
e. Forecast the average price per room for the next twelve months using your fitted model. (Hint: You will need to produce forecasts of the CPI figures first.)

4. We fitted a harmonic regression model to part of the `gasoline` series in Exercise 6 in Section 5.10. We will now revisit this model, and extend it to include more data and ARMA errors.

   a. Using `tslm()`, fit a harmonic regression with a piecewise linear time trend to the full `gasoline` series. Select the position of the knots in the trend and the appropriate number of Fourier terms to include by minimizing the AICc or CV value.
   b. Now refit the model using `auto.arima()` to allow for correlated errors, keeping the same predictor variables as you used with `tslm()`.
   c. Check the residuals of the final model using the `checkresiduals()` function. Do they look sufficiently like white noise to continue? If not, try modifying your model, or removing the first few years of data.
   d. Once you have a model with white noise residuals, produce forecasts for the next year.

5. Electricity consumption is often modelled as a function of temperature. Temperature is measured by daily heating degrees and cooling degrees. Heating degrees is 18°C minus the average daily temperature when the daily average is below 18°C; otherwise it is zero. This provides a measure of our need to heat ourselves as temperature falls. Cooling degrees measures our need to cool ourselves as the temperature rises. It is defined as the average daily temperature minus 18°C when the daily average is above 18°C; otherwise it is zero. Let y_t denote the monthly total of kilowatt-hours of electricity used, let $x_{1,t}$ denote the monthly total of heating degrees, and let $x_{2,t}$ denote the monthly total of cooling degrees.

   An analyst fits the following model to a set of such data:

$$y_t^* = b_1 x_{1,t}^* + b_2 x_{2,t}^* + \eta_t,$$

where

$$(1-B)(1-B^{12})\eta_t = \frac{1-\theta_1 B}{1-\phi_{12}B^{12}-\phi_{24}B^{24}}\varepsilon_t$$

and $y_t^* = \log(Y_t)$, $x_{1,t}^* = \sqrt{x_{1,t}}$ and $x_{2,t}^* = \sqrt{x_{2,t}}$.

a. What sort of ARIMA model is identified for η_t?

b. The estimated coefficients are

Parameter	Estimate	s.e.	Z	P-value
b_1	0.0077	0.0015	4.98	0.000
b_2	0.0208	0.0023	9.23	0.000
θ_1	0.5830	0.0720	8.10	0.000
ϕ_{12}	-0.5373	0.0856	-6.27	0.000
ϕ_{24}	-0.4667	0.0862	-5.41	0.000

Explain what the estimates of b_1 and b_2 tell us about electricity consumption.

c. Write the equation in a form more suitable for forecasting.
d. Describe how this model could be used to forecast electricity demand for the next 12 months.
e. Explain why the η_t term should be modelled with an ARIMA model rather than modelling the data using a standard regression package. In your discussion, comment on the properties of the estimates, the validity of the standard regression results, and the importance of the η_t model in producing forecasts.

6. For the retail time series considered in earlier chapters:

a. Develop an appropriate dynamic regression model with Fourier terms for the seasonality. Use the AIC to select the number of Fourier terms to include in the model. (You will probably need to use the same Box-Cox transformation you identified previously.)
b. Check the residuals of the fitted model. Does the residual series look like white noise?
c. Compare the forecasts with those you obtained earlier using alternative models.

9.8 Further reading

- A detailed discussion of dynamic regression models is provided in Pankratz (1991).
- A generalization of dynamic regression models, known as "transfer function models", is discussed in Box, Jenkins, et al. (2015).

Chapter 10

Forecasting hierarchical or grouped time series

Warning: this is a more advanced chapter and assumes a knowledge of some basic matrix algebra.

Time series can often be naturally disaggregated by various attributes of interest. For example, the total number of bicycles sold by a cycling manufacturer can be disaggregated by product type such as road bikes, mountain bikes, children's bikes and hybrids. Each of these can be disaggregated into finer categories. For example hybrid bikes can be divided into city, commuting, comfort, and trekking bikes; and so on. These categories are nested within the larger group categories, and so the collection of time series follow a hierarchical aggregation structure. Therefore we refer to these as "hierarchical time series", the topic of Section 10.1.

Hierarchical time series often arise due to geographical divisions. For example, the total bicycle sales can be disaggregated by country, then within each country by state, within each state by region, and so on down to the outlet level.

Our bicycle manufacturer may disaggregate sales by both product type and by geographical location. Then we have a more complicated aggregation structure where the product hierarchy and the geographical hierarchy can both be used together. We usually refer to these as "grouped time series", and discuss them in Section 10.2.

It is common to produce disaggregated forecasts based on disaggregated time series, and we usually require the forecasts to add up in the same way as the data. For example, forecasts of regional sales should add up to give forecasts of state sales, which should in turn add up to give a forecast for the national sales.

In this chapter we discuss forecasting large collections of time series that must add up in some way. The challenge is that we require forecasts that are **coherent** across the aggregation structure. That is, we require forecasts to add up in a manner that is consistent with the aggregation structure of the collection of time series. In Sections 10.3–10.7 we discuss several methods for producing coherent forecasts for both hierarchical and grouped time series.

10.1 Hierarchical time series

Figure 10.1 shows a $K = 2$-level hierarchical structure. At the top of the hierarchy (which we call level 0) is the "Total", the most aggregate level of the data. The tth observation of the Total series is denoted by y_t for $t = 1,\dots,T$. The Total is disaggregated into two series at level 1, which in turn are divided into three and two series respectively at the bottom-level of the hierarchy. Below the top level, we use $y_{\text{j},t}$ to denote the tth observation of the series corresponding to node j. For example, $y_{A,t}$ denotes the tth observation of the series corresponding to node A at level 1, $y_{AB,t}$ denotes the tth observation of the series corresponding to node AB at level 2, and so on.

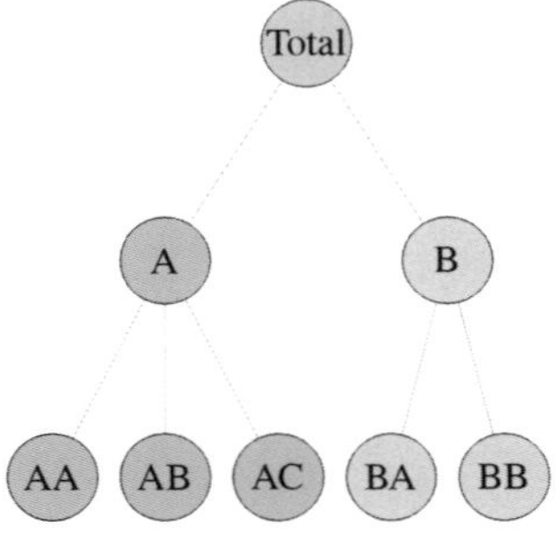

Figure 10.1: A two level hierarchical tree diagram.

In this small example, the total number of series in the hierarchy is $n = 1 + 2 + 5 = 8$, while the number of series at the bottom-level is $m = 5$. Note that $n > m$ in all hierarchies.

For any time t, the observations at the bottom-level of the hierarchy will sum to the observations of the series above. For example,

$$y_t = y_{AA,t} + y_{AB,t} + y_{AC,t} + y_{BA,t} + y_{BB,t} \tag{10.1}$$

and

$$y_{A,t} = y_{AA,t} + y_{AB,t} + y_{AC,t} \quad \text{and} \quad y_{B,t} = y_{BA,t} + y_{BB,t}. \tag{10.2}$$

Substituting (10.2) into (10.1), we also get $y_t = y_{A,t} + y_{B,t}$. These equations can be thought of as aggregation constraints or summing equalities, and can be more efficiently represented using matrix notation. We construct an $n \times m$ matrix $\boldsymbol{S}$ (referred to as the "summing matrix") which dictates the way in which the bottom-level series are aggregated.

For the hierarchical structure in Figure 10.1, we can write

$$\begin{bmatrix} y_t \\ y_{A,t} \\ y_{B,t} \\ y_{AA,t} \\ y_{AB,t} \\ y_{AC,t} \\ y_{BA,t} \\ y_{BB,t} \end{bmatrix} = \begin{bmatrix} 1 & 1 & 1 & 1 & 1 \\ 1 & 1 & 1 & 0 & 0 \\ 0 & 0 & 0 & 1 & 1 \\ 1 & 0 & 0 & 0 & 0 \\ 0 & 1 & 0 & 0 & 0 \\ 0 & 0 & 1 & 0 & 0 \\ 0 & 0 & 0 & 1 & 0 \\ 0 & 0 & 0 & 0 & 1 \end{bmatrix} \begin{bmatrix} y_{AA,t} \\ y_{AB,t} \\ y_{AC,t} \\ y_{BA,t} \\ y_{BB,t} \end{bmatrix}$$

or in more compact notation

$$\boldsymbol{y}_t = \boldsymbol{S}\boldsymbol{b}_t, \tag{10.3}$$

where $\boldsymbol{y}_t$ is an n-dimensional vector of all the observations in the hierarchy at time t, $\boldsymbol{S}$ is the summing matrix, and $\boldsymbol{b}_t$ is an m-dimensional vector of all the observations in the bottom-level of the hierarchy at time t. Note that the first row in the summing matrix $\boldsymbol{S}$ represents Equation (10.1) above, the second and third rows represent (10.2). The rows below these comprise an m-dimensional identity matrix $\boldsymbol{I}_m$ so that each bottom-level observation on the right hand side of the equation is equal to itself on the left hand side.

Example: Australian tourism hierarchy

Australia is divided into eight geographical areas (some called states and others called territories) with each one having its own government and some economic and administrative autonomy. Each of these can be further subdivided into smaller areas of interest, referred to as zones. Business planners and tourism authorities are interested in forecasts for the whole of Australia, for the states and the territories, and also for the zones. In this example we concentrate on quarterly domestic tourism demand, measured as the number of visitor nights Australians spend away from home. To simplify our analysis, we combine the two territories and Tasmania into an "Other" state. So we have six states: New South Wales (NSW), Queensland (QLD), South Australia (SAU), Victoria (VIC), Western Australia (WA) and Other (OTH). For each of these we consider visitor nights within the following zones.

State	Zones
NSW	Metro (NSWMetro), North Coast (NSWNthCo), South Coast (NSWSthCo), South Inner (NSWSthIn), North Inner (NSWNthIn)
QLD	Metro (QLDMetro), Central (QLDCntrl), North Coast (QLDNthCo)
SAU	Metro (SAUMetro), Coastal (SAUCoast), Inner (SAUInner)
VIC	Metro (VICMetro), West Coast (VICWstCo), East Coast (VICEstCo), Inner (VICInner)
WAU	Metro (WAUMetro), Coastal (WAUCoast), Inner (WAUInner)
OTH	Metro (OTHMetro), Non-Metro (OTHNoMet)

We consider five zones for NSW, four zones for VIC, and three zones each for QLD, SAU and WAU. Note that Metro zones contain the capital cities and surrounding areas. For further details on these geographical areas, please refer to Appendix C in Wickramasuriya, Athanasopoulos, and Hyndman (2018).

To create a hierarchical time series, we use the `hts()` function as shown in the code below. The function requires two inputs: the bottom-level time series and information about the hierarchical structure. `visnights` is a time series matrix containing the bottom-level series. There are several ways to input the structure of the hierarchy. In this case we are using the `characters` argument. The first three characters of each column name of `visnights` capture the categories at the first level of the hierarchy (States). The following five characters capture the bottom-level categories (Zones).

```
library(hts)
tourism.hts <- hts(visnights, characters = c(3, 5))
tourism.hts %>% aggts(levels=0:1) %>%
  autoplot(facet=TRUE) +
  xlab("Year") + ylab("millions") + ggtitle("Visitor nights")
```

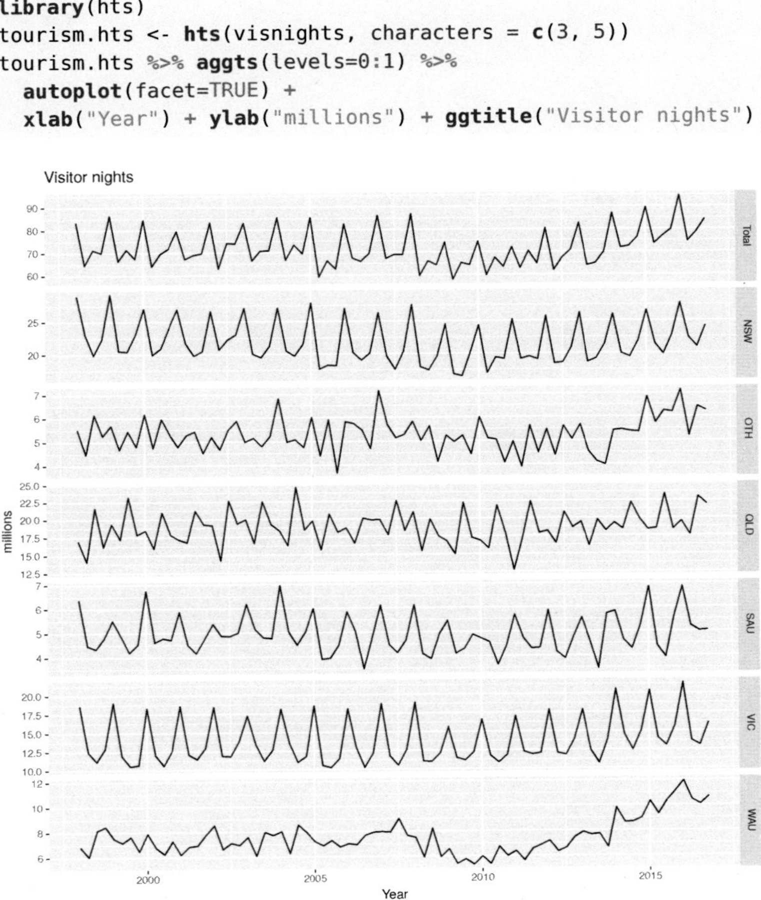

Figure 10.2: Australian domestic visitor nights over the period 1998 Q1 to 2016 Q4 disaggregated by State.

The top plot in Figure 10.2 shows the total number of visitor nights for the whole of Australia, while the plots below show the data disaggregated by state. These reveal diverse and rich dynamics at the aggregate national level, and the first level of disaggregation for each state. The `aggts()` function extracts time series from an `hts` object for any level of aggregation.

The plots in Figure 10.3 show the bottom-level time series, namely the visitor nights for each zone. These help us visualise the diverse individual dynamics within each zone, and assist in identifying unique and important time series. Notice, for example, the coastal WAU zone which shows significant growth over the last few years.

```
library(tidyverse)
cols <- sample(scales::hue_pal(h=c(15,375),
  c=100,l=65,h.start=0,direction = 1)(NCOL(visnights)))
as_tibble(visnights) %>%
  gather(Zone) %>%
  mutate(Date = rep(time(visnights), NCOL(visnights)),
         State = str_sub(Zone,1,3)) %>%
  ggplot(aes(x=Date, y=value, group=Zone, color=Zone)) +
    geom_line() +
    facet_grid(State~., scales="free_y") +
    xlab("Year") + ylab("millions") +
    ggtitle("Visitor nights by Zone") +
    scale_color_manual(values = cols)
```

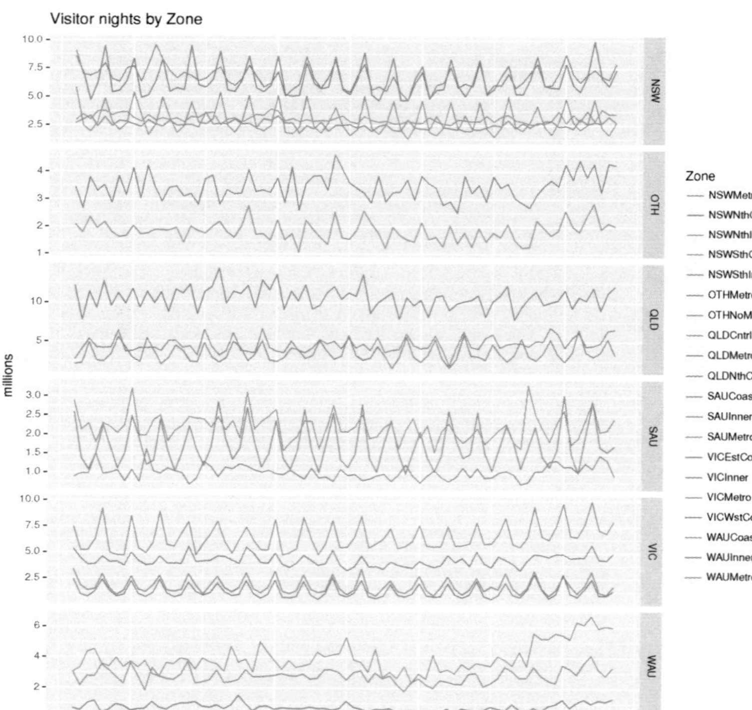

Figure 10.3: Australian domestic visitor nights over the period 1998 Q1 to 2016 Q4 disaggregated by Zones.

To produce this figure, we are using various functions from the **tidyverse** collection of packages[1]. The details are beyond the scope of this book, but there are many good online resources available to learn how to use these packages.

[1] https://www.tidyverse.org/

10.2 Grouped time series

Grouped time series involve more general aggregation structures than hierarchical time series. With grouped time series, the structure does not naturally disaggregate in a unique hierarchical manner, and often the disaggregating factors are both nested and crossed. For example, we could further disaggregate all geographical levels of the Australian tourism data by purpose of travel (such as holidays, business, etc.). So we could consider visitors nights split by purpose of travel for the whole of Australia, and for each state, and for each zone. Then we describe the structure as involving the purpose of travel "crossed" with the geographical hierarchy.

Figure 10.4 shows a $K = 2$-level grouped structure. At the top of the grouped structure is the Total, the most aggregate level of the data, again represented by y_t. The Total can be disaggregated by attributes (A, B) forming series $y_{\mathrm{A},t}$ and $y_{\mathrm{B},t}$, or by attributes (X, Y) forming series $y_{\mathrm{X},t}$ and $y_{\mathrm{Y},t}$. At the bottom level, the data are disaggregated by both attributes.

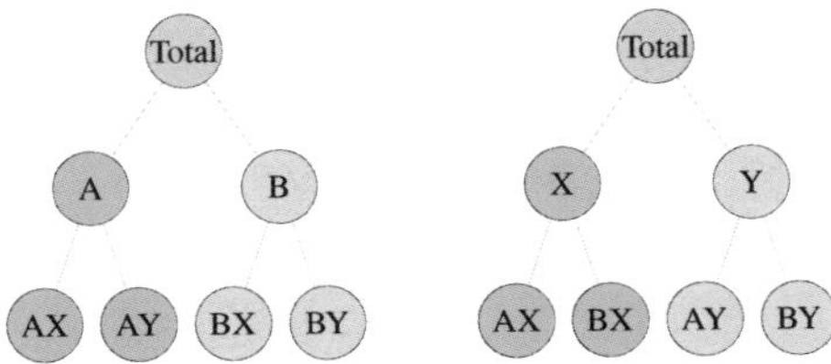

Figure 10.4: Alternative representations of a two level grouped structure.

This example shows that there are alternative aggregation paths for grouped structures. For any time t, as with the hierarchical structure,

$$y_t = y_{\mathrm{AX},t} + y_{\mathrm{AY},t} + y_{\mathrm{BX},t} + y_{\mathrm{BY},t}.$$

However, for the first level of the grouped structure,

$$y_{\mathrm{A},t} = y_{\mathrm{AX},t} + y_{\mathrm{AY},t} \qquad y_{\mathrm{B},t} = y_{\mathrm{BX},t} + y_{\mathrm{BY},t} \tag{10.4}$$

but also

$$y_{\mathrm{X},t} = y_{\mathrm{AX},t} + y_{\mathrm{BX},t} \qquad y_{\mathrm{Y},t} = y_{\mathrm{AY},t} + y_{\mathrm{BY},t}. \tag{10.5}$$

These equalities can again be represented by the $n \times m$ summing matrix S. The total number of series is $n = 9$ with $m = 4$ series at the bottom-level. For the grouped structure in Figure 10.4 we write

$$\begin{bmatrix} y_t \\ y_{A,t} \\ y_{B,t} \\ y_{X,t} \\ y_{Y,t} \\ y_{AX,t} \\ y_{AY,t} \\ y_{BX,t} \\ y_{BY,t} \end{bmatrix} = \begin{bmatrix} 1 & 1 & 1 & 1 \\ 1 & 1 & 0 & 0 \\ 0 & 0 & 1 & 1 \\ 1 & 0 & 1 & 0 \\ 0 & 1 & 0 & 1 \\ 1 & 0 & 0 & 0 \\ 0 & 1 & 0 & 0 \\ 0 & 0 & 1 & 0 \\ 0 & 0 & 0 & 1 \end{bmatrix} \begin{bmatrix} y_{AX,t} \\ y_{AY,t} \\ y_{BX,t} \\ y_{BY,t} \end{bmatrix},$$

or

$$y_t = S\boldsymbol{b}_t,$$

where the second and third rows of S represent (10.4) and the fourth and fifth rows represent (10.5).

Grouped time series can sometimes be thought of as hierarchical time series that do not impose a unique hierarchical structure, in the sense that the order by which the series can be grouped is not unique.

Example: Australian prison population The top row of Figure 10.5 shows the total number of prisoners in Australia over the period 2005 Q1 to 2016 Q4. This represents the top-level series in the grouping structure. The rest of the panels show the prison population disaggregated by (i) state[2] (ii) legal status, whether prisoners have already been sentenced or are in remand waiting for a sentence, and (iii) gender. In this example, the three factors are crossed, but none are nested within the others.

[2] Australia comprises eight geographical areas six states and two territories: Australian Capital Territory, New South Wales, Northern Territory, Queensland, South Australia, Tasmania, Victoria, Western Australia. In this example we consider all eight areas.

To create a grouped time series, we use the `gts()` function. Similar to the `hts()` function, inputs to the `gts()` function are the bottom-level time series and information about the grouping structure. `prison` is a time series matrix containing the bottom-level time series. The information about the grouping structure can be passed in using the `characters` input. (An alternative is to be more explicit about the labelling of the series and use the `groups` input.)

```
prison.gts <- gts(prison/1e3, characters = c(3,1,9),
  gnames = c("State", "Gender", "Legal",
             "State*Gender", "State*Legal",
             "State*Gender*Legal"))
```

One way to plot the main groups is as follows.

```
prison.gts %>% aggts(level=0:3) %>% autoplot()
```

But with a little more work, we can construct Figure 10.5 using the following code.

```
p1 <- prison.gts %>% aggts(level=0) %>%
  autoplot() + ggtitle("Australian prison population") +
    xlab("Year") + ylab("Total number of prisoners ('000)")
groups <- aggts(prison.gts, level=1:3)
cols <- sample(scales::hue_pal(h=c(15,375),
          c=100,l=65,h.start=0,direction = 1)(NCOL(groups)))
p2 <- as_tibble(groups) %>%
  gather(Series) %>%
  mutate(Date = rep(time(groups), NCOL(groups)),
         Group = str_extract(Series, "([A-Za-z ]*)")) %>%
  ggplot(aes(x=Date, y=value, group=Series, color=Series)) +
    geom_line() +
    xlab("Year") + ylab("Number of prisoners ('000)") +
```

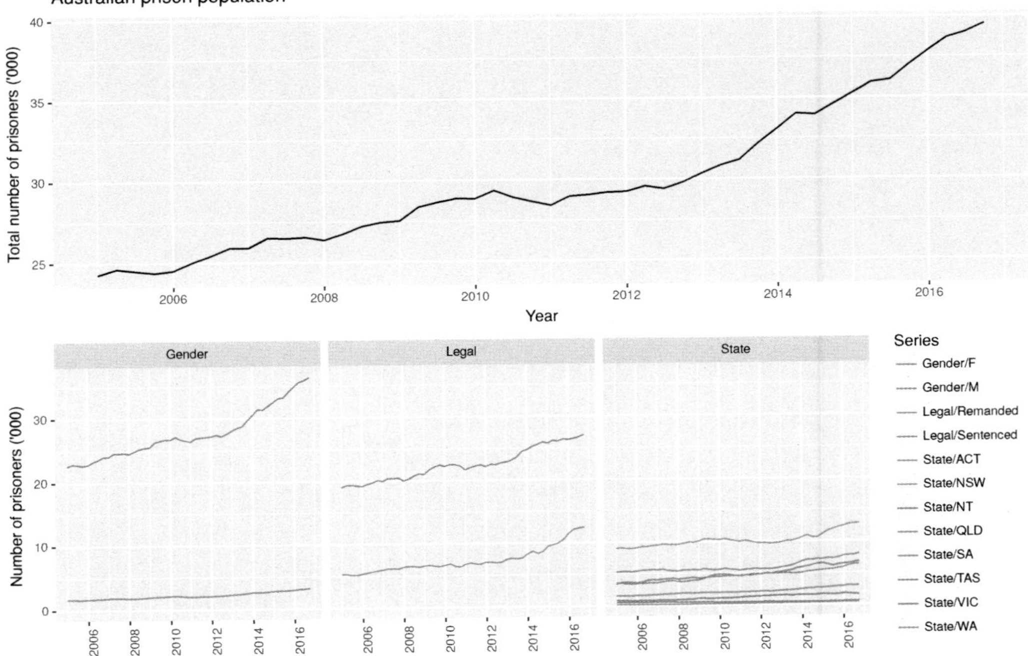

Figure 10.5: Total Australian quarterly adult prison population, disaggregated by state, by legal status and by gender.

```
    scale_color_manual(values = cols) +
    facet_grid(.~Group, scales="free_y") +
    scale_x_continuous(breaks=seq(2006,2016,by=2)) +
    theme(axis.text.x = element_text(angle = 90, hjust = 1))
gridExtra::grid.arrange(p1, p2, ncol=1)
```

Plots of other group combinations can be obtained similarly. Figure 10.6 shows the Australian prison population disaggregated by all possible combinations of two attributes at a time. The top plot shows the prison population disaggregated by state and legal status, the middle panel shows the disaggregation by state and gender and the bottom panel shows the disaggregation by legal status and gender.

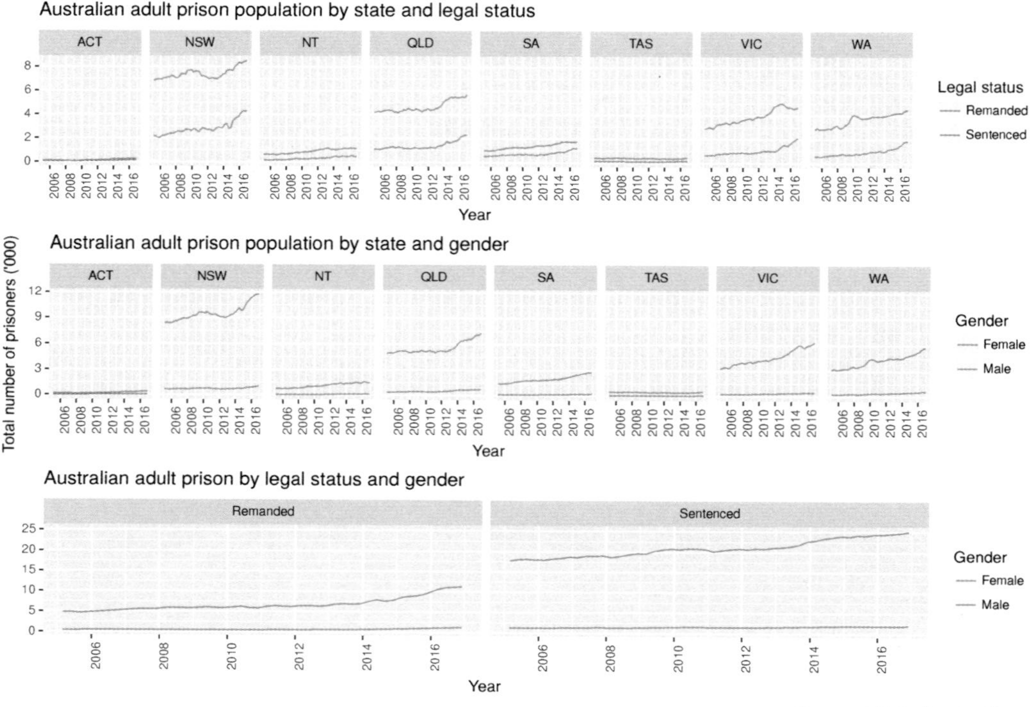

Figure 10.6: Australian adult prison population disaggregated by pairs of attributes.

Figure 10.7 shows the Australian adult population disaggregated by all three attributes: state, legal status and gender. These form the bottom-level series of the grouped structure for the Australian prison population.

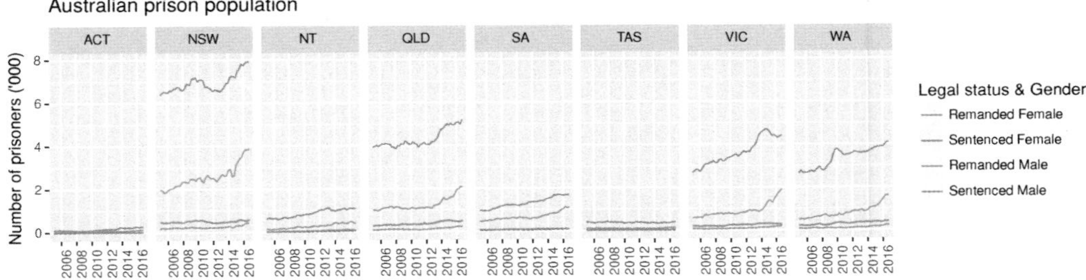

Figure 10.7: Bottom-level time series for the Australian adult prison population, grouped by state, legal status and gender.

10.3 The bottom-up approach

A simple method for generating coherent forecasts is the bottom-up approach. This approach involves first generating forecasts for each series at the bottom-level, and then summing these to produce forecasts for all the series in the structure.

For example, for the hierarchy of Figure 10.1, we first generate h-step-ahead forecasts for each of the bottom-level series:

$$\hat{y}_{\text{AA},h},\quad \hat{y}_{\text{AB},h},\quad \hat{y}_{\text{AC},h},\quad \hat{y}_{\text{BA},h} \text{ and } \hat{y}_{\text{BB},h}.$$

(We have simplified the previously used notation of $\hat{y}_{T+h|T}$ for brevity.) Summing these, we get h-step-ahead coherent forecasts for the rest of the series:

$$\begin{aligned}
\tilde{y}_h &= \hat{y}_{\text{AA},h} + \hat{y}_{\text{AB},h} + \hat{y}_{\text{AC},h} + \hat{y}_{\text{BA},h} + \hat{y}_{\text{BB},h},\\
\tilde{y}_{\text{A},h} &= \hat{y}_{\text{AA},h} + \hat{y}_{\text{AB},h} + \hat{y}_{\text{AC},h},\\
\text{and} \quad \tilde{y}_{\text{B},h} &= \hat{y}_{\text{BA},h} + \hat{y}_{\text{BB},h}.
\end{aligned}$$

(In this chapter, we will use the "tilde" notation to indicate coherent forecasts.) As in Equation (10.3), we can employ the summing matrix here and write

$$\begin{bmatrix} \tilde{y}_h \\ \tilde{y}_{\text{A},h} \\ \tilde{y}_{\text{B},h} \\ \tilde{y}_{\text{AA},h} \\ \tilde{y}_{\text{AB},h} \\ \tilde{y}_{\text{AC},h} \\ \tilde{y}_{\text{BA},h} \\ \tilde{y}_{\text{BB},h} \end{bmatrix} = \begin{bmatrix} 1 & 1 & 1 & 1 & 1 \\ 1 & 1 & 1 & 0 & 0 \\ 0 & 0 & 0 & 1 & 1 \\ 1 & 0 & 0 & 0 & 0 \\ 0 & 1 & 0 & 0 & 0 \\ 0 & 0 & 1 & 0 & 0 \\ 0 & 0 & 0 & 1 & 0 \\ 0 & 0 & 0 & 0 & 1 \end{bmatrix} \begin{bmatrix} \hat{y}_{\text{AA},h} \\ \hat{y}_{\text{AB},h} \\ \hat{y}_{\text{AC},h} \\ \hat{y}_{\text{BA},h} \\ \hat{y}_{\text{BB},h} \end{bmatrix}.$$

Using more compact notation, the bottom-up approach can be represented as

$$\tilde{\boldsymbol{y}}_h = \boldsymbol{S}\hat{\boldsymbol{b}}_h,$$

where $\tilde{\boldsymbol{y}}_t$ is an n-dimensional vector of coherent h-step-ahead forecasts, and $\hat{\boldsymbol{b}}_h$ is an m-dimensional vector of h-step-ahead forecasts for each of the bottom-level series.

An advantage of this approach is that we are forecasting at the bottom-level of a structure, and therefore no information is lost due to aggregation. On the other hand, bottom-level data can be quite noisy and more challenging to model and forecast.

The hts package for R

Forecasts can be produced using the `forecast()` function applied to objects created by `hts()` or `gts()`. The **hts** package[3] has three in-built options to produce forecasts: ETS models, ARIMA models or random walks; these are controlled by the `fmethod` argument. It also use several methods for producing coherent forecasts, controlled by the `method` argument.

[3] https://cran.r-project.org/package=hts

For example, suppose we wanted bottom-up forecasts using ARIMA models applied to the prison data. Then we would use

```
forecast(prison.gts, method="bu", fmethod="arima")
```

which will apply the `auto.arima()` function to every bottom-level series in our collection of time series. Similarly, ETS models would be used if `fmethod="ets"` was used.

10.4 Top-down approaches

Top-down approaches only work with strictly hierarchical aggregation structures, and not with grouped structures. They involve first generating forecasts for the Total series y_t, and then disaggregating these down the hierarchy.

We let $p_1,\dots,p_m$ be a set of disaggregation proportions which dictate how the forecasts of the Total series are to be distributed to obtain forecasts for each series at the bottom-level of the structure. For example, for the hierarchy of Figure 10.1 using proportions $p_1,\dots,p_5$ we get,

$$\tilde{y}_{\text{AA},t} = p_1\hat{y}_t, \quad \tilde{y}_{\text{AB},t} = p_2\hat{y}_t, \quad \tilde{y}_{\text{AC},t} = p_3\hat{y}_t, \quad \tilde{y}_{\text{BA},t} = p_4\hat{y}_t \quad \text{and} \quad \tilde{y}_{\text{BB},t} = p_5\hat{y}_t.$$

Using matrix notation we can stack the set of proportions in a m-dimensional vector $\boldsymbol{p} = (p_1, \dots, p_m)'$ and write

$$\tilde{\boldsymbol{b}}_t = \boldsymbol{p}\hat{y}_t.$$

Once the bottom-level h-step-ahead forecasts have been generated, these are aggregated to generate coherent forecasts for the rest of the series. In general, for a specified set of proportions, top-down approaches can be represented as

$$\tilde{\boldsymbol{y}}_h = \boldsymbol{S}\boldsymbol{p}\hat{y}_t.$$

The two most common top-down approaches specify disaggregation proportions based on the historical proportions of the data. These performed well in the study of Gross and Sohl (1990).

Average historical proportions

$$p_j = \frac{1}{T}\sum_{t=1}^{T}\frac{y_{j,t}}{y_t}$$

for $j = 1, \dots, m$. Each proportion p_j reflects the average of the historical proportions of the bottom-level series $y_{j,t}$ over the period $t = 1, \dots, T$ relative to the total aggregate y_t.

This approach is implemented in the `forecast()` function by setting `method="tdgsa"`, where `tdgsa` stands for "top-down Gross-Sohl method A".

Proportions of the historical averages

$$p_j = \sum_{t=1}^{T}\frac{y_{j,t}}{T}\Bigg/\sum_{t=1}^{T}\frac{y_t}{T}$$

for $j = 1, \dots, m$. Each proportion p_j captures the average historical value of the bottom-level series $y_{j,t}$ relative to the average value of the total aggregate y_t.

This approach is implemented in the `forecast()` function by setting `method="tdgsf"`, where `tdgsa` stands for "top-down Gross-Sohl method F".

A convenient attribute of such top-down approaches is their simplicity. One only needs to model and generate forecasts for the most aggregated top-level series. In general, these approaches seem to produce quite reliable forecasts for the aggregate levels and they are very useful with low count data. On the other hand, one disadvantage is the loss of information due to aggregation. Using such top-down approaches, we are unable to capture and take advantage of individual series characteristics such as time dynamics, special events, etc.

Forecast proportions

Because historical proportions used for disaggregation do not take account of how those proportions may change over time, top-down approaches based on historical proportions tend to produce less accurate forecasts at lower levels of the hierarchy than bottom-up approaches. To address this issue, proportions based on forecasts rather than historical data can be used (Athanasopoulos, Ahmed, and Hyndman 2009).

Consider a one level hierarchy. We first generate h-step-ahead forecasts for all of the series. We don't use these forecasts directly, and they are not coherent (they don't add up correctly). Let's call these "initial" forecasts. We calculate the proportion of each h-step-ahead initial forecast at the bottom level, to the aggregate of all the h-step-ahead initial forecasts at this level. We refer to these as the forecast proportions, and we use them to disaggregate the top-level h-step-ahead initial forecast in order to generate coherent forecasts for the whole of the hierarchy.

For a K-level hierarchy, this process is repeated for each node, going from the top to the very bottom-level. Applying this process leads to the following general rule for obtaining the forecast proportions:

$$p_j = \prod_{\ell=0}^{K-1} \frac{\hat{y}_{j,h}^{(\ell)}}{\hat{S}_{j,h}^{(\ell+1)}}$$

where $j = 1, 2, \dots, m$, $\hat{y}_{j,h}^{(\ell)}$ is the h-step-ahead initial forecast of the series that corresponds to the node which is ℓ levels above j, and $\hat{S}_{j,h}^{(\ell)}$ is the sum of the h-step-ahead initial forecasts below the node that is ℓ levels above node j and are directly connected to that node. These forecast proportions disaggregate the h-step-ahead initial forecast of the Total series to get h-step-ahead coherent forecasts of the bottom-level series.

We will use the hierarchy of Figure 10.1 to explain this notation and to demonstrate how this general rule is reached. Assume we have generated initial forecasts for each series in the hierarchy. Recall that for the top-level "Total" series, $\tilde{y}_h = \hat{y}_h$, for any top-down approach. Here are some examples using the above notation:

- $\hat{y}^{(1)}_{\text{A},h} = \hat{y}^{(1)}_{\text{B},h} = \hat{y}_h = \tilde{y}_h$;
- $\hat{y}^{(1)}_{\text{AA},h} = \hat{y}^{(1)}_{\text{AB},h} = \hat{y}^{(1)}_{\text{AC},h} = \hat{y}_{\text{A},h}$;
- $\hat{y}^{(2)}_{\text{AA},h} = \hat{y}^{(2)}_{\text{AB},h} = \hat{y}^{(2)}_{\text{AC},h} = \hat{y}^{(2)}_{\text{BA},h} = \hat{y}^{(2)}_{\text{BB},h} = \hat{y}_h = \tilde{y}_h$;
- $\hat{S}^{(1)}_{\text{AA},h} = \hat{S}^{(1)}_{\text{AB},h} = \hat{S}^{(1)}_{\text{AC},h} = \hat{y}_{\text{AA},h} + \hat{y}_{\text{AB},h} + \hat{y}_{\text{AC},h}$;
- $\hat{S}^{(2)}_{\text{AA},h} = \hat{S}^{(2)}_{\text{AB},h} = \hat{S}^{(2)}_{\text{AC},h} = \hat{S}^{(1)}_{\text{A},h} = \hat{S}^{(1)}_{\text{B},h} = \hat{S}_h = \hat{y}_{\text{A},h} + \hat{y}_{\text{B},h}$.

Moving down the farthest left branch of the hierarchy, coherent forecasts are given by

$$\tilde{y}_{\text{A},h} = \left(\frac{\hat{y}_{\text{A},h}}{\hat{S}^{(1)}_{\text{A},h}}\right)\tilde{y}_h = \left(\frac{\hat{y}^{(1)}_{\text{AA},h}}{\hat{S}^{(2)}_{\text{AA},h}}\right)\tilde{y}_h$$

and

$$\tilde{y}_{\text{AA},h} = \left(\frac{\hat{y}_{\text{AA},h}}{\hat{S}^{(1)}_{\text{AA},h}}\right)\tilde{y}_{\text{A},h} = \left(\frac{\hat{y}_{\text{AA},h}}{\hat{S}^{(1)}_{\text{AA},h}}\right)\left(\frac{\hat{y}^{(1)}_{\text{AA},h}}{\hat{S}^{(2)}_{\text{AA},h}}\right)\tilde{y}_h.$$

Consequently,

$$p_1 = \left(\frac{\hat{y}_{\text{AA},h}}{\hat{S}^{(1)}_{\text{AA},h}}\right)\left(\frac{\hat{y}^{(1)}_{\text{AA},h}}{\hat{S}^{(2)}_{\text{AA},h}}\right).$$

The other proportions can be obtained similarly.

One disadvantage of all top-down approaches, including this one, is that it does not produce unbiased coherent forecasts (Hyndman, Ahmed, et al. 2011).

This approach is implemented in the `forecast()` function by setting `method="tdfp"`, where `tdfp` stands for "top-down forecast proportions".

10.5 Middle-out approach

The middle-out approach combines bottom-up and top-down approaches. First, a "middle level" is chosen and forecasts are generated for all the series at this level. For the series above the middle level, coherent forecasts are generated using the bottom-up approach by aggregating the "middle-level" forecasts upwards. For the series below the "middle level", coherent forecasts are generated using a top-down approach by disaggregating the "middle level" forecasts downwards.

This approach is implemented in the `forecast()` function by setting `method="mo"` and by specifying the appropriate middle level via the `level` argument. For the top-down disaggregation below the middle level, the top-down forecast proportions method is used.

10.6 Mapping matrices

All of the methods considered so far can be expressed using a common notation.

Suppose we forecast all series independently, ignoring the aggregation constraints. We call these the **base forecasts** and denote them by $\hat{y}_h$ where h is the forecast horizon. They are stacked in the same order as the data y_t.

Then all forecasting approaches for either hierarchical or grouped structures can be represented as

$$\tilde{y}_h = \boldsymbol{S}\boldsymbol{P}\hat{y}_h, \tag{10.6}$$

where $\boldsymbol{P}$ is a matrix that maps the base forecasts into the bottom-level, and the summing matrix $\boldsymbol{S}$ sums these up using the aggregation structure to produce a set of coherent forecasts $\tilde{y}_h$.

The $\boldsymbol{P}$ matrix is defined according to the approach implemented. For example if the bottom-up approach is used to forecast the hierarchy of Figure 10.1, then

$$P = \begin{bmatrix} 0 & 0 & 0 & 1 & 0 & 0 & 0 & 0 \\ 0 & 0 & 0 & 0 & 1 & 0 & 0 & 0 \\ 0 & 0 & 0 & 0 & 0 & 1 & 0 & 0 \\ 0 & 0 & 0 & 0 & 0 & 0 & 1 & 0 \\ 0 & 0 & 0 & 0 & 0 & 0 & 0 & 1 \end{bmatrix}.$$

Notice that $\boldsymbol{P}$ contains two partitions. The first three columns zero out the base forecasts of the series above the bottom-level, while the m-dimensional identity matrix picks only the base forecasts of the bottom-level. These are then summed by the $\boldsymbol{S}$ matrix.

If any of the top-down approaches were used then

$$P = \begin{bmatrix} p_1 & 0 & 0 & 0 & 0 & 0 & 0 & 0 \\ p_2 & 0 & 0 & 0 & 0 & 0 & 0 & 0 \\ p_3 & 0 & 0 & 0 & 0 & 0 & 0 & 0 \\ p_4 & 0 & 0 & 0 & 0 & 0 & 0 & 0 \\ p_5 & 0 & 0 & 0 & 0 & 0 & 0 & 0 \end{bmatrix}.$$

The first column includes the set of proportions that distribute the base forecasts of the top-level to the bottom-level. These are then summed up the hierarchy by the $\boldsymbol{S}$ matrix. The rest of the columns zero out the base forecasts below the highest level of aggregation.

For a middle out approach, the $\boldsymbol{P}$ matrix will be a combination of the above two. Using a set of proportions, the base forecasts of some pre-chosen level will be disaggregated to the bottom-level, all other base forecasts will be zeroed out, and the bottom-level forecasts will then summed up the hierarchy via the summing matrix.

Forecast reconciliation

We can rewrite Equation (10.6) as

$$\tilde{y}_h = \boldsymbol{R}\hat{y}_h,$$

where $\boldsymbol{R} = \boldsymbol{S}\boldsymbol{P}$ is a "reconciliation matrix". That is, it takes the incoherent base forecasts $\hat{y}_h$, and reconciles them to produce coherent forecasts $\tilde{y}_h$.

In the methods discussed so far, no real reconciliation has been done because the methods have been based on forecasts from a single level of the aggregation structure, which have either been aggregated or disaggregated to obtain forecasts at all other levels. However, in general, we could use other $\boldsymbol{P}$ matrices, and then $\boldsymbol{R}$ will be combining and reconciling all the base forecasts in order to produce coherent forecasts.

In fact, we can find the optimal $\boldsymbol{P}$ matrix to give the most accurate reconciled forecasts.

10.7 The optimal reconciliation approach

Optimal forecast reconciliation will occur if we can find the $\boldsymbol{P}$ matrix which minimises the forecast error of the set of coherent forecasts. We present here a simplified summary of the approach. More details are provided in Wickramasuriya, Athanasopoulos, and Hyndman (2018).

Suppose we generate coherent forecasts using Equation (10.6), repeated here for convenience:

$$\tilde{\boldsymbol{y}}_h = \boldsymbol{S}\boldsymbol{P}\hat{\boldsymbol{y}}_h.$$

First we want to make sure we have unbiased forecasts. If the base forecasts $\hat{\boldsymbol{y}}_h$ are unbiased, then the coherent forecasts $\tilde{\boldsymbol{y}}_h$ will be unbiased provided $\boldsymbol{SPS} = \boldsymbol{S}$ (Hyndman, Ahmed, et al. 2011). This provides a constraint on the matrix $\boldsymbol{P}$. Interestingly, no top-down method satisfies this constraint, so all top-down methods are biased.

Next we need to find the error in our forecasts. Wickramasuriya, Athanasopoulos, and Hyndman (2018) show that the variance-covariance matrix of the h-step-ahead coherent forecast errors is given by

$$\boldsymbol{V}_h = \text{Var}[\boldsymbol{y}_{T+h} - \tilde{\boldsymbol{y}}_h] = \boldsymbol{S}\boldsymbol{P}\boldsymbol{W}_h\boldsymbol{P}'\boldsymbol{S}'$$

where $\boldsymbol{W}_h = \text{Var}[(\boldsymbol{y}_{T+h} - \hat{\boldsymbol{y}}_h)]$ is the variance-covariance matrix of the corresponding base forecast errors.

The objective is to find a matrix $\boldsymbol{P}$ that minimises the error variances of the coherent forecasts. These error variances are on the diagonal of the matrix $\boldsymbol{V}_h$, and so the sum of all the error variances is given by the trace of the matrix $\boldsymbol{V}_h$. Wickramasuriya,

Athanasopoulos, and Hyndman (2018) show that the matrix $\boldsymbol{P}$ which minimises the trace of $\boldsymbol{V}_h$ such that $\boldsymbol{SPS} = \boldsymbol{S}$, is given by

$$\boldsymbol{P} = (\boldsymbol{S}'\boldsymbol{W}_h^{-1}\boldsymbol{S})^{-1}\boldsymbol{S}'\boldsymbol{W}_h^{-1}.$$

Therefore, the optimal reconciled forecasts are given by

$$\tilde{\boldsymbol{y}}_h = \boldsymbol{S}(\boldsymbol{S}'\boldsymbol{W}_h^{-1}\boldsymbol{S})^{-1}\boldsymbol{S}'\boldsymbol{W}_h^{-1}\hat{\boldsymbol{y}}_h. \tag{10.7}$$

We refer to this as the "MinT" (or Minimum Trace) estimator.

To use this in practice, we need to estimate $\boldsymbol{W}_h$, the forecast error variance of the h-step-ahead base forecasts. This can be difficult, and so we provide three simplifying approximations which have been shown to work well in both simulations and in practice.

1. Set $\boldsymbol{W}_h = k_h\boldsymbol{I}$ for all h, where $k_h > 0$.[4] This is the most simplifying assumption to make, and means that $\boldsymbol{P}$ is independent of the data, providing substantial computational savings. The disadvantage, however, is that this specification does not account for the differences in scale between the levels of the structure, or for relationships between series. This approach is implemented in the `forecast()` function by setting `method = "comb"` and `weights = "ols"`.

   The weights here are referred to as OLS (ordinary least squares) because setting $\boldsymbol{W}_h = k_h\boldsymbol{I}$ in (10.7) gives the least squares estimator we introduced in Section 5.7 with $\boldsymbol{X} = \boldsymbol{S}$ and $\boldsymbol{y} = \hat{\boldsymbol{y}}$.

2. Set $\boldsymbol{W}_h = k_h\text{diag}(\hat{\boldsymbol{W}}_1)$ for all h, where $k_h > 0$,

$$\hat{\boldsymbol{W}}_1 = \frac{1}{T}\sum_{t=1}^{T}\boldsymbol{e}_t\boldsymbol{e}_t',$$

   and $\boldsymbol{e}_t$ is an n-dimensional vector of residuals of the models that generated the base forecasts stacked in the same order as the data. The approach is implemented by setting `method = "comb"` and `weights = "wls"`.

   This specification scales the base forecasts using the variance of the residuals and it is therefore referred to as the WLS (weighted least squares) estimator using *variance scaling*.

3. Set $\boldsymbol{W}_h = k_h\boldsymbol{\Lambda}$ for all h, where $k_h > 0$, $\boldsymbol{\Lambda} = \text{diag}(\boldsymbol{S}\boldsymbol{1})$, and $\boldsymbol{1}$ is a unit vector of dimension n. This specification assumes that

[4] Note that k_h is a proportionality constant. It does not need to be estimated or specified here as it gets cancelled out in (10.7).

the bottom-level base forecast errors each have variance k_h and are uncorrelated between nodes. Hence each element of the diagonal $\boldsymbol{\Lambda}$ matrix contains the number of forecast error variances contributing to each node. This estimator only depends on the structure of the aggregations, and not on the actual data. It is therefore referred to as *structural scaling*. Applying the structural scaling specification is particularly useful in cases where residuals are not available, and so variance scaling cannot be applied; for example, in cases where the base forecasts are generated by judgmental forecasting (Chapter 4). This approach is implemented by setting `method="comb"` and `weights = "nseries"`,

4. Set $\boldsymbol{W}_h = k_h \boldsymbol{W}_1$ for all h, where $k_h > 0$. Here we only assume that the error covariance matrices are proportional to each other, and we directly estimate the full one-step covariance matrix $\boldsymbol{W}_1$. The most obvious and simple way would be to use the sample covariance. This is implemented by setting `method = "comb"`, `weights = "mint"`, and `covariance = "sam"`.

   However, for cases where the number of bottom-level series m is large compared to the length of the series T, this is not a good estimator. Instead we use a shrinkage estimator which shrinks the sample covariance to a diagonal matrix. This is implemented by setting `method = "comb"`, `weights = "mint"`, and `covariance = "shr"`.

In summary, unlike any other existing approach, the optimal reconciliation forecasts are generated using all the information available within a hierarchical or a grouped structure. This is very important, as particular aggregation levels or groupings may reveal features of the data that are of interest to the user and are important to be modelled. These features may be completely hidden or not easily identifiable at other levels.

For example, consider the Australian tourism data introduced in Section 10.1, where the hierarchical structure followed the geographical division of a country into states and zones. Some coastal areas will be largely summer destinations, while some mountain regions may be winter destinations. These differences will be smoothed at the country level due to aggregation.

Example: Forecasting Australian prison population

We compute the forecasts for the Australian prison population, described in Section 10.2. Using the default arguments for the `forecast()` function, we compute coherent forecasts by the optimal reconciliation approach with the WLS estimator using variance scaling.

```
prisonfc <- forecast(prison.gts)
```

To obtain forecasts for each level of aggregation, we can use the `aggts()` function. For example, to calculate forecasts for the overall total prison population, and for the one-factor groupings (State, Gender and Legal Status), we use:

```
fcsts <- aggts(prisonfc, levels=0:3)
```

A simple plot is obtained using

```
groups <- aggts(prison.gts, levels=0:3)

autoplot(fcsts) + autolayer(groups)
```

A nicer plot is available using the following code. The results are shown in Figure 10.8. The vertical line marks the start of the forecast period.

```
prisonfc <- ts(rbind(groups, fcsts),
  start=start(groups), frequency=4)
p1 <- autoplot(prisonfc[,"Total"]) +
  ggtitle("Australian prison population") +
  xlab("Year") + ylab("Total number of prisoners ('000)") +
  geom_vline(xintercept=2017)
cols <- sample(scales::hue_pal(h=c(15,375),
          c=100,l=65,h.start=0,direction = 1)(NCOL(groups)))
p2 <- as_tibble(prisonfc[,-1]) %>%
  gather(Series) %>%
  mutate(Date = rep(time(prisonfc), NCOL(prisonfc)-1),
         Group = str_extract(Series, "([A-Za-z ]*)")) %>%
  ggplot(aes(x=Date, y=value, group=Series, color=Series)) +
    geom_line() +
    xlab("Year") + ylab("Number of prisoners ('000)") +
    scale_color_manual(values = cols) +
    facet_grid(. ~ Group, scales="free_y") +
    scale_x_continuous(breaks=seq(2006,2018,by=2)) +
    theme(axis.text.x = element_text(angle=90, hjust=1)) +
    geom_vline(xintercept=2017)
gridExtra::grid.arrange(p1, p2, ncol=1)
```

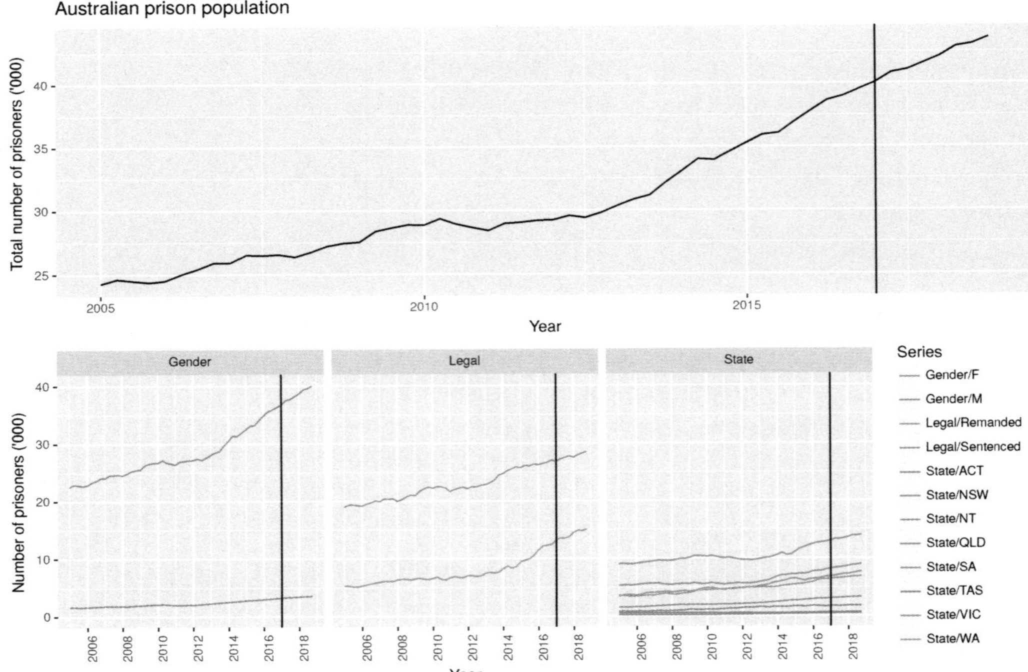

Figure 10.8: Coherent forecasts for the total Australian adult prison population and for the population grouped by state, by legal status and by gender.

Similar code was used to produce Figure 10.9. The left panel plots the coherent forecasts for interactions between states and gender. The right panel shows forecasts for the bottom-level series.

The `accuracy()` command is useful for evaluating the forecast accuracy across hierarchical or grouped structures. The following table summarises the accuracy of the bottom-up and the optimal reconciliation approaches, forecasting 2015 Q1 to 2016 Q4 as a test period.

The results show that the optimal reconciliation approach generates more accurate forecasts especially for the top level. In general, we find that as the optimal reconciliation approach uses information from all levels in the structure, it generates more accurate coherent forecasts than the other traditional alternatives which use limited information.

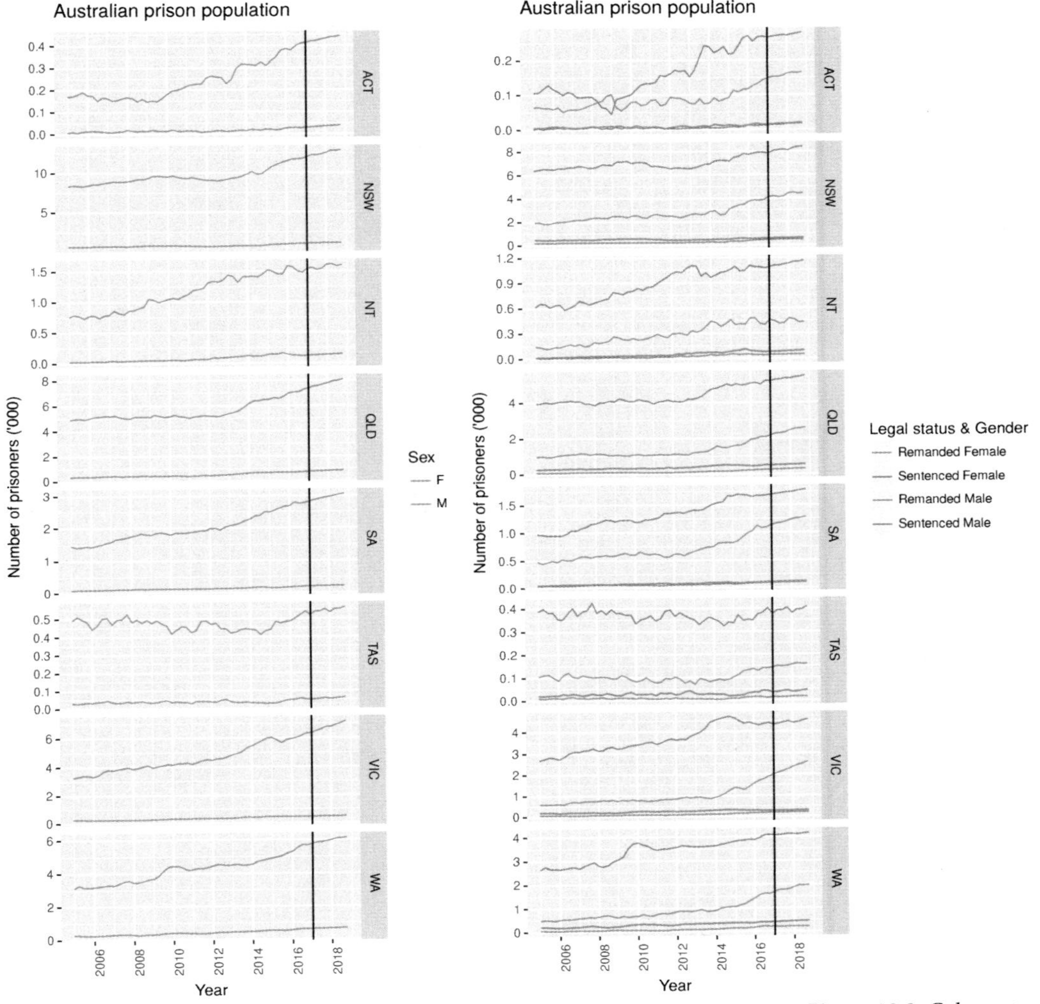

Figure 10.9: Coherent forecasts for the Australian adult prison population grouped by all interactions of attributes.

Table 10.1: Accuracy of Australian prison population forecasts for different groups of series.

	Bottom-up		Optimal	
	MAPE	MASE	MAPE	MASE
Total	5.32	1.84	3.04	1.05
State	7.59	1.88	7.57	1.84
Legal status	6.40	1.76	4.46	1.17
Gender	8.62	2.68	8.63	2.71
Bottom	15.82	2.23	14.82	2.14
All series	12.41	2.16	11.78	2.06

10.8 Exercises

1. Write out the S matrices for the Australian tourism hierarchy and the Australian prison grouped structure. Use the `smatrix` command to verify your answers.
2. Generate 8-step-ahead bottom-up forecasts using ARIMA models for the `visnights` Australian domestic tourism data. Plot the coherent forecasts by level and comment on their nature. Are you satisfied with these forecasts?
3. Model the aggregate series for Australian domestic tourism data `visnights` using an ARIMA model. Comment on the model. Generate and plot 8-step-ahead forecasts from the ARIMA model and compare these with the bottom-up forecasts generated in question 2 for the aggregate level.
4. Generate 8-step-ahead optimally reconciled coherent forecasts using ARIMA base forecasts for the `visnights` Australian domestic tourism data. Plot the coherent forecasts by level and comment on their nature. How and why are these different to the bottom-up forecasts generated in question 2 above.
5. Using the last two years of the `visnights` Australian domestic tourism data as a test set, generate bottom-up, top-down and optimally reconciled forecasts for this period and compare their accuracy.

10.9 Further reading

There are no other textbooks which cover hierarchical forecasting in any depth, so interested readers will need to tackle the original research papers for further information.

- Gross and Sohl (1990) provide a good introduction to the top-down approaches.
- The reconciliation methods were developed in a series of papers, which are best read in the following order: Hyndman, Ahmed, et al. (2011), Athanasopoulos, Ahmed, and Hyndman (2009), Hyndman, Lee, and Wang (2016), Wickramasuriya, Athanasopoulos, and Hyndman (2018).
- Athanasopoulos, Hyndman, et al. (2017) extends the reconciliation approach to deal with temporal hierarchies.

Chapter 11
Advanced forecasting methods

In this chapter, we briefly discuss four more advanced forecasting methods that build on the models discussed in earlier chapters.

11.1 Complex seasonality

So far, we have considered relatively simple seasonal patterns such as quarterly and monthly data. However, higher frequency time series often exhibit more complicated seasonal patterns. For example, daily data may have a weekly pattern as well as an annual pattern. Hourly data usually has three types of seasonality: a daily pattern, a weekly pattern, and an annual pattern. Even weekly data can be challenging to forecast as it typically has an annual pattern with seasonal period of $365.25/7 \approx 52.179$ on average.

Such multiple seasonal patterns are becoming more common with high frequency data recording. Further examples where multiple seasonal patterns can occur include call volume in call centres, daily hospital admissions, requests for cash at ATMs, electricity and water usage, and access to computer web sites.

Most of the methods we have considered so far are unable to deal with these seasonal complexities. Even the `ts` class in R can only handle one type of seasonality, which is usually assumed to take integer values.

To deal with such series, we will use the `msts` class which handles multiple seasonality time series. This allows you to specify all of the frequencies that might be relevant. It is also flexible enough to handle non-integer frequencies.

Despite this flexibility, we don't necessarily want to include all of these frequencies — just the ones that are likely to be present in the data. For example, if we have only 180 days of data, we may ignore the annual seasonality. If the data are measurements of a natural phenomenon (e.g., temperature), we can probably safely ignore any weekly seasonality.

The top panel of Figure 11.1 shows the number of retail banking call arrivals per 5-minute interval between 7:00am and 9:05pm each weekday over a 33 week period. The bottom panel shows the first three weeks of the same time series. There is a strong daily seasonal pattern with frequency 169 (there are 169 5-minute intervals per day), and a weak weekly seasonal pattern with frequency $169 \times 5 = 845$. (Call volumes on Mondays tend to be higher than the rest of the week.) If a longer series of data were available, we may also have observed an annual seasonal pattern.

```
p1 <- autoplot(calls) +
  ylab("Call volume") + xlab("Weeks") +
  scale_x_continuous(breaks=seq(1,33,by=2))
p2 <- autoplot(window(calls, end=4)) +
  ylab("Call volume") + xlab("Weeks") +
  scale_x_continuous(minor_breaks = seq(1,4,by=0.2))
gridExtra::grid.arrange(p1,p2)
```

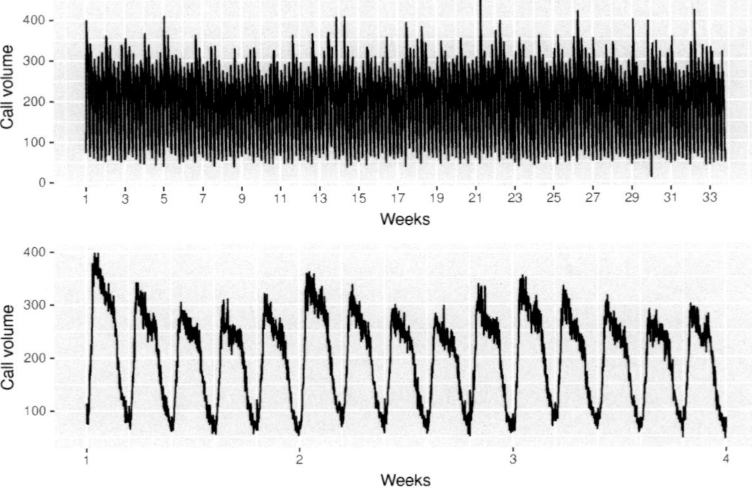

Figure 11.1: Five-minute call volume handled on weekdays between 7am and 9:05pm in a large North American commercial bank. Top panel shows data from 3 March 2003 to 23 May 2003. Bottom panel shows only the first three weeks.

STL with multiple seasonal periods

The `mstl()` function is a variation on `stl()` designed to deal with multiple seasonality. It will return multiple seasonal components, as well as a trend and remainder component.

```
calls %>% mstl() %>%
  autoplot() + xlab("Week")
```

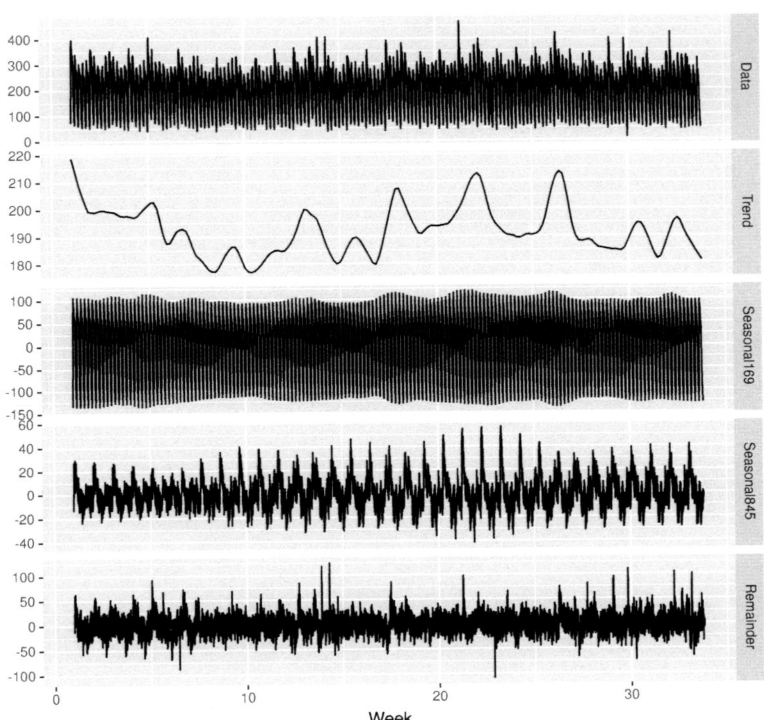

Figure 11.2: Multiple STL for the call volume data.

There are two seasonal patterns shown, one for the time of day (the third panel), and one for the time of week (the fourth panel). To properly interpret this graph, it is important to notice the vertical scales. In this case, the trend and the weekly seasonality have relatively narrow ranges compared to the other components, because there is very little trend seen in the data, and the weekly seasonality is weak.

The decomposition can also be used in forecasting, with each of the seasonal components forecast using a seasonal naïve method, and the seasonally adjusted data forecasting using ETS (or some other user-specified method). The `stlf()` function will do this automatically.

```
calls %>% stlf() %>%
  autoplot() + xlab("Week")
```

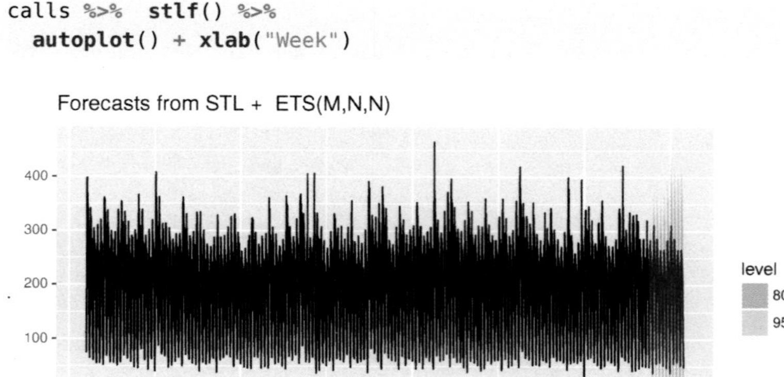

Figure 11.3: Multiple STL for the call volume data.

Dynamic harmonic regression with multiple seasonal periods

With multiple seasonalities, we can use Fourier terms as we did in earlier chapters (see Sections 5.4 and 9.5). Because there are multiple seasonalities, we need to add Fourier terms for each seasonal period. In this case, the seasonal periods are 169 and 845, so the Fourier terms are of the form

$$\sin\left(\frac{2\pi kt}{169}\right), \quad \cos\left(\frac{2\pi kt}{169}\right), \quad \sin\left(\frac{2\pi kt}{845}\right), \quad \text{and} \quad \cos\left(\frac{2\pi kt}{845}\right),$$

for $k = 1, 2, \dots$. The `fourier()` function can generate these for you.

We will fit a dynamic harmonic regression model with an ARMA error structure. The total number of Fourier terms for each seasonal period have been chosen to minimize the AICc. We will use a log transformation (`lambda=0`) to ensure the forecasts and prediction intervals remain positive.

```
fit <- auto.arima(calls, seasonal=FALSE, lambda=0,
         xreg=fourier(calls, K=c(10,10)))
fit %>%
  forecast(xreg=fourier(calls, K=c(10,10), h=2*169)) %>%
  autoplot(include=5*169) +
    ylab("Call volume") + xlab("Weeks")
```

This is a very large model, containing 43 parameters: 7 ARMA coefficients, 20 Fourier coefficients for frequency 169, and 16

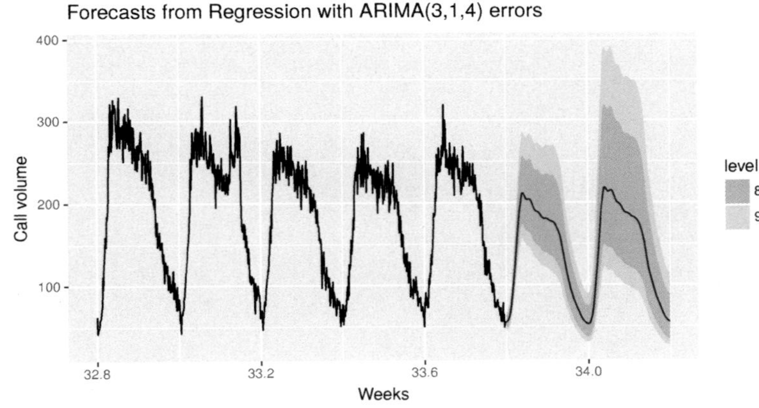

Figure 11.4: Forecasts from a dynamic harmonic regression applied to the call volume data.

Fourier coefficients for frequency 845. We don't use all the Fourier terms for frequency 845 because there is some overlap with the terms of frequency 169 (since $845 = 5 \times 169$).

TBATS models

An alternative approach developed by De Livera, Hyndman, and Snyder (2011) uses a combination of Fourier terms with an exponential smoothing state space model and a Box-Cox transformation, in a completely automated manner. As with any automated modelling framework, there may be cases where it gives poor results, but it can be a useful approach in some circumstances.

A TBATS model differs from dynamic harmonic regression in that the seasonality is allowed to change slowly over time in a TBATS model, while harmonic regression terms force the seasonal patterns to repeat periodically without changing. One drawback of TBATS models, however, is that they can be very slow to estimate, especially with long time series. Hence, we will consider a subset of the `calls` data to save time.

```
calls %>%
  subset(start=length(calls)-2000) %>%
  tbats() -> fit2
fc2 <- forecast(fit2, h=2*169)
autoplot(fc2, include=5*169) +
  ylab("Call volume") + xlab("Weeks")
```

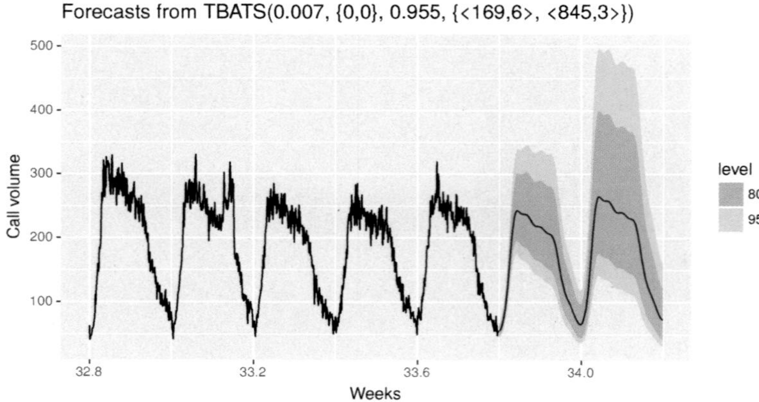

Figure 11.5: Forecasts from a TBATS model applied to the call volume data.

Here the prediction intervals appear to be much too wide – something that seems to happen quite often with TBATS models unfortunately.

Complex seasonality with covariates

TBATS models do not allow for covariates, although they can be included in dynamic harmonic regression models. One common application of such models is electricity demand modelling.

Figure 11.6 shows half-hourly electricity demand in Victoria, Australia, during 2014, along with temperatures for the same period for Melbourne (the largest city in Victoria).

```
autoplot(elecdemand[,c("Demand","Temperature")],
    facet=TRUE) +
  scale_x_continuous(minor_breaks=NULL,
    breaks=2014+
      cumsum(c(0,31,28,31,30,31,30,31,31,30,31,30))/365,
    labels=month.abb) +
  xlab("Time") + ylab("")
```

Plotting electricity demand against temperature (Figure 11.7) shows that there is a nonlinear relationship between the two, with demand increasing for low temperatures (due to heating) and increasing for high temperatures (due to cooling).

```
elecdemand %>%
  as.data.frame() %>%
  ggplot(aes(x=Temperature, y=Demand)) + geom_point() +
    xlab("Temperature (degrees Celsius)") +
    ylab("Demand (GW)")
```

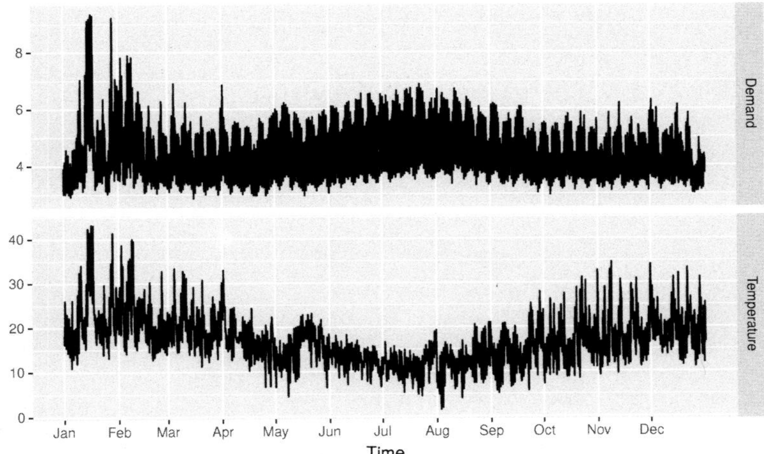

Figure 11.6: Half-hourly electricity demand and corresponding temperatures in 2014, Victoria, Australia.

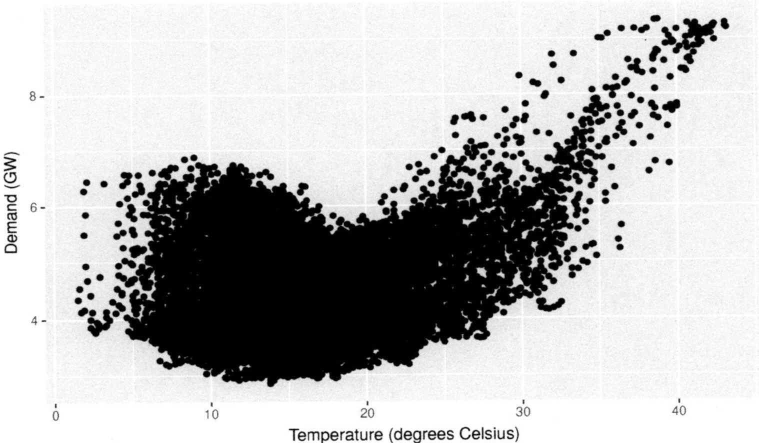

Figure 11.7: Half-hourly electricty demand for Victoria, plotted against temperatures for the same times in Melbourne, the largest city in Victoria.

We will fit a regression model with a piecewise linear function of temperature (containing a knot at 18 degrees), and harmonic regression terms to allow for the daily seasonal pattern.

```
cooling <- pmax(elecdemand[,"Temperature"], 18)
fit <- auto.arima(elecdemand[,"Demand"],
         xreg = cbind(fourier(elecdemand, c(10,10,0)),
                 heating=elecdemand[,"Temperature"],
                 cooling=cooling))
```

Forecasting with such models is difficult because we require future values of the predictor variables. Future values of the Fourier terms are easy to compute, but future temperatures are, of course, unknown. If we are only interested in forecasting up to a week ahead, we could use temperature forecasts obtain from a meteorological model. Alternatively, we could use scenario forecasting (Section 4.5) and plug in possible temperature patterns. In the following example, we have used a repeat of the last two days of temperatures to generate future possible demand values.

```
temps <- subset(elecdemand[,"Temperature"],
          start=NROW(elecdemand)-2*48+1)
fc <- forecast(fit,
        xreg=cbind(fourier(temps, c(10,10,0)),
          heating=temps, cooling=pmax(temps,18)))
autoplot(fc, include=14*48)
```

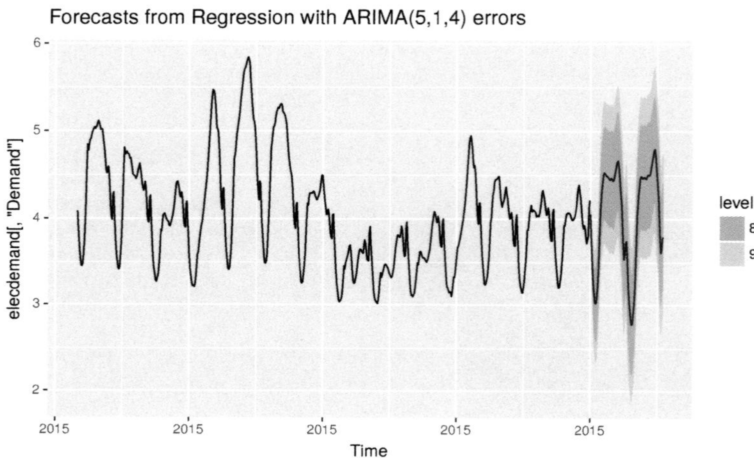

Figure 11.8: Forecasts from a dynamic harmonic regression model applied to half-hourly electricity demand data.

Although the short-term forecasts look reasonable, this is a very crude model for a complicated process. The residuals demonstrate that there is a lot of information that has not been captured with this model.

```
checkresiduals(fc)
```

```
#>
#>  Ljung-Box test
#>
#> data:  Residuals from Regression with ARIMA(5,1,4) errors
#> Q* = 740000, df = 3500, p-value <2e-16
#>
#> Model df: 49.   Total lags used: 3504
```

More sophisticated versions of this model which provide much better forecasts are described in Hyndman and Fan (2010) and Fan and Hyndman (2012).

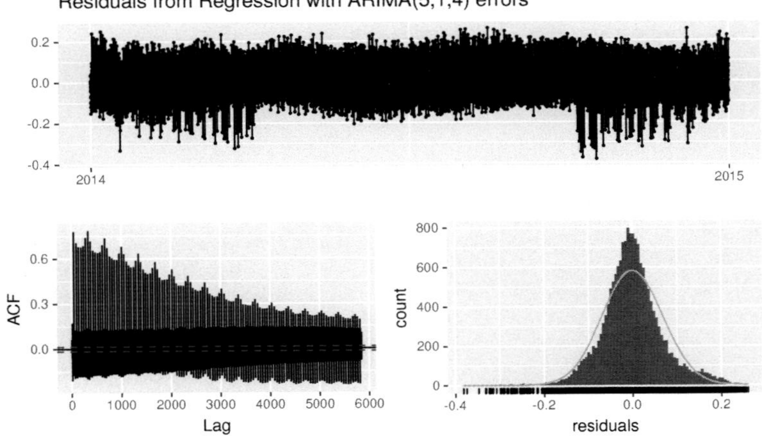

Figure 11.9: Residual diagnostics for the dynamic harmonic regression model.

11.2 Vector autoregressions

One limitation of the models that we have considered so far is that they impose a unidirectional relationship — the forecast variable is influenced by the predictor variables, but not vice versa. However, there are many cases where the reverse should also be allowed for — where all variables affect each other. In Section 9.2, the changes in personal consumption expenditure (C_t) were forecast based on the changes in personal disposable income (I_t). However, in this case a bi-directional relationship may be more suitable: an increase in I_t will lead to an increase in C_t and vice versa.

An example of such a situation occurred in Australia during the Global Financial Crisis of 2008–2009. The Australian government issued stimulus packages that included cash payments in December 2008, just in time for Christmas spending. As a result, retailers reported strong sales and the economy was stimulated. Consequently, incomes increased.

Such feedback relationships are allowed for in the vector autoregressive (VAR) framework. In this framework, all variables are treated symmetrically. They are all modelled as if they all influence each other equally. In more formal terminology, all variables are now treated as "endogenous". To signify this, we now change the notation and write all variables as ys: $y_{1,t}$ denotes the tth observation of variable y_1, $y_{2,t}$ denotes the tth observation of variable y_2, and so on.

A VAR model is a generalisation of the univariate autoregressive model for forecasting a vector of time series.[1] It comprises one equation per variable in the system. The right hand side of each equation includes a constant and lags of all of the variables in the system. To keep it simple, we will consider a two variable VAR with one lag. We write a 2-dimensional VAR(1) as

$$y_{1,t} = c_1 + \phi_{11,1} y_{1,t-1} + \phi_{12,1} y_{2,t-1} + e_{1,t} \tag{11.1}$$
$$y_{2,t} = c_2 + \phi_{21,1} y_{1,t-1} + \phi_{22,1} y_{2,t-1} + e_{2,t}, \tag{11.2}$$

where $e_{1,t}$ and $e_{2,t}$ are white noise processes that may be contemporaneously correlated. The coefficient $\phi_{ii,\ell}$ captures the influence of the ℓth lag of variable y_i on itself, while the coefficient $\phi_{ij,\ell}$ captures the influence of the ℓth lag of variable y_j on y_i.

[1] A more flexible generalisation would be a Vector ARMA process. However, the relative simplicity of VARs has led to their dominance in forecasting. Interested readers may refer to Athanasopoulos, Poskitt, and Vahid (2012).

If the series are stationary, we forecast them by fitting a VAR to the data directly (known as a "VAR in levels"). If the series are non-stationary, we take differences of the data in order to make them stationary, then fit a VAR model (known as a "VAR in differences"). In both cases, the models are estimated equation by equation using the principle of least squares. For each equation, the parameters are estimated by minimising the sum of squared $e_{i,t}$ values.

The other possibility, which is beyond the scope of this book and therefore we do not explore here, is that the series may be non-stationary but cointegrated, which means that there exists a linear combination of them that is stationary. In this case, a VAR specification that includes an error correction mechanism (usually referred to as a vector error correction model) should be included, and alternative estimation methods to least squares estimation should be used.[2]

[2] Interested readers should refer to Hamilton (1994) and Lütkepohl (2007).

Forecasts are generated from a VAR in a recursive manner. The VAR generates forecasts for *each* variable included in the system. To illustrate the process, assume that we have fitted the 2-dimensional VAR(1) described in Equations (11.1)–(11.2), for all observations up to time T. Then the one-step-ahead forecasts are generated by

$$\hat{y}_{1,T+1|T} = \hat{c}_1 + \hat{\phi}_{11,1} y_{1,T} + \hat{\phi}_{12,1} y_{2,T}$$
$$\hat{y}_{2,T+1|T} = \hat{c}_2 + \hat{\phi}_{21,1} y_{1,T} + \hat{\phi}_{22,1} y_{2,T}.$$

This is the same form as (11.1)–(11.2), except that the errors have been set to zero and parameters have been replaced with their estimates. For $h = 2$, the forecasts are given by

$$\hat{y}_{1,T+2|T} = \hat{c}_1 + \hat{\phi}_{11,1}\hat{y}_{1,T+1} + \hat{\phi}_{12,1}\hat{y}_{2,T+1}$$
$$\hat{y}_{2,T+2|T} = \hat{c}_2 + \hat{\phi}_{21,1}\hat{y}_{1,T+1} + \hat{\phi}_{22,1}\hat{y}_{2,T+1}.$$

Again, this is the same form as (11.1)–(11.2), except that the errors have been set to zero, the parameters have been replaced with their estimates, and the unknown values of y_1 and y_2 have been replaced with their forecasts. The process can be iterated in this manner for all future time periods.

There are two decisions one has to make when using a VAR to forecast, namely how many variables (denoted by K) and how many lags (denoted by p) should be included in the system. The number of coefficients to be estimated in a VAR is equal to $K + pK^2$ (or $1 + pK$ per equation). For example, for a VAR with $K = 5$ variables and $p = 3$ lags, there are 16 coefficients per equation, giving a total of 80 coefficients to be estimated. The more coefficients that need to be estimated, the larger the estimation error entering the forecast.

In practice, it is usual to keep K small and include only variables that are correlated with each other, and therefore useful in forecasting each other. Information criteria are commonly used to select the number of lags to be included.

VAR models are implemented in the **vars** package[3] in R. It contains a function `VARselect()` for selecting the number of lags p using four different information criteria: AIC, HQ, SC and FPE. We have met the AIC before, and SC is simply another name for the BIC (SC stands for Schwarz Criterion, after Gideon Schwarz who proposed it). HQ is the Hannan-Quinn criterion, and FPE is the "Final Prediction Error" criterion.[4] Care should be taken when using the AIC as it tends to choose large numbers of lags. Instead, for VAR models, we prefer to use the BIC.

[3] `https://cran.r-project.org/package=vars`

[4] For a detailed comparison of these criteria, see Chapter 4.3 of Lütkepohl (2005).

A criticism that VARs face is that they are atheoretical; that is, they are not built on some economic theory that imposes a theoretical structure on the equations. Every variable is assumed to influence every other variable in the system, which makes a direct interpretation of the estimated coefficients very difficult. Despite this, VARs are useful in several contexts:

1. forecasting a collection of related variables where no explicit interpretation is required;
2. testing whether one variable is useful in forecasting another (the basis of Granger causality tests);
3. impulse response analysis, where the response of one variable to a sudden but temporary change in another variable is analysed;
4. forecast error variance decomposition, where the proportion of the forecast variance of each variable is attributed to the effects of the other variables.

Example: A VAR model for forecasting US consumption

```
library(vars)

VARselect(uschange[,1:2], lag.max=8,
  type="const")[["selection"]]
#> AIC(n)  HQ(n)  SC(n) FPE(n)
#>      5      1      1      5
```

The R output shows the lag length selected by each of the information criteria available in the **vars** package. There is a large discrepancy between the VAR(5) selected by the AIC and the VAR(1) selected by the BIC. This is not unusual. As a result we first fit a VAR(1), as selected by the BIC.

```
var1 <- VAR(uschange[,1:2], p=1, type="const")
serial.test(var1, lags.pt=10, type="PT.asymptotic")
var2 <- VAR(uschange[,1:2], p=2, type="const")
serial.test(var2, lags.pt=10, type="PT.asymptotic")
```

In similar fashion to the univariate ARIMA methodology, we test that the residuals are uncorrelated using a Portmanteau test[5]. Both a VAR(1) and a VAR(2) have some residual serial correlation, and therefore we fit a VAR(3).

[5] The tests for serial correlation in the "vars" package are multivariate generalisations of the tests presented in Section 3.3.

```
var3 <- VAR(uschange[,1:2], p=3, type="const")
serial.test(var3, lags.pt=10, type="PT.asymptotic")
#>
#>  Portmanteau Test (asymptotic)
#>
#> data:  Residuals of VAR object var3
#> Chi-squared = 34, df = 28, p-value = 0.2
```

The residuals for this model pass the test for serial correlation. The forecasts generated by the VAR(3) are plotted in Figure 11.10.

```
forecast(var3) %>%
  autoplot() + xlab("Year")
```

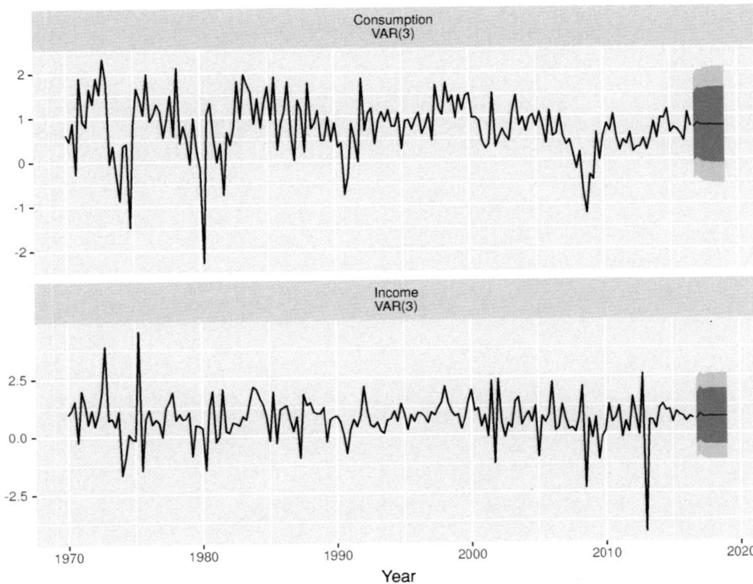

Figure 11.10: Forecasts for US consumption and income generated from a VAR(3).

11.3 Neural network models

Artificial neural networks are forecasting methods that are based on simple mathematical models of the brain. They allow complex nonlinear relationships between the response variable and its predictors.

Neural network architecture

A neural network can be thought of as a network of "neurons" which are organised in layers. The predictors (or inputs) form the bottom layer, and the forecasts (or outputs) form the top layer. There may also be intermediate layers containing "hidden neurons".

The very simplest networks contain no hidden layers and are equivalent to linear regressions. Figure 11.11 shows the neural network version of a linear regression with four predictors. The coefficients attached to these predictors are called "weights". The forecasts are obtained by a linear combination of the inputs. The weights are selected in the neural network framework using a "learning algorithm" that minimises a "cost function" such as the MSE. Of course, in this simple example, we can use linear regression which is a much more efficient method of training the model.

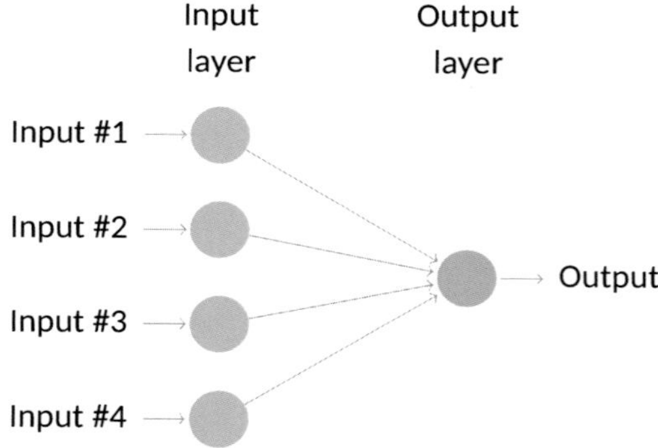

Figure 11.11: A simple neural network equivalent to a linear regression.

Once we add an intermediate layer with hidden neurons, the neural network becomes non-linear. A simple example is shown in Figure 11.12.

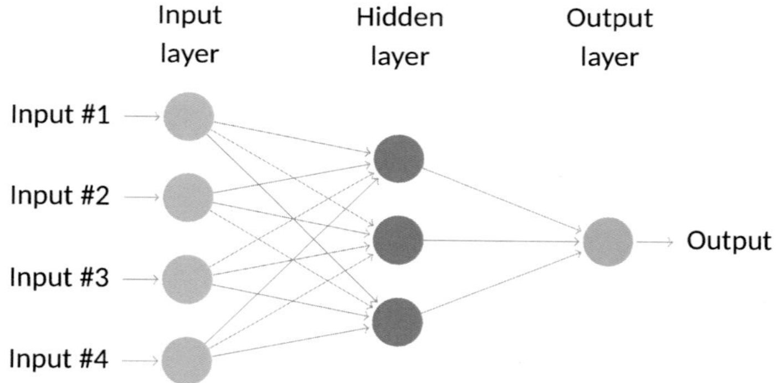

Figure 11.12: A neural network with four inputs and one hidden layer with three hidden neurons.

This is known as a *multilayer feed-forward network*, where each layer of nodes receives inputs from the previous layers. The outputs of the nodes in one layer are inputs to the next layer. The inputs to each node are combined using a weighted linear combination. The result is then modified by a nonlinear function before being output. For example, the inputs into hidden neuron j in Figure 11.12 are combined linearly to give

$$z_j = b_j + \sum_{i=1}^{4} w_{i,j} x_i.$$

In the hidden layer, this is then modified using a nonlinear function such as a sigmoid,

$$s(z) = \frac{1}{1 + e^{-z}},$$

to give the input for the next layer. This tends to reduce the effect of extreme input values, thus making the network somewhat robust to outliers.

The parameters b_1, b_2, b_3 and $w_{1,1}, \dots, w_{4,3}$ are "learned" from the data. The values of the weights are often restricted to prevent them from becoming too large. The parameter that restricts the weights is known as the "decay parameter", and is often set to be equal to 0.1.

The weights take random values to begin with, and these are then updated using the observed data. Consequently, there is an element of randomness in the predictions produced by a neural network. Therefore, the network is usually trained several times using different random starting points, and the results are averaged.

The number of hidden layers, and the number of nodes in each hidden layer, must be specified in advance. We will consider how these can be chosen using cross-validation later in this chapter.

Neural network autoregression

With time series data, lagged values of the time series can be used as inputs to a neural network, just as we used lagged values in a linear autoregression model (Chapter 8). We call this a neural network autoregression or NNAR model.

In this book, we only consider feed-forward networks with one hidden layer, and we use the notation NNAR(p,k) to indicate there are p lagged inputs and k nodes in the hidden layer. For example, a NNAR(9,5) model is a neural network with the last nine observations $(y_{t-1}, y_{t-2}, \dots, y_{t-9})$ used as inputs for forecasting the output y_t, and with five neurons in the hidden layer. A NNAR$(p,0)$ model is equivalent to an ARIMA$(p,0,0)$ model, but without the restrictions on the parameters to ensure stationarity.

With seasonal data, it is useful to also add the last observed values from the same season as inputs. For example, an NNAR(3,1,2)$_{12}$ model has inputs y_{t-1}, y_{t-2}, y_{t-3} and y_{t-12}, and two neurons in the hidden layer. More generally, an NNAR$(p,P,k)_m$ model has inputs $(y_{t-1},y_{t-2},\dots,y_{t-p},y_{t-m},y_{t-2m},y_{t-Pm})$ and k neurons in the hidden layer. A NNAR$(p,P,0)_m$ model is equivalent to an ARIMA$(p,0,0)(P,0,0)_m$ model but without the restrictions on the parameters that ensure stationarity.

The `nnetar()` function fits an NNAR$(p,P,k)_m$ model. If the values of p and P are not specified, they are selected automatically. For non-seasonal time series, the default is the optimal number of lags (according to the AIC) for a linear AR(p) model. For seasonal time series, the default values are $P = 1$ and p is chosen from the optimal linear model fitted to the seasonally adjusted data. If k is not specified, it is set to $k = (p + P + 1)/2$ (rounded to the nearest integer).

When it comes to forecasting, the network is applied iteratively. For forecasting one step ahead, we simply use the available historical inputs. For forecasting two steps ahead, we use the one-step forecast as an input, along with the historical data. This process proceeds until we have computed all the required forecasts.

Example: sunspots

The surface of the sun contains magnetic regions that appear as dark spots. These affect the propagation of radio waves, and so telecommunication companies like to predict sunspot activity in order to plan for any future difficulties. Sunspots follow a cycle of length between 9 and 14 years. In Figure 11.13, forecasts from an NNAR(10,6) are shown for the next 30 years. We have set a Box-Cox transformation with `lambda=0` to ensure the forecasts stay positive.

```
fit <- nnetar(sunspotarea, lambda=0)
autoplot(forecast(fit,h=30))
```

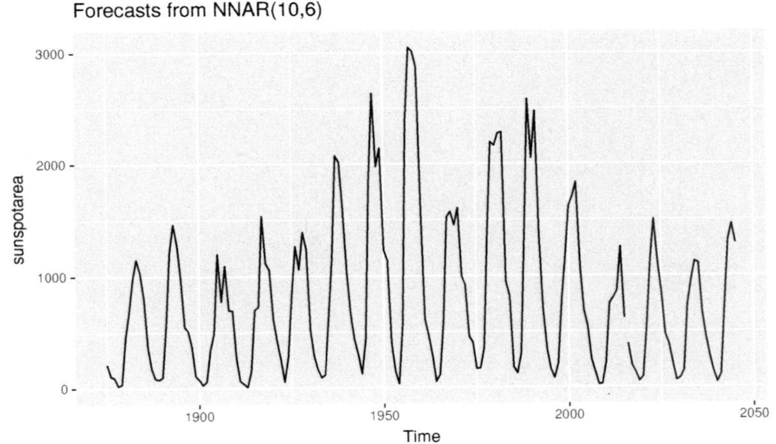

Figure 11.13: Forecasts from a neural network with ten lagged inputs and one hidden layer containing six neurons.

Here, the last 10 observations are used as predictors, and there are 6 neurons in the hidden layer. The cyclicity in the data has been modelled well. We can also see the asymmetry of the cycles has been captured by the model, where the increasing part of the cycle is steeper than the decreasing part of the cycle. This is one difference between a NNAR model and a linear AR model — while linear AR models can model cyclicity, the modelled cycles are always symmetric.

Prediction intervals

Unlike most of the methods considered in this book, neural networks are not based on a well-defined stochastic model, and so it is not straightforward to derive prediction intervals for the resultant forecasts. However, we can still compute prediction intervals using simulation where future sample paths are generated using bootstrapped residuals (as described in Section 3.5).

The neural network fitted to the sunspot data can be written as

$$y_t = f(\boldsymbol{y}_{t-1}) + \varepsilon_t$$

where $\boldsymbol{y}_{t-1} = (y_{t-1}, y_{t-2}, \dots, y_{t-10})'$ is a vector containing lagged values of the series, and f is a neural network with 6 hidden nodes in a single layer. The error series $\{\varepsilon_t\}$ is assumed to be homoscedastic (and possibly also normally distributed).

We can simulate future sample paths of this model iteratively, by randomly generating a value for ε_t, either from a normal distribution, or by resampling from the historical values. So if ε^*_{T+1} is a random draw from the distribution of errors at time $T+1$, then

$$y^*_{T+1} = f(\boldsymbol{y}_T) + \varepsilon^*_{T+1}$$

is one possible draw from the forecast distribution for y_{T+1}. Setting $\boldsymbol{y}^*_{T+1} = (y^*_{T+1}, y_T, \dots, y_{T-6})'$, we can then repeat the process to get

$$y^*_{T+2} = f(\boldsymbol{y}^*_{T+1}) + \varepsilon^*_{T+2}.$$

In this way, we can iteratively simulate a future sample path. By repeatedly simulating sample paths, we build up knowledge of the distribution for all future values based on the fitted neural network.

Here is a simulation of 9 possible future sample paths for the sunspot data. Each sample path covers the next 30 years after the observed data.

```
sim <- ts(matrix(0, nrow=30L, ncol=9L),
  start=end(sunspotarea)[1L]+1L)
for(i in seq(9))
  sim[,i] <- simulate(fit, nsim=30L)
autoplot(sunspotarea) + autolayer(sim)
```

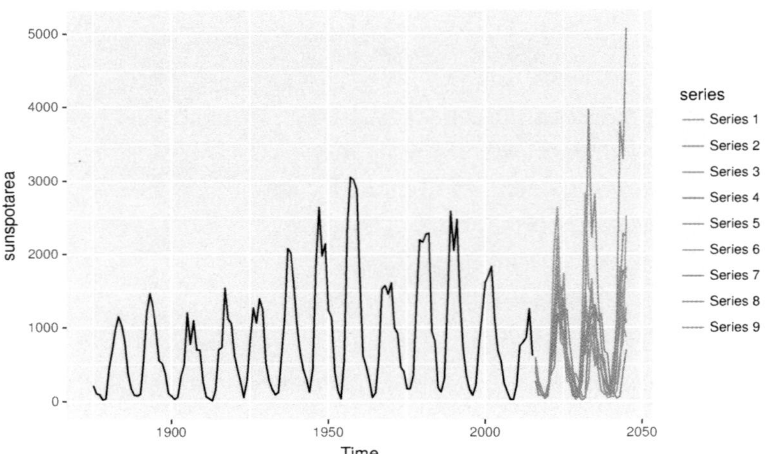

Figure 11.14: Future sample paths for the annual sunspot data.

If we do this a few hundred or thousand times, we can get a very good picture of the forecast distributions. This is how the `forecast()` function produces prediction intervals for NNAR models:

```
fcast <- forecast(fit, PI=TRUE, h=30)
autoplot(fcast)
```

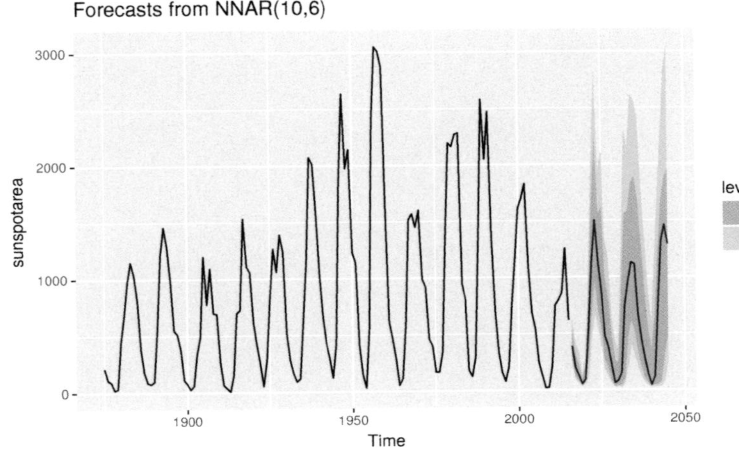

Figure 11.15: Forecasts with prediction intervals for the annual sunspot data. Prediction intervals are computed using simulated future sample paths.

Because it is a little slow, `PI=FALSE` is the default, so prediction intervals are not computed unless requested. The `npaths` argument in `forecast()` controls how many simulations are done (default 1000). By default, the errors are drawn from a normal distribution. The `bootstrap` argument allows the errors to be "bootstrapped" (i.e., randomly drawn from the historical errors).

11.4 Bootstrapping and bagging

Bootstrapping time series

In the preceding section, and in Section 3.5, we bootstrap the residuals of a time series in order to simulate future values of a series using a model.

More generally, we can generate new time series that are similar to our observed series, using another type of bootstrap.

First, the time series is Box-Cox-transformed, and then decomposed into trend, seasonal and remainder components using STL. Then we obtain shuffled versions of the remainder component to get bootstrapped remainder series. Because there may be autocorrelation present in an STL remainder series, we cannot simply use the re-draw procedure that was described in Section 3.5. Instead, we use a "blocked bootstrap", where contiguous sections of the time series are selected at random and joined together. These bootstrapped remainder series are added to the trend and seasonal components, and the Box-Cox transformation is reversed to give variations on the original time series.

Some examples are shown in Figure 11.16 for the monthly expenditure on retail debit cards in Iceland, from January 2000 to August 2013.

```
bootseries <- bld.mbb.bootstrap(debitcards, 10) %>%
  as.data.frame() %>% ts(start=2000, frequency=12)
autoplot(debitcards) +
  autolayer(bootseries, colour=TRUE) +
  autolayer(debitcards, colour=FALSE) +
  ylab("Bootstrapped series") + guides(colour="none")
```

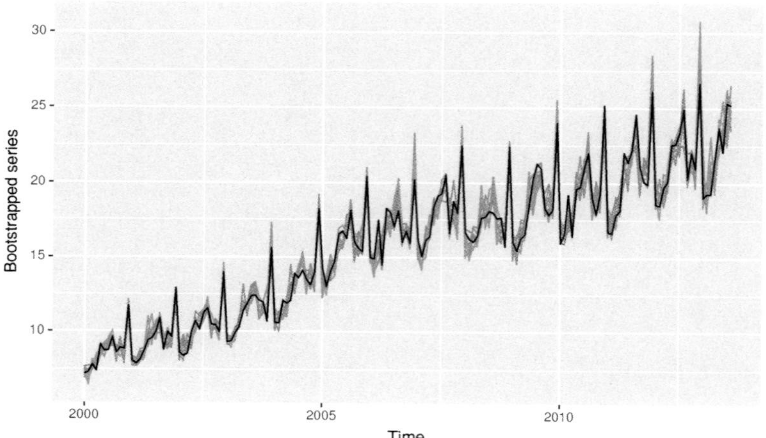

Figure 11.16: Ten bootstrapped versions of monthly expenditure on retail debit cards in Iceland.

This type of bootstrapping can be useful in two ways. First it helps us to get a better measure of forecast uncertainty, and second it provides a way of improving our point forecasts using "bagging".

Prediction intervals from bootstrapped series

Almost all prediction intervals from time series models are too narrow. This is a well-known phenomenon and arises because they do not account for all sources of uncertainty. Hyndman, Koehler, Snyder, et al. (2002) measured the size of the problem by computing the actual coverage percentage of the prediction intervals on test data, and found that for ETS models, nominal 95% intervals may only provide coverage between 71% and 87%. The difference is due to missing sources of uncertainty.

There are at least four sources of uncertainty in forecasting using time series models:

1. The random error term;
2. The parameter estimates;
3. The choice of model for the historical data;
4. The continuation of the historical data generating process into the future.

When we produce prediction intervals for time series models, we generally only take into account the first of these sources of uncertainty. Even if we ignore the model uncertainty and the uncertainty due to changing data generating processes (sources 3 and 4), and we just try to allow for parameter uncertainty as well as the random error term (sources 1 and 2), there are no algebraic solutions apart from some simple special cases.

We can use bootstrapped time series to go some way towards overcoming this problem. We demonstrate the idea using the `debitcards` data. First, we simulate many time series that are similar to the original data, using the block-bootstrap described above.

```
nsim <- 1000L
sim <- bld.mbb.bootstrap(debitcards, nsim)
```

For each of these series, we fit an ETS model and simulate one sample path from that model. A different ETS model may be selected in each case, although it will most likely select the same model because the series are very similar. However, the estimated parameters will be different. Therefore the simulated sample paths will allow for model uncertainty and parameter uncertainty, as well as the uncertainty associated with the random error term. This is a time-consuming process as there are a large number of time series to model.

```
h <- 36L
future <- matrix(0, nrow=nsim, ncol=h)
for(i in seq(nsim))
  future[i,] <- simulate(ets(sim[[i]]), nsim=h)
```

Finally, we take the means and quantiles of these simulated sample paths to form point forecasts and prediction intervals.

```
start <- tsp(debitcards)[2]+1/12
simfc <- structure(list(
    mean = ts(colMeans(future), start=start, frequency=12),
    lower = ts(apply(future, 2, quantile, prob=0.025),
               start=start, frequency=12),
    upper = ts(apply(future, 2, quantile, prob=0.975),
               start=start, frequency=12),
    level=95),
  class="forecast")
```

These prediction intervals will be larger than those obtained from an ETS model applied directly to the original data.

```
etsfc <- forecast(ets(debitcards), h=h, level=95)
autoplot(debitcards) +
  ggtitle("Monthly retail debit card usage in Iceland") +
  xlab("Year") + ylab("million ISK") +
  autolayer(simfc, series="Simulated") +
  autolayer(etsfc, series="ETS")
```

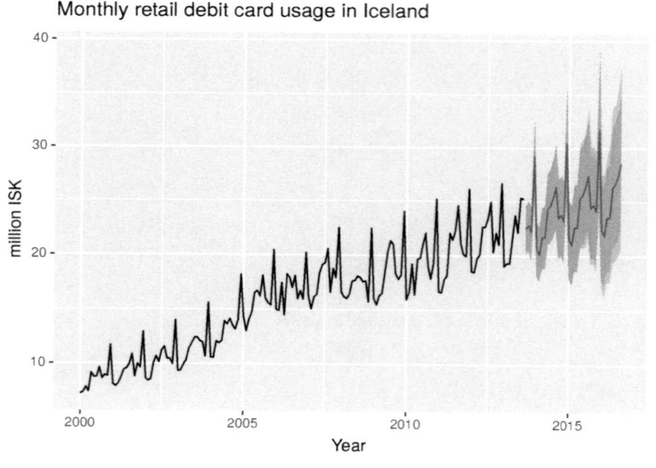

Figure 11.17: Forecasts of Iceland debit card usage using an ETS model with regular prediction intervals along with prediction intervals computed using simulations that allow for model and parameter uncertainty.

Bagged ETS forecasts

Another use for these bootstrapped time series is to improve forecast accuracy. If we produce forecasts from each of the additional time series, and average the resulting forecasts, we get better forecasts than if we simply forecast the original time series directly. This is called "bagging" which stands for "**b**ootstrap **agg**regat**ing**".

We could simply average the simulated future sample paths computed earlier. However, if our interest is only in improving point forecast accuracy, and not in also obtaining improved prediction intervals, then it is quicker to average the point forecasts from each series. The speed improvement comes about because we do not need to produce so many simulated series.

We will use `ets()` to forecast each of these series. Figure 11.18 shows ten forecasts obtained in this way.

```
sim <- bld.mbb.bootstrap(debitcards, 10) %>%
  as.data.frame() %>%
  ts(frequency=12, start=2000)
fc <- purrr::map(as.list(sim),
          function(x){forecast(ets(x))[["mean"]]}) %>%
      as.data.frame() %>%
      ts(frequency=12, start=start)
autoplot(debitcards) +
  autolayer(sim, colour=TRUE) +
  autolayer(fc, colour=TRUE) +
  autolayer(debitcards, colour=FALSE) +
  ylab("Bootstrapped series") +
  guides(colour="none")
```

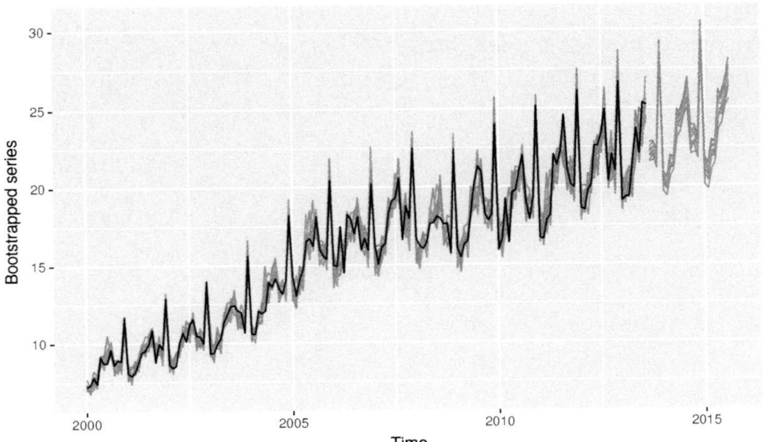

Figure 11.18: Forecasts of the ten bootstrapped series obtained using ETS models.

The average of these forecasts gives the bagged forecasts of the original data. The whole procedure can be handled with the `baggedETS()` function. By default, 100 bootstrapped series are used, and the length of the blocks used for obtaining bootstrapped residuals is set to 24 for monthly data. The resulting forecasts are shown in Figure 11.19.

```
etsfc <- debitcards %>% ets() %>% forecast(h=36)
baggedfc <- debitcards %>% baggedETS() %>% forecast(h=36)
autoplot(debitcards) +
  autolayer(baggedfc, series="BaggedETS", PI=FALSE) +
  autolayer(etsfc, series="ETS", PI=FALSE) +
  guides(colour=guide_legend(title="Forecasts"))
```

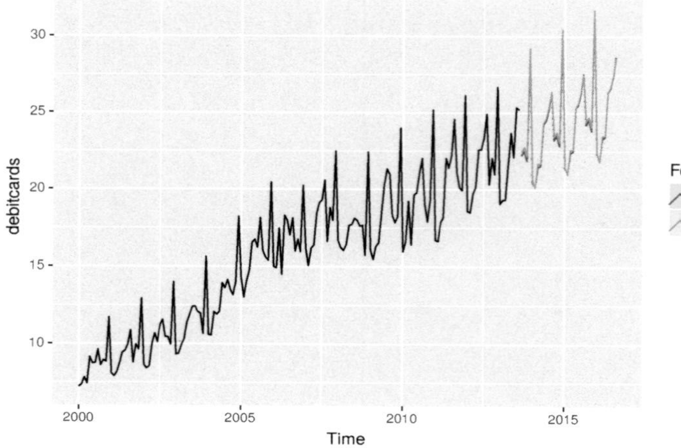

Figure 11.19: Comparing bagged ETS forecasts (the average of 100 bootstrapped forecast) and ETS applied directly to the data.

In this case, it makes very little difference. Bergmeir, Hyndman, and Benítez (2016) show that, on average, bagging gives better forecasts than just applying `ets()` directly. Of course, it is slower because a lot more computation is required.

11.5 Exercises

1. Use the `tbats()` function to model your retail time series.
   a. Check the residuals and produce forecasts.
   b. Does this completely automated approach work for these data?
   c. Have you saved any degrees of freedom by using Fourier terms rather than seasonal differencing?
2. Consider the weekly data on US finished motor gasoline products supplied (millions of barrels per day) (series `gasoline`):
   a. Fit a TBATS model to these data.
   b. Check the residuals and produce forecasts.

c. Could you model these data using any of the other methods we have considered in this book?

3. Experiment with using `nnetar()` on your retail data and other data we have considered in previous chapters.

11.6 Further reading

- De Livera, Hyndman, and Snyder (2011) introduced the TBATS model and discuss the problem of complex seasonality in general.
- Pfaff (2008) provides a book-length overview of VAR modelling and other multivariate time series models.
- Neural networks for individual time series have not tended to produce good forecasts. Crone, Hibon, and Nikolopoulos (2011) discuss this issue in the context of a forecasting competition.
- Bootstrapping for time series is discussed in Lahiri (2013).
- Bagging for time series forecasting is relatively new. Bergmeir, Hyndman, and Benítez (2016) is one of the few papers which addresses this topic.

Chapter 12
Some practical forecasting issues

In this final chapter, we address many practical issues that arise in forecasting, and discuss some possible solutions. Several of these sections are adapted from Hyndsight blog posts[1].

[1] https://robjhyndman.com/hyndsight/

12.1 Weekly, daily and sub-daily data

Weekly, daily and sub-daily data can be challenging for forecasting, although for different reasons.

Weekly data

Weekly data is difficult to work with because the seasonal period (the number of weeks in a year) is both large and non-integer. The average number of weeks in a year is 52.18. Most of the methods we have considered require the seasonal period to be an integer. Even if we approximate it by 52, most of the methods will not handle such a large seasonal period efficiently.

The simplest approach is to use an STL decomposition along with a non-seasonal method applied to the seasonally adjusted data (as discussed in Chapter 6). Here is an example using weekly data on US finished motor gasoline products supplied (in millioins of barrels per day) from February 1991 to May 2005.

```
gasoline %>% stlf() %>% autoplot()
```

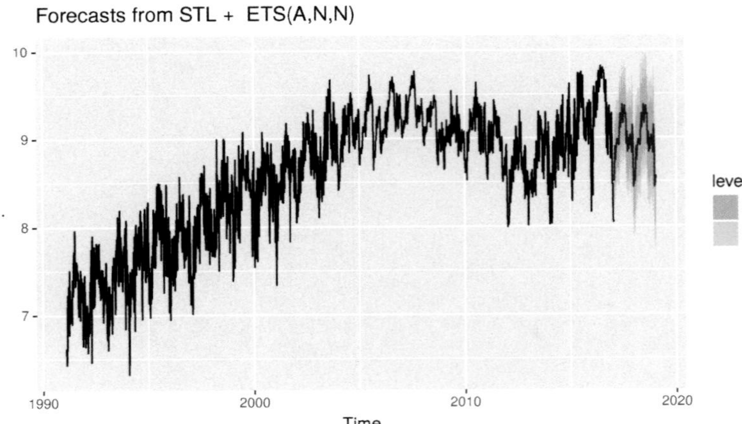

Figure 12.1: Forecasts for weekly US gasoline production using an STL decomposition with an ETS model for the seasonally adjusted data.

An alternative approach is to use a dynamic harmonic regression model, as discussed in Section 9.5. In the following example, the number of Fourier terms was selected by minimizing the AICc. The order of the ARIMA model is also selected by minimizing the AICc, although that is done within the `auto.arima()` function.

```
bestfit <- list(aicc=Inf)
for(K in seq(25)) {
  fit <- auto.arima(gasoline, xreg=fourier(gasoline, K=K),
    seasonal=FALSE)
  if(fit[["aicc"]] < bestfit[["aicc"]]) {
    bestfit <- fit
    bestK <- K
  }
}
fc <- forecast(bestfit,
  xreg=fourier(gasoline, K=bestK, h=104))
autoplot(fc)
```

The fitted model has 13 pairs of Fourier terms and can be written as

$$y_t = bt + \sum_{j=1}^{13}\left[\alpha_j \sin\left(\frac{2\pi jt}{52.18}\right) + \beta_j \cos\left(\frac{2\pi jt}{52.18}\right)\right] + \eta_t$$

where η_t is an ARIMA(0,1,2) process. Because n_t is non-stationary, the model is actually estimated on the differences of the variables on both sides of this equation. There are 26 parameters to capture the seasonality which is rather a lot, but apparently required according to the AICc selection. The total

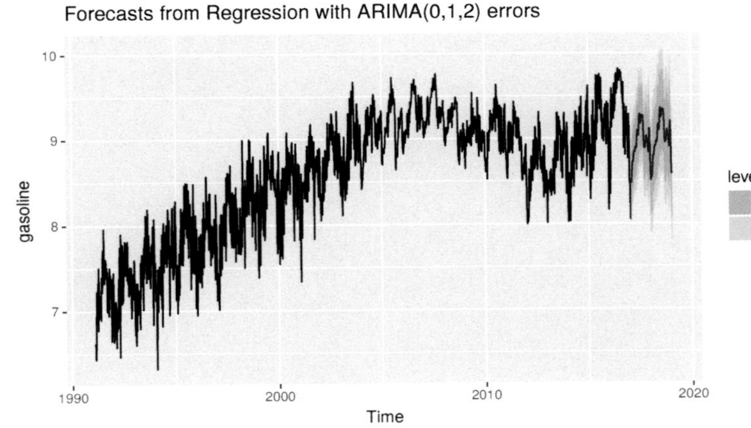

Figure 12.2: Forecasts for weekly US gasoline production using a dynamic harmonic regression model.

number of degrees of freedom is 29 (the other three coming from the 2 MA parameters and the drift parameter).

A third approach is the TBATS model introduced in Section 11.1. This was the subject of Exercise 2 in Section 11.5. In this example, the forecasts are almost identical to the previous two methods.

The STL approach or TBATS model is preferable when the seasonality changes over time. The dynamic harmonic regression approach is preferable if there are covariates that are useful predictors as these can be added as additional regressors.

Daily and sub-daily data

Daily and sub-daily data are challenging for a different reason — they often involve multiple seasonal patterns, and so we need to use a method that handles such complex seasonality.

Of course, if the time series is relatively short so that only one type of seasonality is present, then it will be possible to use one of the single-seasonal methods we have discussed in previous chapters (e.g., ETS or a seasonal ARIMA model). But when the time series is long enough so that some of the longer seasonal periods become apparent, it will be necessary to use STL, dynamic harmonic regression or TBATS, as discussed in Section 11.1.

However, note that even these models only allow for regular seasonality. Capturing seasonality associated with moving events such as Easter, Id, or the Chinese New Year is more difficult. Even with monthly data, this can be tricky as the festivals can fall in either March or April (for Easter), in January or February (for the Chinese New Year), or at any time of the year (for Id).

The best way to deal with moving holiday effects is to use dummy variables. However, neither STL, ETS nor TBATS models allow for covariates. Amongst the models discussed in this book (and implemented in the **forecast** package for R), the only choice is a dynamic regression model, where the predictors include any dummy holiday effects (and possibly also the seasonality using Fourier terms).

12.2 Time series of counts

All of the methods discussed in this book assume that the data have a continuous sample space. But very often data comes in the form of counts. For example, we may wish to forecast the number of customers who enter a store each day. We could have $0, 1, 2, \dots,$ customers, but we cannot have 3.45693 customers.

In practice, this rarely matters provided our counts are sufficiently large. If the minimum number of customers is at least 100, then the difference between a continuous sample space $[100, \infty)$ and the discrete sample space $\{100, 101, 102, \dots\}$ has no perceivable effect on our forecasts. However, if our data contains small counts $(0, 1, 2, \dots)$, then we need to use forecasting methods that are more appropriate for a sample space of non-negative integers.

Such models are beyond the scope of this book. However, there is one simple method which gets used in this context, that we would like to mention. It is "Croston's method", named after its British inventor, John Croston, and first described in Croston (1972). Actually, this method does not properly deal with the count nature of the data either, but it is used so often, that it is worth knowing about it.

With Croston's method, we construct two new series from our original time series by noting which time periods contain zero values, and which periods contain non-zero values. Let q_i be the ith non-zero quantity, and let a_i be the time between q_{i-1} and q_i. Croston's method involves separate simple exponential smoothing forecasts on the two new series a and q. Because the method is usually applied to time series of demand for items, q is often called the "demand" and a the "inter-arrival time".

If $\hat{q}_{i+1|i}$ and $\hat{a}_{i+1|i}$ are the one-step forecasts of the $(i+1)$th demand and inter-arrival time respectively, based on data up to demand i, then Croston's method gives

$$\hat{q}_{i+1|i} = (1-\alpha)\hat{q}_{i|i-1} + \alpha q_i,$$
$$\hat{a}_{i+1|i} = (1-\alpha)\hat{a}_{i|i-1} + \alpha a_i.$$

The smoothing parameter α takes values between 0 and 1 and is assumed to be the same for both equations. Let j be the time for the last observed positive observation. Then the h-step ahead forecast for the demand at time $T+h$, is given by the ratio

$$\hat{y}_{T+h|T} = q_{j+1|j}/a_{j+1|j}.$$

There are no algebraic results allowing us to compute prediction intervals for this method, because the method does not correspond to any statistical model (Shenstone and Hyndman 2005).

The `croston()` function produces forecasts using Croston's method. It simply uses $\alpha = 0.1$ by default, and ℓ_0 is set to be equal to the first observation in each of the series. This is consistent with the way Croston envisaged the method being used.

Example: lubricant sales

Several years ago, we assisted an oil company with forecasts of monthly lubricant sales. One of the time series is shown in the table below. The data contain small counts, with many months registering no sales at all, and only small numbers of items sold in other months.

Year	Jan	Feb	Mar	Apr	May	Jun	Jul	Aug	Sep	Oct	Nov	Dec
1	0	2	0	1	0	11	0	0	0	0	2	0
2	6	3	0	0	0	0	0	7	0	0	0	0
3	0	0	0	3	1	0	0	1	0	1	0	0

There are 11 non-zero demand values in the series, denoted by q. The corresponding arrival series a are also shown in the following table.

i	1	2	3	4	5	6	7	8	9	10	11
q	2	1	11	2	6	3	7	3	1	1	1
a	2	2	2	5	2	1	6	8	1	3	2

Applying Croston's method gives the demand forecast 2.750 and the arrival forecast 2.793. So the forecast of the original series is $\hat{y}_{T+h|T} = 2.750/2.793 = 0.985$. In practice, R does these calculations for you:

```
productC %>% croston() %>% autoplot()
```

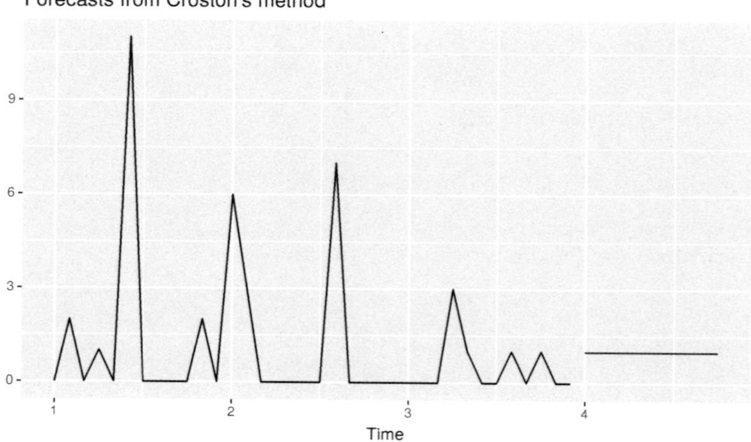

An implementation of Croston's method with more facilities (including parameter estimation) is available in the **tsintermittent** package[2] for R.

[2] https://cran.r-project.org/package=tsintermittent

Forecasting models that deal more directly with the count nature of the data are described in Christou and Fokianos (2015).

12.3 Ensuring forecasts stay within limits

It is common to want forecasts to be positive, or to require them to be within some specified range $[a, b]$. Both of these situations are relatively easy to handle using transformations.

Positive forecasts

To impose a positivity constraint, simply work on the log scale, by specifying the Box-Cox parameter $\lambda = 0$. For example, consider the real price of a dozen eggs (1900-1993; in cents):

```
eggs %>%
  ets(model="AAN", damped=FALSE, lambda=0) %>%
  forecast(h=50, biasadj=TRUE) %>%
  autoplot()
```

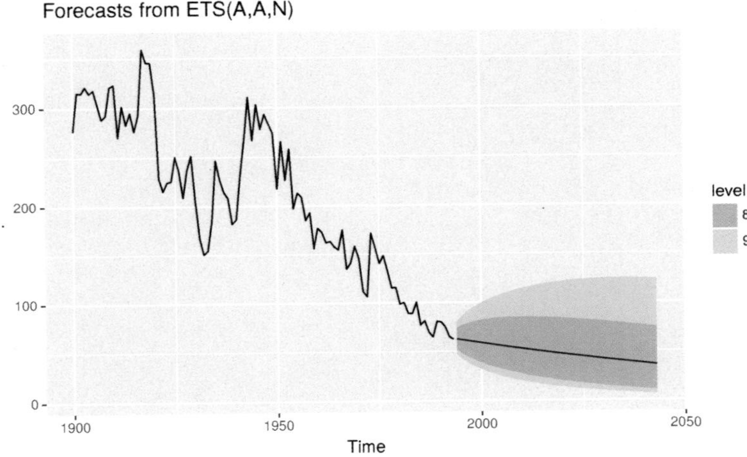

Figure 12.3: Forecasts for the price of a dozen eggs, constrained to be positive using a Box-Cox transformation.

Because we set `biasadj=TRUE`, the forecasts are the means of the forecast distributions.

Forecasts constrained to an interval

To see how to handle data constrained to an interval, imagine that the egg prices were constrained to lie within $a = 50$ and $b = 400$. Then we can transform the data using a scaled logit transform which maps (a, b) to the whole real line:

$$y = \log\left(\frac{x-a}{b-x}\right),$$

where x is on the original scale and y is the transformed data. To reverse the transformation, we will use

$$x = \frac{(b-a)e^y}{1+e^y} + a.$$

This is not a built-in transformation, so we will need to do more work.

```
# Bounds
a <- 50
b <- 400
# Transform data and fit model
fit <- log((eggs-a)/(b-eggs)) %>%
  ets(model="AAN", damped=FALSE)
fc <- forecast(fit, h=50)
# Back-transform forecasts
fc[["mean"]] <- (b-a)*exp(fc[["mean"]]) /
  (1+exp(fc[["mean"]])) + a
fc[["lower"]] <- (b-a)*exp(fc[["lower"]]) /
 (1+exp(fc[["lower"]])) + a
fc[["upper"]] <- (b-a)*exp(fc[["upper"]]) /
 (1+exp(fc[["upper"]])) + a
fc[["x"]] <- eggs
# Plot result on original scale
autoplot(fc)
```

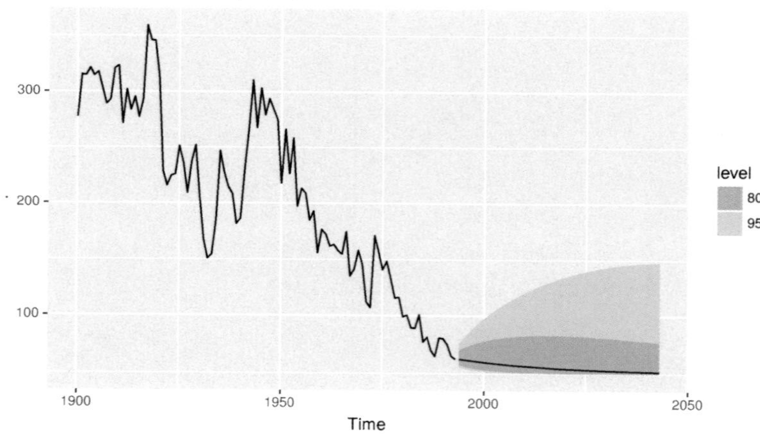

Figure 12.4: Forecasts for the price of a dozen eggs, constrained to be lie between 50 and 400.

No bias-adjustment has been used here, so the forecasts are the medians of the future distributions. The prediction intervals from these transformations have the same coverage probability as on the transformed scale, because quantiles are preserved under monotonically increasing transformations.

The prediction intervals lie above 50 due to the transformation. As a result of this artificial (and unrealistic) constraint, the forecast distributions have become extremely skewed.

12.4 Forecast combinations

An easy way to improve forecast accuracy is to use several different methods on the same time series, and to average the resulting forecasts. Nearly 50 years ago, John Bates and Clive Granger wrote a famous paper (Bates and Granger 1969), showing that combining forecasts often leads to better forecast accuracy. Twenty years later, Clemen (1989) wrote

> The results have been virtually unanimous: combining multiple forecasts leads to increased forecast accuracy. ... In many cases one can make dramatic performance improvements by simply averaging the forecasts.

While there has been considerable research on using weighted averages, or some other more complicated combination approach, using a simple average has proven hard to beat.

Here is an example using monthly expenditure on eating out in Australia, from April 1982 to September 2017. We use forecasts from the following models: ETS, ARIMA, STL-ETS, NNAR, and TBATS; and we compare the results using the last 5 years (60 months) of observations.

```
train <- window(auscafe, end=c(2012,9))
h <- length(auscafe) - length(train)
ETS <- forecast(ets(train), h=h)
ARIMA <- forecast(auto.arima(train, lambda=0, biasadj=TRUE),
  h=h)
STL <- stlf(train, lambda=0, h=h, biasadj=TRUE)
NNAR <- forecast(nnetar(train), h=h)
TBATS <- forecast(tbats(train, biasadj=TRUE), h=h)
Combination <- (ETS[["mean"]] + ARIMA[["mean"]] +
  STL[["mean"]] + NNAR[["mean"]] + TBATS[["mean"]])/5

autoplot(auscafe) +
  autolayer(ETS, series="ETS", PI=FALSE) +
  autolayer(ARIMA, series="ARIMA", PI=FALSE) +
  autolayer(STL, series="STL", PI=FALSE) +
  autolayer(NNAR, series="NNAR", PI=FALSE) +
  autolayer(TBATS, series="TBATS", PI=FALSE) +
  autolayer(Combination, series="Combination") +
  xlab("Year") + ylab("$ billion") +
  ggtitle("Australian monthly expenditure on eating out")
```

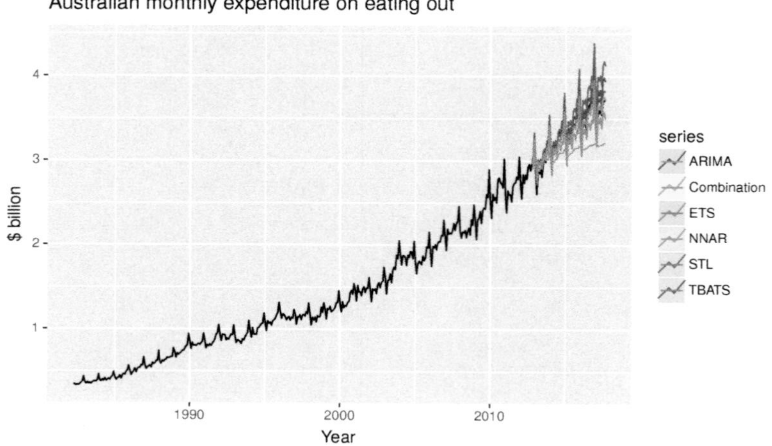

Figure 12.5: Point forecasts from various methods applied to Australian monthly expenditure on eating out.

```
c(ETS = accuracy(ETS, auscafe)["Test set","RMSE"],
  ARIMA = accuracy(ARIMA, auscafe)["Test set","RMSE"],
  STL-ETS = accuracy(STL, auscafe)["Test set","RMSE"],
  NNAR = accuracy(NNAR, auscafe)["Test set","RMSE"],
  TBATS = accuracy(TBATS, auscafe)["Test set","RMSE"],
  Combination =
    accuracy(Combination, auscafe)["Test set","RMSE"])
#>         ETS       ARIMA     STL-ETS        NNAR
#>     0.13700     0.12146     0.21446     0.31768
#>       TBATS Combination
#>     0.09406     0.07165
```

TBATS does particularly well with this series, but the combination approach is even better. For other data, TBATS may be quite poor, while the combination approach is almost always close to, or better than, the best component method.

12.5 Prediction intervals for aggregates

A common problem is to forecast the aggregate of several time periods of data, using a model fitted to the disaggregated data. For example, we may have monthly data but wish to forecast the total for the next year. Or we may have weekly data, and want to forecast the total for the next four weeks.

If the point forecasts are means, then adding them up will give a good estimate of the total. But prediction intervals are more tricky due to the correlations between forecast errors.

A general solution is to use simulations. Here is an example using ETS models applied to Australian monthly gas production data, assuming we wish to forecast the aggregate gas demand in the next six months.

```
# First fit a model to the data
fit <- ets(gas/1000)
# Forecast six months ahead
fc <- forecast(fit, h=6)
# Simulate 10000 future sample paths
nsim <- 10000
h <- 6
sim <- numeric(nsim)
for(i in seq_len(nsim))
  sim[i] <- sum(simulate(fit, future=TRUE, nsim=h))
meanagg <- mean(sim)
```

The mean of the simulations is very close to the sum of the individual forecasts:

```
sum(fc[["mean"]][1:6])
#> [1] 281.8
meanagg
#> [1] 281.7
```

Prediction intervals are also easy to obtain:

```
#80% interval:
quantile(sim, prob=c(0.1, 0.9))
#> 10% 90%
#> 263 301
#95% interval:
quantile(sim, prob=c(0.025, 0.975))
#>  2.5% 97.5%
#> 254.1 311.4
```

12.6 Backcasting

Sometimes it is useful to "backcast" a time series — that is, forecast in reverse time. Although there are no in-built R functions to do this, it is very easy to implement. The following functions reverse a `ts` object and a `forecast` object.

```
# Function to reverse time
reverse_ts <- function(y)
{
  ts(rev(y), start=tsp(y)[1L], frequency=frequency(y))
}
# Function to reverse a forecast
reverse_forecast <- function(object)
{
  h <- length(object[["mean"]])
  f <- frequency(object[["mean"]])
  object[["x"]] <- reverse_ts(object[["x"]])
  object[["mean"]] <- ts(rev(object[["mean"]]),
    end=tsp(object[["x"]])[1L]-1/f, frequency=f)
  object[["lower"]] <- object[["lower"]][h:1L,]
  object[["upper"]] <- object[["upper"]][h:1L,]
  return(object)
}
```

Then we can apply these functions to backcast any time series. Here is an example applied to quarterly retail trade in the Euro area. The data are from 1996-2011. We backcast to predict the years 1994-1995.

```
# Backcast example
euretail %>%
  reverse_ts() %>%
  auto.arima() %>%
  forecast() %>%
  reverse_forecast() -> bc
autoplot(bc) +
  ggtitle(paste("Backcasts from",bc[["method"]]))
```

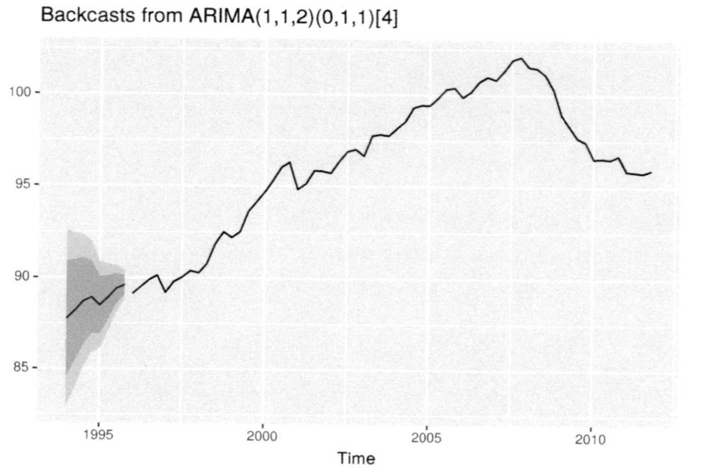

Figure 12.6: Backcasts for quarterly retail trade in the Euro area using an ARIMA model.

12.7 Very long and very short time series

Forecasting very short time series

We often get asked how *few* data points can be used to fit a time series model. As with almost all sample size questions, there is no easy answer. It depends on the *number of model parameters to be estimated and the amount of randomness in the data.* The sample size required increases with the number of parameters to be estimated, and the amount of noise in the data.

Some textbooks provide rules-of-thumb giving minimum sample sizes for various time series models. These are misleading and unsubstantiated in theory or practice. Further, they ignore the underlying variability of the data and often overlook the number of parameters to be estimated as well. There is, for example, no justification whatever for the magic number of 30 often given as a minimum for ARIMA modelling. The only theoretical limit is that we need more observations than there are parameters in our forecasting model. However, in practice, we usually need substantially more observations than that.

Ideally, we would test if our chosen model performs well out-of-sample compared to some simpler approaches. However, with short series, there is not enough data to allow some observations to be withheld for testing purposes, and even time series cross validation can be difficult to apply. The AICc is particularly useful here, because it is a proxy for the one-step forecast out-of-sample MSE. Choosing the model with the minimum AICc value allows both the number of parameters and the amount of noise to be taken into account.

What tends to happen with short series is that the AIC suggests very simple models because anything with more than one or two parameters will produce poor forecasts due to the estimation error. We applied the `auto.arima()` function to all the series from the M-competition with fewer than 20 observations. There were a total of 144 series, of which 54 had models with zero parameters (white noise and random walks), 73 had models with one parameter, 15 had models with two parameters and 2 series had models with three parameters. Interested readers can carry out the same exercise using the following code.

```
library(Mcomp)
library(purrr)
n <- map_int(M1, function(x) {length(x[["x"]])})
M1[n < 20] %>%
  map_int(function(u) {
    u[["x"]] %>%
      auto.arima() %>%
      coefficients() %>%
      length()
  }) %>%
  table()
```

Forecasting very long time series

Most time series models do not work well for very long time series. The problem is that real data do not come from the models we use. When the number of observations is not large (say up to about 200) the models often work well as an approximation to whatever process generated the data. But eventually we will have enough data that the difference between the true process and the model starts to become more obvious. An additional problem is that the optimization of the parameters becomes more time consuming because of the number of observations involved.

What to do about these issues depends on the purpose of the model. A more flexible and complicated model could be used, but this still assumes that the model structure will work over the whole period of the data. A better approach is usually to allow the model itself to change over time. ETS models are designed to handle this situation by allowing the trend and seasonal terms to evolve over time. ARIMA models with differencing have a similar property. But dynamic regression models do not allow any evolution of model components.

If we are only interested in forecasting the next few observations, one simple approach is to throw away the earliest observations and only fit a model to the most recent observations. Then an inflexible model can work well because there is not enough time for the relationships to change substantially.

For example, we fitted a dynamic harmonic regression model to 26 years of weekly gasoline production in Section 12.1. It is, perhaps, unrealistic to assume that the seasonal pattern remains the same over nearly three decades. So we could simply fit a model to the most recent years instead.

12.8 Forecasting on training and test sets

Typically, we compute one-step forecasts on the training data (the "fitted values") and multi-step forecasts on the test data. However, occasionally we may wish to compute multi-step forecasts on the training data, or one-step forecasts on the test data.

Multi-step forecasts on training data

We normally define fitted values to be one-step forecasts on the training set (see Section 3.3), but a similar idea can be used for multi-step forecasts. We will illustrate the method using an ARIMA(2,1,1)(0,1,2)$_{12}$ model for the Australian eating-out expenditure. The last five years are used for a test set, and the forecasts are plotted in Figure 12.7.

```
training <- subset(auscafe, end=length(auscafe)-61)
test <- subset(auscafe, start=length(auscafe)-60)
cafe.train <- Arima(training, order=c(2,1,1),
  seasonal=c(0,1,2), lambda=0)
cafe.train %>%
  forecast(h=60) %>%
  autoplot() + autolayer(test)
```

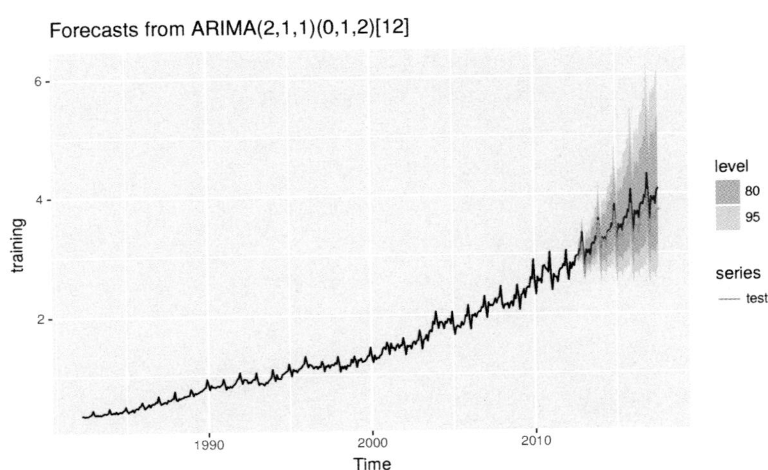

Figure 12.7: Forecasts from an ARIMA model fitted to the Australian cafe training data.

The `fitted()` function has an `h` argument to allow for h-step "fitted values" on the training set. Figure 12.8 is a plot of 12-step (one year) forecasts on the training set. Because the model involves both seasonal (lag 12) and first (lag 1) differencing, it is not possible to compute these forecasts for the first few observations.

```
autoplot(training, series="Training data") +
  autolayer(fitted(cafe.train, h=12),
    series="12-step fitted values")
```

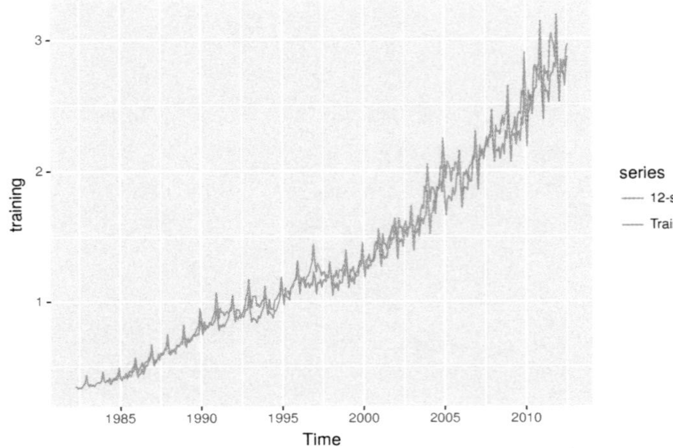

Figure 12.8: Twelve-step fitted values from an ARIMA model fitted to the Australian cafe training data.

One-step forecasts on test data

It is common practice to fit a model using training data, and then to evaluate its performance on a test data set. The way this is usually done means the comparisons on the test data use different forecast horizons. In the above example, we have used the last sixty observations for the test data, and estimated our forecasting model on the training data. Then the forecast errors will be for 1-step, 2-steps, . . . , 60-steps ahead. The forecast variance usually increases with the forecast horizon, so if we are simply averaging the absolute or squared errors from the test set, we are combining results with different variances.

One solution to this issue is to obtain 1-step errors on the test data. That is, we still use the training data to estimate any parameters, but when we compute forecasts on the test data, we use all of the data preceding each observation (both training and test data). So our training data are for times

$1, 2, \ldots, T-60$. We estimate the model on these data, but then compute $\hat{y}_{T-60+h|T-61+h}$, for $h = 1, \ldots, T-1$. Because the test data are not used to estimate the parameters, this still gives us a "fair" forecast. For the `ets()`, `Arima()`, `tbats()` and `nnetar()` functions, these calculations are easily carried out using the `model` argument.

Using the same ARIMA model used above, we now apply the model to the test data.

```
cafe.test <- Arima(test, model=cafe.train)
accuracy(cafe.test)
#>                     ME    RMSE     MAE      MPE  MAPE
#> Training set -0.002622 0.04591 0.03413 -0.07301 1.002
#>                MASE     ACF1
#> Training set 0.1899 -0.05704
```

Note that `Arima()` does not re-estimate in this case. Instead, the model obtained previously (and stored as `cafe.train`) is applied to the test data. Because the model was not re-estimated, the "residuals" obtained here are actually one-step forecast errors. Consequently, the results produced from the `accuracy()` command are actually on the test set (despite the output saying "Training set").

12.9 Dealing with missing values and outliers

Real data often contains missing values, outlying observations, and other messy features. Dealing with them can sometimes be troublesome.

Missing values

Missing data can arise for many reasons, and it is worth considering whether the missingness will induce bias in the forecasting model. For example, suppose we are studying sales data for a store, and missing values occur on public holidays when the store is closed. The following day may have increased sales as a result. If we fail to allow for this in our forecasting model, we will most likely under-estimate sales on the first day after the public holiday, but over-estimate sales on the days after that. One way to deal with this kind of situation is to use a dynamic regression model, with dummy variables indicating if the day is a public holiday or the day after a public holiday. No automated method can handle such effects as they depend on the specific forecasting context.

In other situations, the missingness may be essentially random. For example, someone may have forgotten to record the sales figures, or the data recording device may have malfunctioned. If the timing of the missing data is not informative for the forecasting problem, then the missing values can be handled more easily.

Some methods allow for missing values without any problems. For example, the naïve forecasting method continues to work, with the most recent non-missing value providing the forecast for the future time periods. Similarly, the other benchmark methods introduced in Section 3.1 will all produce forecasts when there are missing values present in the historical data. The R functions for ARIMA models, dynamic regression models and NNAR models will also work correctly without causing errors. However, other modelling functions do not handle missing values including `ets()`, `stlf()`, and `tbats()`.

When missing values cause errors, there are at least two ways to handle the problem. First, we could just take the section of data after the last missing value, assuming there is a long enough series of observations to produce meaningful forecasts. Alternatively, we could replace the missing values with estimates. The `na.interp()` function is designed for this purpose.

The `gold` data contains daily morning gold prices from 1 January 1985 to 31 March 1989. This series was provided to us as part of a consulting project; it contains 34 missing values as well as one apparently incorrect value. Figure 12.9 shows estimates of the missing observations in red.

```
gold2 <- na.interp(gold)
autoplot(gold2, series="Interpolated") +
  autolayer(gold, series="Original") +
  scale_color_manual(
    values=c(Interpolated="red",Original="gray"))
```

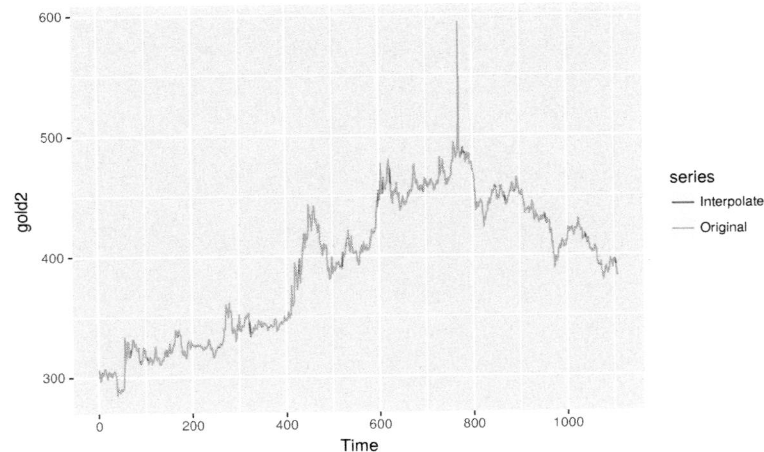

Figure 12.9: Daily morning gold prices for 1108 consecutive trading days beginning on 1 January 1985 and ending on 31 March 1989.

For non-seasonal data like this, simple linear interpolation is used to fill in the missing sections. For seasonal data, an STL decomposition is used estimate the seasonally component, and the seasonally adjusted series are linear interpolated. More sophisticated missing value interpolation is provided in the **imputeTS** package[3].

[3] `https://cran.r-project.org/package=imputeTS`

Outliers

Outliers are observations that are very different from the majority of the observations in the time series. They may be errors, or they may simply be very unusual. (See Section 5.3 for a discussion of outliers in a regression context.) All of the methods we have considered in this book will not work well if there are extreme outliers in the data. In this case, we may wish to replace them with missing values, or with an estimate that is more consistent with the majority of the data.

Simply replacing outliers without thinking about why they have occurred is a dangerous practice. They may provide useful information about the process that produced the data, and which should be taken into account when forecasting.

However, if we are willing to assume that the outliers are genuinely errors, or that they won't occur in the forecasting period, then replacing them can make the forecasting task easier.

The `tsoutliers()` function is designed to identify outliers, and to suggest potential replacement values. In the `gold` data shown in Figure 12.9, there is an apparently outlier on day 770:

```
tsoutliers(gold)
#> $index
#> [1] 770
#>
#> $replacements
#> [1] 494.9
```

Closer inspection reveals that the neighbouring observations are very close to $100 less than the apparent outlier.

```
gold[768:772]
#> [1] 495.00 502.75 593.70 487.05 487.75
```

Most likely, this was a transcription error, and the correct value should have been $493.70.

Another useful function is `tsclean()` which identifies and replaces outliers, and also replaces missing values. Obviously this should be used with some caution, but it does allow us to use forecasting models that are sensitive to outliers, or which do not handle missing values. For example, we could use the `ets()` function on the `gold` series, after applying `tsclean()`.

```
gold %>%
  tsclean() %>%
  ets() %>%
  forecast(h=50) %>%
  autoplot()
```

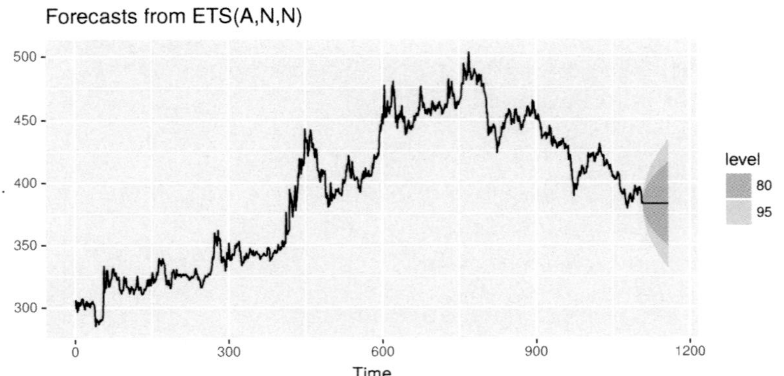

Figure 12.10: Forecasts from an ETS model for the gold price data after removing an outlier.

Notice that the outlier and missing values have been replaced with estimates.

12.10 Further reading

So many diverse topics are discussed in this chapter, that it is not possible to point to specific references on all of them. The last chapter in Ord, Fildes, and Kourentzes (2017) also covers "Forecasting in practice" and discusses other issues that might be of interest to readers.

Appendix: Using R

This book uses R and is designed to be used with R. R is free, available on almost every operating system, and there are thousands of add-on packages to do almost anything you could ever want to do. We recommend you use R with RStudio.

Installing R and RStudio

1. Download and install R.[4]
2. Download and install RStudio.[5]
3. Run RStudio. On the "Packages" tab, click on "Install packages" and install the package **fpp2** (make sure "install dependencies" is checked).

[4] `https://cran.r-project.org/`

[5] `https://bit.ly/rstudiodownload`

That's it! You should now be ready to go.

R examples in this book

We provide R code for most examples in shaded boxes like this:

```
autoplot(a10)
h02 %>% ets() %>% forecast() %>% summary()
```

These examples assume that you have the **fpp2** package loaded (and that you are using at least v2.3 of the package). So you should use the command `library(fpp2)` before you try any examples provided here. (This needs to be done at the start of every R session.) Sometimes we also assume that the R code that appears earlier in the same section of the book has also been run; so it is best to work through the R code in the order provided within each section.

Getting started with R

If you have never previously used R, please first do the free online course "Introduction to R"[6] from DataCamp. While this course does not cover time series or forecasting, it will get you used to the basics of the R language. Other DataCamp courses for R[7] may also be useful. The Coursera R Programming[8] course is also highly recommended.

[6] https://bit.ly/dcintro2r

[7] https://www.datacamp.com/courses/tech:r

[8] https://www.coursera.org/learn/r-programming

You will learn how to use R for forecasting using the exercises in this book.

Bibliography

Numbers on right indicate pages where each reference is cited.

Armstrong, JS, ed. (2001). *Principles of forecasting: a handbook for researchers and practitioners*. Kluwer Academic Publishers. 25

Armstrong, JS (1985). *Long-range forecasting: from crystal ball to computer*. John Wiley & Sons. 65

Athanasopoulos, G, DS Poskitt, and F Vahid (2012). Two canonical VARMA forms: scalar component models vis-à-vis the echelon form. *Econometric Reviews* **31**(1), 60–83. 332

Athanasopoulos, G, RA Ahmed, and RJ Hyndman (2009). Hierarchical forecasts for Australian domestic tourism. *International Journal of Forecasting* **25**, 146–166. 312, 322

Athanasopoulos, G and RJ Hyndman (2008). Modelling and forecasting Australian domestic tourism. *Tourism Management* **29**(1), 19–31. 100

Athanasopoulos, G, RJ Hyndman, N Kourentzes, and F Petropoulos (2017). Forecasting with temporal hierarchies. *European Journal of Operational Research* **262**(1), 60–74. 322

Bates, JM and CWJ Granger (1969). The combination of forecasts. *Operational Research Quarterly* **20**(4), 451–468. 357

Bergmeir, C, RJ Hyndman, and JM Benítez (2016). Bagging exponential smoothing methods using STL decomposition and Box-Cox transformation. *International Journal of Forecasting* **32**(2), 303–312. 346, 347

Bergmeir, C, RJ Hyndman, and B Koo (2018). A note on the validity of cross-validation for evaluating autoregressive time series prediction. *Computational Statistics and Data Analysis* **120**, 70–83. 131

Box, GEP and GM Jenkins (1970). *Time series analysis: forecasting and control*. San Francisco: Holden-Day. 276

Box, GEP, GM Jenkins, GC Reinsel, and GM Ljung (2015). *Time series analysis: forecasting and control*. 5th ed. Hoboken, New Jersey: John Wiley & Sons. 276, 298

Brockwell, PJ and RA Davis (2016). *Introduction to time series and forecasting*. 3rd ed. New York, USA: Springer. 254, 276

Brown, RG (1959). *Statistical forecasting for inventory control*. McGraw/Hill. 185

Buehler, R, D Messervey, and D Griffin (2005). Collaborative planning and prediction: does group discussion affect optimistic biases in time estimation? *Organizational Behavior and Human Decision Processes* **97**(1), 47–63. 91

Christou, V and K Fokianos (2015). On count time series prediction. *Journal of Statistical Computation and Simulation* **85**(2), 357–373. 354

Clemen, R (1989). Combining forecasts: a review and annotated bibliography with discussion. *International Journal of Forecasting* **5**, 559–608. 357

Cleveland, RB, WS Cleveland, JE McRae, and IJ Terpenning (1990). STL: a seasonal-trend decomposition procedure based on loess. *Journal of Official Statistics* **6**(1), 3–73. 174, 183

Cleveland, WS (1993). *Visualizing data*. Hobart Press. 46

Crone, SF, M Hibon, and K Nikolopoulos (2011). Advances in forecasting with neural networks? Empirical evidence from the NN3 competition on time series prediction. *International Journal of forecasting* **27**(3), 635–660. 347

Croston, JD (1972). Forecasting and stock control for intermittent demands. *Operational Research Quarterly* **23**(3), 289–303. 352

Dagum, EB and S Bianconcini (2016). *Seasonal adjustment methods and real time trend-cycle estimation*. Springer. 170, 173, 183

De Livera, AM, RJ Hyndman, and RD Snyder (2011). Forecasting time series with complex seasonal patterns using exponential smoothing. *J American Statistical Association* **106**(496), 1513–1527. 327, 347

Eroglu, C and KL Croxton (2010). Biases in judgmental adjustments of statistical forecasts: the role of individual differences. *International Journal of Forecasting* **26**(1), 116–133. 101

Fan, S and RJ Hyndman (2012). Short-term load forecasting based on a semi-parametric additive model. *IEEE Transactions on Power Systems* **27**(1), 134–141. 330

Fildes, R and P Goodwin (2007a). Against your better judgment? How organizations can improve their use of management judgment in forecasting. *Interfaces* **37**(6), 570–576. 101

Fildes, R and P Goodwin (2007b). Good and bad judgment in forecasting: lessons from four companies. *Foresight: The International Journal of Applied Forecasting* (8), 5–10. 85, 101

Franses, PH and R Legerstee (2013). Do statistical forecasting models for SKU-level data benefit from including past expert knowledge? *International Journal of Forecasting* **29**(1), 80–87. 101

Gardner, ES (1985). Exponential smoothing: the state of the art. *Journal of Forecasting* **4**(1), 1–28. 204, 222

Gardner, ES (2006). Exponential smoothing: the state of the art — Part II. *Interantional Journal of Forecasting* **22**, 637–666. 222

Gardner, ES and E McKenzie (1985). Forecasting trends in time series. *Management Science* **31**(10), 1237–1246. 194

Goodwin, P and G Wright (2009). *Decision analysis for management judgment*. 4th ed. Chichester: John Wiley & Sons. 101

Green, KC and JS Armstrong (2007). Structured analogies for forecasting. *International Journal of Forecasting* **23**(3), 365–376. 94, 101

Gross, CW and JE Sohl (1990). Disaggregation methods to expedite product line forecasting. *Journal of Forecasting* **9**, 233–254. 311, 322

Groves, RM, FJ Fowler, MP Couper, JM Lepkowski, E Singer, and R Tourangeau (2009). *Survey methodology*. 2nd ed. John Wiley & Sons. 97

Hamilton, JD (1994). *Time series analysis*. Princeton University Press, Princeton. 332

Harrell, FE (2015). *Regression modeling strategies: with applications to linear models, logistic and ordinal regression, and survival analysis*. 2nd ed. New York, USA: Springer. 156

Harris, R and R Sollis (2003). *Applied time series modelling and forecasting*. Chichester, UK: John Wiley & Sons. 279

Harvey, N (2001). "Improving judgment in forecasting". In: *Principles of forecasting: a handbook for researchers and practitioners*. Ed. by JS Armstrong. Boston, MA: Kluwer Academic Publishers, pp.59–80. 101

Holt, CE (1957). *Forecasting seasonals and trends by exponentially weighted averages*. O.N.R. Memorandum 52. Carnegie Institute of Technology, Pittsburgh USA. 185, 193, 198

Hyndman, RJ, RA Ahmed, G Athanasopoulos, and HL Shang (2011). Optimal combination forecasts for hierarchical time series. *Computational Statistics and Data Analysis* **55** (9), 2579–2589. 313, 316, 322

Hyndman, RJ and S Fan (2010). Density forecasting for long-term peak electricity demand. *IEEE Transactions on Power Systems* **25**(2), 1142–1153. 330

Hyndman, RJ and Y Khandakar (2008). Automatic time series forecasting: the forecast package for R. *Journal of Statistical Software* **27**(1), 1–22. 244

Hyndman, RJ and AB Koehler (2006). Another look at measures of forecast accuracy. *International Journal of Forecasting* **22**, 679–688. 65, 81

Hyndman, RJ, AB Koehler, JK Ord, and RD Snyder (2008). *Forecasting with exponential smoothing: the state space approach*. Berlin: Springer-Verlag. http://www.exponentialsmoothing.net. 204, 210, 216, 222

Hyndman, RJ, AB Koehler, RD Snyder, and S Grose (2002). A state space framework for automatic forecasting using exponential smoothing methods. *International Journal of Forecasting* **18**(3), 439–454. 342

Hyndman, RJ, A Lee, and E Wang (2016). Fast computation of reconciled forecasts for hierarchical and grouped time series. *Computational Statistics and Data Analysis* **97**, 16–32. 322

James, G, D Witten, T Hastie, and R Tibshirani (2014). *An introduction to statistical learning: with applications in R*. New York: Springer. 134

Kahn, KB (2006). *New product forecasting: an applied approach*. M.E. Sharp. 101

Kahneman, D and D Lovallo (1993). Timid choices and bold forecasts: a cognitive perspective on risk taking. *Management Science* **39**(1), 17–31. 94

Kwiatkowski, D, PCB Phillips, P Schmidt, and Y Shin (1992). Testing the null hypothesis of stationarity against the alternative of a unit root: How sure are we that economic time series have a unit root? *Journal of Econometrics* **54**(1-3), 159–178. 230

Lahiri, SN (2013). *Resampling methods for dependent data*. New York, USA: Springer Science & Business Media. 347

Lawrence, M, P Goodwin, M O'Connor, and D Önkal (2006). Judgmental forecasting: A review of progress over the last 25 years. *International Journal of Forecasting* **22**(3), 493–518. 83

Lütkepohl, H (2005). *New introduction to multiple time series analysis*. Berlin: Springer-Verlag. 333

Lütkepohl, H (2007). General-to-specific or specific-to-general modelling? An opinion on current econometric terminology. *Journal of Econometrics* **136**, 234–319. 332

Morwitz, VG, JH Steckel, and A Gupta (2007). When do purchase intentions predict sales? *International Journal of Forecasting* **23**(3), 347–364. 101

Önkal, D, KZ Sayım, and MS Gönül (2012). Scenarios as channels of forecast advice. *Technological Forecasting and Social Change* **80**, 772–788. 101

Ord, JK, R Fildes, and N Kourentzes (2017). *Principles of business forecasting*. 2nd ed. Wessex Press Publishing Co. 25, 81, 101, 156, 369

Pankratz, AE (1991). *Forecasting with dynamic regression models*. New York, USA: John Wiley & Sons. 298

Pegels, CC (1969). Exponential smoothing: some new variations. *Management Science* **12**, 311–315. 204

Peña, D, GC Tiao, and RS Tsay, eds. (2001). *A course in time series analysis*. New York, USA: John Wiley & Sons. 276

Pfaff, B (2008). *Analysis of integrated and cointegrated time series with R*. New York, USA: Springer Science & Business Media. 347

Randall, DM and JA Wolff (1994). The time interval in the intention-behaviour relationship: meta-analysis. *British Journal of Social Psychology* **33**, 405–418. 98

Rowe, G (2007). A guide to Delphi. *Foresight: The International Journal of Applied Forecasting* (8), 11–16. 91, 101

Rowe, G and G Wright (1999). The Delphi technique as a forecasting tool: issues and analysis. *International Journal of Forecasting* **15**, 353–375. 91, 101

Sanders, N, P Goodwin, D Önkal, MS Gönül, N Harvey, A Lee, and L Kjolso (2005). When and how should statistical forecasts be judgmentally adjusted? *Foresight: The International Journal of Applied Forecasting* **1**(1), 5–23. 101

Sheather, SJ (2009). *A modern approach to regression with R*. New York, USA: Springer. 156

Shenstone, L and RJ Hyndman (2005). Stochastic models underlying Croston's method for intermittent demand forecasting. *Journal of Forecasting* **24**(6), 389–402. 353

Taylor, JW (2003). Exponential smoothing with a damped multiplicative trend. *International Journal of Forecasting* **19**, 715–725. 204

Theodosiou, M (2011). Forecasting monthly and quarterly time series using STL decomposition. *International Journal of Forecasting* **27**(4), 1178–1195. 183

Unwin, A (2015). *Graphical data analysis with R*. Chapman and Hall/CRC. 46

Wang, X, KA Smith, and RJ Hyndman (2006). Characteristic-based clustering for time series data. *Data Mining and Knowledge Discovery* **13**(3), 335–364. 176

Wickham, H (2016). *ggplot2: Elegant graphics for data analysis*. 2nd ed. Springer. 8

Wickramasuriya, SL, G Athanasopoulos, and RJ Hyndman (2018). Optimal forecast reconciliation for hierarchical and grouped time series through trace minimization. *J American Statistical Association* **to appear**. 302, 316, 322

Winters, PR (1960). Forecasting sales by exponentially weighted moving averages. *Management Science* **6**, 324–342. 185, 198

Index